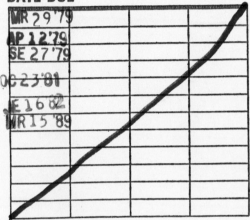

Career Education in Colleges

A Guide for Planning
Two- and Four-Year
Occupational Programs
for Successful Employment

Norman C. Harris

John F. Grede

Career Education in Colleges

 Jossey-Bass Publishers
San Francisco • Washington • London • 1977

CAREER EDUCATION IN COLLEGES
A Guide for Planning Two- and Four-Year
Occupational Programs for Successful Employment
    by Norman C. Harris and John F. Grede

Library of Congress Catalogue Card Number LC 77-82071

International Standard Book Number ISBN 0-87589-342-2

Manufactured in the United States of America

JACKET DESIGN BY WILLI BAUM

FIRST EDITION

Code 7741

The Jossey-Bass Series
in Higher Education

□ □ □ □ □ □ □ □ □ □ □ □ □ □ □ □ □

Preface

The national enterprise in higher education is undergoing rapid change and critical assessment. The problems of the 1960s had barely begun to subside when a new set of challenges associated with the 1970s appeared. The crisis of unbridled growth was replaced by the crisis of the steady state; inflation and economic recession, combined with a sudden loss of public confidence in higher education, brought on an era of financial hardship. By 1975, college graduates were no longer privileged in the market place and hundreds of thousands of them joined the ranks of the unemployed.

Career Education in Colleges views the malaise affecting higher education as resulting from the centuries-old concept and practice that liberal education is for "making a life," vocational education is for "making a living," and "never the twain shall meet." When higher education was only for the select few, such a concept may have been viable; but now that more than half of all youth and millions of adults are in college, a new view of things is in order. For most colleges the times demand a concept of higher education that includes liberal learning and career counseling within a framework of vocational preparation. This concept, although not a new idea, has a new name—*career education*. Career education itself is not actually new; colleges and universities have been engaged in it for centuries for students aspiring to the traditional professions, but it is now time to apply the concept to nearly all programs for nearly all students. Career education then becomes the unifying force, the central thrust, and the rational evolution in higher education.

Despite our advocacy of career education, we do not denigrate liberal education—on the contrary, we value it. Making a living is indeed fruitless unless life has some quality, but life has little quality in a context of poverty and uselessness. For most Americans, a career and economic security are essential ingredients in the recipe for a good life. The flavor, zest, and leavening that liberal learning can impart become merely frustrations and false expectations unless the economic base is there.

We are primarily concerned in this book with career education in colleges for *middle-manpower* development—preparation for careers at paraprofessional, semiprofessional, technical, and very highly skilled levels. More than one third of all jobs in the United States are in middle-manpower occupational groups; the desired preparation for such jobs increasingly includes one or more years of college or other forms of postsecondary education and training. We use the word *college* as an all-inclusive term to cover two-year and four-year colleges and, to some extent, universities as well as technical colleges, technical institutes, and postsecondary vocational-technical schools.

We believe that career education is of overriding importance to higher education and to society for several reasons. First, the complexity of both living problems and work problems increases with each decade. Coping with either set of problems demands greater resources of competence and intellectuality than are ordinarily provided in secondary schools.

Second, proponents of universal higher education have been successful, perhaps beyond their fondest dreams, in promoting the idea of the learning society. The millions so assiduously recruited and eagerly awaited have arrived, but it is apparent that many of them find little in college that they value. A curriculum fashioned for a small group of high school graduates dedicated to academic studies has not suited the needs of a larger and more diverse group. Now that all the new students are here, should higher education serve up the same seven liberal arts, most of which will be left on the plates, or plan a new menu, whose entrée is career preparation?

Third, fiscal prudence demands a critical look at the inputs and outputs of higher education. With an annual public and private dollar input to higher education in excess of $50 billion, Americans are correctly concerned about the returns to be expected on the investment.

Finally, the needs of the nation must be given high priority. The American economy, though it is the most advanced and productive in the world, needs only about one person in five to work at professional and high-level managerial jobs. These persons are educated and trained, and we think exceptionally well-trained, mainly in the baccalaureate and graduate professional schools of our universities. However, middle-manpower jobs involve two workers out of five, and we can no longer ignore the quality of their contributions to American life. In the past we were more or less content to allow these people to "trickle up" (or down) into their jobs, but with the number and severity of crises now facing the nation (energy development, environmental improvement, crime control, health services, national defense, international trade, inflation, food production), such a haphazard policy is no longer tenable. Career education for middle manpower requires the same emphasis on excellence, quality, and competence that colleges have accorded to education for the professions throughout this century.

We support the point of view that colleges are established, funded, and operated by society for the education of students, that the primary function of faculty is to teach and see that students learn, and that resources should be allocated toward ends that will maximize the educational and career rate of return on investment.

We believe that four-year college presidents and deans, program heads and coordinators, faculty and students, and board members should all be concerned with career education issues. Certainly presidents of community colleges and technical institutes, directors of area vocational-technical schools, and administrators and faculty in state colleges are interested in planning for the expansion and improvement of career education. Moreover, legislators and state agency officials, planners in federal bureaus and agencies, and executives in business, industry, and foundations should be thinking about the directions higher education will take in the years ahead.

In our book, which is addressed to all these individuals and to graduate students in higher education and occupational administration, we indicate some of those directions. To deal adequately with issues and ideas at several levels of administration, some repetition has been necessary in certain chapters. For directors and coordinators of programs in business, technology, allied health, or public and human service careers, for example, such issues as curriculum development and manpower supply and demand are dealt with in the chapters of Part Two as they relate to each of these career clusters. The same or related issues are discussed in other chapters from a more global point of view for the consideration of college deans and presidents and for professors and graduate students in higher education.

Our purpose is to challenge decision makers to think, rather than to tell them what to do after decisions are made. We are not so much interested in speedy solutions to problems as we are in identifying and deciding where to attack the problems. We do not believe that bigger is necessarily better, that process is more important than product, or that problems are always most effectively solved by ever-larger appropriations. We firmly believe that career education must be egalitarian in opportunity but that it must also maintain standards of excellence and quality that lead to competence on the job.

Our three goals in writing this book were, first, to give readers the background of fact and discussion for a common perspective on postsecondary career education; second, to delineate in some detail how colleges can initiate and operate career programs in the major occupational clusters related to middle manpower; and third, to reflect about organization, evaluation, and planning in postsecondary career education, closing with a look at what the future may bring. To that end we have organized the book into three parts, each addressed to one of the three tasks we set ourselves.

We acknowledge with gratitude the many contributions of friends and colleagues both in the Center for the Study of Higher Education at the University of Michigan and in the City Colleges of Chicago. Sincere thanks also is due to the many friends, associates, and college administrators from coast to coast who, over the past decade, have encouraged us to write this book. Without their persistent urging it might not have been done.

We especially appreciate the courtesy of all the busy people who took the time to visit with us as we traveled, gathering data, or who responded by telephone or mail to our requests for information about career education programs in their colleges.

Special thanks go also to Mrs. Joyce Dahart for her preparation of the manuscript through many drafts to the final version and to graduate students in higher education seminars who helped us sharpen many of the ideas and issues presented in this book.

July 1977   NORMAN C. HARRIS
                                               Ann Arbor, Michigan

                                               JOHN F. GREDE
                                               Chicago, Illinois

Contents

Preface   ix

The Authors   xix

Figures and Tables   xxiii

Part One. Background, Concepts, and Setting

1. Higher Education in Transition   3

    *The "Depression" in Higher Education • Career
    Education: Definitions and Comment • Why
    College-Level Career Education? • Dichotomy and
    Dialogue • The Dichotomy Challenged • Dialogue
    Replaces Dichotomy • Summary*

2. Students in Search of Careers   26

    *Who Goes to College? • The Learning Society • Shift to
    Career-Oriented Studies • Some Problems of Diversity •
    Students as a Class • Summary*

3. Stability and Change in the Labor Force   43

    *Manpower Development and the Labor Force •
    Occupational Structure: Twenty Years of Change •
    Education for Middle Manpower • Summary*

4. Institutional Settings 64

*Institutions and Agencies for Manpower Development •
Community and Junior Colleges • Technical Institutes •
Area Vocational-Technical Schools and Technical
Colleges • Private Business, Trade, and Technical
Schools • Four-Year Colleges and Universities • Summary*

Part Two. Career Programs: A Cluster Analysis

5. Business and Office Careers 101

*Scope of Business Employment • Office Careers • Careers
in Finance, Insurance, and Real Estate • Sales Careers •
Hospitality Careers • Agri-Business Careers •
Management Careers and Career Paths • Guidelines and
Conclusions*

6. Careers in Engineering, Science, and
Industry-Related Technologies 131

*Trends in Technical Education • The Technician's Place
in Industry • Manpower Forecasts and Educational
Programs for Technical Occupations • Current Trends
in Technical and Technological Program
Development • Guidelines for Planners*

7. Allied Health Careers 166

*Health Team Approach to Health Care • Manpower
Needs in Allied Health • Programs for Allied Health
Careers • Advantages of a Core Semester—Student
Selection • Career Ladders in Allied Health • Other
Issues in Allied Health Education*

8. Public and Human Service Careers 197

*Manpower Needs in Public and Human Services •
Programs in Public and Human Services • Issues in
Public and Human Service Education*

9. Career Potentials for the Liberal Arts   227

*Developing the Economic Dimension • Career Outlets for
Two-Year College Liberal Arts Programs • Career
Prospects for Liberal Arts Baccalaureate Graduates •
Cooperative Education for Liberal Arts Students •
Providing the Link Between Education and Work •
Conclusion*

Part Three. Planning, Finance, and Governance

10. Planning and Operating Successful
    Programs   251

*Competence and Quality in Career Education •
Curriculum Content for Competence • Faculty •
Estimating the Demand for Middle Manpower •
Occupational Surveys • Determining Drawing Power
and Projecting Enrollments • Utilizing Advisory
Committees • Planning the Level and Breadth of Each
Program • Deciding on Teaching and Learning Systems •
Implementing Work Experience • Using Support
Services • Summary and Guidelines for Planners*

11. Career Education in Urban Community
    Colleges   291

*Emergence of Urban Community College Systems •
Looking Outward to the City • Handmaiden to the
Establishment? • Specialization Versus
Comprehensiveness • Articulation • Granting Credit for
Prior Learning • Attitudes of Minorities Toward Career
Education and Job Training • Financial
Considerations • Summary*

12. Economics of Career Education in Colleges   316

*Education and American Society • Cost-Benefit
Considerations in Higher Education • Returns on
Career-Oriented Education • Long-Term Trends •
Implications for Career Education • Summary and
Suggestions for Planners*

13. Futurism and Career Education: The Road
    to 1990   351

*A Vantage Point for Viewing the Future • Three
Scenarios: A Look at 1990 • Seven Future Issues for
America and for Career Education • Challenges to
Career Education • Accountability in Career Education •
Quality and Excellence in Career Education • Financing
Career Education • Governance and Administration •
Trends in Governance • Summary and Conclusions*

References   387

Index   408

The Authors

NORMAN C. HARRIS is professor of higher education at the Center for the Study of Higher Education, University of Michigan, and has been coordinator of Community College Development at the center since 1970. Prior to joining the University of Michigan faculty in 1961, he was dean of technical education at Bakersfield College in California. During the 1950s he was chairman for three years of the California State Committee on Vocational-Technical Education in the Junior College, a group which led the move toward programmatic comprehensiveness in the state's junior colleges at that time.

Norman Harris has been a visiting professor at San Diego State College (1951); the University of Hawaii (1966 and 1976); and a senior specialist at the East-West Center, Honolulu (1970). His books include *Modern Air Conditioning Practice* (1959, 1974), *Updating Occupational Education* (Ed., 1973), *Experiments in Applied Physics* (1963, 1972), *Introductory Applied Physics* (with E. M. Hemmerling, 1955, 1963, 1972), and *Technical Education in the Junior College* (1964). In addition, he has authored numerous monographs and articles on higher education and technical education and on higher education and manpower development.

At the University of Michigan he teaches graduate courses and seminars on the community college, technical education, higher education, and manpower development and is a consultant to community and technical colleges. In fields other than education, he has been an air conditioning consulting and design engineer, a consultant on manpower development policies in Southeast Asia, and an officer in the U.S. Navy, in which he holds the rank of Commander, USN (Retired).

Norman Harris received the bachelor's degree in physics from UCLA in 1935 and the master's degree from the University of California, Berkeley, in 1940.

Awards and honors include the presidency of a campus chapter and later a field chapter of Phi Delta Kappa; an Outstanding Service Award from the American Society of Tool and Manufacturing Engineers, Detroit Chapter; a Distinguished Service Award from the Council of North Central Community Colleges; a senior specialist in-residence award from the East-West Center, Honolulu; and an honorary doctorate from the University of Pangasinan, Dagupan City, Philippines.

He and his wife Pauline live in Ann Arbor, Michigan, as do one son and one daughter. Two older sons reside on the West Coast, one in Seattle and one in San Francisco.

JOHN F. GREDE is Vice Chancellor for Career and Manpower Programs at the City Colleges of Chicago. Prior to his present position, he taught at the University of Michigan (1969–1971), was director of Occupational Education at the City Colleges of Chicago (1966–1969), and president of Chicago's Southeast Junior College, now Olive-Harvey, (1959–1966). He was founding president of the National Council for Occupational Education and currently serves on the executive board. He is also a member of the Curriculum Commission of the American Association of Community and Junior Colleges. The American Council on Education recently appointed him to its National Commission on Educational Credit, following his two years of service on the council's Task Force on Educational Credit.

John Grede has taught social science and economics at Chicago's Crane Junior College, now Malcolm X, and courses on occupational education, the community college, multicampus administration, and collective bargaining at the Center for the Study of Higher Education, University of Michigan. He has also taught graduate courses on the community college at Northern Illinois University and the University of Illinois, Urbana. In another role, he has been a member of the board negotiating team for the City Colleges of Chicago since 1966; in 1975 he served as chief negotiator.

His publications include a number of articles on occupational education in the *Journal of Higher Education,* the *Community and Junior College Journal,* The U.S. Office of Education's *Essays on Career Education,* and the Jossey-Bass series on *New Directions for Community Colleges.* He has also written about collective bargaining, including an article for the *Academic Collective Bargaining Handbook* (1977).

John Grede earned his bachelor's degree in political science in 1938, his master's degree in international relations in 1947, and his doctorate in history in 1962, all from the University of Chicago. Although his graduate work was in the social sciences, his later interests and administrative experiences have been in occupational education.

He and his wife Katie live in Palos Heights, Illinois. A married daughter and son both live in the southwest suburbs of Chicago.

We dedicate this book to our wives,
Pauline Harris and Kathleen Grede

Figures and Tables

Figures

1. Middle-Manpower Jobs Located on a Manipulative-Cognitive Scale.   54

2. Levels of Technological Occupations, by Task, Mix of Manipulative and Cognitive Skills, Sources of Training, and Degree Level.   138

3. Typical Baccalaureate Technology Curriculums of Differing Objectives.   158

4. Relationships Among Several Aspects of Public and Human Services.   198

5. Manpower Development for Energy Independence: Two Alternatives for Technical Educators.   272

6. Place of Career Counseling and Educational Advising Within Two-Year Career-Oriented College Programs.   281

xxiii

7. The Linking-Pin Concept of the Community College in Career Education Articulation. 307

8. Comparison of College-Going Trends with Growth in Professional Occupations, United States, 1900–1990. 330

9. Suggested Administrative Organization for a Two-Year College, Illustrating the "Career Division" Concept. 384

Tables

1. Percent of New High School Graduates Attending Higher Education Institutions, 1962–1973. 28

2. Estimated and Projected Program Enrollments in the Noncollegiate Sector of Postsecondary Education, 1970 and 1980. 31

3. Percent of Total Enrollment by Program Among 216,338 Students at 157 Two-Year Colleges, 1973–1974. 34

4. Percent of the United States Population in Selected Age Groups, 1975 and 2000. 46

5. Percent of the Civilian Labor Force of the United States in Major Occupational Groups, and Women in the Labor Force, Selected Years, 1954–1974. 48

6. Estimated Distribution of the Employed Labor Force by Occupational Groups, 1960 and 1975. 52

7. Estimated Number of Postsecondary Noncollegiate Private Schools (Excluding Technical Institutes) Offering Occupational Programs, by Type and Control, 1970–1971. 85

8. Workers in Selected Business and Office Careers, by Industry, 1970. 103

9. Percent of Incoming Freshmen Planning on Majors or Careers in Business Fields, by Level of Institution, Fall 1975. 105

10. Persons Employed in Selected Office Occupations, 1960 and 1970. 107

11. Employment in Selected Technical Occupations, 1960 and 1970. 136

12. Estimated Manpower Requirements and Supply in Allied Health, 1975 and 1980. 171

13. Percent of Incoming Freshmen Planning on Majors or Careers in Allied Health Fields, by Level of Institution, Fall 1975. 179

14. Persons Employed in Selected Service Occupations, 1960 and 1970. 200

15. Certificates and Degrees Awarded in Liberal Arts and Occupational Fields, 1973–1974. 229

16. Present Value of Lifetime Earnings of Males
    and Females for Two Age Cohorts, by Race
    and Years of Schooling Completed,
    Discounted at 2 Percent, 1972.   328

17. Estimated Sources of Economic Growth,
    United States, 1927–1957 and 1960–1980.   334

◨ ◨ ◨ ◨ ◨ ◨ ◨ ◨ ◨ ◨ ◨ ◨ ◨ ◨ ◨ ◨ ◨ ◨

Career Education in Colleges

A Guide for Planning
Two- and Four-Year
Occupational Programs
for Successful Employment

I

Background, Concepts, and Setting

1 ◨ ◨ ◨ ◨ ◨ ◨ ◨ ◨ ◨ ◨ ◨ ◨ ◨ ◨ ◨

Higher Education in Transition

> *If we do not change our direction, we are quite certain
> to end up where we are heading.*
>
> Chinese Proverb

America's love affair with higher education has spent its passion.
The marriage itself is still secure, but its stability and balance now
depend on support mandated by law rather than on assurances
ingenuously sought and sustenance freely given. The honeymoon
of the 1960s—when enrollments soared upward, when education
was seen as the cure for all the nation's ills, and when money for
every "need" seemed to be either at hand or readily available at
the next session of the legislature—that golden age of "happy talk"
is over. Now higher education is being put to the same political,
social, and financial tests that properly challenge all democratic
institutions. For those who long for the return of "normal times"
in higher education, relax—these *are* normal times, and the 1960s
were the free-spending euphoric weekend.

The "Depression" in Higher Education

Some educators cry out against the "new depression" in higher education (Cheit, 1971) and allege shortsightedness and parsimony on the part of legislators and taxpayers. But rather than lamenting the halcyon days of the past and becoming mired in a swamp of recrimination and accusation, it makes more sense to set about the task of making colleges and what they offer more valuable to more people. If fewer people elect to invest time and money in college than before, the reason may be simply that many Americans have come to the conclusion that other investments than higher education are better for them, and that other social goals should now have higher priority for funding—for example, environmental improvement, energy development, crime control, urban assistance, unemployment compensation, social security, health, and welfare. Beyond this competition for investment, the decline of public confidence in higher education involves at least five other factors, none of them necessarily a manifestation of legislative evil intent.

First, steeply escalating college costs have brought demands for accountability and the end of the "blank check" era. Second, the increased militancy of teachers has brought collective bargaining and even strikes patterned after industrial models, and union contracts resulting in higher pay for fewer hours of work. Third, legislators, taxpayers, and citizens generally became convinced that higher education promised more than it could possibly deliver. They realized that the record of education as a problem solver for the economic and social ills of the nation had left much to be desired. There was a feeling that its central function, learning and teaching, had been pushed into the background and a resolve to direct higher education back into the activities for which it was founded and funded—learning, teaching, and basic research.

Fourth, there was an uneasy feeling on the part of the public and their elected representatives that educational needs and demands were not closely related. During the growth crises of the 1960s, educators had claimed that when and if they ever got caught up and their institutions entered a period of enrollment stability, they would put their major effort back into the thrust for quality, where it belonged. But it didn't work that way. When enrollment pressures finally did relax, most colleges immediately put maximum effort into recruiting more students rather than into improving quality.

And fifth, there was the very evident imbalance by 1975 between manpower demands on the one hand and college students' fields of study on the other. By that year, college graduates were no longer privileged in the marketplace, as hundreds of thousands of them joined the ranks of the unemployed. Exemplified most dramatically by the oversupply of prospective teachers, the imbalance was almost as readily apparent in nearly all liberal arts fields. Legislators were quick to question the advisability of continued high levels of funding for colleges and programs that remained insensitive to manpower trends and changes in the economy.

The slowing of the enrollment growth rate in four-year colleges and universities which began in the early 1970s has been ascribed to a variety of causes including (1) smaller high school graduating classes in many regions of the nation; (2) economic and inflationary factors affecting decisions about college attendance; (3) removal of the draft threat, as America's participation in the Indochina war ended; (4) changing value systems and life styles of young people; (5) serious questioning, on the part of many youth and their parents, of the economic value of a traditional college degree in the arts and sciences; (6) increased interest in occupational studies (Greene, 1974); and (7) saturation effects and the operation of the law of diminishing returns. The economic value of a college degree inevitably shrank when participation in higher education by college-age youth edged past the 50 percent mark in many states and reached as high as 60 to 70 percent in a few states. Combined with inflation and economic recession, this slowdown in growth brought on an era of financial hardship for colleges and universities. The dimensions of this slowdown threatened the very existence of many colleges as the 1970s moved past their midpoint.

Glenny (1973, p. 1) summarizes the survey research findings regarding public support of higher education.

"With the exception of a few states, the proportion of the state budget going to higher education will be no greater in 1980 than it is now [1973]—whether there are boom times or bad, Republicans or Democrats in office. . . . The major trend which forces less funding growth for higher education is the establishment of a new set of social priorities in which higher education drops to a much lower position than previously held. . . . Unless some national catastrophe occurs for which higher education is believed to be the principal salvation, colleges and universities will not regain their favored position of the 1960s—at least not during the next twenty years."

If all the verbiage and rhetoric about the support of higher education is stripped away, the primary if not sole reason for public investment in colleges and universities is the expectation that, in broadest terms, a better society will result. The term *public funds* has been used so often and so glibly that we tend to forget that it means taxes—taxes paid by citizens generally, many of whom make no direct use of higher education services. Funds for higher education, whether they be in the form of taxes, gifts, or tuition, are supplied willingly only if people expect a satisfactory rate of return on their investment. Returns on investment in higher education can be *social* (nonpecuniary), as manifested by such parameters of social progress as increased participation in civic affairs, enlightened leadership, better family life, less crime, greater tolerance, and generally increased levels of activity in improving the human condition; or they can be *economic,* as manifested by increased earning power of graduates and the concomitant replenishment of the public treasury as a result of their productivity and tax payments. But unless policy-makers and the public are convinced that these returns on investment in higher education are adequate, colleges and universities not only will not regain their former status as Glenny foresees, but also may see their support erode even further.

Consider how cost-benefit concepts influence public attitudes toward higher education. First, with respect to social or nonpecuniary returns, there has been little, if any, objective, measurable, and convincing evidence that increased college attendance results in a significantly better society (Jacob, 1957; Withey, 1973; Juster, 1975). Indeed, some persons have thought the social returns from higher education to be negative in recent years. Political and social conservatives point to campus violence, deterioration in manners and morals, the high incidence of crime in and around major university centers, the apparently close connection between college students and the counter culture, increasing drug abuse, and continuing attacks by some students and professors on capitalism and representative democracy as examples of a negative return. Put bluntly, many Americans of conservative and middle-of-the-road social and political views feel that they have been "conned" into paying for a higher education establishment that is inculcating a set of values diametrically opposed to their own. And since programs, curriculums, course content, and teaching methods are not subject to citizen control, they resort to the only recourse left to them—fiscal control.

Second, with regard to economic returns, it has been a widely held conviction for the past several decades that "going to college" was a sort of automated highway to upward occupational mobility and preferred socioeconomic status. Evidence is now mounting, however, that a college degree per se is no longer a ticket to upper income brackets and preferred jobs—or, for that matter, to any job at all (see Chapter Two). A Bureau of Labor Statistics study as far back as 1972, for example, revealed that nearly 40 percent of recent college graduates were employed, if at all, in jobs having no direct relation to their major field of college study; among social science majors the figure was 67 percent.

The dilemma is obvious: Should we continue to invest billions of dollars annually in an enterprise that promises a meager (or possibly negative) rate of economic return and at the same time compound the problems of society by producing millions of disillusioned college graduates who may be underemployed or unemployed; or should we assay the distasteful and highly unpopular alternative of curtailing public investment in higher education with the dashed expectations and apparent discrimination that such a course would entail? Perhaps neither alternative is acceptable in the extreme, and a compromise may be the chosen course of action.

There is little doubt that higher education will encounter further erosion of public confidence and eventually a real depression if educators do not carefully evaluate the terrain ahead and seek new directions. Higher education cannot continue cost escalation without concomitant and demonstrable productivity increases. The teaching profession cannot continue to demand higher pay and less work while backing up this demand with strikes, dissension, and violence. Colleges cannot allow further politicization of their programs, students, and faculty. They cannot continue their aggressive and almost hucksterish recruiting policies of the past few years just to keep their head-count and generated credit hours up. They cannot continue to emphasize quantity without equal emphasis on quality—for example, open admissions or egalitarian entry—without meritocratic exit and demonstrated competence of graduates. And most important, they cannot continue to turn out millions of liberal arts graduates unprepared for any kind of significant economic activity.

In short, rather than a time of depression, this is a time of transition in higher education—a time for taking bearings, for evaluating trends and conditions, and a time to seek new directions and renewed public confidence. Among the several critically important issues that should influence the future direction of higher education, none is more important than career education. It is to that topic that we now turn.

Career Education: Definitions and Comment

Career education is a term popularized by Sidney P. Marland, Jr., U.S. Commissioner of Education during the early 1970s. Central to the idea of career education as enunciated by Marland is the concept that all education, from the early grades on into college, can and should be associated with the individual's future career. The necessity to do away with the centuries-old dichotomy between "practical" education and "academic" education is inherent in the use of the term *career education.* Also a part of the career education concept are such ideas as the dignity and worth of all work, the career ladder concept, and the increasing necessity for postsecondary and collegiate-occupational education for millions of Americans. Marland (1974, p. xiii) puts the challenge in these words: "Our society is asking that our schools and colleges sustain our heritage of academic rigor, and concurrently adapt teaching and learning more explicitly to the useful pursuits of the economic and professional world. This slow turn is now beginning."

Career education is seen as beginning in the lower grades, perhaps as early as the second, and continuing through high school and into colleges, community colleges, and other postsecondary institutions. Actually, many baccalaureate and advanced degree programs in colleges and universities are also career education, but the currently popular usage of the term does not include graduate programs in universities for traditional professional-level careers. There are, however, many new occupationally oriented baccalaureate degree programs that are a part of career education.

Career education is intended, among other things, to provide the same kind of opportunities to "emerging" and "new" students (Clarke, 1971) as have been afforded to inner-directed and highly motivated college and university students for decades. Since it contains a special thrust for emerging students, career education must have within its structure strong elements of career counseling and career exploration, including, if possible, cooperative work experience or internships. Continuous educational guidance and counseling must be a strong feature to insure that students' course elections are reasonably consistent with their interests and academic abilities.

In a restricted sense, career education might be regarded merely as a new euphemism for "vocational-technical" or "occupational" education. It is different, however, in that it is more comprehensive, involving all facets of career preparation, and in that it proposes to involve the common schools (K–12) at all levels in an all-out educational effort to give focus and status to career preparation by providing exploratory experiences, career guidance, and occupational training. The career education concept implies that the traditional emphasis on academic subjects only, in elementary and secondary education, will end and that youngsters will be given early and continuous instruction in practical studies and will learn about careers at all levels.

Career education also involves colleges, postsecondary schools, and institutes. Realizing that a substantial part of career preparation, in both its academic and its specialized practical aspects, must occur at postsecondary levels, career education calls for good articulation between K–12 school systems and postsecondary educational institutions.

An example of the vertical integration implied in the career education concept is the model program that was developed from 1972 to 1975 in Orange County, California. Three school districts, including fifteen schools ranging in level from kindergarten through community college, formed the Orange County Consortium Career Education Project (Hamilton, 1975) and, with the aid of federal and state funding, developed a "working model" for career education. Some twenty-eight thousand students, over eight hundred teachers, and twenty-six hundred businesses and industries were involved in the three-year project. The Santa Ana Community College was the postsecondary institution providing college-level career education for the project. Vertical curriculum coordination and integration emphasized a "career ladder" concept. Career counseling, educational advisement, and aptitude and interest testing were all improved. Advisory committees were increased in number and provided with support to make them more effective. Field trips and guest speakers at the elementary school and junior high school levels and cooperative work experiences and internships at the senior high school and community college levels were maximized, in order to give students the greatest possible knowledge about and experience in a variety of career activities. Business and industrial firms were heavily involved in the project and proved to be a major factor in lending realism to its career education thrust.

When a new term is introduced, a mystique of sorts frequently develops around it and tends to color and confuse its meaning. *Career education* is no exception. Certain groups within education have given the term an aura of magic, suggesting that a heretofore unattainable threshold in education has been crossed and that any school system or college that will adopt their particular version of career education will almost automatically achieve new levels of educational excellence. Actually, all the elements implied in *career education* have been known (and applied by some teachers in some schools) for years. The *new* idea is that they should be applied in all schools by all teachers, as a planned, national effort.

For a few careers, postsecondary education and training is not indicated (or at least not essential), and career education ends with high school. For many careers, however—those in the occupational classifications of professional, managerial, paraprofessional, semiprofessional, technical, and very highly skilled—postsecondary or college education and training is essential or highly desirable. We estimate that currently these job classifications involve over 50 percent of the labor force in the United States and that this figure will increase slowly over the next decade. Colleges, then, constitute the capstone in the structure of career education for millions of American citizens.

William J. Micheels, the former president of University of Wisconsin-Stout (1973, p. 153) emphasizes the necessity for colleges to get involved in career education: "The career education movement is creating a groundswell of activity at every educational level, perhaps as one reflection of the temper of the times. Higher education cannot remain aloof from these new realities."

Why College-Level Career Education?

Education is dedicated to the eradication of ignorance and incompetence. But in any honest evaluation of education's contributions to job competence, the judgment would have to be less than commendatory. Across the entire range of the work force in America, there are too many persons who are not really competent in their jobs, who have not mastered the combination of knowledge and skills needed to perform effectively. All too many mechanics do not really understand the machines they work on; too many cooks really do "spoil the broth"; too many carpenters are indeed "wood butchers"; too many managers make bad decisions; too many school teachers really could not do anything else; and too many doctors do "bury their mistakes."

In every kind of work activity, there is more muddling through than there ought to be, and it is an interesting and troublesome observation that serious gaps between actual performance and expected performance occur more frequently at the level of ordinary, easily perfectible tasks than at levels near the frontiers of knowledge and performance. Space missions, for example, are rarely "scrubbed" because of scientifically sophisticated problems, but more often because a valve leaks, dirt gets into a fuel cell, or an electrical connection comes unsoldered.

We are very good, it seems, when we operate near the cerebral and physiological limits of the human organism. But sadly, the record is not impressive with respect to the mundane tasks that are the livelihood of most citizens and that form the base of the national economy. As a people we tend to admire the new idea, the theoretical concept, and the complex "system" and to regard with disdain or at best grudging acceptance the more mundane ideas, skills, and mechanisms that promote a high standard of living and have built a great nation. Moreover, the lamentable fact is that most of us do not understand very well the sophisticated bases of new discoveries, and we do not perform very well the practical tasks that determine our everyday well-being.

Why can fantastically difficult problems be readily accomplished, when routine administrative, management, and technical tasks are often bungled? One reason is that highly talented professionals have traditionally been *selected, educated,* and *trained* for their jobs while we have been content to allow middle manpower jobs to be filled by persons who merely "trickle up" (or down) into them. We take very seriously the education and training of those extremely talented individuals who conceive and operate the complex systems of society, providing for them in the most prestigious universities and colleges of the land. But we have been less concerned, perhaps downright unconcerned, about competence in the middle range of the occupational structure: the range of jobs that we associate with middle manpower and that account for about one third of all jobs in the labor force.

Part of this problem stems from the quickening pace of change. In a former time, changes in most jobs came slowly, almost imperceptibly, and people could adjust to them by a kind of cultural osmosis that kept them in step with the relatively incremental new discoveries they encountered. A carpenter of the seventeenth century, for example, would have had little difficulty in adjusting to the work of a construction crew in 1900; the tailor of Napoleon's time would have felt at ease in a shop in the 1920s; and the clerk who kept accounts in colonial Williamsburg could easily have balanced the books for a wholesale business in San Francisco as late as 1935. But those days are now history, and recent decades have been characterized by change so rapid that we seem never to catch up. The industrial revolution came, and before we had quite adjusted ourselves to its pace, the technological-scientific revolution or "age of automation" took its place. Now, still reeling from the impact of automated technology, we find the cybernetic revolution upon us and realize that we are hardly ready to cope with it.

The central theme of this book is that society cannot continue to muddle through with regard to middle manpower. Well-planned, competency-based educational programs for paraprofessionals, semiprofessionals, and technicians are just as essential to good job performance in the middle manpower segment of the labor force as specialized and rigorous graduate training is to the future astrophysicist. And it must be emphasized that to meet today's demands, most of the education for these careers should take place in colleges. The idea that training for careers is a function of colleges is widely accepted today, but it is a rather recent development. For centuries higher learning avoided "vocationalism" as one would avoid the plague. Practical arts belonged in the "lower schools," while the liberal arts constituted the only proper curriculum for colleges. The legacy of this divisive dichotomy continues to affect present policy debates, and a review of this dichotomy is essential for understanding these debates and planning rationally for the future.

Dichotomy and Dialogue

Only four decades ago, when the middle-aged and senior citizens of today were college undergraduates, no jet plane had yet flown, television was unheard of, and the only earth-orbiting satellite was the moon without footprints. The iron horse still ruled the rails, Dalton's atom was still indivisible (except in a few research laboratories), and most Americans supported or at least accepted these five ideas about higher education: (1) a college is a community of scholars; (2) college is for the academically gifted; (3) only the wealthy can afford college; (4) only those with professional career goals need a college education; and (5) higher education should concern itself only with the arts, sciences, humanities, and established professions, and not with practical vocational studies. In the past forty years nearly everything that directs our lives has changed. A population of 125 million in the 1930s has increased to one of 215 million in the 1970s. Rural and small-town living patterns have been superceded by urban and suburban metropolitan areas, with attendant problems of unemployment, drug addiction, crime, and urban decay. A society divided into a small educated elite and a large mass of unskilled workers has evolved into one with a dominant middle class and with great mobility among classes, all of them seeking the freedom that the American system provides. The "melting pot" concept has not worked: the opportunities, challenges, and disappointments of a free society have produced not the generic American but a nation of different kinds of people, still retaining many of the ethnic, cultural, social, and political attributes of their lands of origin, many of them unhappy with the American system but all of them demanding the affluence that the system offers.

In terms of technology, the iron horse and even its rails have rusted. The threat of energy shortages augurs an uncertain future for transportation in a society in which mobility has been essential to the pursuit of happiness. Dalton's atom not only has been divided but its fission energy provides a promise for the future that its fusion energy can either assure or destroy. Communication has become so nearly instantaneous and all-pervasive that we often hear, read, and see more than we really want to know. And though currently under attack on some fronts, the new technology has created a demand for greatly increased education of citizens generally—especially in practical and technical subjects.

Internationally, a relatively isolated nation on the periphery of world affairs has become the hub around which world affairs revolves, and the centrifugal force thus generated creates inner tensions with great potential for conflict. The free society, dimly perceived by the framers of the Magna Carta, eloquently expressed in the documents establishing this nation, and highly prized by native-born and immigrant alike for 200 years, is now threatened by challenges from without as well as by apathy and agitation from within.

Can higher education respond effectively to all of these changes—particularly those related to economic and social viability—to the matching of people's talents to jobs, and to a future in which a less bountiful environment must be offset by greater individual productivity? Can the age-old dichotomy between the liberal arts and the practical arts be resolved? Can we finally arrive at an attitude that makes no pejorative distinctions between "clean" school subjects on the one hand and "dirty" fields of study on the other or between "academic education" and "occupational training," or the "good students" and the "vocational students"?

Some scholars of education are doubtful. They note that events and institutions of the past receive a peculiar kind of adulation and acquire the same sort of mystic patina that supposedly makes old silver more desirable than new. Higher education, as it developed in Europe through the Middle Ages and the Renaissance, acquired such a patina: it was intended for a select few, and it emphasized the arts and sciences and preparation for the professions. This quality became firmly imbedded in the philosophy of American higher education over two centuries. Despite the challenge of the land-grant colleges after 1862 and of the public junior colleges since the early 1930s, the idea that higher education should concern itself with the liberal arts, the sciences, and the humanities, has persisted to the present day.

Dualism in education thus remains very much with us. The dichotomy between liberal learning and occupational training is alive and well. The liberal arts still constitute the generally accepted body of knowledge with which colleges are expected to concern themselves; and the practical arts, though they are tolerated as economic necessity from time to time may require, are still relegated to a lower station by genteel members of the higher education family. Somehow it is intellectually respectable to study and deliberate about Democritus' primitive notions of the structure of matter, but it is less than fully respectable for colleges to offer courses in how electrons can be harnessed to serve man's needs. It remains in the best traditions of higher education to study the contributions of Euclid to geometry, Archimedes to physics, Newton to the calculus, or Lord Kelvin to thermodynamics, but the suggestion that higher education should engage in teaching technicians the practical applications of these discoveries is an anathema to many in the professoriate.

Let us briefly examine some of the basic sources of the dichotomy. Educational dualism has its roots in Greco-Roman philosophy. It was Aristotle who is supposed to have said that "the aim of education is the wise use of leisure." And since, in his time, only the elite few had any leisure, it is clear that he considered education to be only for the elite: the rulers, the thinkers, the wealthy, and the highly born. This concept of education is rooted in the general dualism of ancient societies (the gods versus man; good versus evil; guardians versus slaves; kings versus commoners; heaven versus earth), where freemen were few and slaves were many. Plato, in *The Republic*, goes one step beyond dualism and envisions three social classes: guardians, warriors, and workers (slaves). Guardians were freemen, those whose political status by right of birth gave them the authority to proclaim the law and fashion the government and whose economic status allowed them the leisure to study, deliberate, and debate. It was for the guardian class that liberal education was intended. Our word *liberal* comes from the Latin word *liber*, meaning *free*. Liberal education was education for the "free" man, the leisured man, the ruling class, and it was very early contrasted with the kind of training that came to be known as the "practical arts" and was intended for workers and warriors. Commercial knowledge to train tradesmen in accounts, craft training to impart the skills of construction, and military training (for the warriors) to insure success in battle—these practical arts were in no way related to the liberal arts for free men.

Epictetus (c. A.D. 100) is credited with remarking that "Only the educated are free." Noble as this thought is (and it is found on more than a few college cornerstones today), in Epictetus' time it would have been decently honest to have reversed it to say, "Only the free are educated." Although we may disagree with the Greek idea of education as the prerogative of the leisure class, they (the leisured ones) applied themselves so enthusiastically to study and schooling that their word for leisure, σχολή, became so nearly synonymous with scholarly activity that it translates into modern (Western European) words for school—*escuela, école, schüle* (Brubacher, 1965).

Originally, in the heyday of Greek civilization, the liberal arts consisted of the disciplines of grammar, rhetoric, and logic, a group known later (in Roman times) as the *trivium.* During the first millenium of the Christian era four other disciplines acquired respectability and were, one by one, brought into the fold of the liberal arts. These four—the *quadrivium*—were arithmetic, geometry, music, and astronomy. By the twelfth century A.D. the accepted studies of higher education were known as the seven liberal arts; and although modification and expansion, branching and bunching, new discoveries and new problems, and new needs of new societies have by now filled college catalogs with hundreds of separate courses, the old dualism still persists.

The dichotomy between the liberal and practical arts has been a convenient vehicle in America for class distinction. In a politically classless society, one in which "low" or "high" birth has had only minimal effect on one's social mobility and in which economic acumen and the Horatio Alger complex have often been determinants of financial success, there has been a certain usefulness, for ego-building purposes, in the pursuit of the liberal arts. Some have found the road to becoming a philosopher-king far easier and more to their liking than the road to business success or to competence in a profession or vocation in which hard work and competition are essential components. And, along with the pursuit of "things of the mind," all too often has come the denigration of the activities of the hand. Work tends to fall into disrepute (Faltermeyer, 1974), and "thinking" is enthroned. And, tragically, in this hierarchy of values, second-class thinking becomes better than first-class work.

A rather serious problem with respect to curriculum-spawned class distinction arose on college and university campuses in the 1960s. Faculty and students in liberal arts and humanities fields adopted increasingly arrogant and supercilious attitudes toward their colleagues and fellow-students who were in scientific and technical fields of study. By peculiar modes of reasoning based on unexamined premises, persons studying the liberal arts and the humanities exhibited an antitechnology syndrome, equating themselves with the "good guys" and the business, engineering, agriculture, and science students with the "bad guys" (Branscomb,

1971). The study of the humanities somehow implied that you were going to render some service of incalculable value to humanity; whereas the study of business, science, engineering, or technology implied that you intended to exploit your fellowman and probably despoil the earth at the same time. The scorn of the self-proclaimed intellectual for the very persons who make his life of free inquiry possible is one of the sharp tragedies of dualistic thinking in higher education today. The much discussed antiintellectualism in America is not fiction—there really is a sense of pent-up anger toward some intellectuals on the part of many working people and in no small measure it is backlash against the contempt in which they—the workers—have been regarded by some intellectuals. Antipathy toward "hard-hats" and constant denigration of "middle-class values" by intellectuals have finally exhausted the patience of millions of "ordinary" Americans. One of the office posters so popular these days speaks wisely to this issue. "All Americans should get a good education so that people won't look down on them and then get enough more that they won't look down on people."

S.I. Hayakawa (1970, p. 18) expresses his concern about elitism in college and university circles. "The ancient Greek prejudice against work is reflected to this day in the American university in the scorn of many liberal arts professors of (what they call) 'vocationalism,' and in the contempt of many English majors for such subjects as commerce, engineering, or agriculture. Laden with such prejudices the verbalists find it easy to *define themselves* as an intellectual aristocracy—an elite class—and to begin to act like one" (emphasis added).

Higher education is one of those institutions that for centuries has been guided by tradition. Even when, on occasion, tradition was set aside to meet a societal need (for example, the establishment of land-grant colleges under the Morrill-Land Grant Colleges Act of 1862 for practical higher education in agricultural and mechanical arts) it soon reasserted itself and redirected higher education onto paths of the past. Nearly every A. and M. college in the nation deemphasized its role in practical arts education during the period between 1940 and 1970 in order to become a "regular" university. But a basic fact about American society is that it is not tradition-directed, and with each passing year it is increasingly evident that tradition-directed, liberal-arts-oriented higher education has not been responsive to the needs and demands of present-day society.

Why must dichotomy give way to dialogue in higher education? Here are a few reasons: (1) the increasing complexity of everyday life in an industrialized society characterized by growing urbanization. (2) The impact of technology, automation, and the flow-process industries on production, jobs, and people. (3) The explosion of scientific and technical knowledge, which increases exponentially with time. (4) The alarming increase in sophistication and complexity of jobs at all levels, to a point where almost all jobs have a considerable cognitive component. (5) The fact that education beyond high school is a prerequisite to nearly half the jobs provided by capital-intensive industries (including agriculture). (6) The virtual disappearance of unskilled (common labor) jobs. (7) The needs of business and industry for middle manpower—semi-professionals and technicians. (8) The "disaster gap" that has opened up between those of our citizens with advanced education and those with little education. (9) An awareness of the fact that if indeed "only the educated are free," then all the free must be educated. (10) The certain knowledge that, even in a dynamic and affluent society, there are definite limits to the number of philosopher-kings a society can support. And (11) the need for millions of citizens who can both think and do—citizen-workers who realize that the road to both economic security and personal satisfaction has a foundation of both academic study and practical experience.

The Dichotomy Challenged

We have come then to the realization, after a thousand years, that higher education is not a cult for the few but a necessity for the many—that it is a driving force behind the economic and cultural development of nations. We know now that "liberal" education can be taken to mean not only the liberation of the mind through intellectual inquiry, but also liberation from poverty and uselessness and exploitation through education for occupational competence. As Marvin Feldman (1976, p. 1) puts it: "We don't believe people are enslaved when they learn skills. We believe they are enslaved when they have no skills."

The Aristotelian concept of education only for a leisure class is as barren today as the very idea of a leisured class. In America—and the same is true of most advanced industrial societies—rich and poor alike work, tycoons of industry and members of the recognized professions in many instances setting themselves a far more demanding pace than that expected of laborers or production-line factory workers. In our society, education may in part be preparation for leisured moments and for interludes of contemplation, but it is also preparation for work.

As technological development proceeds, work becomes more and more like education. The cognitive content of work at all levels and in all spheres of economic activity increases. Whereas at one time disciplines such as English, mathematics, economics, psychology, and the sciences would most certainly not have been regarded as vocational subjects, today selected content from these disciplines is essential to the occupational competence of the majority of the work force. This change in the relationship between work and education prompted Grant Venn (1963, p. 1) to write, in a report for the American Council on Education: "It is the thesis of this report that technology has created a new relationship between man, his education, and his work in which *education is placed squarely between man and his work* (emphasis added). Although this relationship has traditionally held for *some* men and *some* work (on the professional level, for example), modern technology has advanced to the point where the relationship may now be said to exist for *all* men and for *all* work."

A liberal education today is markedly different from the liberal education of Cicero's time or of Woodrow Wilson's time, for that matter. There is one thread of commonality, however, and that is that a truly liberal education should prepare a person for the life he is to lead. In a former time this may have meant preparation for leisure and for ruling and directing the lower classes. Today, it means preparation for one's life work, be that in business, science, military service, industry, politics, the arts, or in helping one's fellow man. All of these are vocations in life, and in a real sense all education is vocational education. Richard Millard (1973, p. 2) says, "In this broader concept of vocation . . . may well lie the key to reforming, restructuring, and revitalizing not just vocational education . . . but education as a whole. Putting *vocation* or preparation for a career back as the *central aim of education*, a number of things begin to fall into perspective, and some of the broad dichotomies drawn in the past begin to disappear."

Adler and Mayer (1958, p. 102) pose the question with clarity as they put words in the mouth of the "modernist." "How can the 'traditionalist' say, on the one hand, that human society has been revolutionized by democracy, industry and science and, on the other, that the education appropriate to pre-industrial aristocracy or feudalism is appropriate today?" Pursuing the same theme, they quote John Dewey's concept of a liberal education (in Adler and Mayer, 1958, p. 103). "A truly liberal and liberating education would refuse today to isolate vocational training on any of its levels from a continuous education in the social, moral, and scientific context within which wisely administered callings and professions must function."

In the same vein, Brubacher (1965, p. 58), as he explores some bases for policy in higher education, states: "When only the few were free, they did no work; consequently there grew up a tradition of exalting general or liberal education and denigrating special or vocational education. Clearly such an educational tradition became incongruous in a democratic society where all men are free and all work. . . . modern liberal education must find a worthy place for work in its curriculum, not grudgingly, nor of necessity, but willingly and enthusiastically."

Dialogue Replaces Dichotomy

American higher education is seeking new bases for policy and is properly engaged in a careful examination of long-held premises. Certainly higher education for leisured man is hardly a fitting role for that vast enterprise in which America is already investing over $50 billion annually. The "liberal education" needed by college students today is that which will liberate them from ignorance and ineptitude, from uselessness and poverty, from arrogance and brittle intellectualism; that which will free them from dichotomous ideas about work and leisure and from dualistic thinking about "humanistic" studies and "practical" studies; that which will prepare them for a life of productivity in a world that needs the best possible contribution from every capable individual. This kind of education is *vocational* education in the real meaning of the term—preparation for vocation, for one's *calling* in life. (The word *vocation* comes from a Latin root meaning "a summons" or "a calling," as in the religious sense when one is "called" to a life's work.) If American higher education has no stake in this venture, then it really deserves the loss of public confidence that seems apparent in this decade (Marland, 1973a). To use a popular 1960s expression, perhaps the American people "are trying to tell us something."

As dialogue replaces dichotomy most, if not all, of the following changes will occur in the concept and operation of colleges and career education programs.

First, education for careers will become not only a respectable and normal function of most colleges—it will be the central focus of college programs, with arts and sciences education in essential supporting roles. Second, colleges with comprehensive postsecondary education programs will cease to have two faculties and two student bodies—departments (or divisions) and student enrollments will be organized around career fields, not grouped separately as "arts and sciences" and "vocational" (Lombardi, 1973). Third, courses in two-year colleges will not be rigidly divided into liberal arts (transfer) and vocational (nontransfer) categories.

Fourth, there will be recognition of a ladder concept of education and careers—that is, that no educational program or career level should be considered a "dead end." Fifth, career (or vocational) programs will operate at appropriate levels of quality and rigor and will cease to be dumping grounds for the unprepared, the unmotivated, and the inept. Sixth, as teachers of the liberal arts come to recognize the importance of career education, so will "vocational teachers" realize that liberal learning is vitally important to students in search of careers.

Seventh, the position advanced by some writers that education in liberal arts and professional fields is a just and equitable charge on society, but that education and training for jobs of less-than-professional status should be paid for either by the individual or by business and industrial employers, will be recognized for what it is—a crude claim of privilege made by those already privileged more than they perhaps should have been. Eighth, as liberal arts programs and career education programs achieve equal prestige, enrollment in the former only for status reasons will drop off, with beneficial effects for all of higher education and for society generally. Ninth and finally, it eventually may come to pass that most students, in search of meaningful careers, will plan the education for those careers around both liberal learning and practical learning, fully recognizing the values in each.

Alfred North Whitehead (1949) said it best nearly sixty years ago in his presidential address to the Mathematical Association of England: "There can be no adequate technical education which is not liberal, and no liberal education which is not technical."

Summary

The current "depression" in higher education results from the interaction of several factors: (1) a decline in the rate of growth of enrollment, especially of college-age youth, that has seemed almost as disastrous as an actual enrollment decline, since capital outlays, staffing, program development, and long-range planning were predicated on extrapolations of the abnormally high growth rates of the 1960s; (2) a decline in federal funds for basic research and development; (3) a slower rate of increase in state funding in most states, combined with frequent failures of local millage proposals in community college districts; (4) a relative decline in the preferred status of higher education as other social issues and problems have claimed greater attention and increased funding; and (5) alarmingly escalating costs, due in part to significantly increased faculty and staff compensation and in part to the general inflation which affects all operating costs.

These factors point not to an actual depression in higher education but to a slowing down of growth and a period of financial restraint after a decade of frenetic growth and feverish activity in which higher education, like the phantom horseman, rode off in all directions. If there is a real depression in American higher education today, it is not one of enrollment collapse, although the current steady state is perhaps a less comfortable condition than steady growth. Neither is it one of collapsing revenue structures, since revenues, even in constant dollars, have more than kept pace with enrollments. Instead, the depression is a state of mind, a way of thinking about higher education, a loss of public confidence in higher education, and a keen sense of disappointment over that loss. Many Americans feel that higher education promised a great deal and somehow did not deliver that much, that higher education was elitist in a populist era, and that higher education failed to meet the challenge of career preparation.

The challenge to higher or postsecondary education is to accept eagerly and convincingly the concept of career education and to co-opt a major share of this educational thrust for colleges. There must be continuous, not episodic, interest in and support of career education by academic administrators as well as faculty. Colleges and universities already have the major role in professional education at the baccalaureate level and beyond, while community colleges and collegiate-level technical institutes have most of the market for paraprofessional and technical education. Some four-year colleges are also quite active in technician education and in providing baccalaureate programs at the technologist level.

Humanists are apt to be severely critical of this new vocationalism. They feel that the purpose of higher education is not to train people to make a living but to educate people to make a life. In contrast, we agree with Harbison and Myers (1964, pp. 12–13) who seek a middle road between humanism and narrow job training and who contend that "the purely humanistic approach, like the limited economic approach to human resource development, distorts the true meaning of the aspirations of modern man and modern societies."

Higher education has been in a boom-and-bust cycle for the past fifteen years. The boom was a real joy-ride, which made the bust appear to be disastrous. In reality, however, it is not as grim as the literature and the banquet speakers suggest. Actually, public funding of higher education is at an all-time high; enrollments, except for those of college-age youth in regular full-time study, are up substantially, not down. Public confidence in the enterprise, though eroded somewhat compared to its high point in the early 1960s, is still strong. The American people want what higher education can provide, and they still have a great deal of respect for higher education institutions. They are insisting, however, on improved accountability, increased productivity, and a closer compatibility between the goals of college and the goals of America as they see them. The cry of "relevance," so popular among students in the 1960s, is precisely what the American public is expressing now. And among all the education thrusts that are relevant to this nation, career education occupies a signally important position. Higher education should welcome career education as a major force in determining the direction along which the path of future progress lies.

2 🔲🔲🔲🔲🔲🔲🔲🔲🔲🔲🔲🔲🔲🔲🔲

Students in Search
of Careers

> *There is a tide in the affairs of men,*
>> *Which, taken at the flood, leads on to fortune;*
>> *Omitted, all the voyage of their life*
>> *Is bound in shallows and in miseries.*
>> *On such a full sea are we now afloat;*
>> *And we must take the current when it serves*
> *Or lose our ventures.*
>
> William Shakespeare, *Julius Caesar*

In any recent year, ten million or more students have been enrolled or about to enroll in American colleges and universities, hoping that higher education is the tide "which, taken at the flood" will lead them on to fortune, a satisfying career, and a full life. Increasing numbers of them have been seeking career-oriented education as it became evident in the early 1970s that liberal arts graduates, even those with advanced degrees, were having difficulty in finding jobs—any jobs, let alone one suited to their level and field of education.

The phenomenal growth of two-year colleges and technical institutes; the opening of admissions to "new" students whose socioeconomic backgrounds and high school records would have precluded college attendance in former years; the return to school of housewives and other women as they have sought new status; and the seeking after further education by persons in mid-career—all of these trends have brought significant changes to the higher education student body in the past decade. College administrators—presidents, deans, and program directors—are facing many new realities. College age youth no longer crowd the gates of the academy clamoring for admission. On the contrary, many an academic scouting party is now sent forth to locate, influence, and sign up prospective learners. *Recruitment,* an invidious term once used to castigate the coaching staff, is now a legitimate entry in the lexicon of academicians. The "hunt for bright young minds," though still in full cry, now has its counterpart in the hunt for minds neither bright nor young; and the milieu in which learning and learners interact is often so unstructured that the simple question: Who is a student? has no ready or simple answer.

Who Goes to College?

Certainly the traditional view of college students—eighteen to twenty-four years of age, engaged in a one-time quest for knowledge that will serve for a lifetime—is no longer valid. Students are no longer predominantly white males from middle- and upper-income families seeking degrees and credentials that will authenticate their entry into professional and white-collar status.

Women are attending college in great numbers. In 1974 they comprised nearly 45 percent of total enrollments in four-year colleges and 46.2 percent in two-year colleges, and their rate of attendance will probably soon be equal to that for men.

Blacks and other minorities are enrolling by the thousands, realizing that higher education offers a chance at upward occupational and social mobility. For example, in 1960 only 4.2 percent of the nonwhite population between the ages of eighteen and thirty-four years was enrolled for degree credit in college, but by 1972 this figure had grown to 13.4 percent (U.S. Department of Health, Education and Welfare, 1974a). (Comparable figures for the total population, both white and nonwhite, of eighteen to thirty-four year olds were 7.7 percent in 1960 and 16.2 percent in 1972.)

Youth from poor families, low-income workers, housewives, the aged, members of the armed forces, people in hospitals, prisons, and rest homes, and thousands from the ranks of the unemployed—all now have an opportunity to enroll in college because of free and low-tuition community colleges and extensive federal, state, and private grants and loans.

Moreover, "enrollment" in colleges today does not necessarily imply enrollment in structured, formalized courses for degree credit. Hundreds of thousands of persons are enrolled in short-term, adult and continuing education courses, many of them with a career education objective. Nontraditional study in "storefront colleges," "satellite learning centers" and "colleges without walls" is increasingly common.

The age-mix of college students is shifting rapidly too, with an increase in older and part-time students but a decrease in the percentage of new high school graduates who are attending college. As Table 1 shows, the percentage of new high school grad-

Table 1. Percent of New High School Graduates Attending Higher Education Institutions, 1962–1973.

Year	Total	Men	Women	Whites	Blacks
1962	49	55	43	51	34
1963	45	52	39	46	38
1964	48	57	41	49	39
1965	51	57	45	52	43
1966	50	59	43	52	32
1967	52	58	47	53	42
1968	55	63	49	57	46
1969	54	60	47	55	37
1970	52	55	49	52	48
1971	53	58	50	54	47
1972	49	53	46	49	48
1973	47	50	43	48	35

Source: U.S. Department of Labor, Bureau of Labor Statistics (1974c).

uates going on to postsecondary education reached a peak of 55 percent in 1968 and has been decreasing ever since. For two decades after World War II, their participation rate in college increased at about one percent a year, but since 1968 it has decreased at about the same rate. Various reasons have been advanced for the decrease, including economic and inflationary factors, the end of American involvement in the Indochina war and of the military draft, and the changing value systems and life styles of young people in the 1970s; but because the causes for the fall-off cannot be accurately pin-pointed, it is impossible to predict whether or not it will continue. But combined with smaller numbers of college age youth, this trend means that enrollments of young students probably are now at their peak and will decline year by year for the foreseeable future.

It is a known demographic fact that the age cohort of eighteen and nineteen year olds reached a peak in 1976 and will fall off for at least the next seventeen years (Poulton, 1975). For example, the number of high school age youths between fourteen and seventeen years old will drop from a 1975 top of 16.8 million to 14.3 million in 1985—a decrease of 14.9 percent for the decade (U.S. Bureau of the Census, 1973).

With the birth rate presently at a low point for this century (fifteen live births per thousand of the mid-year population as of 1975), and with many young adults currently interested in zero population growth, any projection of "college age" enrollments in regular-day programs must, of necessity, be one of no-growth or even decline as far into the future as the mid-1990s. The college students of 1994 are already born, and the only factor that could change this projection would be a marked increase in their participation rate—but as noted above, this rate is going down rather than up.

Offsetting this no-growth scenario for youth, however, is the almost phenomenal resurgence of a cyclical phenomenon—the idea of "lifelong learning." The proportion of older students in the college population, especially in the age range of twenty-five to thirty-four years, is increasing rapidly. In 1950, when there were about 2.3 million degree-credit college students in the United

States, only 18 percent of them were in the twenty-five to thirty-four age group. During the 1973–74 college year, however, nearly 25 percent of the 8.5 million degree-credit students (U.S. Department of Health, Education and Welfare, 1975a) were in this age cohort. In fact, many community colleges and technical institutes report that the median age of their students is now twenty-six years or more. Almost imperceptibly at first, then steadily, and now in a flood, "nontraditional"—part-time degree-credit and nondegree-credit—students are seeking postsecondary education either on campus, at satellite centers, or in classes held in factories, libraries, community centers, churches, prisons, union halls, corporation offices, and Indian reservations, because, as the Carnegie Commission puts it, "people want more options among work, education, and leisure throughout their lives; more opportunities to assess possibilities and change directions; more extension of the potentialities of youth into age" (1973b, p. 14).

Table 2 gives some idea of the magnitude of the kinds of programs and institutions that now exist outside of traditional academic higher education. It may be a surprise to many that the number of students engaged in "noncollegiate" postsecondary education settings is six times that enrolled in "regular" colleges in degree-credit programs. Nearly one of every three persons over age eighteen is enrolled in some form of postsecondary education at some time during the year. Other observers predict even greater participation in the "learning force" than does the Carnegie Commission. Stanley Moses, for example, in 1971 estimated that by 1975, more than 80 million adults would be engaged in continuing education programs of some kind. Somewhat less astronomical totals are obtained by projecting total head-count enrollment (degree credit and nondegree credit) in two-year and four-year colleges, technical institutes, and postsecondary area vocational-technical schools, over the next twenty years. Mangelson (1974) has plotted projections (from the Carnegie Commission, the U.S. Bureau of the Census, the U.S. Department of Health, Education and Welfare, and other individual researchers) that indicate that postsecondary enrollments thus defined will peak at between ten to thirteen million by 1980 and hold steady until 1993, when they may again begin to rise if the birth rate begins to rise in the re-

Table 2. Estimated and Projected Program Enrollments in the
Noncollegiate Sector of Postsecondary Education,
1970 and 1980.

Kind of Institution Or Program	Enrollments[a]		Percent Change, 1970 to 1980
	Estimated, 1970	Projected, 1980	
Employers and Associations	31,800,000	40,900,000	29%
Proprietary Schools (except Correspondence Schools)	3,800,000	8,000,000	111
Armed Forces	3,050,000	3,300,000	8
Correspondence Schools	2,000,000	3,500,000	75
Public Postsecondary Schools (Does not include community colleges)	1,000,000	2,500,000	150
Government Programs (Work Incentive, Agricultural Extension, etc.)	750,000	850,000	40
Prisons	200,000	200,000	0
Unions	100,000	150,000	50
Other Organized Programs (TV, Churches, Synagogues, Community Centers, Libraries, Museums, etc.)	10,000,000	15,000,000	50
Totals	52,700,000	74,400,000	41%

[a]Number of persons participating at some time during the year, excluding informal or unorganized learning. These numbers may overstate the number of separate persons by a factor of approximately 1.3 because of multiple program enrollments during the year.

Source: Carnegie Commission on Higher Education (1973, pp. 46–47).

maining years of the 1970s. If these projections prove to be anywhere near correct, we will indeed be well on the way to becoming a "learning society."

The Learning Society

Lifelong learning is not a new idea. Dating from the time of Socrates and Plato through the intervening centuries to Veblen in the 1920s, Hutchins in the 1930s, and on to the present day, the ideal of the learning society has had many advocates. Each age and place have given the notion a special meaning, and many past trends can be followed into current discussions of the subject.

For a variety of reasons this Utopian learning society has never been fully attained, but the idea reappears from time to time, and it is now with us again in the form of a renewed and multifaceted interest in and commitment to continuing education. Workers in mid-career see advantageous lateral or upward occupational moves as possible results of further education; women sense that new opportunities await them if additional education is obtained in a time when affirmative action is one of the nation's top priorities; ethnic minority groups often have similar motivations; and in a time of economic recession and high unemployment thousands of persons return to school partly from boredom and partly in the hope that further education will enhance chances for employment. The added inducement of stipends from federally sponsored manpower projects attracts many poor and disadvantaged students, and GI benefits attract many veterans. Early retirement—moving the retirement age from sixty-five down to sixty for professionals, and from sixty down to fifty-five for industrial workers, with "thirty-and-out" retirement and pension plans—is already producing millions of potential enrollees for colleges, some of whom may have retraining for a second career in mind and others of whom seek further education for cultural or recreational reasons. And finally there are the thousands of senior citizens, retired and with no further career aspirations in an economic sense, who are just becoming aware of the values that education has for them in the sometimes lonely afternoon of their lives. All of these factors, combined with the findings of the relatively new field of educational gerontology, are beginning to set in motion trends which could shift the emphasis in cradle-to-the-grave education farther from the cradle and nearer to the grave.

From lifelong learning, we can realize both *consumer* goods (values that enhance the sense of individual well-being or merely satisfy the desire to know) and *economic* goods (advanced training for better-paying jobs). Both constitute worthy reasons for seeking higher education. (Wise said it well in the title of his omniscient little book, *They Come for the Best of Reasons* [1958].) Almost any reason for wanting more education is a good reason—upward job mobility, preparation for greater service to society, increased cultural attainment, learning a new hobby or recreational pursuit. All are worthwhile, but perhaps the best reason of all is purely and simply the desire to know. There is no greater satisfaction than scholarly activity in the arts and sciences and humanities when studied for their intrinsic values, and there is no doubt that these disciplines will continue to be the major interest of millions of students in the future. For millions of other students, however, the central purpose in going to college is the expectation of a satisfying career at high pay. For this group—and it is a much larger group than the other—the entire concept of higher education must change.

Shift to Career-Oriented Studies

In recent years, a significant shift of interest has occurred among college students toward career-oriented programs. Beginning in the 1950s, community colleges began emphasizing occupational education for middle-manpower jobs, and since 1960, enrollment in occupational programs of these institutions has more than tripled. According to the American Association of Community and Junior Colleges, nearly 50 percent of students enrolled in community colleges in 1972–1973 were studying in occupational fields ("Training More People . . .," 1973). And the trend continued into 1974, as evidenced by reports collected by Garland Parker (1974, p. 469) from a sample of 157 two-year colleges that indicated 56.8 percent of their students were enrolled in career-oriented curriculums. The figures represent a significant departure from the long-accepted rule of thumb prior to 1970 that two-thirds of the students in two-year colleges chose transfer programs rather

Table 3. Percent of Total Enrollment by Program Among 216,338 Students at 157 Two-Year Colleges, 1973–1974.

Program	Percent of Total Enrollment
Arts and Humanities	32.5
Technical	14.8
Business Office	13.7
Trade and Industrial	12.4
Business Management and Marketing	8.7
Public Service (Social Science)	8.2
Health	7.3
Natural Sciences	2.5
Total	100.2

Source: Parker (1974, p. 469).

than occupational specialties. Undoubtedly affecting these statistics is the fact that now, in contrast to the past, students in many two-year occupational programs can transfer to a large number of four-year colleges without losing credits.

Parker's data for 1973–1974 show that at the 157 two-year colleges students distributed themselves by programs as indicated in Table 3. Similar trends are much in evidence at four-year colleges and universities, with a pronounced movement since 1971 into career-oriented majors and the professional schools. By 1975, for example, among 186,406 college freshmen surveyed by Astin at 366 institutions to get a representative sample of freshman opinion, nearly 70 percent of those who had already decided on a major had chosen an occupational field of study rather than the arts and sciences. Fully 80 percent of the freshmen at two-year institutions were occupationally inclined, and even among those at four-year colleges and universities, at least 62 percent planned occupational majors. Twenty percent of the freshmen men and 17.5 percent of the women planned to major in business—a higher proportion than in any other field—with engineering the second most popular major among men at 14 percent, and education in second place for women at 15.5 percent. Among these freshmen, 51 percent indicated that their belief that college "will help me get a better job" was a very important reason in their choice of college—a reason checked by more of them (including 50 percent of the men and 52 percent of the women) than any other, and even more than the "very good academic reputation" of their college, which was in second place with 47.5 percent.

Beyond their choice of majors, in terms of choice of future occupation nearly 14 percent of these freshmen indicate one or another area of business as their probable career (17.2 percent of the men and 10 percent of the women). Over 18 percent seek work in the health professions (12.1 percent of the men and 26 percent of the women), while 10 percent of the men plan to enter engineering and 11 percent of the women plan to teach (Astin, King, and Richardson, 1976, pp. 18–42).

Occupational training is also of most importance to adults who seek further education. In a national survey of adults no longer in school or college, researchers for the Educational Testing Service found that among those who were interested in studying any subject, 46 percent of them were interested in vocational subjects, as compared to only 13 percent interested in general academic subjects, another 13 percent interested in hobbies and recreational topics, and the rest who were interested in such other fields as personal development, home and family, public affairs, and religion. Seventy-eight percent of these adults reported at least some interest in further vocational study, with 26 percent seeking improved business skills, 22 percent interested in one or another industrial trade, 19 percent interested in technical skills, 16 percent in management, and 14 percent in computer science (Carp, Peterson, and Roelfs, 1974, pp. 18–19). These data and evidence from other surveys and continuing education enrollments belie the claims of some critics who contend that the interests of adults in further education are limited to such avocational pursuits as square dancing, rope twirling, and fly tying.

Some Problems of Diversity

This diversity of college students—in age, in life style, in educational and career aspirations—and the rapid relative increase in participation among women, minority racial groups, and part-time and off-campus students would seem to present challenge enough to collegiate institutions, but the most critical issue posed by diversity is yet to be examined. It is the range of aspirations and academic ability presented by the "new" students, whose background and secondary school achievement would almost automatically have excluded them from higher education as recently as a decade ago.

Up to about 1950, isolated examples of many forms of diversity could easily be found in most colleges. There were some older students, some from poor families assisted by scholarships, and some women, blacks, and Spanish-surnamed students. There was considerable diversity, in many colleges at any rate, of educational goals and aspirations, with many students in liberal arts and professional programs of course, but significant numbers also in occupational education programs. In one respect however, diversity was notably absent: "going to college" two decades ago was generally limited to persons who were judged to be "of college caliber." Academic ability was evaluated from high school grades in academic subjects, and from scores made on academic aptitude tests. Using, for example, IQs and high school grades as measures of academic ability, not very many fully matriculated students before 1950 would have been found with standings much below an IQ of 105 and a high-school grade average of B in academic subjects in four-year colleges and an IQ of 95 and a C average in high school in junior colleges. If the currently popular academic aptitude test of the American College Testing Program (ACT), had been in general use twenty-five years ago, a cutting score of 20 probably would have been common for admission to four-year colleges, and 15 for two-year institutions. But currently, the *median* score for first-time enrollees in two-year colleges nationally is about 15, and thousands of entering students score below 10.

High-school counselors of the 1950s advised, if indeed they did not admonish, students with less than a B average in high school against going to any kind of college at all. Beginning in the late 1950s, however, there began to be voiced the idea of "universal higher education." The community colleges especially became in the 1960s "open door colleges." In the early 1970s, when enrollments of "college caliber" students at four-year colleges and universities began falling off markedly, more than a few of these "senior" colleges suddenly made arrangements to accommodate persons whose applications would have been rejected on academic grounds a few years earlier.

As a consequence of these trends—either commendable or deplorable, depending on one's concept of the mission of higher education—colleges today are not at all like the colleges of a decade ago. As an example of the pervasiveness of low academic ability, one state survey reveals that nearly three fourths of all public junior-college freshmen enrolled in English and mathematics courses in that state in the late 1960s were in courses of noncollege level. Another research study reveals that, of all students enrolled in developmental and remedial courses in California public two-year colleges in the mid-1960s, the failure rate ranged from 40 to 60 percent (Roueche, 1968). And the steady increase in the number of universities and four-year colleges that are establishing "general colleges" or "vestibule programs" of one kind or another bears testimony to the fact that the phenomenon of the academically unprepared college student is not limited to the two-year college.

The issue here is not whether academically underqualified students should be *admitted* to college—that step has already been taken. Egalitarianism and meritocracy are in a continual tug of war on many fronts, but in the arena of college *admissions* egalitarian ideas have won the day. Community colleges are committed to open access, to the second chance, and to the "late bloomer." It should be emphasized strongly, moreover, that this must not be a hollow commitment. Having made the commitment, community colleges must do their utmost to render it meaningful. Operationally, this means basic education programs, developmental/remedial programs, vestibule programs, quasitutorial teaching-learning systems, new media learning laboratories, performance-based learning, and learning systems in which achievement is the constant and time is the variable. Egalitarian entrance is a defensible educational philosophy in a nation committed to equal opportunity, but if it is not matched by the goal of meritocratic exit, mediocrity will be the inevitable result.

The issue we are trying to sharpen here is perhaps the most critical in higher education today. It transcends the problems of finance, governance, and control, important as they are; it is much more basic to the purposes of education than are issues related to collective bargaining and conditions of faculty employment. The issue of quality within diversity focuses on whether or not we can successfully provide open access to higher education and still retain a climate of excellence and unmitigated standards of performance. We need only to review the last thirty years of the American high school to predict what could happen to higher education unless the commitment to open access and equal opportunity for students is matched by a determined commitment to quality, excellence, and standards of performance for retention in programs and for eventual program completion with the appropriate degree.

It is certainly to be hoped that, with newer concepts of teaching and learning, the aid of educational technology, and the assistance of an entire new generation of teachers interested in and trained to work with the "new students," millions of them will succeed. But the cost of their success must not be the deterioration of the higher learning in America. Happily, it is not an either/or situation. With dedication to the student and his needs, but with an equal commitment to the disciplinary demands of college study and the performance demands of careers, we can plan and operate college programs (each with its proper level of cognition and skill attainment) that will allow each student to learn as much as he is capable of learning and perform as well as he is capable of performing. The chances of success for all will be enhanced, but success for everyone cannot be guaranteed.

Students as a Class

It was mentioned on an earlier page that with respect to higher education today, the question "Who is a student?" has no simple answer. Since the twelfth century when the early universities at Paris and Bologna were established, students of the higher learning have tended to regard themselves as a special class of people. Banding together at first to protect themselves against real or imagined economic pressures from the local merchants and landlords, they soon formed guilds of a more structured nature to regulate the activities of their professors. Meyer (1965) relates how the student guilds controlled lecture hours, the semester's schedule, and even professors' elocutionary and reading styles.

Partly as a result of their own demands and partly because the society of that time awarded them a station apart from ordinary citizens in return for a commitment to the sometimes grubby and often ascetic life of the scholar, university students in those early days became a clearly recognizable privileged class. In England, for example, they paid no taxes and did not have to serve in the King's armed forces. In Europe, the local police did not extend civil law onto the campus and student law breakers were disciplined either by the university or by the church. Eventually, the idea of students as a class easily crossed the Atlantic and established itself in the early American colleges. This "pedestal syndrome" for students was enhanced, of course, by the fact that almost all students in the early American universities were preparing for prestigious professions in the service of mankind—the ministry, the law, and teaching—and were therefore, as students, granted an advance payment on the respect and esteem which would later be theirs as professionals. Through the eighteenth and nineteenth centuries and up to perhaps World War II, American college and university students were usually "the best and the brightest"; they were generally well-behaved and well-mannered; they were ordinarily oriented toward the professions and thus were already beginning to accumulate a patina of what H. Becker (1962), has called "honorific symbolism." On the other hand, they were young, most of them were away from home, and they had to be "protected" from the temptations and problems of the real world. The concept of the university's being *in loco parentis* gained ground rapidly in America, especially after colleges began enrolling significant numbers of young women. Student housing, student unions or commons, student health services, student grants, fellowships, and loans, student discounts, student insurance, and during stressful times student draft exemptions and work-study programs—all are examples of ways in which the larger society has not only permitted but encouraged the consideration of students as a class in our society.

During the 1960s, students were not loath to make their class power felt. Pressure tactics, confrontations, riots, and violence across a broad front were skillfully orchestrated by "student leaders"—many of whom were indeed leaders but not students. Students everywhere moved to throw off the constraints of *in loco parentis* and at the same time to demand increased rights as a class. The fact that a newly espoused right for one group of students violated the rights of other students seemed not to boggle many minds. As new rights were claimed, old responsibilities were shunned, until by the end of the 1960s being a "student" (on many campuses at least) seemed to have only a casual relationship to scholarship and preparation for a career. For a vocal minority of students the ultimate right was the right to malign the society which had provided them the opportunity for higher education. They called for its overthrow while basking in its amenities.

The late 1960s was also an era in which an anti-technology syndrome gripped most campuses (Lessing, 1971). Science, technology, engineering, business, agriculture—all of these were considered grubby. Working with things was to be avoided; only work with people or ideas made for an acceptable life style. Making a living was regarded as materialistic and many students arrived easily at the opinion that society owed them a living simply because they were students. Being a student became a way of life for some—membership in the student class was so satisfying and the environs of the university so compatible with the chosen lifestyle that graduation was not an event to be anticipated but one to be postponed, unless one could stay on by going right into graduate school. Tonsor (1971) refers to "intellectual spastics" among students who eschewed science, engineering, business, or the law and chose education "in the defunct tradition of the gentleman"—in short, a "class education."

Happily, this particular form of madness seems now to have subsided. There is a noticeable recommitment to scholarship among students of the mid-1970s. For whatever reasons—economic necessity; America's withdrawal from the Indochina war; a realization that the difference between affluence and poverty may be only one generation of idle, rebellious youth; a recognition that work, after all, adds meaning to life; or just the end of a curious cycle whose beginnings were not clear—students today are studying seriously again and enrolling in the disciplines and programs that prepare for professions and for occupations at paraprofessional, technical, and highly skilled levels.

Market forces are, of course, a part of the reason for the increased seriousness of purpose and for the shift to job-oriented fields. The rapid increase in numbers of older persons in college has also led to greater job orientation among college students, since older students see themselves only partly as students and their roles as parents, citizens, and productive workers are more sharply defined for them than is that of student. Unlike the youthful students of the 1960s, whose rite of passage to student-class status consisted of completing their registration, setting up their parent-provided campus bank accounts, and settling in to four years of state-supported study, midcareer students of today plan their college programs within the context of job and family responsibilities, social and citizenship obligations, and the realities and sacrifices of life as participants in the larger society.

The new diversity of college student bodies may, at long last, be leading us out of the centuries-old custom of regarding college as an enclave for a protected group of elite young people and students as a privileged class to be supported by others so they may become philosopher-kings and critics of society. In an era when differences between full-time students and part-time students are nebulous, when young people often stop-out for a sample of adult life before completing their undergraduate programs, when commuting students outnumber resident students, when nearly 50 percent of new high school graduates elect to go to college, and when half of all college students are in career-oriented programs, the idea of students as a separate social class is anachronistic. Being a student is not being some one *apart* from society—it is rather becoming a *part* of society, and a productive part at that. Rather than standing aloof as a critic of society, it means participating in the economic, social, and political life of the nation. At last, paraphrasing Commodore Oliver Hazard Perry (and later, the cartoon character Pogo), more and more college students are coming to say, "We have met the people, and they are us."

Summary

The enterprise of postsecondary education is incalculably vast. Ten million students are involved in the collegiate sector alone, and by 1980, the annual cost of this sector may be in the range of $55 million to $60 million dollars, amounting to nearly one-tenth of the nation's gross national product depending on inflationary factors. But size, either in enrollments or costs, is only one measure of the enterprise. A second is its complexity: higher education now serves a more diverse group of students in terms of age, ability, and interest than ever before; and the impact of these new students on higher education, already great, will be even greater over the next twenty years. For example, there is no doubt that the arts and sciences and humanities—the traditional content of the higher learning—will continue to be the major interest of millions of students in the future; and when studied for their intrinsic values there is no greater satisfaction than scholarly activity in these disciplines. But for millions of other students, the central purpose in going to college is the expectation of a satisfying career at high pay rather than the sheer enjoyment of scholarly pursuits for their own sake. For this group—already much larger than the first and still growing—the entire concept of higher education must change. Course content, instructional methods, relationships with the "outside" world, accountability for inputs and outputs, standards of admission, retention, and graduation—all are having to be viewed from a different perspective. Tomorrow's students will more and more expect an economic return on their educational investment. Cost-benefit considerations are already implicit in student planning, and they need to be included as well in the plans administrators make for colleges. Career education offers an answer to these career interests. Although it poses more challenges for institutions than the cloistered study of the liberal arts, educators must be prepared to meet these challenges. They must offer effective and efficient career education programs for the millions of Americans who, a few decades ago, would have been content to end their formal education with secondary school or less but who now have no intention of doing so.

3 ▣▣▣▣▣▣▣▣▣▣▣▣▣▣▣

Stability and Change in the Labor Force

> *It must be considered that there is nothing more difficult to carry out, nor more doubtful of success, nor more dangerous to handle, than to initiate a new order of things.*
>
> Niccolò Machiavelli, *The Prince*

One of the recurring problems of the twentieth century has been the gap between man's productive capabilities and society's needs. The quickening pace of change, the continuing initiation of a new order of things, has dictated that manpower development become an explicit responsibility of educational institutions rather than remaining a haphazard process of individual adjustments to changing labor needs.

Manpower Development and the Labor Force

The importance of educated manpower in the economic development of nations has been recognized since the early days of economic theory. Adam Smith, in his classic volume, *The Wealth of*

43

Nations, identified land, labor, and capital as the essential ingredients of economic power. Beyond that, however, he pointed out that the education and training of the labor force becomes a part of capital and that the cost of training a more efficient labor force, like money spent for improved machinery, is a capital investment. Speaking of *talents* in the sense that we would use *abilities* today, Smith (1939, pp. 265–266) wrote in 1776: "The acquisition of such talents, by the maintenance of the acquirer during his education, study, or apprenticeship, always costs a real expense, which is a capital fixed and realized, as it were, in his person. Those talents, as they make a part of his fortune, so do they likewise of that of the society to which he belongs."

Just as Smith recognized the value of investment in education both to the individual and to society, in a similar manner, Alfred Marshall (1949, p. 216), the eminent British economist of the late nineteenth century, writing in 1890, stated: "We may then conclude that the wisdom of expending public and private funds on education is not to be measured by its direct fruits alone. It will be *profitable as a mere investment,* to give the masses of the people much greater opportunities than they can generally avail themselves of. . . . And the economic value of one great industrial genius is sufficient to cover the expenses of the education of a whole town; for one new idea, such as Bessemer's chief invention,* adds as much to England's productive power as the labour of a hundred thousand men" (emphasis added).

The "productive power" that Marshall mentioned is today ordinarily called *manpower*—that is, the total productive power of a people for producing goods and services at all levels of work and in all aspects of the economy.** Manpower development is the process by which the knowledge, skills, experiences, and attitudes of people are maximized for the best possible productive effort.

---

*A new process at that time for making steel.

**Although the term *human resources* is often used in the same sense as *manpower,* there is no suitable non-sex-linked term to supplant *manpower. Personpower, people power,* and similar terms are contrived and unsatisfactory. Throughout this book the contributions of women to economic development and the necessity for equality of opportunity for women are recognized and encouraged, but the use of such terms as *manpower, manpower development,* and *middle manpower* is unavoidable.

Manpower (or human resources) development occurs not only through schools and colleges which provide formal, mainstream education, but also through proprietary schools, correspondence study schools, industry and military training programs, educational programs operated by prisons or other social agencies, apprenticeship and internship programs, and educational television and other communications media. As noted in Chapter Two, estimates by the Carnegie Commission (1973) and by Moses (1971) of the magnitude of this noncollegiate sector of postsecondary education indicate that, in the aggregate, the total contribution to manpower development by this sector may far exceed that made by the formal collegiate sector.

The contribution of various types of postsecondary institutions to manpower development will be the subject of Chapter Four. This present chapter lays the groundwork for that and later chapters by explaining the sources, composition, and classification of the American labor force. And because any country's labor force is directly dependent on the characteristics of its population, recent and current population trends in the United States must be discussed first.

U.S. Population Trends. The United States has not had a high birth rate during this century, and recently its birth rate has fallen below the "replacement" or "zero population growth" rate figure of 2.11 live births per family (Davis, 1973) to about 2.05 in 1973 and 1974. In terms of another birth-rate statistic, "births per 1,000 women at completion of child-bearing," this rate has declined from a high in 1959–1960 of nearly 3,600 to a low for this century in 1972 of about 1,900 ("Burgeoning Benefits," 1973). These statistics should not be taken to mean, however, that the population of the United States has ceased to grow. Due to such demographic factors as increased life expectancy, increased rates of family formation resulting from the high birth rate up to 1965, lower incidence of infant and child mortality, and in-migration, the replacement birth rate now attained will not result in an actual stable population for another seventy years. Even if the present low rate of fertility continues, demographers thus estimate that it will be around the year 2040 before the U.S. population reaches a maximum and levels off, probably at a figure in excess of 300 million, compared to 1975's 214 million and a projected 264 million in the year 2000 ("How Your Life Will Change," 1975).

Of special interest to educators and manpower planners is the shift in age occurring in the population. The median age, which was 28.1 years in 1972, will increase to 34 years by the turn of the century. As a result, the so-called "youth cult" of the last several decades will have less impact on society, labor force participation rates will probably increase, and productivity may also increase since a greater proportion of the labor force will be mature and experienced. Of even more significance than the median age is a breakdown of the membership in each age group. Assuming a replacement level birth rate from 1975 on to the end of the century, age-group membership is expected to shift as shown in Table 4.

Note that we are not to become a society of senior citizens. The "over 65" group increases by only one percentage point in the twenty-five year period. The data in Table 4 do show, however, that we will move away from the youth-oriented society which we have been since the founding of the Republic, toward a "middle-aged" society by the year 2000.

Several effects of these population trends on schools and colleges can be deduced with some degree of confidence. Elementary and secondary school enrollments will continue their steady decrease, and "regular-day" enrollments in college of college-age youth aged eighteen to twenty-five will probably continue to fall until the early 1990s, when the children of persons born in the 1955–1960 "baby-boom" will begin entering college. For the com-

Table 4. Percent of the United States Population in Selected Age Groups, 1975 and 2000.
(Approximations)

Age Group	1975	2000 (estimate)
0–19 years	35%	30%
20–34 years	24%	21%
35–49 years	16%	23%
50–64 years	15%	15%
Over 65	10%	11%

Source: Abstracted from data in "How Your Life Will Change" (1975).

ing twenty years, therefore, colleges desirous of maintaining or increasing their enrollments will have to do so from cohorts of the population above thirty years of age, or by increasing the college-going rate among those whose interest in and success with high school education was minimal.

The Labor Force. Defining the labor force is a complex matter, but as an oversimplification, the U.S. labor force in a given week can be considered comprised of all those persons sixteen years of age and older who are gainfully employed or who are actively seeking employment. Members of the armed forces are included, but people engaged in personal housework, retired persons, students in full-time school attendance, and persons unable to work are not. The *total* labor force is often subdivided for analysis purposes, into the *civilian* labor force and the members of the armed forces. (The *Handbook of Labor Statistics 1975, Reference Edition,* U.S. Department of Labor, Bureau of Labor Statistics, 1975, pp. 1–4, gives a complete discussion of the labor force and the methods by which its size and composition are determined throughout the year.)

As noted above, it can be inferred from Table 4 that, between now and the year 2000, the labor force will get increasingly older with each decade. The backbone of the labor force throughout most of the period will be the thirty-five to forty-nine year-old group. The youth segment (twenty to thirty-four) will account for a decreasing percentage; and although the senior segment (fifty to sixty-four) will hold its own at 15 percent of the population, early retirement among professionals and "thirty-and-out" plans for industrial workers will tend to reduce the participation rates of these older workers.

Women are entering the labor force in rapidly increasing numbers at all occupational levels, and no doubt this trend will continue into the future. The impact may be of such magnitude as to render highly inaccurate most labor force projections made in the early 1970s, but whether it will have its greatest effect in younger cohorts or in the thirty-five to forty-nine-year-old cohort cannot yet be predicted. This will depend upon the attitudes toward marriage and family formation of young women during the next two decades.

The size and occupational distribution of the civilian labor

Table 5. Percent of the Civilian Labor Force of the United States in Major Occupational Groups, and Women in the Labor Force, Selected Years, 1954–1974.

Occupational Groups	1954	1960	1965	1970	1974
Professional and Technical Workers	8.9%	10.8%	12.0%	13.8%	14.0%
Managers and Administrators	9.8	10.2	9.9	10.2	10.1
Sales Workers	6.4	6.5	6.5	6.1	6.3
Clerical Workers	13.1	14.5	15.4	17.4	17.5
Craftsmen and Foremen	13.6	12.9	12.7	12.8	13.3
Operatives	20.7	18.6	18.9	18.2	16.7
Service Workers	11.1	12.6	13.1	12.5	13.4
Farmers and Farm Managers	6.0	4.0	3.0	2.0	1.8
Laborers, including Farm Workers	10.4	9.9	8.4	6.7	7.0
Total Labor Force	100.0%	100.0%	99.9%	99.7%	100.1%
(number)	64,000,000	70,150,000	75,000,000	82,200,000	90,330,000
Women in the Labor Force (number)	19,700,000	23,400,000	26,320,000	31,240,000	35,440,000
(percent)	31%	33%	35%	38%	39%

Note: Numbers and percentages are rounded. "Civilian labor force" includes the employed, classified by current job, and the "unemployed but looking for work," classified according to their latest civilian job.
Source: Adapted from U.S. Department of Labor, *Handbook of Labor Statistics 1975*, (p. 41).

force in selected years from 1954 to 1974 is shown in Table 5. In terms of size, the labor force grew from 64 million in 1954 to some 90 million in 1974—an increase of 41 percent in two decades. Department of Labor analysts expect it to grow from 91 million in 1975 to nearly 122 million by the year 2000—an increase of about 33 percent for the last two and a half decades of this century. Drucker (1976) claims that we may soon enter a long period of chronic labor shortage, since beginning about 1979 the last of the "baby boom" children will enter the labor force and from then on into the 1990s only the "baby bust" children of the 1960s and 1970s will be entering. But the increasing rate of women participating in the labor force and the steady (and somewhat alarming) increased participation of immigrants and aliens may more than balance this eventual shortage of young entrants to the labor force.

Occupational Structure: Twenty Years of Change

As the era of mass production merged into the "age of automation" in the 1950s and on into the cybernetic age (the computer's invasion of the domain of human brainpower) in the 1960s and 1970s, the occupational structure of the United States has undergone noticeable change. Jobs demanding increased education and training have, over time, been on the increase, while jobs that emphasize manual skills and minimize cognitive abilities have decreased as a percentage of the labor force. For example, note in Table 5 that the greatest proportional increase between 1954 and 1974—in terms of the standard occupational groupings used by the U.S. Department of Labor—was in the two groups of "professional and technical workers" and "managers and administrators." Combined, these two groups increased from 18.7 percent of the labor force in 1954 to 24.1 percent in 1974. The other groups that grew appreciably as a percentage of the total were clerical workers and service workers. In contrast, the proportion of unskilled and farm laborers within the work force fell sharply.

The often-heard statement that "the most rapidly growing segments of the labor force are those requiring advanced education" thus certainly seems to have been true over the twenty-year period to 1974. However, the rate of growth of these segments slackened somewhat from 1970 to 1974, which—when combined with the flood of college graduates in those years—was a factor in the recent and current soft job market for college graduates, and there is some doubt whether this generalization will hold for the next decade. Recent (1973–1976) events contain the implication of a possible leveling off in the nation's need for high-talent manpower. Some manpower analysts feel that the soft job market for college graduates of the mid-1970s was merely a transient phenomenon occasioned by the economic recession that began in 1973. But other analysts take a more negative view and insist that the United States is entering a period where the supply of high-talent manpower has exceeded the long-term demand and that economic recovery will not correct for years of "overinvestment in college education" (Freeman and Hollomon, 1975, p. 24).

Certainly there has been change in the occupational distribution of the labor force over the past twenty years, and colleges must be responsive to those changes. But a considerable degree of stability is also evident from Table 5, and college programs should reflect this stability as well. At the undergraduate level, educators should note that employment in the distribution group of jobs (management, sales, and clerical) has been growing steadily. Nearly one in three workers was employed in these categories in 1974. While it is true that offices are being automated, increased levels of office technology are not likely to have a major inhibiting influence on the growth of these occupational groups, since new jobs requiring new skills evolve constantly, requiring larger numbers of personnel every year.

In addition, service jobs are on the increase, and educators need to emphasize preparation for these jobs. There is an image problem here of course, but as America moves further into an economy in which machines can produce some things cheaper and better than people can, more and more people will have to occupy themselves doing the things machines cannot do—providing the kinds of personal and public service that other people need and are willing to pay for. Guidance counselors in schools and colleges can help students learn more about opportunities in the service occupations. However, there is a limit to the percentage of the labor force which can be employed in jobs which render services to others. These are not basic jobs as economists define them; they do not produce wealth but rather consume it. In the vernacular, "taking in other people's laundry" depends on two factors: (1) how much laundry is there to do?; and (2) how much are people willing to pay to have it done? Educators will thus have to also provide realistic information to students about limits to opportunity in these occupations.

Data agglomerations such as those of Table 5, though useful for drawing broadly general conclusions such as these for educators, are of limited value for college curriculum planning. Occupational clusters related to paraprofessional and technical jobs cannot be pulled out of them for ready identification and analysis. The data-gathering efforts of such federal agencies as the Census Bureau and the Department of Labor still appear to be keyed to the tacit assumption that there are three basic levels of jobs—cognitive, skilled-manual, and unskilled—and incidentally, just three basic levels of education—elementary school, high school, and four-year college. The emergence of middle manpower as a fourth major segment of the work force, and the explosive growth of the two-year college as a fourth and distinct level of education—two fifths of all college enrollments in 1975 were in two-year colleges— are developments that, as yet, seem to have made only minimal impact on manpower analysts in the government agencies.

Take, for example, the occupational category, professional and technical workers. Presumably all the semiprofessional, paraprofessional, subprofessional, and technical workers in business, industry, science, health, agriculture, and natural resources, are included in this classification. Hidden in the clerical and sales classifications are thousands of semiprofessionals and technicians, and subsumed under craftsmen and foremen are many more thousands of technicians, first-line supervisors, estimators, draftsmen, inspectors, and designers whose middle manpower identity is lost in the general categories.

Middle Manpower. The concept of "middle manpower" dates back to the early 1960s and refers to the rapidly increasing segment of the manpower spectrum which lies between the recognized professions on the one hand and the manual trades and crafts on the other. Educationally, the middle manpower occupations can be loosely categorized as demanding education and training beyond high school, but ordinarily not to the level of the baccalaureate degree. Sharp distinctions cannot be made, of course, and many persons prepare for middle manpower jobs without formal college training through work experience, home study, and military training schools. By the opposite token, and for a variety of reasons, many four-year college graduates also become a part of the middle manpower work force, as Chapter Four will show.

The term *middle manpower* subsumes a number of other designations frequently encountered, such as paraprofessional, semiprofessional, subprofessional, technician, foreman, middle management, engineering aide, and even some of the very highly skilled trades and crafts. It does not include semiskilled occupations. Taken together, middle manpower occupations made up an estimated 35 percent of the U.S. labor force during the middle 1970s. Table 6 presents data on the employed labor force, with middle manpower occupational groups broken out and highlighted.

Table 6. Estimated Distribution of the Employed Labor Force by Occupational Groups, 1960 and 1975.

Occupational Group	1960	1975
Professional Workers and High-Level Managers	12%	14%
Middle Manpower Occupations	(24)	(35)
Paraprofessionals, Semiprofessionals, and High-Level Technicians	2	6
Middle-Level Technicians, Middle-Level Managers, Foremen, and Leading Men	6	8
Skilled Clerical, Sales, and Kindred Workers	10	15
Very Highly Skilled Craftsmen and Journeymen	6	6
Skilled Tradesmen and Craftsmen	10	7
Semiskilled Operatives	20	17
Semiskilled Clerical and Sales Workers	12	9
Service Workers, Semiskilled and Unskilled	14	12
Laborers, including Farm Workers	8	6
	100%	100%

Note: All percentages are approximate and rounded.

Another way to look at the middle manpower occupations is to consider the relative balance between manipulative activity and cognitive activity as the worker goes about the daily job routine. Figure 1 presents a "manipulative-cognitive scale" laid out on a percentage continuum. On such a scale, middle manpower jobs generally lie in the range from about 50 percent cognitive to perhaps 80–85 percent cognitive. (The shaded areas in Figure 1 indicate that there is a great deal of overlap at the interfaces between job levels. The spectrum of jobs from "all manual" to "all cognitive" is continuous, not discontinuous.)

Within the middle manpower fields, paraprofessionals (also frequently called semiprofessionals and subprofessionals) work directly with or immediately under professionals in the same or allied field. They may and often do assume a considerable amount of initiative and responsibility in their work, which involves cognitive activity (see Figure 1). Educational programs for career preparation at this level include a significant theoretical base and general education content, along with the specialized collegiate-technical courses making up the major. Educational programs for paraprofessionals sometimes lead to the baccalaureate degree, and the normal minimum expectation is the completion of an associate degree in a recognized (accredited) program of college-level work. There seems to be a tendency to use the term *paraprofessional* more often when the job field is in the public and human services or the allied health field; *semiprofessional* or *subprofessional* are terms often used in other fields.

Technicians, leading workers, and foremen work with and for professionals, but they often have a day-to-day working relationship also with skilled or semiskilled workers or both. Their work may vary in complexity and sophistication from fairly routine and repetitive tasks (as in testing) to extremely innovative and insightful contributions to research and design. The work of technicians is often associated with the use of such sophisticated instruments, tools, and test equipment as oscilloscopes, spectrographs, chromatographs, and laser devices. The kind of work done and the equipment used varies, of course, from one field of activity to another. Workers at this level often become a part of middle manpower as they assume the responsibilities of foremen and section

Figure 1. Middle-Manpower Jobs Located on a Manipulative-Cognitive Scale.

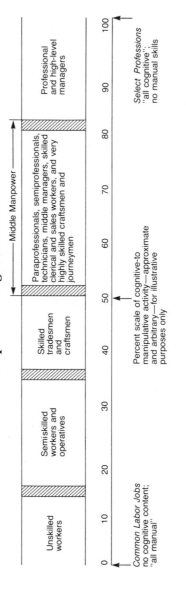

leaders, thus filling a liaison role between management (professionals) and the general work force (skilled, semiskilled, and unskilled workers) in the enterprise.

Many technicians reach this occupational status from "trickle up" procedures related to job experience, ambition, inherent qualities of leadership, and so on. Increasingly, however, it is recognized that such background methods will not supply either the numbers or the quality of technicians needed across all fields of economic activity. In the future the recognized preparation of most technicians will include the completion of a specialized postsecondary technical program of one or two years duration, ideally a two-year associate degree program.

Very highly skilled workers comprise an occupational group difficult to define in terms of formal education. Workers have attained this status through many routes—union-related apprenticeship programs, on-the-job training, training received in military service, training courses in secondary schools, trade schools, and area skill centers. In recent years, however, many job clusters at this level have received the attention of community junior colleges and postsecondary vocational-technical schools. Hundreds of programs with the purpose of producing skilled workers have been established at postsecondary levels in the past two decades. Some are joint enterprises with a local union, others have little connection with organized labor. For the most part these are certificate programs of less than two years duration, but some contain the twin features of the journeyman's card (from the union) and the associate degree (from the college) on successful completion of a planned program. Such a program may be four or more years in length, in order that on-the-job and apprenticeship requirements may be met while college or technical school studies are conducted on a part-time basis.

These skilled workers, as their name implies, work at jobs requiring a high degree of manipulative competence. Their jobs ordinarily do not include management or decision-making roles. Their work is somewhat repetitive but not stultifying. The use of precision equipment and machines is often a key factor in this job cluster, although that feature varies among the fields of economic activity. In today's labor force most highly skilled workers have attained that status without going to college. This situation is steadily changing, however, as pointed out above, and career education for them increasingly will become one of the responsibilities of postsecondary education.

Hundreds of different jobs and millions of workers are involved in middle manpower, and clear-cut distinctions with regard to job titles and levels cannot always be made. Manpower analysts may agree that the responsibility level and skill content of a particular job justifies a "skilled worker" designation, but persons who work at that job may regard themselves as paraprofessionals or, indeed, may speak of "their profession" when alluding to their jobs. This tendency toward unilateral upgrading of jobs is a normal human penchant, since a person's job is often regarded as a status symbol carrying judgmental overtones about one's value to society and supporting one's sense of personal worth.

We agree with Flanders (1970), that even by 1980, only 20 percent of all jobs will require a four-year college degree. Such a statement requires interpretation, however. In terms of the actual demands of the job—what a person must know or must be able to do to perform at a satisfactory level—it is quite true that not more than one job in five requires the skills and knowledge associated with college graduates. Indeed, the occupational group classification, professional and technical, accounted for only 14 percent of the labor force in 1974; and if the classification, managers and administrators, is added the two groups together make up only 24 percent of the labor force. But there is another trend—the tendency toward artificial "educational upgrading" of jobs (Carnegie Commission, 1973a). In response to social pressures, supply-demand factors, and problems inherent in labor-management relations, there has recently been a subtle but steady reclassification of entry requirements for many jobs. The jobs themselves have not changed—just the stated educational requirements for entry to the job. Whether such moves will drastically alter the relationship between professional jobs and semiprofessional and technical jobs in the future cannot be foretold at present. Currently, there is definite evidence of the "puppy-dog's tail phenomenon" at the interface between postsecondary education and jobs. For example, the 1950s and 1960s demanded millions of persons capable of performing at semiprofessional-technical levels. Higher education responded with an explosive growth of occupational programs at the two-year college level. Higher education marketed its image so well in the 1960s that there was an overproduction of baccalaureate degree graduates in many fields—especially the liberal arts. Industry, business, and government responded by "educationally upgrading" many of the semiprofessional-technical jobs that formerly did not require a baccalaureate degree.

Therefore, in the early 1970s a "new level" of jobs appeared to be emerging (whether real or artificially created only time will tell)—a level between the traditional professions and the semiprofessions of the 1960s. Higher education responded by creating a new level of baccalaureate degree occupational education, best exemplified by the new degree structures in business (Bachelor of Business Management), health (Bachelor of Applied Science), engineering (Bachelor of Engineering Technology), and industry (Bachelor of Industrial Technology). These four-year "quasi-professional" educational programs will be examined in detail in a later chapter. Whether they belong in "middle manpower education" or in "professional education" is moot at the moment. With four-year occupational education programs opening up at scores of state colleges and universities, many two-year colleges responded by restructuring their associate degree occupational programs, originally intended for immediate employment and competence on the job. These programs became transfer programs for the so-called "two-plus-two" baccalaureate degree technologist and "quasi-professional" curriculums.

As a result of real and artificially created factors, educational requirements for nearly all jobs are rising. The 35 percent figure shown in Table 6 for middle manpower might well be 40 percent by the mid-1980s, unless significant numbers of jobs are reclassified as professional in the years ahead.

Knowledgeable observers of the present supply-demand situation regarding middle manpower jobs could agree on most, if not all, of the following statements as of the mid-1970s.

First, the critical shortage in the 1960s of scientific, engineering, and industrial technicians has abated, and the current supply-demand situation appears to be pretty well balanced. We may enter a shortage cycle again by 1980, however, if an all-out national program for energy resources development gets under-way in this decade (Harris, 1975). Second, well-qualified secretaries and office workers are still in demand in nearly all regions of the nation. Third, the middle management field in business is cur-rently in a near-balance situation as regards workers in such areas as accounting, marketing, finance, insurance, real estate, advertis-ing, and store management.

Fourth, computer technology, including data programming and processing, has passed through its period of peak demand, and in some areas of the nation data processing technicians (op-erators) are in oversupply for the time being. Programmers, sys-tems analysts, and computer technicians are still in demand, how-ever. Opportunities are especially good for qualified women in computer fields. Fifth, the health occupations continue to require increasing numbers of paraprofessionals and technicians. Sixth, the relatively new area of the human service occupations, although "experts" have been forecasting critical needs for several years, has not yet provided large numbers of middle manpower jobs. Needs are evident, but demand—backed up by budgeted job openings—has not increased very rapidly.

And seventh, agriculture and natural resources is a field with many paradoxes. Mechanization in agriculture continues apace, and although production trends go upward every year, employ-ment continues downward. The big push for environmental im-provement and conservation of natural resources, although these areas represent potential employment for technicians in the future, has not yet resulted in a significant demand for middle manpower workers because of low funding priorities.

Women and Middle Manpower. One of the most evident socio-economic characteristics of American life in recent decades has been the phenomenal increase in the labor force participation rate by women—as Table 5 indicated, from 31 percent of the total labor force in 1954 to 41 percent by 1976, with a numerical increase from less than twenty million to thirty-eight million over the same period. Nearly 48 percent of all women between the ages of 18 and 60 are now in the labor force—that is, either employed outside the home or actively looking for work.

Ellis (1971) provides some interesting data about women in

the work force: Into the 1980s, women will be entering the labor force at a rate of more than a half-million a year; nine out of ten women will work outside the home sometime during their lifetime; and 75 percent of working women will work full-time.

Two factors have been primarily responsible for the increase in women employed outside the home: (1) the inflationary spiral, which has made one income insufficient for a satisfactory life style for thousands of families; and (2) the women's liberation movement, which has diminished sex stereotyping in jobs and has opened up hundreds of careers to women that were, until recently, effectively closed to them. At all levels and in nearly all fields, employment of women is increasing rapidly. The health and business fields have always attracted a high proportion of women, but women are now entering management, engineering, and several technologies in significant numbers. And although female factory workers have been common ever since "Rosie the riveter" crafted airplanes in World War II, female auto mechanics, welders, electricians, and coal miners are no longer curiosities (Minter and Cacciola, 1976).

Women's advocates point out, however, that despite these encouraging developments, only a small percentage of women are employed in the upper levels of middle-manpower occupations or in professional ranks. Many of the gains have been made instead largely in sales and clerical level jobs. Ellis (1971) notes, for example, that in 1970, women represented only 11 percent of all science and engineering technicians in the United States. And S.M. Smith (1973, p. 33), in terms of improved careers for women, admits some small gains but claims that "movement is not synonymous with freedom and that participation is not clear evidence of opportunity. What the dissenters are saying is that the relationship of the contemporary woman to the world in which she lives is essentially the same as it was a century ago. Only the number of her activities has changed; her sphere really has not been opened."

Despite the disappointment of such women's advocates that career opportunities for women do not seem to be improving fast enough, the fact is that they are improving and will undoubtedly continue to do so over the next decade. Such pronouncements mask some very real gains that have been made and that are readily apparent even to the most casual observer, as evidenced by women managers of steel mills, research laboratories, banks, and invest-ment conglomerates ("Women at Work," 1976). They also fail to point out, for that matter, that only some 14 percent of all work-ers—both men and women—were employed in professional and technical jobs as recently as 1974. But it is true that employment of women in professional and high-level middle-manpower occu-pations—and particularly in technical fields—is still low, partly as a result of discrimination and overt sex stereotyping in the past, and partly as a result of attitudes held by women themselves.

Because new and emerging technologies have as yet not as-sumed either a male or female stereotype, Ellis suggests that fields like bio-medical equipment technology, laser and electro-optical technology, nuclear medical technology, noise abatement technol-ogy, and similar fields offer much promise as careers for women. To this list can be added nearly all of the science-based technolo-gies as well as those that are based on mathematics, such as com-puter programming and systems analysis.

It appears that sex discrimination in employment is waning rapidly, both because of legal mandates and because of the simple realization that women are excellent employees. Colleges of all kinds and levels should plan for a future in which women will be welcome in all career education programs; their career develop-ment centers and career counselors should be the starting point for women's awareness of new opportunities; and their faculty members should be prepared for increased numbers of women en-rolees in career fields. Two cautions need to be observed in the process, however. In the rush to equalize career opportunities for women, it would not be wise to create a climate of social pressure or "reverse stereotyping" on young women that would force them to choose careers that formerly had a male stereotype. Also, re-cruiting thousands of women into career programs that have little employment potential would do no more for women than it would for men.

Education for Middle Manpower

Already 35 percent of the labor force works at middle man-power occupations that require some education beyond high school, and by the year 2000 as many as 50 percent may be so employed. But there is little indication that the "meat and potatoes" middle manpower occupations are going to disappear. Far from it. Despite continued evolution of professional jobs and the likely appearance in the future of many professions unknown in 1970, the next decade will find us with a work force whose structure will not be drastically different from that today. We will still need hundreds of thousands of accountants, electricians, insurance agents, mechanics, salesmen, secretaries, and technicians in current middle manpower occupations as well as thousands more in new middle manpower jobs that the future will bring. And two-year and four-year institutions increasingly will be the training grounds for these workers.

There is absolutely no hard evidence to support the often encountered statement: "Today's training for today's jobs is a waste of time." In this connection it is instructive to recall some of the alarmist statements of the early 1960s. Silberman (1961, p. 48), for example, in a remarkable flight of fancy more than fifteen years ago, took this view of the future: "It is impossible to predict today what skills will be needed ten years from now. Nothing could be more wildly impractical therefore . . . than an education designed to prepare people for specific vocations and professions. . . . To be practical, an education now must prepare a man for work that doesn't yet exist, and whose nature can't even be imagined." It would be an interesting exercise to calculate how many millions of workers in 1976 would not have had any education and training for their jobs if such advice had been followed in the 1960s. We suggest that similar alarmist predictions being made now by some futurists will have about the same accuracy as Silberman's 1961 forecast.

Although the decade ahead will undoubtedly bring shifts in the occupational structure, the changing demands within each job family will not be cataclysmic in the sense that they will render millions of workers obsolete. New demands will appear gradually, and on-the-job training will provide the "mobility" many older workers need. Formal retraining programs in community colleges, technical institutes, and adult schools will assist those whose jobs do, in fact, become victims of technological change. And colleges at all levels will respond to the new career education thrust with carefully conceived and timely educational programs to keep pace with manpower in transition.

Regarding technological change, productivity, and employment, the National Commission on Technology, Automation, and Economic Progress (1966, p. 1) stated "According to one extreme view, the world—or at least the United States—is on the verge of a glut of productivity sufficient to make our economic institutions and the notion of gainful employment obsolete. We dissent from this view. . . . Our broad conclusion is that the pace of technological change has increased in recent decades and may increase in the future, but a sharp break in the continuity of technical progress has not occurred, nor is it likely to occur in the next decade."

Some alarmists and many futurists claim that career education for jobs that exist now is a waste of time. They extol the liberal arts and the humanities as the only viable approach to occupational education for the future, thus saying in effect that to prepare for the dynamic, technological, cybernated future we should pattern higher education after the remote, pastoral, slow-moving past. Career education in colleges is concerned with a solid grounding in knowledge and a cluster of skills and competencies. The youth who, after career education in college, joins the labor force and retires in 2015 will be better prepared to face changes in his work and challenges to his humanity because of his training than today's senior citizen who drew his first paycheck in 1925 and retired yesterday.

Summary

As the era of mass production merged into the age of automation in the 1950s and on into the cybernetic age in the 1960s and 1970s, the occupational structure of the United States has undergone a steady shift in the direction of professional, managerial, and service occupations and of employment at middle-manpower levels. At the same time, the labor force itself has been changing. By 1975, it included 91.3 million persons; but Department of Labor analysts expect it to grow to nearly 122 million by the year 2000—an increase of about 33 percent over the remaining quarter of the century. During these years, the labor force will get increasingly older, and women will undoubtedly continue to enter the labor force in increasing numbers and in an increasing variety of careers.

There is change in the labor force to be sure; but there is also stability. Technology sometimes eliminates jobs, but it does not eliminate work; and although the economy's need for particular specialized skills is affected by new technologies, careers based on a broad cluster of knowledge and skill competence are not. Career education in colleges is concerned with broadly based education and training. Career education not only has no fear of technology; it uses and even fosters technology. It can help produce the new technology that will solve the problems the old technology has created.

4 ▣ ▣ ▣ ▣ ▣ ▣ ▣ ▣ ▣ ▣ ▣ ▣ ▣ ▣

Institutional
Settings

We shape our institutions and then they shape us.
Winston Churchill

In pluralistic America, it is not surprising to find great diversity in postsecondary education. The early development of higher education in the United States followed the European two-track model of academic institutions for entry to the prestigious professions, and practical institutions for entering other occupations. These were characterized by the classical liberal arts college on the one hand and polytechnic institutes, normal schools, and agricultural and mechanical institutes on the other. In the nineteenth century, however, American colleges began to reject this two-track approach. At Union College, Eliphalet Nott introduced engineering and science courses to the college curriculum; Harvard and Yale organized programs for the emerging technologies in the Lawrence Scientific School and the Sheffield Scientific School; and the enactment of the Morrill Land-Grant Colleges Act of 1862 assured that public colleges would offer both the liberal arts and preparation for many occupations. That Act initiated experimentation

64

with new forms and levels of postsecondary education that continues to this day and has resulted in a complex but flexible system of interacting and interrelated kinds of levels of institutions beyond the high school.

Perhaps the greatest departure from European tradition is the feature of this system that allows students to keep their options open. Transferring from one college to another, or among public postsecondary institutions in general is fairly common and relatively easy; a change in major, though it often delays a student's progress, is not unacceptably onerous; and students may drop out or "stop out" for extended periods, losing little if any academic credit when they return. Students who start in vocational programs can, with additional academic work and some loss of time, change to arts and science or preprofessional studies. Conversely, those who suddenly realize that the economic dimension is absent from their liberal arts program can either switch entirely to career education taking extra time for specific skill preparation, or incorporate some occupationally oriented courses into an academic major—such as the mathematics student who elects a computer science option or the economics major who elects courses in business management or banking and finance.

America has thus avoided the social trap of the two-track-and-no-switching-yard system of education so common in countries based on the European model. Slowly, and with more than a little resistance from some quarters, we have moved toward an acceptance of Millard's thesis that preparation for a vocation is "the central aim of education" (1973, p. 2). And we have provided a flexible, diverse structure of higher education within which a multitude of career ladders can be planned and effectively scaled.

Institutions and Agencies for Manpower Development

Manpower development—that is, the process by which the knowledge, skills, experiences, and attitudes of people are maximized for the best possible productive effort—occurs not only through the formal education of youth and adults in schools and colleges and in cooperative work-study programs between educational institutions and employers but also in on-the-job training in business and industry, in apprenticeship and internship programs, in military training, by home study and correspondence education, and more recently through educational television and other communications media. The magnitude of the noncollegiate sector of human resource development is often forgotten by college officials. As Table 2 in the second chapter indicates, the Carnegie Commission on Higher Education estimated that nearly 53 million American adults were engaged in continuing education programs of some kind outside of schools or colleges in 1970—compared to 8.9 million full-time college students. Some 31 million of these people were participating in programs run by their employers and associations, while another 10 million were engaged in programs run by community organizations and the mass media. Looking to 1980, the commission anticipated that these nonacademic enrollments will increase 41 percent to 74 million while full-time degree-credit enrollments in colleges and universities will rise only 29 percent to between 11 and 12 million.

In short, in terms of the number of individuals involved, the total contribution to human resource development being made by noncollegiate postsecondary programs far exceeds that made by collegiate institutions. But in terms of the length, breadth, and depth of manpower development, colleges and universities will continue to offer the major opportunity for systematic vocational preparation.

One might think that with such varied sources of training, postsecondary institutions and noncollegiate programs would assume the leadership in "vocational" education. To understand why this is not the case, one must go back to 1917 and the enactment of the Smith-Hughes Act. With the entry of the federal government into job preparation under that act, the term *vocational education* took on restricted and special meanings. Rather than referring to all education which prepares a person for life's work, regardless of what that work is to be, it became closely associated with specific programs supported by federal funds that were distributed through state directors of vocational education, acting as officers of the several state departments of education. Vocational education soon became the empire of vocational educators within secondary education, and for many decades its programs were defined in federal guidelines and in state plans for vocational education as being of "less than college grade." Vocational education, as the domain of the secondary school, has been concerned, for the most part, with activities more manual than cognitive and with those jobs that are ordinarily categorized as semiskilled and skilled, in such fields as trades and industry, business, agriculture, and home economics. It has generally aimed at training, as distinguished from education, and has been surrounded by prescriptive rules governing clock hours of instruction, limitations on general education, and on certification for those permitted to teach in or administer federally reimbursed programs. Over the years, it has tended to acquire the image of an important educational movement—important, that is, for other people's children (Millard, 1973).

The vocational education establishment as exemplified by the American Vocational Association has been gradually disassociating itself since 1963 from the "less-than-college-grade" image of Smith-Hughes times and has been promoting the theme that "vocational education is gradeless" partly in order to extend its influence and control over technical and occupational education in colleges. Having resisted the idea for fifty years that colleges should have much of a role in vocational education, vocational educators have recognized that the real "action" now and in the future will take place at postsecondary levels. They moved rapidly, first with the Vocational Amendments of 1968 and then with the Education Amendments of 1972, to make sure that a large piece of that action would be theirs.*

But because of the connotations that vocational education acquired from 1917 until the 1960s, college educators have come to prefer "occupational education" as a generic designation for

---

*This trend toward emphasis on postsecondary activities can be noted by comparing Sections 4 and 5 of Public Law 88–210 (The Vocational Education Act of 1963) with Sections 104 (a-5 and b-1) and 108 (1 and 2) of Public Law 90–576 (The Vocational Amendments of 1968).

postsecondary activities and experiences that lead to gainful employment. The American Association of Community and Junior Colleges, for example, wants the term *occupational* to be used in future federal vocational education acts specifically to designate postsecondary career education activities (*Community and Junior College News,* 1975). *Occupational education* seems a useful term for this purpose, since it is not limited by the connotations of federal reimbursement and supervision at the secondary-school level inherent in *vocational education* and has come to mean the totality of all education-for-work activities of colleges and postsecondary institutions (Harris, 1964).

Occupational education has broader connotations than technical education. As first used and popularized by technical institutes in Europe and America, the term *technical education* had a specialized and limited meaning. Prior to the 1960s, it referred to postsecondary education programs for training persons to work with engineers and scientists on research, development, and production tasks requiring the application of scientific and engineering knowledge and the manipulative skills to use sophisticated tools, instruments, and test equipment. In the 1960s, however, with hundreds of community colleges entering the middle manpower field and with federal interest having been asserted by the National Defense Education Act of 1958, the term *technical education* began to be used more loosely (Harris, 1964). In fact, as the 1960s progressed, both *technical education* and *technician* became almost household words. Since they were popular and carried the image of upward occupational mobility, colleges and schools, including high schools, developed so-called technical education programs by the hundreds, many of them entirely unrelated to science and engineering and at levels of cognition often little greater than those required by the semiskilled and service occupations. Very soon there appeared the vocational-technical or technical-vocational combination to differentiate less scientifically based programs from engineering-technical programs.

In short, technical education has lately been co-opted by schools of all kinds to mean whatever they want it to mean and now loosely refers to a broad area of occupational education intended to prepare students for jobs in industry that lie anywhere between the semiskilled and the professional levels. But two-year technical institutes, as well as many sectors of industry and government, still use the term as it was originally intended—an education based on a science and engineering curriculum. Occupational education is a much broader designation, covering preparation for all fields of work, not just industrial and engineering-related jobs.

By 1970, it was apparent that traditional colleges and universities were of questionable value in meeting the emerging needs for occupational education. Several prestigious reports, among them the Report of Higher Education of the United States Department of Health, Education, and Welfare taskforce chaired by Frank Newman (the so-called "Newman Report") and a number of the studies and reports of the Carnegie Commission on Higher Education (such as *New Students and New Places, The Open Door Colleges,* and *Less Time, More Options*) emphasized the gap between the aspirations of new groups of students and the conventional policies and practices of academic institutions. Either higher education had to change or the new students would be mostly dropouts. The increasingly obvious need for college-level occupational education for middle manpower jobs also pointed to a gap that traditional colleges had been slow to fill. Higher education thus opened itself to the criticism of being elitist and irrelevant for the times.

The politics of 1972 demanded that the higher education establishment be chastised for its insensitivity to the needs of students and the economy. As a result, during the hearings on and the writing of the Education Amendments of 1972, *higher education,* in the sense of colleges and universities, was purposely down-graded, and *postsecondary education,* including all educational institutions beyond the high school, was introduced and highlighted—with the intent, in the words of Gladieux and Wolanin (1976, p. 226), "to break the stereotype that education beyond high school means a four-year academic program leading to a baccalaureate degree."

With the backing of influential members of Congress and with support from federal and state education bureaucracies, "postsecondary education"—rather than merely "higher education"—has now become the object of federal attention and largess, and federal funds are flowing both to collegiate institutions and to noncollegiate schools that are accredited by nationally recognized agencies. Thus, besides the nation's nearly 3,000 collegiate institutions of higher education, the definition of postsecondary education in the Education Amendments of 1972 includes over 7,000 noncollegiate occupational schools, (including technical institutes, business schools, hospital schools of nursing, and—most numerous of all—schools offering cosmetology training or flight instruction) whose students are eligible to participate in federal aid programs; plus an estimated 3,500 unaccredited schools ineligible for federal funds that offer instruction in occupational and recreational fields ranging from real estate sales and professional modeling to social dancing and mountain climbing. Statistics on enrollments in unaccredited schools are not accurate but the nearly ten thousand institutions eligible to participate in federal programs enrolled nearly eleven million students in 1973 (National Commission on the Financing of Postsecondary Education, 1973, pp. 14–20.)

The central concern of this volume is with middle manpower development in postsecondary collegiate institutions, rather than with either occupational preparation by business, industry, and the military services, or with secondary-school vocational training and skill development offered by unaccredited schools. Consequently we deal for the most part with postsecondary schools and colleges in which programs for middle manpower careers are paramount. These include (1) community and junior colleges, (2) technical institutes, (3) area vocational-technical schools and technical colleges, (4) private business, trade and technical schools, and (5) certain four-year colleges and universities that emphasize career programs at middle manpower and quasiprofessional levels. The remaining sections of this chapter describe each of these five types of institutions in turn.

Community and Junior Colleges

For the past twenty years, the major institutional factor in middle manpower development has been the community (junior) college. More than 1,000 of these publicly supported two-year colleges are now in operation, and they represent a magnificent educational resource for middle manpower training.

Space does not permit a review of the growth of the community college movement since the first junior college was established in 1901 at Joliet, Illinois. Today, every state has such colleges; California alone has 109 of them, enrolling more than one million (head-count) students as of 1975. An extensive body of literature exists about these institutions—works by Monroe (1973), Medsker and Tillery (1971), and Thornton (1972) are good examples—and the American Association of Community and Junior Colleges publishes an annual directory that provides basic information on all members of the Association.*

Two-year colleges were at one time called *junior colleges*, and some public and private institutions still retain that legal designation. But most of the public institutions have adopted the *community college* label as they have sought to serve more community residents than merely college freshmen and sophomores; and some have dropped both *junior* and *community* designations and now call themselves simply colleges—for example, Bakersfield College and San Francisco City College, both in California.

Besides public community colleges, over 200 private or independent junior colleges are in existence, many of which provide excellent career education programs. But the public institutions enroll the great majority of students and offer the widest spectrum of programs and services. They range in size from mammoth systems like the Los Angeles Community College District, with nine campuses and over 135,000 students in 1975, to small semirural and small-town colleges with no more than 300 students. Their annual budgets can run well over $100 million for some, to less than $1 million for others. Urban and metropolitan area colleges generally offer a full range of arts and sciences courses parallel to those taught at four-year institutions, as well as scores of occupational programs. The City Colleges of Chicago, for example, offer 180 different associate-degree and certificate programs and have nearly half of their students enrolled in occupational courses, while rural community colleges of necessity offer a limited variety of

*The 1976 edition of the *Directory* (American Association of Community and Junior Colleges, 1976) lists 1,230 institutions with a total head-count enrollment of 4,069,279 students. Not all of these institutions are called community or junior colleges: many are technical colleges and institutes or area vocational schools, and some are business colleges and two-year branches of four-year colleges.

programs and usually have a much higher percentage of their students enrolled in regular-day arts and sciences transfer programs. Nationally, as Table 3 in Chapter Two indicated, Parker found from a sample of 157 two-year colleges of all types (not just community colleges) in 1974 that 56.4 percent of their head-count enrollments were in occupational programs.

Common Characteristics. Publicly supported community colleges generally exhibit most or all of the following characteristics.

First, admission to the college is usually "open door" for high school graduates or for persons over age eighteen whether or not they have graduated from high school. Some colleges even allow entry to all programs on an open-door basis rather than restricting enrollments to students meeting certain qualifications or demonstrating particular competence.

Second, tuition is low, normally not exceeding one third of the actual cost of instruction. In some states, no tuition is charged for in-state residents, but fees may be substantial.

Third, educational offerings are comprehensive, providing not only transfer programs in the arts and sciences, and occupational programs, but also developmental or remedial education, general education, adult and continuing education, community services, career guidance and educational advisement, placement, and other student services.

Fourth, most have an atmosphere conducive to lifelong learning, with well-qualified faculty members, good instructional resources, and excellent facilities. Well-equipped laboratories, shops, and classrooms provide the latest in up-to-date "hardware" and "software" to assist students in acquiring both knowledge and skills.

Fifth, they either have or are actively seeking accreditation on an institutional basis by one of the regional accrediting associations and often on a programmatic basis for specialized career offerings by relevant specialized accrediting agencies.

Sixth, they are locally supported in many states and are community-based, with a localized mission. Many have a commitment to *community service*—a term that is not clearly defined and that is the subject of much controversy but that tends to include such activities as community forums; workshops for business, industry,

and government groups; counseling clinics; child-care centers; and senior citizen services.

Seventh, for the most part they serve commuter students of all ages and with diverse educational and career objectives. The median age of their students as of 1975 was about twenty-six years and increasing. Enrollments of part-time and evening students often exceed those of full-time regular-day and college-age students (Knoell, 1976). In this sense, community college students are more mature and less "junior" than those in so-called senior colleges. More of their students are already facing adult challenges and responsibilities than are the traditional college-age students at liberal arts colleges.

Eighth, they generally attract a large proportion of minority students, partly because many are in urban locations and partly because of their relatively low cost. Women, too, find them attractive, both for career preparation and for lower-division arts and sciences programs. (In 1974–1975, women accounted for over 46 percent of their head-count enrollments.) Their students generally come from families with lower incomes than those enjoyed by the families of four-year college students, and a much larger proportion of their students are employed full-time while going to college than is true of liberal arts college students. In addition, the flexibility and open options of community colleges encourage attendance by so called new students—those who previously have not done well in school (Cross, 1971)—as do their developmental and guidance services, their career education programs, their core-and-ladder organization of curricular offerings, and their "second-chance" opportunities to succeed. All of these programmatic features no doubt constitute major reaons for their continued growth in enrollments during a period in which other types of colleges have experienced steady or declining enrollments.

Ninth, they enroll large numbers of students whose educational and career goals are not well-focused, whose aspirations and abilities are not well-matched, and whose scores on tests of academic ability as measured by such standardized instruments as the Scholastic Aptitude Test or the ACT Assessment are well below the national average for college students. As a result, these colleges must devote much of their energy to counseling and remediation.

And tenth, unfortunately they have developed the image (not justified, but popularly held nonetheless) of being places where learning is easy, where almost anyone can succeed in almost any subject, even though he has failed it somewhere else, and where degrees and certificates are sometimes awarded, like high school diplomas, on the basis more of accumulated credit hours than of demonstrated proficiency or achievement.

Most community colleges do not confine instruction strictly to their campuses. Indeed, Wayne County Community College in Detroit currently (1976) has no facility that could be called a campus, although one or more are being planned. Its programs are offered city-wide in "store-front" learning centers, in leased space in high schools, libraries, church basements, and other locations convenient to inner city residents. The City Colleges of Chicago operate Chicago City Wide College (CCWC), a college without a campus, which offers both occupational and college parallel courses and programs at dozens of locations throughout the city in response to the needs and demands of students and city agencies and employers. Pioneer Community College performs a city-wide non-traditional learning-teaching function for the Metropolitan Community Colleges of Kansas City. On the West Coast, both Los Angeles (where a New Dimensions College has been proposed) and Peralta Community College District in Alameda County, California, with its Peralta College for Non-Traditional Study, are addressing themselves to the unique needs of urban populations for education and training under less formalized structures than traditional college campuses can provide.

In terms of their career programs, community colleges offer occupational packages of many and varied levels and lengths and in a great variety of settings. But most of their job-oriented programs can be grouped into three general categories: (1) two-year, associate-degree, collegiate-technical level career programs, preparing paraprofessionals, semiprofessionals and high-level technicians and midmanagement personnel. These programs usually include a core of general education, amounting to about one fourth of the total credit hours. (2) One-year or two-year programs with the major emphasis on skill development, preparing persons at skilled-craft and foreman levels. Some of these lead to the associate degree, some to a certificate or diploma. General education is sometimes included in these programs as well. And (3) one-year or shorter programs emphasizing specialized skills, trade-training, retraining, the service occupations, and special programs for the unemployed. Certificates are sometimes awarded even for these short-term programs, but general education is not usually included.

As a result of several factors unique to community college operations—open-door access; low tuition; comprehensive programs; multilevel programs of career education as well as college-parallel and preprofessional programs; emphasis on career guidance and educational advisement; and recent attempts to improve placement services and enhance the career-ladder concept—these colleges are coming to be recognized as the key element or linchpin in the entire postsecondary education enterprise in America (DeBernardis, 1973). Whether they will, in fact, earn and deserve that designation will depend on what is done in the next few years about some very evident operational weaknesses, for despite their great promise for middle manpower career development, there are troublesome signs that they are falling short of their potential on several fronts.

Common Problems. First, some community colleges still are run by administrators and faculty who regard education and training for an economic purpose as being somehow a mechanism for class distinction. A few community-college presidents and some social critics have claimed, for example, that the career education movement in community colleges is merely a device to keep minorities or women or both in menial jobs of low social status (for example, Karabel, 1972).

Second, in their occupational programs, community colleges are making less than optimum use of advisory committees as a means of relating program development to the ongoing and changing employment needs of local communities, and work-experience or internship programs often receive only minor attention. As a result, not only faculty members but also students are more isolated from actual job demands and conditions than is desirable, and their programs are thus less effective and efficient than necessary.

Third, the lack of rigor or quality and standards of performance in courses and programs is a growing concern. All too many community colleges have opted for such socially popular concepts as *open access, noncompetitive learning, nonpunitive grading, humaneness in education, learner-directed curriculums,* and similar euphemisms for the collapse of academic rigor. Even if such concepts were viable for experimentation in the liberal arts, they certainly are not acceptable in occupational education. Just as objective job standards are used to measure performance (or lack of it) on the job, so must objective performance standards characterize career education in colleges. Open access or open-door admissions can be defended on egalitarian grounds, but college degrees and credits can be defended only on meritocratic grounds. Egalitarian entry to career programs is acceptable and commendable only to the extent that meritocratic exit is the end result. Recent moves toward competency-based programs (Gleazer, 1974), mastery learning (Bloom, 1970), and the identification of performance objectives in occupational education (D. Brown, 1974) are reassuring signs that these self-defeating policies have perhaps run their course. Corcoran (1972) alluded to some of these problems when he referred a few years ago to community colleges as the "coming slums of education."

And fourth, limited attention is given to placement and follow-up of graduates. Community college placement offices (when they exist) often are more concerned with finding part-time jobs (casual placement) for students to earn money while they are in college than they are with placing graduates of the career education programs in the jobs for which they have prepared themselves. Similarly, follow-up of and continued contact with graduates gets only minor attention in most community colleges (Grede, 1973a).

If public community colleges are to fulfill the expectations of the American people who support them and serve as a major national resource for career education, they will have to give more attention to improving the quality and standards of attainment in all programs at all levels, providing for mastery of the required job competencies through a performance objectives approach to teaching and learning (Mager, 1970), and providing programs at several levels of rigor and of differing lengths of time to suit job-oriented students (short-term, certificate programs) as well as career-oriented students (associate degree programs). They must retain realistic general education and theoretical course content in associate degree programs but restructure short-term, certificate programs and specific job training programs to emphasize necessary manual skills. The latter programs should limit general education requirements to those necessary for the job. They must provide effective career counseling and educational advisement that is somewhat directive, thus helping students to choose programs and courses at entry points where success will be probable. The community colleges should also improve work-experience and internship programs, make broader and more effective use of advisory committees, and provide a placement office that really works at placing students as they complete career education programs. They must build the image of the community college as the place to go for career education, instead of the image that it now all too often has as the place to go if you can't make it somewhere else, and a place where learning is easy, and where everybody passes and nobody fails. The image of the community college as a community service agency that should tackle any and all social ills of the community and the nation must go. Community colleges are *educational* institutions, and as such they are domains for learning and teaching, for quality and excellence, for standards of attainment and realistic levels of performance. Colleges of themselves do not solve the economic and social problems of the community, the city, or the nation; but they educate and train people who do— if those people are given the kind and quality of education that they have every right to expect.

Technical Institutes

Technical institutes began to emerge in the United States as early as 1822, the Gardiner Lyceum in Gardiner, Maine, having been established in that year. Often called "mechanics institutes," they sought to meet the demands of the new industrial surge in America for draftsmen, machinists, toolmakers, supervisors, and designers. The oldest of these institutes still in existence was founded in Cincinnati in 1828 as the Ohio Mechanics Institute and now operates as the Ohio College of Applied Science of the University of Cincinnati.

Graney (1965, p.9) describes these early technical institutes in this way: "They geared their instruction to the maturing technology of the time, laying emphasis upon application with intensive instruction during short periods of less than four years. If they tended to prepare artisans to some degree, it was because such artisans . . . were qualified themselves to bridge the gap between practice and theory." The key words in this description—and they still apply to the technician and to technical institutes today—are "to bridge the gap between practice and theory." Technical institute program planners and technical institute graduates regard this as their primary function.

Many of the early private technical institutes did not survive the rapid growth of and competition from public education at secondary and college levels in the late nineteenth and early twentieth centuries; and the creation of state agricultural and mechanical colleges militated against their further growth until well after the turn of the century. From the 1920s on into the 1960s, however, the number of technical institutes steadily increased until in the late 1960s there were nearly 100 of these specialized collegiate-level technical schools operating in the United States. Many of them are private, not-for-profit, corporations. A few fall into the realm of private-for-profit ventures. Some are publicly supported as two-year branches of state or municipal universities.

Common Characteristics. Most, if not all, of the following criteria describe the college-level technical institutes under discussion here: (1) The educational programs are usually closely related to engineering and scientific research and development, and to industrial production. (2) A selective admissions policy, not open door admissions, usually governs. Applicants are expected to have reasonably good aptitudes in science, engineering, mathematics, and related fields, as demonstrated by good high-school grades in these subjects. (3) Programs are of two or sometimes three years in length and are quite rigorous. Engineering technology programs leading to the associate degree may total seventy to seventy-six semester credit hours, with many laboratory courses, and may necessitate as much as thirty hours per week under instruction in classrooms and laboratories. (4) Theory and application receive almost equal attention so that graduate technicians can bridge the gap between the scientist/engineer on the one hand and the crafts-

man/production worker on the other. (5) Internships or field experiences are common features of their programs. (6) General education is not neglected; about one fourth of the student's total
credit hours are in liberal studies. (7) Programs are planned and
staffed with the expectation that they will meet the accreditation
standards of the Technical Institute Division of the Engineers
Council for Professional Development (ECPD). Most technical institutes are also accredited by one of the regional accrediting associations. (8) Tuition, except at publicly-supported schools, is
usually rather high, since quality technology education programs
are expensive. (9) Courses and programs are for the most part,
competency-based and stress excellence, the primary objective being
to graduate well-qualified technicians to work with engineers and
scientists (American Society for Engineering Education, 1962).

Technical institutes, as a group of educational institutions,
should be distinguished from certain other kinds of schools with
similar names. Some states (notably Ohio) have state systems of
technical colleges, which, although they may and frequently do
provide programs for engineering technicians, also provide programs in business, health, public and human services, and sometimes agriculture. Such colleges are more properly classified as
comprehensive technical colleges or polytechnical institutes than
as technical institutes. Another very large group of institutions, the
area vocational-technical schools, will be treated in another section since their mission is considerably different from that of technical institutes.

The technical institute is concerned primarily with engineering technology education, and the central purpose of engineering
technology education is "support for the practical side of engineering achievement with emphasis on the end product rather
than the conceptual process" (American Society for Engineering
Education, 1972 p. 14). The *Final Report* of the Engineering Technology Education Study, sponsored by the American Society for
Engineering Education further characterizes engineering technology education: "In contrast to engineering education where capacity to design is the central objective, engineering technology
education develops capacity to achieve a practical result based
upon an engineering concept or design either through direct as-

sistance to an engineer, in supervision of technically productive personnel, or in other ways." Again, the emphasis on bridging the gap between theory and practice and the emphasis on technology as it relates to engineering and industry should be noted.

It should not be inferred from the present discussion that technical institutes monopolize engineering technology education. On the contrary, about 65 percent of all colleges offering engineering technology programs are community colleges and 15 percent are senior colleges or universities. Of all postsecondary institutions offering engineering technology education, only about 20 percent are technical institutes of the type under discussion in this section. There is no authoritative list of technical institutes as such, since there is no rigorous definition that clearly sets them apart from similar institutions. According to the Engineering Manpower Commission, about 550 institutions offered collegiate-technical curriculums in 1970 (American Society for Engineering Education, 1972), but it is suggested that not more than eighty to one hundred of these institutions are technical institutes as defined here.

Enrollments in technical schools are in a definite upward trend. Parker, in his annual survey of two-year institutions, reports that, in 1975–1976, technical schools as a group (within the total two-year college group) reported the largest enrollment jump—up 32 percent over the previous year (Parker, 1976). Parker obtained data from 776 two-year colleges; he classified 79 of these as technical institutes and 38 as technical-vocational schools. The rest are presumably community junior colleges. Parker (p. 7) comments, on the basis of his findings, that "the educational tide still is running exceedingly high" for career-oriented programs.

Common Strengths and Weaknesses. The technical institute in America has several attributes to recommend it: (1) There is close association with engineering, science, and industry—the student gets the feel of moving into a respected career. (2) Programs are, for the most part, of excellent quality, and the rigor is influenced by the required job competencies. Students are selected for entry with the academic requirements of the program in mind. The emphasis is on hard work, and evaluation (grading) is directly related to absolute, not relative, standards of performance. (3) Placement services are generally excellent as a result of industry contacts, cooperative work experience programs, and placement directors who realize that getting jobs for the graduates is the key to continued prosperity for the institute. (4) Most technical institutes are accredited, either institutionally by a regional accrediting association or programatically by the Engineers Council for Professional Development (ECPD). And (5) associate degree graduates of these institutions enjoy a very high rate of placement (90–95 percent even in recent "recession" years) and top salaries for semiprofessional and technical level jobs.

There are, of course, a few concerns as well: (1) Generally, tuition is fairly high—very high in the private institutions. (2) Career counseling, educational guidance, and developmental/remedial education are not emphasized since the institutes try to select applicants who seem to be goal-oriented toward technology and who have good high-school grades. And (3) technical institutes are not numerous enough to make attendance easy or inexpensive. Added to tuition and other in-school costs for most students is the expense of living away from home.

On balance, and for the specialized purposes for which they are intended, technical institutes represent a postsecondary career education resource that renders a good service to society. They are proving their value in the market place of student decision as enrollments trend upward each year.

Area Vocational-Technical Schools and Technical Colleges

Several states operate systems of postsecondary regional or area vocational-technical schools (AVTSs) and technical colleges. Wisconsin, Minnesota, Ohio, Indiana, South Carolina, Alabama, Connecticut, and New York (Ag-Tech Colleges) are examples. (An excellent description of Wisconsin's Vocational, Technical, and Adult Education [VTAE] system is given in a recent issue of *Technical Education Newsletter* [1976]). Some states (Indiana and South Carolina, for example) have elected to develop postsecondary education through vocational-technical schools rather than through a commitment to publicly supported community colleges (see *Indiana Plan for Postsecondary Education*, 1973), whereas others (New York, Minnesota, New Jersey, Ohio, for example) have both community college systems and vo-tech or technical college systems. Many other states have systems of vocational-technical schools—postsecondary in some instances and combination secondary and postsecondary in others.

Since 1963, massive amounts of federal funding (appropriations from the Vocational Education Acts of 1963 and 1968, and the Education Amendments of 1972) have been earmarked for postsecondary vocational-technical education. Throughout the period, there has been a great deal of competition for these funds among the various types of institutions and agencies offering postsecondary vocational-technical education. Perhaps the sharpest controversy erupted between community college groups and agencies on the one hand (governed by "higher education" boards in many states) and vocational school groups and agencies (under the State Department of Education—K-12 programs) on the other. The relative merits of the two positions have frequently been submerged in the mire of politics, and educational decisions have been made in response to lobbying pressures from groups and associations favoring one side or the other in the controversy. More than a few members of Congress have attained national prominence over the years as a result of championing one side or the other in this on-going contest for federal dollars.

The result of the competition has often been counterproductive and wasteful. Funds intended by the Congress for program development and for learning and teaching have been spent to further the cause of one side or the other, to staff up state agencies for more intensive competition, and to establish a claim or a territory by building a campus before the other system does. In some states a dual system of postsecondary career education has developed, with unnecessary and destructive competition; duplication of campuses, programs, and equipment; high-pressure recruiting of potential students; skyrocketing costs; and citizen-taxpayer disillusionment bordering on outrage.

For years enrollments at some postsecondary vocational-technical schools were disgracefully low, with very high unit costs. With the swing back to vocational education in the late 1960s, however, enrollments in these schools trended upward for several years in almost all regions of the country. Very recently, however, Parker

(1975) has found that, based on a limited sampling (not statistically definitive) of vocational schools, enrollments had levelled off or had even declined slightly from 1974 to 1975. All other types of two-year postsecondary institutions showed significant enrollment gains over the same period. If indeed enrollments in these institutions are trending downward again, a serious inquiry into the causes will have to be made.

Characteristics. State-operated area vocational-technical schools (AVTSs) are often tuition free, and persons who have already made a career decision, who do not need remediation, and who want "hands-on" technical training in as short a time as possible in an institution where the very atmosphere is industry-oriented, should do well in area vocational-technical schools. Such students are sometimes negatively affected by what they hear about the general education requirements and the extra time required for them at community colleges; and about the purportedly less effective placement services. The serious, goal-oriented student, eager to become qualified for a job in the shortest possible time, does not want to be delayed by course requirements that he considers unnecessary nor by classmates who are either undecided or perhaps unable to profit from the instruction or both (Research Coordinating Unit for Vocational Education, 1972). Many such students will continue to choose specialized vo-tech schools and technical colleges over comprehensive, open-door community colleges. It should be remarked that such a choice may not necessarily be in their long-term best interests, but it seems the better choice to them at the time.

Strengths and Concerns. For a future in which career education is popular, area vocational technical schools would seem to have an assured clientele. They offer courses and programs students want; their facilities and equipment are first rate; tuition is either low or absent altogether; placement of graduates is usually good; and the present political climate favors them at the expense of liberal arts colleges. For a certain kind of student—inner-directed, goal-oriented, anxious to get trained and get to work—these institutions offer the kind of postsecondary education that they demand. Nor are they any longer the "dead end" schools that they once were. Many provide programs for the associate degree, and more and more four-year colleges are accepting some of the work taken at an AVTS for credit toward certain new degrees in occupational fields (see a later section of this chapter).

Some serious concerns remain, however. Principal among them is the tacit assumption that specific job-oriented training is a proper solution to problems of manpower development. Narrowly-focused job training may be what the student wants now, but his career prospects often suffer in the process. Further, in many area vocational schools there is a serious lack of developmental-remedial education, with the result that the student does not develop the basic learning skills which will be needed for upward, or even lateral, job mobility. The often-heard statement that "today's worker will have to change jobs and retrain at least five times in his working lifetime," has some truth in it. It also has some of the elements of a self-fulfilling prophecy when it is so eagerly espoused by proponents of vocational-technical schools.

Private Business, Trade, and Technical Schools

Since 1970, there has been increasing interest in and development of private schools in the career education field. They were identified in the Education Amendments of 1972 as "recognized" components of postsecondary education in the United States (U.S. Congress, 1972) eligible to participate in federal financial aid programs provided they are accredited or approved by a federally recognized accrediting agency. Both private nonprofit and "proprietary" (that is, chartered for profit) schools are included in this category of institution, with proprietary schools by far the most numerous. Although there is no authoritative list of private schools that are serving postsecondary career-education and job-training needs of youth and adults, the National Center for Educational Statistics estimated that there were nearly 5,000 accredited proprietary schools and nearly 800 accredited private nonprofit schools, apart from technical institutes, offering postsecondary occupational education in the United States in 1970–1971 (National Commission on the Financing of Postsecondary Education, 1973, p. 17).

Characteristics. As shown in Table 7, these schools run the gamut from industrial technical-vocational schools to business,

Table 7. Estimated Number of Postsecondary Noncollegiate
Private Schools (Excluding Technical Institutes) Offering
Occupational Programs, by Type and Control, 1970–1971.

Type of School	Nonprofit	Proprietary	Total
Technical/Vocational School	40	423	463
Business/Commercial School	20	940	960
Cosmetology School	2	1475	1477
Flight School	10	1332	1342
Trade School	34	509	543
Correspondence School	1	112	113
Hospital School	681	47	728
Other	10	20	30
Total	798	4858	5656

Source: National Commission on the Financing of Postsecondary Education (1973, p. 17).

beauty, flight, and trade schools to correspondence schools offering commercial art, electronics, and other instruction and hospital schools of nursing and applied health sciences. Illustrative of the numbers is a report of the Michigan State Department of Education (1973) indicating that 204 licensed private occupational schools were operating in Michigan in 1973.

These private occupational schools exist in every state and city and even in many small towns. They range from such nationally known institutions as the Katherine Gibbs schools specializing in business and office careers to locally based trade schools enrolling only a handful of students. But the 5000 accredited institutions that offer postsecondary career education of certifiable quality constitute only a small segment of the total universe of private occupationally oriented and recreational schools, estimated by Clark and Sloan (1966) at more than 35,000 in the mid-1960s and offering every conceivable subject, skill, and behavior from ballroom dancing to ventriloquism. (For an analysis of proprietary schools within this universe of private institutions, see Erwin, 1975, and Trivett, 1974.)

Reliable data on the number of students enrolled in all these thousands of private schools are not available, since reporting mechanisms are not well developed for nonaccredited institutions. But estimates of the 1973 enrollments in the 5000 accredited institutions range from 1.2 million to 1.8 million students, with preference given to the larger figure as probably more nearly accurate (Erwin, 1975). The importance of these institutions as educational enterprises can be appreciated by noting that in 1973 the nation's 2,720 colleges and universities enrolled some 9.6 million students, and thus the accredited private schools enrolled approximately one student for every five attending "collegiate" institutions.

Strengths and Weaknesses of Proprietary Schools. Erwin (1975) and Trivett (1974) have studied separately the impact on collegiate institutions of the proprietary schools among these accredited private schools. Among their findings and conclusions are.these:

First, (1) These schools constitute a valuable educational resource for the nation. (2) Because of their relatively high tuition, they will probably not attract large numbers of economically disadvantaged, federally assisted students. (3) They probably will continue to attract large numbers of students who want no-nonsense occupational training that prepares for entry jobs in a minimum time. Trivett (1975) notes that one of the reasons most often given by proprietary school students for not enrolling in a community college is the requirement by the latter of a core of general education. (4) In order to compete with proprietary schools, "regular" colleges may be subjected to increased pressure to add or expand programs of subbaccalaureate occupational education. (5) The ability of proprietary schools to respond quickly to learner needs and their serious and continuous concern with placement are attributes of these institutions that "regular colleges" would do well to emulate. (6) Whatever serious impact proprietary schools may have on collegiate institutions is most likely a problem for the future rather than the present.

We would be remiss, as this section concludes, if certain negative aspects of these schools were not also pointed out. Some of the problems mentioned below have been subjects of press overkill, and some have not been written about enough. Some are unique to proprietary schools; others show up frequently in public colleges as well.

First, some proprietary schools are accused of engaging in aggressive, hard-sell recruiting; using misleading advertising about courses, programs, faculty, facilities, and placement of graduates on jobs; maintaining unsatisfactory refund policies for students who drop out early in the course; and providing unsatisfactory quality control over the teaching and learning process. Recognized accrediting associations within the proprietary school sector are continually forcing improvement on these matters, however, and caveat emptor is, happily, no longer the essential watchword in dealing with most proprietary schools.

In addition, many private schools and correspondence schools are not chartered to grant college credits and degrees. The competencies attained from study at these schools often lack the legitimacy that comes from transcripts of credit and from associate or baccalaureate degrees. Without the credit and degree structures of regular colleges, educational career ladders cannot easily be put together. Although seen as an advantage by many students, the very lack of college-level general education in most proprietary school curriculums militates against evaluating competencies attained in these schools for credit to apply toward a degree in a "regular" college.

Moreover, proprietary schools have not generally been considered eligible for accreditation by the regional accrediting agencies. There is an extensive network of specialized accrediting groups serving groups of schools of the same type, as, for example, the Engineers Council for Professional Development (ECPD), the accrediting agency for technical institute programs and the National Association of Trade and Technical Schools (NATTS), serving trade and technical schools. Business colleges have their accrediting group, as do schools of podiatric medicine, medical laboratory technology, drama and theater, correspondence schools, and so on. But each of these accrediting agencies and their accrediting activities must be approved by the U.S. Commissioner of Education before federal assistance can be made available to students attending member schools.

Finally, some proprietary schools have from time to time engaged in questionable practices with regard to awarding diplomas, certificates, and degrees. Now that the "external degree" movement has attained some popularity and even a considerable degree of federal government support, the temptation to cash in on this trend is strong, and no doubt some schools will yield to it. Proprietary schools are not the only sinners in this matter, however. The unseemly haste with which some regular colleges have moved into the external degree business in recent years augurs ill for the integrity of higher education in the collegiate sector as well. The logical result of unethical practices with regard to external degrees by either proprietary schools or regular colleges will be a new spate of government regulation (McNett, 1976).

In summary, private schools are a significant resource for job-specific training in the United States. Their contribution to career education is somewhat limited by the difficulty of transferring their certificates, diplomas, and degrees into the traditional collegiate sector. As pointed out elsewhere, however, traditional credits and degrees are no longer the certain keys to upward economic mobility that they once were. Today there is increased emphasis on competence and demonstrated ability to do the job. Artificially determined degree standards for jobs are being challenged in the courts at the same time that the nationwide interest in performance objectives and competency-based education is beginning to be a programmatic reality. Both the private school and the regular collegiate sectors should welcome these developments and redouble their efforts to provide career education of high quality for a price that will enable students to realize a satisfactory return on their investment.

Proprietary schools as a group have had a somewhat tarnished image because of the unethical practices of a few, but accrediting agencies and other forces within the proprietary sector, plus stricter federal and state rules and regulations, are bringing about steady improvement in the ethical practices of these institutions. A familiar penchant of sinners is to point the accusatory finger at other sinners, and proprietary schools are always eager to justify a questionable practice by noting that "regular" colleges are engaging in it, too. One sin, of course, does not justify another, but the fact that the accusing finger can be pointed so often and with unerring accuracy should be a source of grave concern to the public collegiate sector.

Four-Year Colleges and Universities

For decades a small number of four-year colleges have been concerned with career education at middle manpower levels. Most of the agricultural and mechanical universities and certain specialized colleges like Ferris State College in Michigan, University of Wisconsin-Stout, Rochester Institute of Technology in New York, and California Polytechnic State University at San Luis Obispo have produced thousands of highly competent graduates at paraprofessional and semiprofessional levels as well as many thousands at the professional level. It is only recently, however, that four-year colleges as a group have moved aggressively into career education for middle manpower. The score or more technologically oriented colleges like those identified above have in the past few years been joined in this effort by hundreds of four-year colleges and universities of a type that until recently were characterized by the term *state colleges*.

Characteristics. There are more than 280 of these "colleges of the forgotten Americans" (Dunham, 1969); and in 1969 they enrolled 21 percent of all students in higher education.

Prior to 1940 the majority of these institutions were teachers' colleges, but after World War II the name change to state colleges began, and this was the mode until the early 1960s when a stampede began to incorporate the word *university* in the names of these institutions. Their roles were changing rapidly, also, and their enrollments skyrocketed during the twenty years from 1947 to 1967. Many of them added bona fide graduate professional schools and became real universities; others became universities in name only. Perhaps the best generic name for this group of institutions is "regional state colleges and universities" (Harcleroad, Molen, and Rayman, 1973, p. 1). Their national association is the American Association of State Colleges and Universities (AASCU) with offices in Washington, D.C.

In their 1973 study of these colleges and universities, Harcleroad, Molen, and Rayman (p. 31) concluded that "one of the most significant trends verified through the collection of degree program data is the phenomenon aptly described as 'occupational pluralism'." They noted the rapid expansion of baccalaureate and subbaccalaureate programs in business, engineering and industrial technology, health sciences, and the public and human services at these institutions between 1968 and 1973. One can speculate at length about the reasons for such a rapid growth of career education programs in institutions that, only a few years ago, were tending to become more academic and liberal-arts oriented. Their move into occupational education came about as the result of a number of trends and events. First, college enrollment growth of the 1960s tapered off in the early 1970s especially with respect to college-age youth. Since continued growth was the name of the game, something had to be done to get new students, and these new programs attracted many—both freshmen and two-year college transfers. Second, generally negative feelings of legislators and taxpayers toward higher education in general and liberal-arts programs in particular increased into the 1970s. State legislatures and the U.S. Congress seemed to be saying, "career education is worthy of public support, but we are beginning to have doubts about liberal arts programs." These colleges may have decided to get involved in areas where continued public financial support seemed more likely.

Third, many of these colleges had hundreds of unfilled dormitory rooms. Mortgage payments were due, and the lack of rental money from the unused rooms made a shambles of debt retirement schedules. More students was the only answer, and new career programs could conceivably attract them. Fourth, many associate degree technology graduates, either directly upon graduation or after working for a few years, were very much interested in going on for a baccalaureate degree. Since their occupational courses in the community college or technical institute did not prepare them for upper division work toward a regular professional degree, a new kind of program and a new degree had to be devised. State colleges, whose role in education for the traditional professions (other than teaching) had been somewhat tenuous, were ready and eager to participate in the identification of and preparation for a new level of occupations requiring the baccalaureate degree. The timing for such a move was right, since artificial educational upgrading of jobs had already begun by 1970 in both the public and the private sectors (Carnegie Commission on Higher Education, 1973a).

Fifth, in order to achieve the immediate goal of enrolling more students, admissions requirements had to be appreciably lowered. Colleges that had been moving toward more rigorous arts and sciences courses in the 1960s, now had to initiate programs more suited to the interests and academic levels of the "new students" (Trachtenberg and Levy, 1973). And sixth, students themselves forced changes in state college programs. With dismal employment prospects in the teaching field and almost equally negative feedback from other liberal-arts fields, students began to demand educational programs for career fields in which job prospects were brighter.

Not all occupationally oriented baccalaureate degree programs are new phenomena. The Bachelor of Engineering Technology (BET) and Bachelor of Industrial Technology (BIT) programs have been around for more than a decade. Baccalaureate programs for selected careers in the health field—clinical laboratory technology and baccalaureate degree nursing, for example—have been in operation for many years. Other and somewhat newer fields for baccalaureate-level career education include several specialties in industrial management, several different degrees in business (not to be confused with the traditional degree in business administration), many new specialties in the public and human services field, additional specialties in the health field, and programs for careers in conservation of natural resources and environmental improvement (Rinehart, 1973).

Since 1970, however, baccalaureate degree programs with career objectives have flowered like marigolds in a summer garden. Ninety-five such programs were reported operating in the field of engineering technology alone, according to a 1973 survey by Moore and Will (1973). Nearly 4,000 graduates of BET programs were reported in June 1972, and the recency of the phenomenon is attested to by the fact that over a third of the institutions reported on in the Moore and Will study had not operated the program long enough to have had any graduates.

Questions About Four-Year Career Programs. A number of questions are developing with regard to these new baccalaureate degree structures. Where will the graduates fit into the economic, occupational, and social structure of the nation? As practitioners, will they be regarded as professionals or paraprofessionals? Will some

such new term as *quasiprofessional* come into use? Will they constitute an occupational wedge that displaces professionals or one that
pushes aside semiprofessional technicians? What relative salaries
will they receive? Is there actually a new occupational terrain that
requires knowledges and skills at a level in between the traditional
professional on the one hand and the paraprofessional and technician on the other? Or is this terrain being artificially created by
sociocultural attitudes shared by students, employers, and educators alike? Are these new baccalaureate graduates welcomed by
corporate management partly as ploys in the labor relations game?
Exactly what new and advanced competencies are produced by the
two upper-division years? Answers to these questions will come
only with time and experience.

Currently, there appears to be a brisk job market for graduates of these career-oriented baccalaureate degree programs.
With programs in business, public and human services, technical
and applied arts, and health fields, aggregating 21 bachelor of science curriculums and totalling 748 graduates in 1974–1975, Ferris
State College in Michigan reports excellent placement in "directly
related" employment in all fields, ranging from a high of 92 percent in technical and applied arts curriculums to 72 percent in business curriculums (Ferris State College, 1975). Only 8.4 percent of
Ferris graduates were still seeking employment four months after
graduating in June 1975. Beginning salaries clustered around
means for the different fields ranging from $750 per month up
to $929 per month.

University of Wisconsin-Stout (1975) reports equally good
placement for its baccalaureate degree graduates in such fields as
business, industry, and government in their *1974–1975 Placement
Report*. Of 498 graduates in these broad fields in 1975, 324 were
placed within three months of graduation. As of August 1975, only
forty-one were still "reported available" for employment. Salary
means ranged from $7,160 to $10,957 annually, with some isolated
"highs" in the $18,000 range.

Similar reports are available from scores of these regional
colleges and universities, and generally they tell about the same
story. Placement of career program graduates in jobs related to
their training ranges from good to excellent in nearly all regions
of the country—far better than the placement record for arts and

sciences bachelor's degree graduates. Salaries for the graduates of these new programs are sometimes disappointing, however, especially in the "people-related" or "helping professions" fields. Even in business and technical fields salaries tend to cluster at the $9,000 to $13,000 level—not significantly above those being reported for many associate degree graduates from community colleges and technical institutes. Whether this means that employers generally regard the new baccalaureate degree graduate as a sort of "super-technician," worth only a modest sum more than the two-year technician, or whether they feel that these neoprofessionals can actually fill the jobs that used to go to graduates of the traditional professional schools and that they can be obtained for less money are questions we will not have answers to for several years. In the meantime, there is a demand at reasonably good salaries for the graduates of baccalaureate degree career education programs.

Two-Plus-Two Programs. Some state colleges and universities are designing baccalaureate programs in the applied arts and sciences as upper division programs only, aimed at providing a career ladder for associate degree graduates through the *capstone* or two-plus-two program concept. Many associate degree graduates in career fields later decide to seek further education to prepare for careers with greater responsibility and (expected) higher income. The upper division programs now in operation and those planned for the future will facilitate further education and upward occupational mobility. Two-plus-two programs are an excellent example of cooperation between four-year and two-year colleges. They are, in a sense, "upside-down" baccalaureate degree programs, in that the student gains specialized and saleable skills first and adds theoretical and general education and management courses later.

Some four-year colleges, on the other hand, aware of the popularity and growth of community colleges and technical colleges and interested in getting maximum state head-count appropriations for their own programs, have decided to challenge two-year colleges on their own ground and have instituted new career programs beginning with the freshman year. The associate degree can be attained at the two-year point, either as a career option or on the way to the baccalaureate degree. Not a few four-year colleges have practically eliminated academic admissions requirements and have joined community colleges as open-door colleges. Some have added the kinds of counseling and guidance services, developmental/remedial education programs, and community outreach programs found in community colleges. At a recent conference in the Midwest a four-year college president ended his presentation with the remark, "Anything a community college can do, we can do better."

Questions About Less-Than-Four-Year Programs. The trend toward providing both upper and lower division instruction in new career programs at four-year colleges, competitive though it often is with respect to the associate degree programs of nearby community and technical colleges, does not engender nearly as much controversy as has the recent move of some baccalaureate-level institutions to establish and recruit students for two-year associate degree and certificate level occupational education programs. A 1973 survey by the American Association of State Colleges and Universities reports that nearly 40 percent of its 370 member colleges were then offering one- and two-year certificate and associate degree programs (Watkins, 1973). In some instances, such programs have been initiated within a few miles of a community or technical college with the same or a similar program already operating.

These often duplicative educational ventures pose difficult problems for articulation that will not be solved overnight. Four-year colleges, many of them in need of more students and aware of student interest in and the nationwide trend toward more practically oriented education, defend their two-year programs by saying they are merely responses to the need of the times. Community colleges and technical colleges, with qualified faculty and costly laboratory facilities already on hand, accuse the four-year colleges of pirating "their students" away from them. And the fact that new associate-degree programs at four-year colleges sometimes operate with inadequate facilities and with a faculty reassigned from teacher training programs adds fuel to the fire of two-year college criticism. And, to make the controversy all the more bitter, aggressive recruitment policies at some four-year colleges have featured appeals to prospective students based on such themes as the "advantages of attending a *real college*."

Complex and potentially acrimonious as these issues are, they must be faced and quickly solved, preferably by the colleges themselves. Legislative appropriations committees, state boards of higher education, taxpayer groups, and citizens in general are not disposed to allow further destructive competition, aggressive and often disgraceful recruiting policies (*College Board News,* 1975), and costly and wasteful duplication of effort. These problems will be resolved one way or the other—through either effective self initiated articulation or state-imposed regulations. To take leadership in their resolution, four-year colleges should concentrate on two-plus-two programs providing upper division theoretical, general, and *advanced* specialized education that builds directly on the associate degree programs and diplomas of two-year colleges and area vocational-technical schools. They should initiate complete four-year career programs only in fields in which the community colleges and vocational-technical schools of the region are not providing or cannot provide the first two years. They should avoid creating one-year and two-year certificate and associate degree programs unless there are no community colleges or vocational-technical schools in the area to provide them. They should discontinue one-year and two-year programs directly competitive with those already offered in two-year institutions in the region. And they should work cooperatively with these institutions so that career ladders will be readily available to students and workers who want to upgrade themselves. Their upper-division programs should follow an "upside-down" plan so that students in two-year programs can meet transfer requirements but at the same time develop competencies for entry-level employment. Over the years, guidelines for articulation been junior and senior colleges have been developed cooperatively to permit easy transfer of arts and science majors (American Council on Education, 1967). They can be used, with some modifications, to solve articulation problems in career education as well.

Above all, four-year institutions should not contemplate starting career education programs just to utilize empty facilities or to retain faculty in the face of falling enrollments. As an illustration, the initiation of Bachelor of Engineering Technology (BET) or Bachelor of Industrial Technology (BIT) programs would be ill-advised if they utilized for the most part industrial arts shop facilities and the former industrial education faculty. Career-oriented programs of high quality require specially planned facilities and, often, newly acquired equipment, and more often than not require new faculty as well, with education and experience directly related to career preparation.

As senior institutions in the system of postsecondary education, four-year colleges should be expected to exhibit model behavior for the rest of the system, emphasizing quality and productivity instead of open-door admissions and escalating enrollment figures. Head counts and student credit hours generated are not outputs of the educational process; learning, knowledge, performance, competence, and placement of graduates in jobs are.

Summary

America is fortunate indeed to have the diversity and educational opportunity provided by the mix of public and private schools and colleges described in this chapter. These institutions make career education available in every region of the country under many differing formats and at tuition costs from as much as $4,000 a year down to merely a modest fee for registration. With better articulation between levels of institutions, they are developing career-ladder opportunities in many fields, providing for employable skills at several levels of career development, and arranging their curriculums so that students who enter the labor market after earning a certificate or diploma can return for associate and baccalaureate degrees later with little time or effort lost. The drop-in/stop-out feature of many of their programs encourages participation in career education by employed adults and promotes the concept of lifelong learning. By any considered judgment these diverse institutions constitute a career education system that is a recognized national asset.

The system is a very costly one to maintain, however, and in the cost-benefit, tax-conscious climate of the 1970s more and more citizens are demanding accountability, productivity, elimination of unnecessary duplication and competition, and the assurance of a reasonable social and economic rate of return on investment. In the private sector, market forces usually take care of these matters. Hundreds of proprietary schools "go broke" or phase out every year as a result of such factors as poor management, inadequate demand for their programs, poor quality education, lack of placement of graduates, or excessive competition. In the public sector, however, the market does not govern with such certainty, and shaping up the system must be accomplished either by the state, through a combination of legislative enactments and fiscal restraints, or preferably in-house by educators themselves.

II

Career Programs:
A Cluster Analysis

5 🔲🔲🔲🔲🔲🔲🔲🔲🔲🔲🔲🔲🔲🔲🔲

Business and
Office Careers

The business of America is business.

Calvin Coolidge

Many Americans might disagree with the Coolidge thesis, but business, by whatever name—whether in trade, commerce, manufacturing, construction, or finance—is essential to society in general and to each of us as individuals in particular. It has always been so since that unknown day in prehistory when some individual of less combative bent conceived the idea that, instead of fighting for or stealing a coveted possession, he would barter one of his belongings for it. The jobs that generate income, the commerce that brings the necessities of life, the commodity markets that supply food and raw materials, the wholesale and retail trade outlets we patronize daily, the financial transactions we require, the standard of living that allows the arts and the humanities to flourish, and the taxes that pay for all the services of government—all of these depend on business. A prominent European economist remarked a few years ago that "when American business sneezes, the economy of Europe gets pneumonia." If the level of American business

101

affects Europe that much, its effect on our own daily lives needs little elaboration.

Scope of Business Employment

No matter what industry or sector of the economy is being considered, business and office careers—in terms of transactions involving goods and services, paper work, management and administration—are indispensable. Business is important not just to "businessmen" but to everyone.

Table 8 breaks the economy down into the nine industrial categories commonly used by such government agencies as the Departments of Commerce and Labor in gathering statistics on employment in such industries as agriculture, forestry, and fisheries; mining; construction; and manufacturing. It also shows the number of Americans employed in several business and office occupations in each of these sectors in 1970—secretaries, computer specialists, bookkeepers, salesmen and sales clerks, managers, and administrators. Some people may think of business careers as being limited to certain industries such as manufacturing and trade and assume that other industries do not involve business. Agriculture for example, may connote cowboys and field hands to them, while mining and construction implies miners, welders, and hardhat equipment operators. But business and office work is involved in all of these industries. Farms and mines have business offices— although the farmer's office may be merely a few pigeonholes and drawers in a desk—and even the service industries, including non-profit hospitals and colleges, require thousands of "business office" employees. In fact, the figures in Table 8 indicate that while the service industries employ 26 percent of the nation's workers at large, they employ fully 40 percent of America's secretaries. In other words, business activity and office work is present in every industry or sector of the economy—private or public, profit or nonprofit.

Indeed, as the United States has moved over the past two decades into an economy where the production and delivery of services is as important as the production of material goods, business and office workers in white-collar jobs have increased as a

Table 8. Workers in Selected Business and Office Careers, by Industry, 1970.

Industry	Secretaries	Computer Specialists	Bookkeepers	Salesmen and Sales Clerks	Self-Employed Managers	Salaried Administrators[a]
Agriculture, Forestry, & Fisheries	12,235	312	15,103	11,079	8,273	10,101
Mining	17,406	2,573	9,777	4,491	6,215	21,984
Construction	78,135	2,353	67,767	30,627	143,678	243,935
Manufacturing	511,567	92,189	257,265	411,757	65,319	645,528
Transportation, Communication & Other Public Utilities	113,698	14,110	90,811	53,987	23,289	235,297
Wholesale & Retail Trade	308,357	16,746	652,934	3,357,838	481,207	880,750
Finance, Insurance, & Real Estate	385,051	27,612	214,790	5,462	23,016	155,331
Service Industries	1,077,411	68,913	292,063	139,262	150,560	404,801
Public Administration & Government	198,239	29,728	69,300	7,028	0	242,704
Total in All Industries	2,672,099	254,437	1,534,768	4,019,531	895,342	2,840,431

[a]Includes salaried managers and administrators and public officials, but not office managers.
Source: U.S. Bureau of the Census (1972).

percentage of the total labor force at the expense of manual laborers in blue-collar work. Today, more persons are employed in the service industries than in either manufacturing or trade—the next two largest industries in terms of manpower—and by 1985 half of the nation's workers are expected to be in white-collar occupations. Farming, mining, and manufacturing become more efficient each passing year due to mechanization and automation, and as they produce more with fewer workers and as their need for management, marketing, distribution, and communication increases with increased production, they require more business jobs.

Moreover, there are currently about four active workers in the labor force for every retiree over age 65,—in actual numbers, 85 million to 23 million as of 1975—but by 1985, this worker-to-retiree ratio will be only about three to one—as the numbers grow to 95 million and 30 million respectively (Drucker, 1976). Since senior citizens require many services provided by business and office workers—from investment management, travel bookings, and tourist accommodations to social security benefits, pension checks, and welfare services—it seems safe to predict an increasing demand in business and office occupations for the 1980s.

Even though the field of business enterprise is not likely to generate a large number of new job *titles* over the next decade, it will generate hundreds of thousands of jobs annually. Professional and managerial personnel in business are likely to face the same kind of need for semiprofessionals that confronted scientists and engineers two decades ago, and they will need greatly increased numbers of middle-manpower workers to gather data, staff communications systems, operate computers, prepare graphic analyses, write technical reports, manage offices, arrange credit, plan travel, run restaurants and hotels, and operate financial institutions.*

*This analysis is, of course, predicated on a healthy full employment economy that will, in turn depend on a satisfactory solution to the energy problem by 1985. Full employment does not, of course, mean 100 percent employment. In the United States, a full employment economy is considered to be one in which unemployment is 4 percent or below. The 4 percent figure is termed *structural* unemployment and includes those persons "in between jobs" at any given time, persons who supposedly want a job but who refuse it when offered, and persons with so little ability or training or dependability that they cannot hold down any job, even when there are plenty of jobs available.

Thus, continuing the trend of the past thirty years, there will be more jobs for middle-manpower workers in business and office occupations than in any other field. And, it should be emphasized, in contrast to the mistaken statements so often seen in "scare" news stories, *business jobs are not being automated out of existence.* While jobs are sure to change and persons in them will have to acquire new knowledge and skills to cope with the increasing complexities of industrial, institutional, and agency life, these changes in skills and knowledge will not be so sudden and dramatic that today's well-prepared graduates in business and office skills programs will suddenly be obsolete and unemployable. Preparation for today's jobs in business is not a waste of time—in fact, it is probably the best preparation for "tomorrow's" jobs as well. Indeed, the major current change is one of increased opportunity for women: business is now a wide-open career field for qualified women as well as men, and the number of women entering the business world—not just in the traditional role of secretary—is increasing dramatically.

At both the two-year and four-year college level during 1975, college freshmen picked business fields as their first choice for program of study or major (19 percent) and for career (14 percent), according to the annual survey of incoming freshmen by the Cooperative Institutional Research Program of the University of California at Los Angeles and the American Council on Education (Astin, King, and Richardson, 1976). As Table 9 shows, business programs and careers are of particular interest to two-year college

Table 9. Percent of Incoming Freshmen Planning on Majors or Careers in Business Fields, by Level of Institution, Fall 1975.

	Majors			Careers		
Level of Institution	Men	Women	Total	Men	Women	Total
Two-Year Colleges	21.5	29.6	25.2	18.7	12.7	16.0
Four-Year Colleges	19.9	10.2	14.9	16.7	7.7	12.1
Universities	18.3	10.4	14.6	15.3	9.4	12.6
All Institutions	20.1	17.5	18.9	17.2	10.0	13.8

Source: Astin, King, and Richardson (1976, pp. 20, 32, 44).

freshmen, compared to those in four-year colleges and universities. This same study indicated that, ending a long estrangement from business careers, black students and women students are now enrolling in business programs in large numbers. Business as a major was favored by 22 percent of the freshmen at the predominantly black colleges that were sampled, and although more women freshmen continue to plan careers in the health fields (26 percent) and teaching (11 percent) than in business (10 percent), women were choosing business majors more often than those in the health professions—a reversal from 1973 findings.

Education and training for business careers is offered by nearly all public vocational-technical schools, two-year and four-year colleges, and universities and by hundreds of private business colleges—probably by more different institutions than any other branch of career education. In some two-year colleges, more students are enrolled in business programs than in *all* other career programs combined. Partly because business programs were "clean" white-collar programs, partly because they could be offered without highly-specialized and expensive shops or laboratories, and partly because they had been popular and successful in high school, they were the first vocational subjects to gain a foothold in the early junior colleges. Now the fields of marketing and sales promotion, banking, finance, insurance, and real estate are also represented by widely distributed curriculums in two-year and four-year institutions in most states. Agri-business programs are found throughout the major agricultural states in both rural and suburban two-year colleges and agricultural-technical schools. Among business and office fields, only hospitality career programs are geographically limited to a relatively small number of institutions: hotel and restaurant management and tourism programs remain concentrated in or near resort areas or very large cities where conventions are "big business."

Business and office career education programs can be classified in many different ways. For convenience, the following sections of this chapter examine first the office careers that include clerk-typist, stenographer, secretary, and computer specialist or data programmer; then careers in finance, including banking, real estate and insurance; then marketing; hospitality careers; agri-business; and, finally, business management, both for self-employed entrepreneurs and for salaried managers and administrators.

Office Careers

Despite the growth of automation and electronic communication, the need for office workers throughout the economy continues to increase. In business, industry, and government, the flow of paper work continues unabated. Every new development that is touted as a solution to the problem of records, accounts, and communication seems to generate its own volume of traffic, and when the dust settles from these claims, more rather than fewer office workers are needed.

Table 10 shows the increase among several of the major office occupations between 1960 and 1970. While the number of clerical and kindred workers at large increased nearly 46 percent over the decade, most of these occupations increased far more (except for stenographers, whose numbers declined by 47 percent). Computer specialists, not listed in Table 10 because they were not enumerated in 1960, numbered 254,537 by 1970.

Table 10. Persons Employed in Selected Office Occupations, 1960 and 1970.

	1960	1970	Percent Change
File Clerks	132,926	356,660	+168.3%
Typists	521,240	977,446	+ 87.5
Stenographers	269,759	127,957	− 47.4
Secretaries	1,463,731	2,702,099	+ 84.6
Office Machine Operators	304,952	552,580	+ 81.2
All Clerical and Kindred Workers	9,303,231	13,568,260	+ 45.8

Source: U.S. Bureau of the Census (1962, 1972).

As of 1974, nearly 15 million Americans were employed as office workers of one kind or another, and it is expected that employment opportunities for nearly all kinds and levels of office workers will rise appreciably during the 1980s. The level of sophistication of their jobs will probably increase, however, and many relatively unskilled and semiskilled clerical jobs may indeed be eliminated by automation. The challenge to educators in postsecondary business office education is to continually upgrade the knowledge and skills of their students in order to match the job requirements of the business offices of the future.

The short career ladder that exists in office occupations, whereby workers can advance from one job to another as they gain greater experience and training, begins with clerk-typist, or general office worker, and rises to office manager as its top rung. Two-year colleges operate programs for all levels of these careers, as illustrated by the following major types of program.

Clerk-Typist. Usually this is an open-door program in that no prior experience or demonstrated competence is required for admission, although some programs assume a modest typing ability. The program is usually only one academic year in length, leading to a certificate. It should be competency-based, however, so that students can "test out" of those courses for which they can already demonstrate proficiency, and the graduation certificate should clearly state the competencies attained by the student. Normally expected minimum performance levels include: typing fifty words per minute with no more than three errors per page; spelling words commonly used in business practice with no errors; setting up and maintaining a simple filing system; and demonstrating general office skills both by satisfactory performance of office routines and the operation of office machines and by satisfactory ratings from the work-experience or co-op supervisor.

A typical certificate program leading to these competencies for recent high-school graduates is outlined below. Many variations in course names, content, and hours of credit are possible. Special sequences may be desirable for older students and students with prior work experience who are now returning to the job market.

Certificate Level Clerk-Typist Program

Semester I	Credit Hours	Semester II	Credit Hours
English/Communication Skills	3	Intermediate (or Advanced) Typing	3
Beginning (or Intermediate) Typing	3	Business Accounting	3
		Secretarial Practice	3
Business Mathematics	3	Records Management	2
Office Procedures	3	Co-op Work Experience	3
Office Machines	3	Elective	2
	15		16

Stenographer. This typical two-year, associate degree level program emphasizes typing speed and accuracy plus capable handling of shorthand and electronic transcription systems. Shorthand shows some signs of phasing out, with electronic transcription and other forms of shorthand eventually taking its place. Competency levels expected on graduation are: typing of 60 to 70 words per minute with no errors, and shorthand at 100 words per minute with no errors in the finished transcription. Not an open-door program, this curriculum assumes some office skills already developed in high school and requires good-to-excellent capability in English.

The clerk-typist may move up the career ladder to stenographer, after working awhile, by concentrating in a second college year on typing, shorthand, and business English. Attaining the 110 words-per-minute rate in shorthand, however, may require more than two semesters of course work.

Secretary. This word often is used loosely to refer to persons working in many different office jobs. Accurately used, the term *secretary* means an office worker who handles all correspondence for an executive and manages all the important detail work related to the executive's assignment. Etymologically, it comes from the same root as *secret,* and the secretary-executive relationship, in fact, still does imply "one to be trusted with secrets or confidences of an employer" (*Webster's Seventh New Collegiate Dictionary*).

Several variations of associate degree secretarial programs are commonly found—legal secretary, technical secretary, medical secretary, executive secretary, and so on. Most are built around a two-year curriculum that emphasizes typing, shorthand (not all curriculums now require shorthand), filing, and general office practice plus the skills and knowledge required by the specialty, as law, medicine, or science. In addition to these skills, however, the secretarial program stresses general and liberal education and requires a high level of ability in English. The program is quite definitely not open-door. The first and necessary requirement is basic intelligence and verbal ability as demonstrated by a good academic record from high school. Second, the basic office skills already must have been attained if the program is to be completed in two academic years. Applicants for such programs should already type forty WPM, no errors, and be able to take dictation at eighty to ninety WPM and transcribe it without error.

Graduates of associate degree secretarial programs should be able to demonstrate skills of typing seventy to ninety words per minute with no errors and taking shorthand at 110 words per minute with no errors in the finished transcription; or if shorthand is not required, demonstrating accuracy and speed in transcribing perfect copy from dictating machines is necessary. In terms of other competencies, graduates must be capable of performing all office tasks and routines including reception, customer contact, telephone, itineraries and appointments, duplication of copies, correspondence, and confidential matters. Personality, appearance, and dependability are attributes of paramount importance.

A sample program is shown below, but many variations can be found.

Associate Degree Level Secretary Program

First Year

Semester I	Credit Hours	Semester II	Credit Hours
English Composition I	3	English Composition II	3
Office Procedures	3	Intermediate Shorthand	4
Business Correspondence	3	Advanced Typing	3
Records Management	2	Office Machines Laboratory	2
Economics	3	American History	3
Elective	2		
	16		15

Associate Degree Level Secretary Program (Continued)

Second Year

Advanced Shorthand	4	Political Science	3
Principles of Accounting	4	Office Management	3
Transcription	2	Co-op Work Experience	3
Speech	3	Electives	6
Elective	3		
	16		15

The electives can be chosen with either a specialty, such as legal or medical secretary, or an eventual baccalaureate degree objective in mind. By careful choice of electives, up to forty credit hours of the above two-year program could be acceptable for transfer to some four-year colleges in such stipulated programs as business education teaching or professional secretary. The career-ladder concept can function fairly well in the business office fields if students and career counselors select the elements of the students' two-year programs carefully, with the requirements of four-year colleges in mind from the beginning.

Careers in Finance, Insurance, and Real Estate

The outlook for jobs in these fields is good to excellent. Sixty thousand or more new jobs will open up annually for beginning white-collar workers in banks, savings and loan institutions, credit unions, and similar offices. Credit counseling, accounting and computer programming, and insurance are good fields for two-year college career programs in this area, while business management programs at the four-year college level should find good employment opportunities for their graduates in banking and finance.

Many middle-manpower jobs exist in banking, insurance, real estate, and investment firms—jobs that do not require a bachelor's degree, although larger banks, finance companies, and insurance companies place more emphasis on college degrees, as usual, than do smaller financial institutions. Most associate degree programs by themselves, however, do not provide the competencies required for most of these jobs, and thus career ladders for two-year college graduates must feature "steps" of practical experience. In contrast to other business and office occupations, most of which place much emphasis on preemployment education through formally structured curriculums, the fields of banking, investment, insurance, and real estate are heavily oriented toward the further education of persons already employed. Tellers and other counter personnel therefore may not need college training; and vertical mobility in the banking, finance, and real estate fields is not entirely dependent on earning advanced degrees, although a baccalaureate or graduate degree can often make the promotion path much smoother.

Large firms usually have their own executive development plans, and these are often operated cooperatively with colleges and universities. In some instances, the master's degree in business administration with appropriate concentration in banking and finance may be almost a requirement for moving up the executive ladder, but in smaller establishments with less structured management concepts, capable and ambitious associate degree graduates can move right up the career ladder, combining their on-the-job experience with professional-association courses, industry-sponsored seminars, and regular college courses taken on a part-time basis while regularly employed. Thus colleges and universities should be as concerned with offering continuing education in these areas as they are with preprofessional training. For both adults continuing their career development and college-age students planning careers in these fields, computer experience is becoming almost a "must" in the financial world.

Banking. Banks have recently begun to tap the potential of associate degree holders (Wiggs, 1970), but traditionally they have been oriented either to four-year college graduates or to filling middle-management positions by promotions from within. The American Institute of Banking, beginning in 1900, has developed its own series of courses for management training, and colleges can use in these in cooperative continuing education programs. Community colleges sometimes enter into joint agreements with local chapters of the Institute to offer associate degree and continuing education programs in banking. These cooperative training programs feature courses and seminars dealing with such topics as corporation finance, investments and trusts, business law, bank organization, credit management, personnel management, and computer operations in banking. They lead to such advancement jobs as credit manager, branch bank manager, tax and investment analyst, and bank statistician. Large banks often develop their own training programs in cooperation with local colleges, instead of using the American Institute of Banking materials.

Real Estate. Real estate has specific training and experience routes—the steps of which are usually specified by law—to the attainment of salesperson or broker status. Salesperson and broker status can both be attained in most states without pursuing a degree program, although it is probable that in the relatively near future states will begin to stipulate degree requirements at least for the broker's license. Now, although the requirements vary from state to state, most states specify the completion of one or more stipulated courses in real estate plus the passing of the state board examination for a salesperson's license. In addition, some states require "sponsorship" by a licensed broker. After a stipulated period of experience as a salesperson and the completion of other specified courses, one can sit for the state board examination for a broker's license. Only after these steps of education, experience, and licensing are completed can one become a realtor.

Consequently, the role of postsecondary education in the real estate field is cooperative rather than prescriptive. Real estate courses are offered, usually in cooperation with a local group of realtors, one of whom well may be the instructor. The elementary courses are usually "tailored" to the state board examination, while advanced courses may specialize in such subjects as appraisal, finance, investment, economics, and law.

Some community colleges offer an associate degree program in "real estate science," but enrollments in and especially completion of such programs tend to be low. The great majority of students in such programs are mature adults, including many women. The course that prepares for the state salesperson's license is given early in such degree programs so that the students can actually begin selling real estate. The rest of the program is made up of advanced real estate courses, along with a generous infusion of liberal arts and business management courses. Since the program is usually taken on a part-time basis in the evenings, by the time it is completed (perhaps after several years), the person well may be ready to sit for the broker's examination. Students in specialized real estate programs should be encouraged to complete at least the associate degree. If all but the specialized courses are chosen from liberal arts and transfer-course lists, a great deal of the program would be creditable toward a baccalaureate degree if that later should become the student's objective.

Insurance. Insurance also is a field where practical experience is just as important as formal education. One of the professional associations in this field—Chartered Life Underwriters—has developed its own training program for the life insurance field. Two-year colleges can join cooperatively with a local or regional chapter in providing these courses. A typical associate degree program designed to prepare students for entry into the insurance field would include courses and laboratory work of the following kinds:

Associate Degree Level Insurance Program

First Year

Semester I	Credit Hours	Semester II	Credit Hours
Introduction to Business I	3	Introduction to Business II	3
Accounting I	3	Accounting II	3
English I	3	English II	3
Marketing I	3	Marketing II	3
Introduction to Insurance I	3	Introduction to Insurance II	3
Business Mathematics	3		
	18		15

Second Year

	Credit Hours		Credit Hours
Introduction to Insurance III	3	Introduction to Insurance IV	3
Economics	3	Applied Psychology	3
Speech	3	Business Law	3
Mathematics of Finance	3	Co-op Work Experience	3
Introduction to Computer Science	3	Elective	3
	15		15

Such programs, particularly if the cooperative work experience is realistic, can lead to entry level jobs, such as claims analyst or claims adjuster, policy clerk, computer programmer, premium clerk, or insurance salesperson.

Sales Careers

The five million workers employed in sales and marketing jobs as of 1974 were about evenly divided between retail sales-workers (53 percent) and wholesale and "outside" salesmen (including persons selling real estate, insurance, and securities) and manufacturers' representatives (47 percent). Every economic portent points to a steady growth in the employment of sales workers in "outside" selling, but the trends in automated and self-service retail selling point to leveling off or no-growth in jobs for retail sales workers.

College-trained merchandising majors are generally aiming at such management positions as buyer, department manager, or store manager. Outside salesmen or manufacturer's representatives, however, need additional and extensive sales training in industry and technical knowledge of the products or services being sold. The business management and marketing/salesmanship curriculums in community colleges are specifically planned to produce such salesmen, but work experience or internships must be an integral part of the program. Courses in real estate, insurance, or finance provide for preparation in these selling specialties.

The importance of work experience, internships, and on-the-job training cannot be overemphasized in all business education fields, but this is especially true in sales. Community colleges and vocational-technical schools have incorporated internships into their programs for years, but even greater emphasis should be placed on this feature of marketing education (ERIC Junior College Research Review, 1970).

Hospitality Careers

Americans are notorious tourists. Long before the age of flight the most popular automobile body style was the "touring car." With the advent of jet travel and superhighways, travel for business, pleasure, and health reasons has grown to a point where it almost seems that nobody stays at home. In the winter, it is skiing for some and sun fun for others; in the summer, vacation trips for the whole family.

All of this mobility has caused a geometrical rate of growth in hotels, motels, restaurants, resorts, clubs, and other facilities to accommodate the vacationing and traveling public. These activities taken in the aggregate—hotels, restaurants, resorts, and the travel agents and tour guides that assist in the planning—are now called the "hospitality industry." It is one of the four largest industries in the United States, with annual sales in 1975 of over $60 billion. It provides 800 million meals a week, employs about 3.5 million workers, and in a few states is the biggest of all industries. The Council on Hotel, Restaurant, and Institutional Education in Washington, D.C. estimates that the industry's manpower needs over the next decade will approximate 250,000 new employees each year to take care of growth and provide replacements for those who retire or leave the field.

Jobs in the industry range across a broad spectrum from dishwasher to short-order cook to restaurant manager and from hotel chef to general manager or president of a hotel or restaurant chain; and from ticket agent to director of tourism for an entire state (Almarode, 1968). Many of these are middle-manpower jobs for which postsecondary career education programs are the optimum preparation. There are hundreds of new jobs annually at the professional level also, and a number of four-year colleges and universities provide nationally known programs in hotel and restaurant management. At the other end of the job spectrum are the semiskilled and unskilled jobs for which a brief period of on-the-job experience or a short course in a vocational skill center will provide the necessary training. Our interest here is primarily in the semiprofessional, technical, and highly-skilled jobs for which associate degree and certificate programs are provided in community junior colleges, technical colleges, and area vocational-technical schools.

The future of the tourism sector of this industry may be negatively affected because of its dependence on travel fueled by petroleum. Another oil embargo or severe increases in fuel prices could stop or reverse growth trends in this area quite dramatically, and colleges should be prepared to aid the lateral occupational mobility of graduates of these programs in case the industry falls on hard times.

Associate-Degree Programs. In general, two-year associate degree programs are management-oriented, in contrast to one-year certificate programs, which are skills-oriented. As an example, the hotel and restaurant management curriculum outlined below, offered by a technical college in a southeastern resort area, has a three-fold purpose: first, to provide a good base of management theory; second, to provide at least reasonable familiarity with some of the skills of food preparation and service and of hotel operation; and third, to provide approximately 430 hours of actual on-the-job experience, half in restaurant operations and half in hotel operations.

Associate Degree Level Hotel and Restaurant Management Program

First Year

Semester I	Credit Hours	Semester II	Credit Hours
English	3	Restaurant Management (laboratory)	6
Business Mathematics	3	Speech	2
Introduction to Hospitality Management	3	Advertising and Promotion	2
Principles of Accounting	3	Restaurant Accounting	2
Introduction to Quantity Food Preparation (laboratory)	3	Front Office Procedures	2
Sanitation	1	Purchasing	2
	16		16

Second Year

	Credit Hours		Credit Hours
American History	3	Political Science	3
Business Law	3	Human Relations	2
Hotel Accounting	2	Hotel Management	3
Menus and Nutrition	2	Advanced Food Service Laboratory	2
Co-op Work Experience (Restaurant)	4	Beverage Service Laboratory	2
		Co-op Work Experience (Hotel)	4
	14		16

There are, of course, many different approaches to curriculum development. Some programs specialize in one field or the other—restaurant management or hotel management—in which case the depth in the one field can be much greater, but the job market opportunities might not be as good, especially in a locality where the hotels and motels are relatively small and a hired manager or franchise owner will have to manage both lodging and food-service operations.

With respect to vertical mobility up a career ladder a student completing an associate-degree program like the one above currently cannot expect a great deal of transfer credit into a hotel and restaurant management baccalaureate-degree program. Better articulation is needed to improve career ladder potentials in the field. In the meantime, the amount of transfer credit could be maximized by selecting all the English, mathematics, social studies, speech, and accounting courses from the college-parallel group of two-year college courses. Beyond these courses, totalling perhaps twenty-four credits, the transfer credit allowed for the specialized hospitality career courses might vary from none in certain prestigious university programs to perhaps twenty or more at some four-year colleges.

Certificate Programs. Certificate programs of one year or less are usually skill-oriented, but occasionally they concentrate on a narrow management specialty such as sales promotion, purchasing, or cafeteria management. Skill-oriented programs also tend to concentrate in such specialized fields as baking, short-order cooking, or beverage service.

The objective of certificate programs is immediate employment in a specialized field. The training is intensive, with as much as 1,500 hours of instruction and work experience in a typical program. The programs rely heavily on laboratory work and cooperative work experience, and only a few credits for electives might be allowed in the typical thirty-two- to thirty-six-credit-hour program.

For career ladder reasons, certificate programs should be planned so that they are open-ended. That is, anyone completing the one-year program should be able to continue on to earn the associate degree by satisfactorily completing general education re-

quirements and additional career-oriented courses totalling together not more than one additional academic year of work.
Advisory Committees. Starting a hospitality program without an active local or regional advisory committee would be unthinkable. An excellent example of advisory committee participation is that at the Kapiolani Community College in Honolulu (Kalani, 1975).

Agri-Business Careers

Agriculture, over the past half-century, has been America's most efficient economic activity. In many nations of the world, 70 percent or more of the total labor force (including women and very young children) must be engaged in agriculture to produce enough food for the population. But one American farmer, with the benefits of mechanization, scientific production methods, and managerial business "know-how" produces enough food for forty other people.

Much of agriculture in this country has a business base. On family-owned farms, cattle ranches, orchards, and vegetable farms, as well as corporate farms, business methods are almost as important as the actual tilling of the soil. Colleges have responded to this need with business-oriented programs in agriculture, most of which have been developed within the past twenty years. In general, four-year colleges and universities prefer the term *agricultural economics* for these programs, while community colleges and postsecondary technical schools use the term *agri-business.*

Agri-business programs are usually a joint effort between the business and the agriculture departments in two-year colleges and technical schools. The typical offering is a two-year associate degree program consisting of some thirty credit hours of specialized agri-business courses, twelve credits of basic agriculture courses, perhaps fifteen credits of general education, and eight credits of co-op work experience, for a total of about sixty-five credits.

Agri-business programs prepare for "off-the-farm" jobs closely related to the production, sale, and distribution of farm products. Examples of career fields are management of an agriculture-related business; working with banks and insurance companies in farm-related credit, investments, and insurance; dealing in farm commodities or in farm equipment and services; market analysis and forecast work; and in a wide range of sales jobs. Associate degree programs as offered at community and technical colleges feature content similar to the following:

Associate Degree Level Agri-Business Program

First Year

Semester I	Credit Hours	Semester II	Credit Hours
English I	3	English II	3
Introduction to		Introduction to	
Business I	3	Business II	3
Accounting I	3	Accounting II	3
Agricultural Economics	3	Introduction to Animal	
Soil Science	3	Husbandry	3
		Introduction to Data	
		Processing	3
	15		15

Second Year

	Credit Hours		Credit Hours
Applied Psychology	3	Agricultural Finance	3
Farm Management	3	Agricultural Marketing	3
Crop Production	3	Co-op Work Experience	8
Agricultural Machinery	3	Elective	3
Political Science	3		
	15		17

With a judicious selection of the general education and basic agriculture courses, nearly one half of the program can be transferable to a baccalaureate program. As always, the academic ability of the student is an important factor in deciding to take university-parallel courses, and of course the specific requirements of the four-year college or university that the student has in mind must be adhered to.

Many community colleges offer short-term certificate programs on a continuing education basis for persons already in agriculture, for various fields of agri-business. Such specialties as "fertilizers and pesticides" and "farm accounting" are not uncommon. Such programs may be cosponsored by farm cooperatives, granges, and dealers in agricultural equipment and supplies. Credits earned in these courses should be applicable to an associate degree program if the student later decides to take another step up the career ladder. Enrollment of employed adults on a part-time or evening basis is characteristic of these programs.

Management Careers and Career Paths

Coast to coast, hundreds of thousands of small businesses, from hamburger stands to camera shops, are owned and operated by entrepreneurs or owner-managers who need all the knowledge and skill they can get to operate their business profitably. In addition, bigger firms employ many persons in middle-management positions for which training in two-year colleges and technical schools is excellent preparation. Opportunities for young men and women trained in associate-degree business management programs are good now and should improve over the next ten years. But as Table 8 earlier in this chapter showed, there are many managers and administrators employed in salaried positions in corporations, associations, and government. Among large organizations there is currently rather general recognition that the bachelor's degree in business administration (BBA) is an important step on the road to an administrative career and that the master's degree (MBA) is the professional degree.

The management of business as a discipline or science is called business *administration,* and such professional programs are properly offered in four-year colleges and universities. Further, the prestige programs in the profession are generally offered by colleges or schools of business administration accredited by the American Association of Collegiate Schools of Business (AACSB). The majority of graduates of these programs at the BBA and MBA level go into "big business" or corporate firms as managers, and a few enter their family firm eventually to become the owner, the president, or a partner.

At present, and regrettably, the dichotomy between "practical business training" at the two-year level and "professional business administration" at the four-year and graduate level is pronounced.

Although this picture could change over the next decade, as it is currently beginning to do in the health field (see Chapter Seven), it is still almost impossible to develop a career ladder approach to business management involving two-year, four-year, and graduate professional programs. There is no neat career ladder in the business world that educators can use as a template for coordinated curriculum and program development. Two-year colleges can, and many do, offer the first two years of business administration programs. But business administration as a university-level professional program is very prescriptive during its first two years, and most AASCB-accredited colleges of business administration either discourage transfer students or insist that they take no more than their freshman year in any other institution. Thus two-year college or business college programs in business management ordinarily are not accepted for transfer except to some of the bachelor's degree programs that have been initiated in recent years at some state colleges, technological colleges, and newly-designated state universities that award the bachelor's degree in business management (BBM). Rinehart (1973, p. 98) sums up the lack of a career-ladder approach in this area and emphasizes the difficulty of transferring practical business management courses taken in the two-year college to business administration programs in four-year colleges and universities by commenting, "Changing one's mind on the *level* of education in business is almost as expensive in time and effort as changing to a different career field."

Since much of business is entrepreneurial and small-scale in character rather than corporate, management plays a number of different roles. In the entreprenurial business, the individual proprietor organizes the business, hires and fires employees, manages day-to-day operations, assumes the risks, and takes the profits, if any. This is owner-managership, and it is representative of thousands of firms in all kinds of business from coast to coast.

There are few hard and fast criteria for the education and training of entrepreneurs. Persons with only a fourth-grade education have owned and operated their own businesses successfully and in some cases have built them into million-dollar-a-year enterprises, while others with graduate degrees in business administration sometimes have gone broke. Too many variables exist in the business world to enable anyone to propose the "right" educational program to assure success as an entrepreneur, although there is considerable agreement among manpower experts that everyone interested in a business management career, even in small business, should have some background in computer technology (Houston, 1975) and that preemployment programs should feature internships. Community colleges should have a wide offering of specialized courses for persons already in business, since not many people go into business for themelves immediately upon completing a business management program in the way that people who complete a nursing program immediately "go into nursing." The business opportunity must be there, capital (that is, money to start and operate the business until it will carry itself) must be arranged, a suitable location must be found, franchises or other sources of merchandise must be secured, and credit provided for.

Thus much of the formal education for owners of small businesses comes after the business has been founded. Colleges and business schools everywhere provide extension courses, evening courses, seminars, clinics, and workshops for owners of these businesses. Subjects include accounting, marketing, taxation, purchasing, finance, insurance, personnel management, credit management, computer technology, advertising and sales promotion, and, of course, small business management. Courses of these kinds can be arranged in a pattern leading to an associate or even a baccalaureate degree in business management, if the student and a competent educational adviser plan carefully together.

Associate Degree Programs. A variety of associate-degree programs with somewhat different career objectives come under the general heading of business management programs, since besides concentration in small business management, students can specialize in such fields as accounting, banking and finance, and real estate. This is particularly true at such large community colleges as Golden West College in Huntington Beach, California, where the number of different courses offered in these fields varies from eighty to one hundred and ranges from "Introduction to Business" to "Securities and Investments."

An associate degree curriculum from a two-year college in a southern state is shown below as illustrative of programs in small business management. Such programs are not open-door, since students are expected to undertake college-level work in accounting and economics in their first semester.

Associate Degree Level Business Management Program

First Year

Semester I	Credit Hours	Semester II	Credit Hours
Business English	3	Speech	3
Introduction to Business	3	Marketing	3
Economics	3	Principles of	
Business Mathematics	3	Management	3
Introduction to		Human Relations	3
Computers	3	Electives	4
	15		16

Second Year

	Credit Hours		Credit Hours
Political Science	3	American History	3
Proprietorship		Accounting II	3
Accounting I	3	Business Management	
Credit and Finance	3	Laboratory	2
Advertising and Sales		Internship	8
Promotion	3		
Field Project	3		
	15		16

It is quite probable that a specialized job-oriented program like that outlined above would not provide for more than about thirty transfer credits in most four-year programs. Students and their career advisors should explore this possibility carefully if further study toward the baccalaureate degree is contemplated.

Bachelor of Business Management Programs. At certain four-year colleges of the "state college" type the transfer of well-qualified graduates from associate degree programs in business management has been facilitated in recent years. For example, Ferris State College in Big Rapids, Michigan, grants 100 quarter-credit hours (one half its bachelor of science program requirements) to Associate in Applied Science graduates of accredited two-year colleges through its "two-plus-two" curriculum arrangement. The Bachelor of Science in Business Management at Ferris State may be attained by associate degree graduates by completing two upper-division academic years (100 quarter credits) in a program with content somewhat as follows:

Upper Division Bachelor of Science Business Management Program

Fields and Courses	*Quarter Hours*
Management	(21)
Principles of Management	3
Industrial Management	4
Personnel Management	4
Financial Management	4
Management Problems and Policies I and II	6
Information Systems	(24)
Managerial Accounting	12
Statistics	8
Data Processing	4
Business Environment	(16)
Financial Institutions	4
Marketing	4
Advertising	4
Business and Government	4
Business Economics	(8)
Business Forecasting	4
Management Economics	4
Psychology	(7)
General Psychology	3
Applied Psychology	4
Co-op Work Experience and Electives	(24)
Co-op Work Experience	16
General Education Electives	8

Such two-plus-two programs provide an opportunity for associate degree middle management workers to move up the career ladder into baccalaureate level management positions in many fields of industry and business.

In addition to two-plus-two programs, nearly all state colleges and universities offer all four years of business management or business administration. As pointed out above, business schools accredited by the American Association of Collegiate Schools of Business call their programs "business administration," and the first degree they award is the Bachelor of Business Administration (BBA). It is again emphasized that transfer from two-year college business programs into BBA programs at these schools is quite difficult, with very little if any credit being allowed for the two-year college business management courses.

In concluding this brief look at prospects for business management, some emphasis should be given to the rapidly growing importance of international trade. American-owned firms have innumerable foreign branches and—a new phenomenon—more and more foreign-owned firms are establishing both sales and manufacturing operations in the United States. Personnel with business training plus fluency in another language, special training in telecommunications, or special knowledge of the culture and economic needs of other peoples will probably be in great demand.

Guidelines and Conclusions

Three characteristics of all good career education programs—work experience, laboratory work, and advisory committees—are particularly important in business and office careers.

Work Experience. The internship or work-experience component is extremely important for students without prior or current experience in business. According to Robert Brown (1971, p. 6), "Schools must respond to the impetus of business needs. The demand for greater relevancy should put the school in high gear, not bring it to a halt. Work experience rounds out education, eases the progression from knowledge to performance, and satisfies the need for reality in learning."

The key phrase here is "eases the progression from knowledge to performance." An internship provides the opportunity to apply the knowledge that has been acquired and to begin evaluative and judgmental processes in the context of actual day-to-day business practice. All of these important aspects of learning can take place on the employer's premises, in a business venture operated with the employer's capital, before one's own money (or credit) is "on the line." Although the emulation of successful businesses is the goal of the college program, a chance to observe the operations of some struggling businessmen should not be denied the students. We learn from failures as well as successes. *Business Management Laboratory: Simulation.* In the business world managers play a variety of roles and are involved in more areas of decision-making than other staff. To prepare prospective managers for this kind of responsibility, many teachers of business management have adapted the case study methods pioneered by the Harvard Graduate School of Business Administration for their own instructional programs at the undergraduate level. The cases are written for small and medium-sized business ventures, "mom and pop" stores, and entrepreneurships typical of those found on the local scene, as well as for the complex corporate ventures of "big business."

A variant of the case-study method that is used very effectively in many community colleges, technical colleges, and business colleges is business simulation. The course listed as Business Management Laboratory in the business management program earlier in the chapter is often used as a vehicle for simulating problems in small business organization and operation. In one of the Ohio technical colleges it meets for four hours a week during the same semester as the internship, so that actual problems encountered in the work-experience situation can be used as a backdrop against which to project the case studies of the simulation laboratory.

Sprick (1973, p. 61) describes business simulation as denoting "either a theoretical framework for industry or a hypothetical business situation in which students assume predetermined semistructured roles. Players are typically required to resolve a major business issue or 'operate' a company in a dynamic market environment." The business simulation activity typically divides the class into small groups, each of which is the "management group" for a hypothetical business firm. For example, an appliance dealership might be simulated. Students in a group of five might take on the following roles: owner and president; vice president and controller; sales manager; service manager; and personnel manager. The instructor will have prepared in advance the essential dimensions of and ingredients in the case study. A series of "problems" is then posed, which may run the gamut from sales slumps to personnel problems, including such issues as opening another store, taking on other lines of merchandise, a threatened strike of union employees, a suit for damages involving a company truck driver who is accused of a hit-and-run accident, and so on.

All the elements of small group instruction can be brought to these sessions. Conference methods, printed case discussions, buzz sessions, role playing, visits to sites, and calling in "experts" can all be used. During the semester each person might work on three or four different management teams representing different businesses and cope with as many as ten or a dozen typical problems of business management. One of the great advantages of simulation is that it forces each student out of a passive role as a learner and requires him or her to function in an active role (Sprick, 1973). When each case is resolved, it is reviewed in detail with the instructor, who will point out other possible outcomes, different courses of action, and elements of success and failure. Definite time limits should not be set on cases. The object is to learn as much as possible about business management, not to complete a set number of cases. Each case, however, should be satisfactorily resolved before "reshuffling the management" to take on another case.

The simulation approach is strongly recommended, but it must be carefully planned by instructors who are experienced in both small-group instruction methods (Olmstead, 1974) and small-business management practices. A suitable laboratory, with its own small library and media resources center, is very nearly essential to the success of such a method. The laboratory should be kept open so that the several "management teams" can schedule its use as needed for their work. A small conference room and business office suite (functional, but not elaborate) are desirable. If a computer is available, the "game" can simulate management decision-making on very complex issues (Mayhew, 1974).

Advisory Committees. The importance of advisory committees has been stressed continually for all of career education, but even more emphasis needs to be given to their use as business management programs are planned and operated. Administrators and coordinators of programs should make a special effort to get a good cross section of local businessmen on the advisory committee. A variety of different kinds of businesses—production, processing, service, financial, wholesale, and retail—should be represented. William O. Haynes (1968, p. 12), coordinator for a large food distribution curriculum at Western Michigan University, states the case for advisory committees as he writes, "A guiding precept in the development of a successful program is a full utilization of a well-organized advisory committee. It is truly amazing what an effective advisory committee can do for a program."

The reason for this emphasis on work experience, laboratory, and advisory committees for business programs stems from the fact that in education for business careers, just as in most other postsecondary career education fields, the problem of standards of attainment and quality of the programs is critical.

The Problem of Quality in Business Programs. The open-door policies of many colleges, combined with the recently noted decline in the academic aptitude of young high-school graduates, as evidenced by reports from the College Entrance Examination Board (CEEB) and the American College Testing Program (ACT), have posed serious problems for business education programs dedicated to excellence and competency on the job. As unprepared students choose business courses on an open-door basis, often without the basic learning skills to cope with the work, a kind of academic Gresham's law sets in that if allowed to govern, will inevitably lower standards to the point where program credibility will be in doubt.

One should make a clear distinction here between the open-door college, which is a good idea, and the open-door course, which often is not (Trivett, 1976). In business programs, as in all other career education programs, the very essence of the instruction is eventual competence on the job. There can be no compromise with that principle. Recent moves in the direction of competency-based education, mastery learning, and performance objectives constitute encouraging evidence that postsecondary career education does not intend to allow its credentials to become meaningless.

Developmental-remedial programs can assist the ill-prepared. Open laboratories, autotutorial systems, and increased use of the media can assist the slow learner as we again adopt the principle of "making learning the constant and time the variable"

(Roueche, Herrscher, and Baker, 1976). The development of various levels of programs is to be encouraged—short-term, specific job training; one-year certificate; two-year diploma or associate degree; paraprofessional or midmanagement programs at associate degree or baccalaureate levels; and graduate professional programs. The career ladder concept can be applied to some programs, degrees, and job levels, but each level must maintain its integrity and its own performance standards. The challenge to business educators is, first, to know what these standards of quality are and, second, to so plan the programs, courses, learning systems, and admissions criteria that when a given program level is completed, the required minimum competencies can be demonstrated by all students.

Guidelines for Planners. Many of the suggestions to be found in Chapter Ten on planning and operating successful career education programs are applicable to planners of programs in business and office fields, as are the suggestions in the final chapter on the administration of these programs through a "career division" administrative structure. Specialists in business education should review those ideas as well as noting the importance for quality business programs of these particular guidelines: (1) Do not plan any business education program without an effective advisory committee representing a cross-section of employers in the community. (2) Be sure to conduct periodic business-careers surveys to determine the needs and demand for business program graduates. (3) Adopt a competency-based approach to instruction, establish performance objectives for each course in the program, and award credits and degrees only when these objectives are attained. (4) Provide instructional systems compatible with a competency-based approach, including case studies and simulation techniques and cooperative work experience. (5) Offer good career counseling, educational advisement, and developmental remedial programs and other student services. And (6) plan the steps on career ladders in business in cooperation with high schools and other colleges, to assure continued opportunities for occupational advancement. In business careers, as in most others, preparation for today's jobs is not a waste of time but may be the best preparation for tomorrow's jobs as well.

6 ▣▣▣▣▣▣▣▣▣▣▣▣▣▣▣

Careers in Engineering, Science, and Industry-Related Technologies

There is an unfortunate tendency to view pragmatism and realism as somehow opposed to high promise and humanism. But we have reached a point at which high promise and humane concern can be responsibly expressed only through operational performance which is pragmatic and realistic. To continue to pretend otherwise would be unrealistic.

Elliot Richardson (1973)

This is an age of anomalies—a time when the abnormal becomes the norm, when emotions supplant rationality, and mythologies challenge science as a means of bringing order to human affairs. In an age when science and technology landed us on the moon and probed the solar system, astrology suddenly has more followers than astronomy; mystics claim millions of converts; and the university, for centuries the fortress of reason, is now a haven for antirationalists who claim that the higher learning should emphasize the affective domain rather than the domain of the intellect.

At the very time when reason, intellectual rigor, science, and technology are urgently needed to meet critical national goals, there is a significantly large and effectively vocal segment of society that demands a turning away from technology and a return to the simple life. The needs for energy development, food production, national defense, and the rising expectations of the poor notwithstanding, a kind of antitechnology syndrome affects millions of Americans, rendering them unproductive in a society that desperately needs their productivity. In 1971, Lewis M. Branscomb, then director of the National Bureau of Standards, associated this denigration of technological and scientific achievement with the guilt complex that has seemed to haunt many Americans in the past decade as he wryly commented, "Science is, perhaps, some kind of cosmic apple juice from the Garden of Eden. Those who drink it are now doomed to carry the burden of original sin."

Evidence of the war on technology abounded in the early 1970s—cut-backs in aerospace and science research; injunctions against atomic energy development and new power plants; withdrawal of insecticides and agriscience products from the market; and legal power plays to prevent the development of new petroleum fields are only a few examples. In concert with such overt acts, there were throughout the late 1960s and early 1970s continual references to technology as the major cause of the world's troubles. The result, in the United States at least, was a dangerous slowdown in the rate of research and development, a loss in economic productivity (quickly taken advantage of by other industrial nations), and plummeting enrollments in the early 1970s in science, engineering, and the technologies in universities, colleges, and technical schools.

In contrast to those who fear technology, members of the scientific and technical community take a more balanced view. They admit that technology causes problems but know that it also solves problems. Most of the critical problems that have plagued mankind for centuries were solved or alleviated through technology—disease, famine, drudgery, ignorance, communication, and transportation, to name only a few. In solving these problems, others have been created, to be sure, but these too can be solved through technology. "Technology solves the problems technology creates" is not an idle slogan but a proven factor, and America needs more, not fewer, well-trained technicians to solve these and other problems. By 1976, the anti-technology movement had lost some of its momentum. As energy crises became real instead of mere future predictions, as the U.S. economy slowed to depression levels, and as the threat of famine stalked vast regions of the world, people began to realize that "the call to the simpler life" really has appeal only when affluence accompanies simplicity. Well-being for most people comes only from effective participation in economic activity with all the help which science, engineering, and technology can provide. As a result, there is now a perceptible swing back to engineering and technology in colleges and technical schools and there are even some signs of increasing enrollments in the pure sciences in colleges and universities. Some softness in the job market still remains for scientists, engineers, and technicians, but it is now quite clear that a realistic commitment to the nation's goals (Lecht, 1969) will, over the next decade, require hundreds of thousands of well-educated and highly trained scientists, engineers, and technicians.

Consistent with the theme of career education for middle manpower, this chapter explores the field of science and technology at paraprofessional and technical levels. Therefore, it deals primarily not with scientists or professional engineers but with occupations, occupational clusters, and career training programs for semiprofessionals and technicians, including the relatively new baccalaureate degree level engineering and industrial technology programs and the jobs their graduates fill.

Trends in Technical Education

Technical or technological education may have had its beginnings in Germany about 1766, when a technical mining school was established in Freiburg, but some historians cite the creation of the École Polytechnique in France in 1794 as its origin (American Society for Engineering Education, 1972). In the United States, schools for technical education—called "technical institutes"—began operating as early as 1822, when the Gardiner Lyceum in Gardiner, Maine, was established; many others started before 1850. Engineering schools began operating in the United States at about the same time, with Union College, Harvard, and Yale all having engineering programs prior to 1850. By 1900, forty-two engineering colleges or programs were in operation in this country.

During the late nineteenth and early twentieth centuries, dozens of technical institutes were started, some publicly supported, others as private nonprofit institutions, and still others as proprietary or profit-making institutions. These technical institutes tended to be special-purpose institutions that limited their programs and courses to fields and jobs in business, industry, and government for which practical training associated with theoretical knowledge of science, mathematics, and engineering was essential. Today, scores of technical institutes and technical colleges continue to function, most of them still somewhat specialized in their offerings, concentrating on associate degree programs related to semiprofessional and technician jobs (Graney, 1965; Henninger, 1959).

Following World War II, with the entry of the community junior college into this level of education, technical education began a sequence of "boom-and-bust" cycles. The period from 1946 to 1954 was one of explosive growth, as veterans sought education and training which would prepare them for satisfying middle-level jobs in engineering and industry-related fields. In the period from 1954 to 1957, however, college students (mostly new high school graduates) turned away from technology and science, and enrolled heavily in the humanities and the arts. Then came Sputnik I in 1957, and the sudden realization that America had lost much ground in both the space race and the cold war. Congress passed the National Defense Education Act (NDEA) of 1958, with funds for both institutional programs and student stipends. All the stops were pulled out for a nationwide promotional campaign to popularize scientific, engineering, and technical fields.

The early and mid-1960s constituted another period of rapid growth for both technician utilization in the work force and postsecondary technical education programs. These years, devoted to space exploration and to putting men on the moon before 1970, placed critical demands on technical manpower. Industry required modernization, with automation and computers controlling manufacturing processes; research and development funds flowed freely in both the private and public sectors; scientists, mathematicians, engineers, and technicians were in continual demand. As late as 1970, the National Industrial Conference Board published an important study emphasizing the nation's shortage of technical manpower and urging young people to consider careers in scientific and technical fields.

Another "down-cycle" occurred from about 1969 through 1974, associated with a wave of antitechnology, antiindustry, and antieconomic development feeling referred to above and related to the environmental-ecology movement, resistance to the Indo-China war, and the aftermath of the student disaffections of the 1960s. The severe economic recession of 1973–1976 and the drastic reduction in research and development funds for such purposes as space exploration, national defense, industrial modernization, and advances in "pure" science both contributed to a falling off of employment in technical occupations.

In 1976, however, another era was under way. The nation's dire need for energy resources development was driven home in no uncertain terms by the oil embargo of 1974 and the subsequent high prices for petroleum. American industry urgently needed retooling and modernizing; national defense again regained a high priority for federal spending; and such national needs as health care, environmental improvement, increased food production, and modernization of the merchant marine came to be recognized as problems that could not be solved without technology. Consequently, we are at the beginning of another cycle of need for scientists, engineers, and technicians. Just how rapidly these needs will be translated into demands, with plenty of job offers for new science and engineering graduates, cannot be predicted. At the technician level however, during the mid-1970s, demand has remained steady. The growth of some of these careers between 1960 and 1970 is shown from Bureau of the Census data in Table 11,

Table 11. Employment in Selected Technical Occupations,
1960 and 1970.

	1960	1970	Percent Change
Air Conditioning, Heating, and Refrigeration Mechanics and Repairmen	63,101	117,592	+86.4%
Automobile Mechanics and Repairmen	684,228	909,694	+33.0
Foremen and Leading Men	1,174,314	1,444,526	+23.0
Electrical and Electronic Technicians	92,541	150,934	+63.1
Other Engineering and Science Technicians	185,354	285,361	+54.0

Source: U.S. Bureau of the Census (1962).

with the increase ranging from a low of 23 percent for foremen to a high of 86 percent for air conditioning, heating, and refrigeration mechanics and repairmen.

The U.S. Department of Labor forecasts a 1985 requirement of 1,050,000 engineering and science technicians of all kinds and levels, compared to a 1972 employment of 707,000. This represents a 49 percent increase for the 1972–1985 period, with the average number of new openings per year (including growth and replacement) approximately 40,000 (U.S. Department of Labor, 1974a). Graduates of associate degree programs in engineering and industrial technology have not really experienced a serious unemployment situation. According to the Engineering Manpower Commission of the Engineers Joint Council, only 11 percent of June 1975 associate degree technician graduates had "no offers or plans" by graduation day (*Scientific, Engineering, Technical Manpower Comments,* 1975).

The Technician's Place in Industry

The technician is a middle-manpower worker whose usual employment involves both theoretical knowledge and manipulative skills that lie between those of the professional scientist or engineer on the one hand and the skilled craftsman on the other. The theoretical knowledge is most often drawn from the disciplines of the sciences, mathematics, and engineering, and the manipulative skills from such fields as drafting, metal and wood working, bench work, and machine operation. Since many technicians serve as members of a science/engineering/industry team, there is a communications or liaison dimension to their work also, and human relations skills are important for effective functioning on the job.

A satisfactory definition of the technician's work has been formulated by the U.S. Department of Labor (1962, p. 2):

> Technicians work with engineers and scientists in virtually every aspect of engineering and scientific work. One of their largest areas of employment is in research, development, and design. Technicians in this type of activity generally serve as direct supporting personnel to engineers or scientists. In the laboratory they conduct experiments or tests; set up, calibrate, and operate instruments; and make calculations. They may assist scientists and engineers in developing experimental equipment and models, do drafting, and frequently assume responsibility for certain aspects of design work under the engineer's direction.

Just as middle manpower occupations constitute a segment of the total occupational spectrum, so do technical occupations constitute a segment of the job spectrum that is related to the industry/engineering/science complex. The word *technician* means many things to many people, and any number of paradigms or graphical schemes have been devised to portray the relationships between and among the various levels of technicians. One such graphical portrayal is shown in Figure 2.

As this figure shows, workers in technology can be conceived of as being at five different levels—craftsmen or skilled tradesmen, industrial technicians, engineering technicians, engineering and industrial technologists, and engineers and scientists. The heavy line sloping upward from left to right across the five categories gives a general indication of the mix of manual skill and cognitive skill, or theoretical and technical knowledge required of workers

Figure 2. Levels of Technological Occupations, by Task, Mix of Manipulative and Cognitive Skills, Sources of Training, and Degree Level.

The Spectrum of Technical and Scientific Jobs

————— Middle-Manpower Fields —————

	Tradesmen and Craftsmen	Highly Skilled Industrial Technicians	Semiprofessional Science and Engineering Technicians	Engineering and Industrial Technologists	Professional Scientists and Engineers
Characteristics, Tasks, and Responsibilities	Production jobs requiring manual skills of a high order. Some need for technical knowledge. Construction, maintenance, repair, and service jobs. Most trades are controlled by unions, and training programs are often coordinated by joint apprenticeship committees.	Install, test, maintain, and repair complex equipment such as electronic instruments and gear. Drafting, detailing, estimating. Some production of prototype equipment. Balance between manual skills and technical knowledge.	Research and design in support of the activities of scientists and engineers. May work independently on some assignments. May engage in sales work as a manufacturer's representative. With experience, may move into middle-management positions. Needs some manual skills, but emphasis is on technical and engineering knowledge.	Research, design, and some management. May be in charge of "practical" production engineering problems. Plant layout and supervision. Cost analysis and production efficiency analysis. Still some question as to the exact "place" or "niche" for graduates of these programs.	Basic research and design. Direction of research, design, and production projects. Members of this group can be and are licensed by states to practice their profession as entrepreneurs. After suitable experience, advancement to management or to professional assignments is common. Often work at the frontiers of knowledge.

Highly Manipulative → Highly Cognitive

Sources of Preparation	Trade schools, skill centers, vocational-technical schools, adult evening schools, apprenticeship programs, in-plant training, armed forces schools	Community colleges, area vocational-technical schools, apprenticeship programs, in-plant training, armed forces schools	Technical institutes, community junior colleges, technical colleges, university branches	State colleges or "new" state universities. Some technical institutes and technical colleges. Some traditional universities	Traditional universities and graduate schools. Institutes of science and technology
Educational Level of Program	High school diploma	Certificate or associate degree	Associate degree	"New" bachelor's degrees	Traditional degrees

at each level. Across the bottom of the chart is an indication of the kinds and levels of schools in which education and training are offered for the several levels.

It must be emphasized that such a chart is a crude device at best. The complexities and nuances of job skills, knowledge, experience, and judgment cannot really be reduced to a paradigm. The levels overlap at all the neatly drawn lines, and the terminology for them is not universally accepted. Very few workers like to be pigeon-holed or characterized by titles in rectangles of such a matrix. Despite the weaknesses of chart construction, however, if they are admitted and kept in mind, such a figure is a useful tool in understanding the hierarchy of technician careers and in explaining it to potential students in search of careers.

As pointed out earlier, middle manpower careers are those that fall between the extreme left-hand (tradesmen and craftsmen) column and the right-hand (professional scientists and engineers) column. They include the three career levels in between: (1) highly-skilled industrial technicians; (2) science and engineering technicians, and (3) engineering and industrial technologists.

Highly Skilled Industrial Technicians. These technicians usually exhibit the following characteristics. First, they work at jobs which relate to repetitive testing, installation, repair, or maintenance of equipment or systems, rather than design and development. Second, they may be called "technicians" (as in "automotive service technician" or "appliance repair technician") just because the word is a popular one when, in fact, their jobs are actually related to crafts or mechanics.

Third, they frequently are members of a collective bargaining labor organization and ordinarily are paid an hourly wage. Fourth, they may reach technician status by "working up" on the job, with little formal postsecondary training. Fifth, they may graduate from associate degree programs, but often their postsecondary educational background is one year or less, for which a certificate of some kind is awarded. Generally their training program has only a minimal content of theoretical, scientific, and general education components.

Semiprofessional Science and Engineering Technicians. These semiprofessional technicians usually exhibit most if not all of the following characteristics. First, they work in close association with, or under the immediate supervision of, professionals on jobs related to design, research and development, planning, analysis, or interpretation. Second, they may belong to the national association for engineering technicians and often are in a salaried or management group rather than being a member of an organized labor union. And third, they ordinarily hold an associate degree from a community junior college or technical institute, having completed a two-year program of collegiate-technical work with a strong math-science-engineering base.

A landmark report entitled *Characteristics of Excellence in Engineering Technology Education,* published by the American Society for Engineering Education (1962), clarifies the concept of the engineering technician. "Engineering technology is that part of the engineering field which requires the application of scientific and engineering knowledge and methods combined with technical skills in support of engineering activities; it lies in the occupational area between the craftsman and the engineer at the end of the area closest to the engineer." Science technicians serve the same function in scientific research as do engineering technicians in engineering practice.

Engineering and Industrial Technologists. These members of a relatively new occupational group have four years of technical and quasiengineering education, ordinarily culminating in a bachelor's degree (Rinehart, 1973). They occupy (and perhaps created) a niche between the associate degree level science/engineering technician and the graduate level professional scientist or engineer. For the most part, they share the following characteristics. First, they work in close association with professionals and after gaining experience may function in many ways as a professional, except where a license is required. The term *quasiprofessional* is sometimes used to describe their status, but the term probably is not acceptable to the group. Second, their status as a group is still somewhat uncertain as concerns level, salary, certification, and so on—the niche is still being carved out.

Third, they often enter upper-division study after completing an associate degree technician or preengineering curriculum. Fourth, they more often than not hold their baccalaureate degrees from state colleges or technical colleges rather than from professional engineering schools. The degrees themselves are not professional engineering degrees. And fifth, their upper division programs are characterized by advanced (but practical) mathematics, applied physics, engineering and industrial courses and laboratory work, and courses in management, along with general education and courses in the humanities.

The difficulties and uncertainties of categorizing or pigeonholing people in these three levels of jobs is recognized, as is the fact that employers generally may not apply the same criteria to job levels and titles as educators and manpower analysts do. But, despite these problems, there are educationally sound reasons for considering technical work within these three frameworks. Job analysis of the entire technical occupation field supports the distinctions between (1) a large group of technicians whose day-to-day work deals mostly with job-oriented specific manual skills with only minor infusions of theoretical and scientific knowledge; (2) a somewhat smaller group working at research, design, and development jobs in close association with scientists and engineers where engineering and technical knowledge are at a premium and manual skills may be needed only occasionally; and (3) a new family of jobs for which advanced technological and industrial training at the baccalaureate level is needed—or at least desired—by a significant number of employers.

Although, as mentioned above, some technicians and technologists have prepared for their jobs entirely through on-the-job or in-plant training buttressed by night school or correspondence courses, most of them have been, and in the future will be, educated and trained in formal two-year or four-year college and technical school programs.

Manpower Forecasts and Educational Programs for Technical Occupations

There is a good deal of manpower analysis and forecasting in America. The Department of Labor through reports of its Bureau of Labor Statistics, the U.S. Office of Education, the annual *Manpower Report of the President,* and periodic research studies and reports by such agencies as The Conference Board, the American Society for Engineering Education, the National Science Foundation, the National Association of Manufacturers, and the U.S. Chamber of Commerce—all are good sources of information about supply and demand factors related to technician careers. In all such projections, two overriding considerations govern: (1) the general level of activity of the economy, and (2) the political and social climate *vis a vis* expenditures for research and development on the one hand, and a reduction of those expenditures in favor of welfare, health services, pensions, crime control, and similar social programs on the other.

There is quite general agreement that, for the period to 1985, there should be a steady demand for new workers in technical occupations. If American national policy over the next decade includes all or most all of the following elements, careers in technical occupations will grow steadily as a proportion of the total occupational spectrum: (1) a determined effort to reach energy independence by 1985 or 1990; (2) an equally determined effort to maintain and improve the national defense; (3) in response to world need, greatly expanded agricultural production; (4) expanded world trade, paced by increased productivity and cost effectiveness in world markets, coupled with expansion of the U.S. merchant marine; and (5) breakthroughs in health care and medical services featuring sophisticated instrumentation and biomedical engineering techniques and apparatus.

Based on the assumption that all of these goals will be tenaciously pursued, the following paragraphs offer a brief employment analysis and forecast for a number of technical occupations, synthesizing studies and reports made in recent months by many of the above-enumerated agencies, and then discuss education for these occupations.

Highly Skilled Industrial Technicians. The need for technicians at this level is directly related to the level of manufacturing activity, especially in the durable goods industries. During this decade, the manufacturing sector of the economy is not expected to increase its employment any faster than will the economy as a whole. The expected average annual growth rate in employment between 1972 and 1980 is 2.2 percent (U.S. Department of Labor, 1974a). Employment forecasts for industrial technicians vary from field to field as these nine examples illustrate.

Machine Tool Technicians. Job prospects are only fair. Careful local surveys are advised before making a decision to start a training program.

Industrial Management Technicians—Foremen. Job prospects are good, but in-plant training is essential. Because foremen are usually promoted from within, most training programs provide management and other specialized knowledge and skills to persons already employed as technicians, rather than for the young and inexperienced.

Instrument Repair Technicians. Prospects are good as instrumentation and modernization of industrial processes move on apace. Successful programs combine theory courses at college with in-plant training. This is an excellent field for women.

Appliance Repair Technicians. Job prospects are excellent for competent men and women who are willing to work carefully and efficiently. Good appliance mechanics are scarce everywhere. Income is good in most locations. Colleges can give most of the training in their own labs and shops if funds are available to keep the equipment and tools up to date.

Auto Service Technicians (Auto Mechanics). Prospects are excellent, with competent men and women needed in almost all localities. A rolling adjustment plan is necessary, however, to anticipate new developments in the industry.

Air-Conditioning, Heating, and Refrigeration Technicians. This would be a heavy demand field were it not for the possibility that an energy crisis would restrict electricity and natural gas for heating and refrigerated cooling. "New energy" technologies—solar, wind, geothermal, oceanographic—will demand new technicians also, and inservice training to allow lateral movement into the new technologies by already employed technicians will be needed.

Detail Draftsmen. Reasonably good propsects exist for men and women who are neat and fast in drafting. These are not design-level people, but they must be good on the board.

Mining Technicians (Mechanics). Prospects are slow now, but this may be a growing job field if a major share of energy production shifts back to coal.

Construction Technicians (Skilled Craftsmen and Estimators). Prospects are good: there are never enough really competent journeymen and leading men in the building industry. However, the training program must be a cooperative venture, combining theory and general education in college with practical experience on the job, usually through union-coordinated apprenticeships.

Overall, the annual potential for new entrants into the labor force at the highly skilled industrial technician level is very large—of the order of several hundred thousand jobs. Many of these jobs, however, are influenced or controlled by organized labor and seniority considerations, union rules, and in-plant or union-managed training programs are common practice, following the "trickle-up" theory of technician training. Colleges should find ways to participate in the education and training of these workers, but control of the programs may have to be shared with employers and labor unions. Competition from private trade technical schools and public area vocational technical schools will be keen, and colleges will have to be extremely practical and very flexible if they are to have much of a role at this level of middle manpower technical training.

For the most part, industrial technician-level jobs are best undertaken by persons with at least one year of postsecondary technical training, while two years in an associate degree program is even better. Industrial technician programs emphasize "hands-on" training rather than much abstract science, engineering, and mathematics. Hence they can be undertaken successfully by students of considerably less academic ability than that required for science and engineering technician programs.

Community junior colleges and postsecondary area vocational-technical schools (AVTSs) are the primary sources of formal in-school training for industrial technicians. Curriculums may be of one- or two-years duration and may lead to either a certificate or an associate degree. Certificate programs are job-specific and minimize theoretical knowledge and general education, while associate-degree programs are more discipline-oriented, ordinarily requiring a core of theoretical courses and a sampling of general education courses.

Large, comprehensive community colleges like the C.S. Mott

Community College in Flint, Michigan may enroll hundreds of students each year in industrial technician programs and provide as many as twenty different specialities in such varied industrial fields as air conditioning, architectural drafting, automotive mechanics, aviation, building construction, electrical power, electronics, hydraulics, industrial controls, machine tool, mechanical technology, metallurgy, and surveying. In order to cover all the knowledges and skills required to produce competent technicians in these fields, in such colleges the division of applied science (as it is often called) may offer upwards of one hundred different specialized courses, not counting general education or such basic theory courses as chemistry, applied physics, or technical mathematics.

The following outline of a one-year certificate program in machine drafting as offered in a Midwest public community college illustrates the emphasis on entry-level competence in manual skills and the specialized knowledge typical of one-year programs.

One-Year Certificate Level Machine Draftsman Program

Courses	Semester Credit Hours
Technical Mathematics	4
Technical Drawing Fundamentals	3
Machine Drawing	3
Descriptive Geometry	3
Hydraulics and Pneumatics	2
Manufacturing Processes	3
Metallurgy	4
Electives or Co-op Work Experience	8
Total	30

Note the complete absence of general education and the lack of basic sciences and advanced mathematics in this certificate program as compared with the following two-year associate degree program at the industrial technician level in air conditioning and refrigeration offered by a community college on the West Coast. This program includes not only specialized technical courses in the major but also a balance between skill courses and theoretical (supporting) knowledge and a background in general education.

Two-Year Associate Degree Program in Air Conditioning/Refrigeration Technology

Specialized Courses in the Major	*Semester Credit Hours*
	(33)
Introduction to Refrigeration	3
Intermediate Refrigeration	3
Commerical Refrigeration I	3
Commercial Refrigeration II	3
Air Conditioning I	3
Air Conditioning II	3
Applied Electricity (Controls)	3
Heating I	3
Heating II	3
Specifications Writing	3
Air Conditioning/Refrigeration Codes	3
Theory and Support Courses	(15)
Elementary Algebra	3
Technical Mathematics	3
Technical Physics	6
Introduction to Technical Drawing	3
General Education Courses	(15)
Communications I and II	4
Introductory Biology	2
Social Science Survey	2
Introduction to the Behavioral Sciences	2
American Government	3
Human Relations Seminar	2
Total	63

It should be noted that even in this associate degree program the job-oriented emphasis of industrial technician training is clear. Such programs put heavy emphasis on the skills necessary to perform repetitive technical tasks—in this case, installing, operating, trouble-shooting, and repairing heating and cooling systems. The element of system design and development, typical of science and engineering technician programs, is absent.

Colleges and postsecondary vocational-technical schools have found that both certificate and associate degree programs at the industrial technician level can be operated on an open-door or open admissions basis. Aptitude and interest testing is important, however, followed by a realistic assessment by a qualified career counselor of ability and interest. And since many persons interested in technician training possess no more than fifth or sixth grade reading and mathematics skills, remedial/developmental programs are an essential part of all open-door programs. To avoid inordinately high attrition rates, remediation should proceed concurrently with an actual beginning in some of the course work and laboratory/shop work of the technician program.

Semiprofessional Science and Engineering Technicians. This level of technical work was one of the fastest growing segments of the labor force in the 1950s and 1960s. From 1950 to 1968, its rate of growth averaged 7 percent annually, compared to only about 1.5 percent for the employed civilian labor force as a whole (National Industrial Conference Board, 1970). By 1970 some 980,000 technicians were at work in the United States assisting some 450,000 scientists and 1,200,000 engineers. That year, the ratio of technicians to scientists and engineers was about two to three, or sixty-six technicians for every hundred engineers and scientists. (The much heralded "needed" ratio of three technicians to every engineer, which was frequently proposed in the mid-sixties, was never reached, and it obviously was not needed.)

After 1968, the demand slackened, and for the past several years there has not been a serious shortage of science and engineering technicians. But neither has there been an oversupply, and it appears that the demand for technicians will remain steady over the rest of this decade and into the 1980s for several reasons. First among them is the fact that the number of first professional degree engineering graduates decreased from nearly 45,000 annually in 1970 to only about 29,000 in 1976–1977 (Engineering Manpower Commission, 1972), at the very time that the demand for engineers has been rising. In 1976 in fact, the number of engineering graduates was the lowest in twenty years. Science graduates also will be relatively few in the late 1970s. Consequently, industry and government both may have to resort to employing well-qualified technicians to back-stop and maximize the work of scientists and engineers. In addition, the urgent national problems facing the United States referred to above—the energy crisis, increased food needs, improvement of the environment, further exploration of space, mass transportation, health care, and national defense—all require the combined efforts of scientists, engineers, and technicians.

While the overall employment outlook for new science and engineering technicians is thus expected to be very good on into the 1980s, according to the 1976–1977 *Occupational Outlook Handbook* of the U.S. Department of Labor, graduates of collegiate technical programs will have the best job prospects. For associate degree technicians, salaries are generally very good and opportunities for women are excellent. With affirmative action procedures in effect in all sectors of the economy, public and private employers are actively seeking qualified women technicians in nearly all fields. Salaries, under affirmative action regulations, are comparable to those paid to men. The expectation is that the number of women enrolling in science and engineering technical programs will increase markedly during the rest of this decade.

With regard to the demand for specific types of science and engineering technicians, the following fields are worthy of separate comment.

Aerospace Technicians. As a speciality, this is one to be cautious about. Demand depends on aerospace and national defense commitments, and it currently is low, but it could increase markedly if military and space research are stepped up.

Chemical Technicians. Demand may be steady but not brisk. The tendency in the chemical industry is to put graduate (baccalaureate) chemists to work at technician-level jobs for a year or two and to up-grade skilled craftsmen in the industry to technician status. If coal-conversion and water- and air-pollution programs get massive funding, prospects for chemical technicians will be greatly enhanced.

Civil Engineering Technicians. Prospects are fair to good. If mass transit, public housing, large-scale environmental improvement, energy development, and similar "national needs" projects are funded, the prospects here will be excellent.

Electronics and Electrical Technicians. Prospects are excellent, even with no exotic new developments. Nearly all industries in both private and public sectors need competent electronic and electrical technicians. This is a good field for women.

Mechanical Engineering Technicians. Prospects are good to excellent. American manufacturing is going to have to retool and reorganize if it is to remain competitive on the world scene. The scientist/engineer/technician team is the key to success in that effort.

Drafting (Design) Technicians. Prospects are good for well-trained associate-degree graduates as draftsmen. At least 15,000 new design draftsmen per year will be needed for the foreseeable future. This is also an excellent field for women.

These listings represent only a few of the many science and engineering technician job titles. It will be noted that no exotic specialties, such as laser-optics technician, thermonuclear fusion technician, biomedical electronics technician, geothermal technician, and electronic computer technician have been listed, since these are limited-demand fields, necessitating highly specialized training that is expensive and difficult to provide in college laboratories, and the numbers of personnel needed in such narrow specialties would be a matter for purely local determination. There is also a very real question as to whether a specific goal-oriented approach to engineering technician curriculum development for such specialties is as good as a more general discipline-oriented cluster approach.

It cannot be emphasized too much that technicians for these science and engineering jobs must be capable, competent, and well trained. The associate degree from rigorous two-year curriculums is the desired preparation. Colleges wishing to contribute to this middle manpower need will have to select students for these programs carefully and keep standards of attainment high. There can be no substitute for excellence in the programs or for competence in the students and the graduates. Engineering technology programs of this kind have stood the test of time. They really do produce graduates who move into industry, business, and government jobs to perform capably at entry levels and qualify for career ladders with rungs leading to very responsible and nearly professional jobs. Entry salaries of $9,000 annually are not uncommon, and salaries in the $16,000 and up bracket after eight to ten years' ex-

perience are not unusual. Even in the economic recession of 1972–
1975, colleges and technical institutes reported very little trouble
in placing their engineering technology graduates. In 1974, for
example, Delta College in Michigan, found that placement of its
associate degree technician graduates was running at the 79 percent level one month after graduation, with entry salaries ranging
from $8,500 to $10,000 in the face of massive 15 percent unemployment in Michigan. And among nineteen graduates in electronics technology in 1975 from Vincennes University Junior College in Indiana, only one was unemployed two months later. Their
mean entry salary was $9,000, and the highest was $13,000 (Report
of Career Division, 1976).

Community colleges, technical colleges and technical institutes all offer associate-degree programs to prepare science and
engineering technicians. Technical institutes, however, have been
the leaders at this level of technical education for the past fifty
years. Associated with the American Society for Engineering Education (ASEE) and with the Engineers Council for Professional
Development (ECPD), they have set the pace for engineering technology curriculum development.

In its landmark report, *Characteristics of Excellence in Engineering Technology Education* (1962), the ASEE concluded that "the
engineering technician of tomorrow must be educated at a higher
level than he has been in the past. Though it is difficult to accomplish in the short span of two years, there are certain areas (such
as mathematics, physics, humanistic-social studies) in which the student must be given a broader base than has heretofore been the
common practice." Among the ASEE criteria or "characteristics"
of excellence in engineering technology education, the following
four are worth special mention.

First, admission requirements to such programs should include secondary school graduation with at least three units of English, two units of mathematics (algebra and plane geometry), one
unit of physical science (physics or chemistry) with laboratory, and
a "C" average or better in all high school work.

Second, mathematics and physical science should be the twin
foundations of engineering technology programs. Both the mathematics and the applied physics must be college level, although

they may emphasize problem solving and applied concepts rather than principles and theory exclusively.

Third, engineering technology programs cannot be successfully planned and operated unless there are graduate engineers on the faculty. At least half of the faculty members teaching technical specialties should be engineers, and practical experience in industry should be reflected in the backgrounds of most faculty.

Fourth, technical specialty and theory courses should be accompanied by extensive laboratory work featuring sophisticated modern equipment and should emphasize the measurement of physical phenomena and the gathering, analysis, and presentation of data. Each laboratory exercise should be as near to an engineering or technical investigation as possible.

Specialized accreditation for engineering technology programs is conducted by ECPD, and most colleges that claim to operate programs at this level either have already sought ECPD accreditation or plan to do so when their programs approach the criteria of excellence spelled out in the 1962 ASEE report. So far, ECPD-accredited programs are relatively few in number compared with non-ECPD level programs. ECPD recommends that the two-year engineering technology curriculum be planned somewhat as follows, with the courses distributed among three kinds of content—basic science and mathematics, technical courses, and general education (Defore, 1974b).

Associate Degree Engineering Technology Program

	Semester Credit Hours	*Percent of Total*
Basic Science and Mathematics	(20)	(27%)
Mathematics (algebra, trigonometry, applied calculus, advanced topics)	12	16
Physical Science (applied physics, chemistry, thermodynamics)	8	11
Technical Courses (the major)	(38)	(51)
Technical Skills (drafting, bench		

Associate Degree Engineering Technology Program (Continued)

	Semester Credit Hours	*Percent of Total*
work, manufacturing processes)	6	8
Technical Specialties (the specialized courses of the major)	32	43
General Education	(16)	(22)
Communications (English, speech, technical report writing)	6	8
Humanistic-Social Studies (economics government, literature)	6	8
Behavioral Sciences (psychology, human relations, management)	4	6
Totals	74	100%

In 1968, the U.S. Office of Education established its criteria for technician education, based on several years study of postsecondary programs and the needs of industry for technician-level employes (U.S. Department of Health, Education and Welfare, 1968). Its analysis of thirty-two selected technician curriculums in twenty-five two-year colleges and technical schools revealed the following breakdown of subject content, based on a mean total credit hour requirement of seventy-one semester credit hours for the associate degree.

	Credit Hours	*Percent of Total*
Mathematics	9	13%
Applied science	9	13
Supporting technical courses	7	10
Technical specialty courses	35	49
General education	11	15
Totals	71	100%

The relative emphasis placed on each subject group is not much different from the ECPD plan. The actual difference between ECPD-accredited curriculums and programs based on the Office of Education Criteria is the level of the courses themselves: the calculus, engineering physics, and technical courses in ECPD curriculums are heavily science and mathematics based, and the general education courses are college transfer level. Reflecting this rigor, selective student admissions is a critical factor for ECPD programs if untenable attrition is to be avoided, while a somewhat more open admissions policy can be followed with the Office of Education criteria.

Associate degree engineering technology definitely should not be an open-door program. Success in this level of technology requires good secondary school preparation (The Conference Board, 1972) and an aptitude and liking for mathematics, physical science, and engineering. Few students with ACT mathematics scores of 18 or below have succeeded in this level of program. Remedial or developmental assistance at the outset can bring some highly motivated students up to a point where they can succeed (Defore, 1974a), but there is no escaping the fact that the program is rigorous, academically demanding, and not for everybody. Admitting academically weak students into the program is not good educational practice.

Finally, perhaps as many as half of all students now desiring technician education are older persons who have been out of high school for several years and who have gained considerable job experience. Many are currently employed and able to attend classes only part-time, and often they have family and civic responsibilities which limit their study time. Traditional "regular day" programs designed for new high school graduates who lack practical experience are inappropriate for these older working students. In order to accommodate them several variations in the usual curriculum must be initiated: (1) Provision must be made for "testing-out" and granting credit for skills and knowledge already possessed by the older student. (2) Necessary basic and remedial education must be provided, if possible, on an auto-tutorial, time-as-the-variable, basis. (3) Work-experience credit should be granted for current employment. (4) Off-shift and Saturday classes in the required courses should be scheduled. And (5) counseling and guidance services for these students should be at least equivalent to those provided regular-day students. *Engineering and Industrial Technologists.* As yet this occupational group is so new and their place in the hierarchy of industrial and engineering jobs so unclear that there is little basis for predicting future demand. Educators and manpower analysts refer to these workers as "technologists," but employers generally make no such nice distinctions. A 1972 report by the American Society for Engineering Education revealed that the titles of industrial positions employers offered to baccalaureate engineering technology graduates usually had the word *engineer* in the title, such as junior engineer, sales engineer, customer engineer, and maintenance engineer, but this survey "did not disclose a single title using the words 'technician' or 'technologist,' although these titles do appear in descriptions of certain civil service positions" (p. 29).

Such fragmentary data as are available suggest that these new bachelor's degree technologists (by whatever job title) are being well received. A recent Engineering Manpower Commission survey included them with graduate engineers and associate-degree technicians. Reporting on the results of this survey and exploring the field generally, the staff of *SET Manpower Comments* (1975, p. 1) stated recently that, "Such baccalaureate degree technology programs have been growing more rapidly in recent years than have the traditional engineering curricula; but *the role of their graduates in industry is not yet clearly defined"* (Emphasis added).

It is known that the number of colleges offering baccalaureate technology programs is increasing rapidly and so is the number of graduates from these programs. Moore and Will (1974) reported 5,383 graduates from 79 collegiate institutions in 1974 and indicated a brisk demand for them as evidenced by starting salaries averaging $10,572 annually for the 4,824 graduates reported in 1973; and placement of graduates of industrial technology programs is reported to be good to excellent in placement office reports from such colleges as Rochester Institute of Technology in New York, the University of Wisconsin-Stout, and Ferris State College in Michigan.

Future demand will undoubtedly be influenced by such factors as (1) the general level of the economy and especially of manufacturing and research and development activities; (2) whether or not there is a shortage of engineering graduates from professional programs, which may well be the case between 1977 and 1985; (3) the extent to which employers engage in artificial educational upgrading of jobs in response to social pressures and their known penchant to hire persons with college degrees even when the job does not require it; and (4) the extent to which employers can avoid union labor problems by hiring college graduates instead of technical school graduates for "technician" jobs.

Asking for more education than a job actually requires ("credentialism") is a well-known penchant of employers, but this practice of subjecting technical jobs to educational upgrading by using the baccalaureate degree as a screening device or as a device to bypass union influence on technician jobs has been under scrutiny by the courts in recent years as a result of suits initiated under the Civil Rights Act of 1964. In 1971, the U.S. Supreme Court ruled that employment practices, including degree requirements, that "cannot be shown to be related to job performance" are contrary to the 1964 Act (*Griggs and others* v. *Duke Power Company*). This decision could possibly have a restrictive impact on the growth of baccalaureate degree technology programs if employers cannot show that the additional two years of training beyond the associate degree is a legitimate aid to job performance.

Nevertheless, over one hundred colleges and state universities are now offering programs leading either to the Bachelor of Engineering Technology (BET) or the Bachelor of Industrial Technology (BIT). For the most part these are either technological colleges and universities, or new state universities that, until recently, went under the name of "state colleges." Many of them offer teacher education programs to prepare teachers of technical education in area vocational-technical schools and community colleges (Bolick, 1974), and many draw heavily on graduates of two-year institutions for their upper-division students. Some of them have structured their BET and BIT programs entirely as upper division programs, designed to accept as third-year students associate degree graduates of engineering-technican and industrial-technician programs from technical institutes and community junior colleges. These two-plus-two programs are excellent examples of articulation between two-year and four-year institutions.

Bachelor of Engineering Technology (BET) programs are oriented toward the support of engineering activities, while Bachelor of Industrial Technology (BIT) programs are "oriented toward production management" (American Society for Engineering Education, 1972, p. 24). Accordingly, there is great variability among BET and BIT degree requirements and programs and between them and baccalaureate programs for the preparation of technical education teachers. Both the ASEE and the ECPD exercise considerable influence over the structure and general objectives of BET and BIT curriculums.

Based partly on actual programs demonstrated to be successful, partly on the recommendations of the ASEE and the ECPD, and partly on perhaps the best study to date of BIT curriculums and policies—one completed by a task force of the then California State Colleges in 1970 and entitled, *Industrial Arts/Industrial Technology* (California State Colleges, 1970)—"median" curriculums have been proposed for both BET and BIT programs. These are presented in Figure 3.

Currently, it seems that baccalaureate programs in engineering technology and in industrial technology are prospering. Associate degree graduates do want a track open to a bachelor's degree, and they are enrolling in these programs by the hundreds. In some states, community junior colleges report that over one-third of their associate degree technician graduates are transferring to four-year colleges for BET, BIT, or upper-division technical teacher training. Although some question the new level, wondering if there is really a need for it and feeling that jobs considered somewhat "beneath" the engineer can be performed very capably by two-year technicians, other employers, whatever their motivations, are hiring the graduates of these programs into entry jobs, and reporting that they prefer them over associate degree technicians. One plant manager has even been quoted as toying with the idea of switching the roles of engineers and engineering technologists by "relegating the analytical engineer as a 'support' person to the engineering technologist, who is concerned with solving the problems in an operating situation" (American Society for Engineering

Figure 3. Typical Baccalaureate Technology Curriculums of Differing Objectives.

INDUSTRIAL TECHNOLOGY
Median Four-Year IT Curriculum

Social Science	Non-technical Elective	Technical Specialty	Technical Elective	Management, Ind. Relations	Fourth Year
Human-ities	Technical Science	Technical Specialty	Technical General	Management, Accounting	Third Year
Communi-cations	Mathe-matics Science	Non-technical Elective	Technical General	Management, Economics	Second Year
General Education	Mathe-matics	Science	Technical General	Non-technical Elective	First Year

Oriented Toward
Production Management

INDUSTRIAL TECHNOLOGY

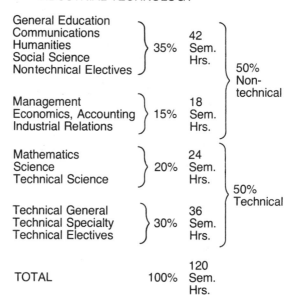

General Education
Communications
Humanities   } 35% 42 Sem. Hrs.
Social Science
Nontechnical Electives

Management
Economics, Accounting } 15% 18 Sem. Hrs.
Industrial Relations

                                          } 50% Nontechnical

Mathematics
Science   } 20% 24 Sem. Hrs.
Technical Science

Technical General
Technical Specialty } 30% 36 Sem. Hrs.
Technical Electives

                                          } 50% Technical

TOTAL   100% 120 Sem. Hrs.

ENGINEERING TECHNOLOGY
Median Four-Year ET Curriculum

Fourth Year	Social Science	Non-technical Elective	Technical Specialty	Technical Specialty	Technical Elective
Third Year	Humanities	Technical Science	Management	Technical Specialty	Related Technical Study
Second Year	Communications	Mathematics Technical Science	Technical Science	Technical Specialty	Related Technical Study
First Year	General Education	Mathematics	Science	Technical Core	Technical Core

Oriented to Support
Engineering Activities

ENGINEERING TECHNOLOGY

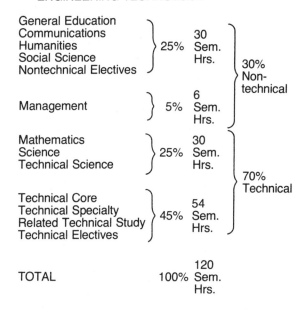

General Education
Communications
Humanities   } 25% 30 Sem. Hrs.
Social Science
Nontechnical Electives

Management   } 5%   6 Sem. Hrs.

} 30% Nontechnical

Mathematics
Science   } 25% 30 Sem. Hrs.
Technical Science

Technical Core
Technical Specialty
Related Technical Study } 45% 54 Sem. Hrs.
Technical Electives

} 70% Technical

TOTAL   100% 120 Sem. Hrs.

Education, 1972, p. 51). With over one hundred colleges now offering such programs, and with several thousand graduates each
year and many thousands of students "in the pipeline," it thus
seems that BET and BIT programs are here to stay.

Current Trends in Technical and Technological Program Development

The tendency of associate degree technician graduates to
continue on into upper division work and an eventual baccalaureate degree has caused a great deal of reassessment of the goals,
purposes, and content of two-year technician programs. For decades these programs have been employment oriented. Job competence, not upper division study, was the essential criterion for
program development. But as BET and BIT programs developed
at four-year colleges the following chain of events could be observed in many localities: First, these programs start out as two-
plus-two programs, offering only upper-division work, with entry
requirements flexible enough to accommodate associate degree
transfers from almost any technician program. Then certain course
and content requirements, which are not covered by associate degree programs, gradually are introduced, and two-plus-two becomes "two-plus-two-and one-half." At about this time, especially
if overall enrollments at the four-year college have been decreasing, the institution decides to offer the first two years of the
program. Competition for students with regional two-year colleges
and technical institutes then ensues, as students begin to enroll as
freshmen at the baccalaureate-level institution, some to avoid
transfer problems and some because attendance there seems more
prestigious. Finally, the two-year colleges are forced into curriculum changes that will "smooth out transfer problems" or, even
though they may not change their curriculum as printed in the
catalog, their students may be advised to make substitutions to suit
transfer requirements, even at the risk of not attaining realistic job
competency as technicians.

As a result of these trends some associate degree technician
programs have become homogenized and are now quasitransfer

programs, with courses offered for their transferability rather than for their applicability to technical competence on the job. Some two-year colleges have so drastically changed their course requirements that their "technician" curriculums consist of only about 40 percent specialized technical subjects and up to 60 percent transfer-level arts and sciences courses. Such an arrangement does help the one-third who may transfer, but it plays havoc with the two-thirds who do not—increasing their attrition rate and not providing job competence for those who seek employment directly from the two-year college.

The Core and Ladder Approach in Technical Education. The ultimate solution here is probably a core curriculum of some kind or a core-and-ladder approach as it is practiced in some two-year colleges. At most community colleges and area vocational-technical schools, the number of students adequately prepared for and interested in engineering technician programs is relatively small compared to those in industrial technician programs. The more academically capable students will exhibit a strong preference for the baccalaureate degree, especially now that four-year institutions provide the BIT and BET degrees. At the same time, the job demand continues to be good for highly skilled graduates of industrial technician programs. It is difficult, however, to track students at the very outset into two streams—one for engineering technicians, with a four-year bachelor's degree as an optional goal, and the other a definitely terminal program for industrial technicians leading directly to jobs in manufacturing and service occupations. As a consequence of this dilemma, many colleges have turned to an "upside down" core curriculum that places early emphasis on job competence and hands-on training, while providing the opportunity to move into more demanding academic work later. Evidence over a thirty-year period shows that the attrition of students who need remediation in basic skills is about 65 percent during the first college year. Remedial and developmental studies should be combined with laboratory and shop training to give students an employable skill by the end of the first year and permit the award of a one-year certificate, with the option left open for students to complete the theoretical and general education courses required for the associate degree at some later time.

In other words, given the academic ability of the majority of students entering two-year postsecondary institutions today, it is a mistake to set the level of industrial technician programs too high and to not develop employable skills of some kind early in the program. Thus after initial testing, assessment, and counseling, technician students should enroll in a first-semester core comprised mainly of technical and skill courses that can lead to immediate employability. During the second core semester, students begin specialized courses in electronics, mechanical, civil, refrigeration, or other technology along with introductory technical mathematics and applied physics and any remedial or developmental education they need. During this semester, students have the opportunity to settle some of the uncertainties about their career plans themselves and decide which level of credential to aim at—one-year certificate, two-year associate degree, or four-year baccalaureate. For those who leave after one year with a certificate, the road back to the career ladder should be kept open if they eventually decide to move on up. And for those who elect a second year, a choice is open at the start of that year—the employment-oriented associate degree technician curriculum, concentrating in its second year on specialized engineering or industrial technology subjects, with more mathematics, physics, and general education, or a transfer-oriented program containing some additional work in the technical specialty but more heavily loaded with arts and sciences transfer courses. The associate degree technician graduate has immediate employability as he steps off the career ladder at the end of this year. He can get back on the ladder at any time by completing those arts and sciences courses which may be required for junior standing at a four-year college or university if he chooses to work toward the baccalaureate. Meanwhile, the technology transfer student can probably find employment if he so desires, but his normal move is on up to further study. If unsuccessful with upper division work, he still has a measure of employability, which he can improve by in-plant training or by returning to the two-year college for evening or Saturday courses.

Such a core-and-ladder approach, although not entirely without discontinuities, is appearing in many regions of the country as two-year and four-year college educators and employers work cooperatively to make career ladders in technical education a reality. *Competency-Based Instruction.* A healthy trend is now under way toward setting standards of performance in all technical programs. Since the very purpose of occupational education is to prepare students for effective job performance, it is not to educators' credit that it has taken this long to adopt a competency-based philosophy. But beginning with Bloom's concept of "learning for mastery" (Bloom, 1970), and abetted by Mager's work in the field of task analysis and instructional objectives (Mager, 1975), college administrators and teachers in career education programs have moved with some determination in recent years to a "performance objectives" approach. Several states have moved toward a performance objectives approach for all of career education, with Michigan's Performance Objectives Development Project, completed in 1974, a good example of these efforts (D. Brown, 1974).

Using a performance objective approach, a job is analyzed in the field; its tasks are evaluated with regard to difficulty of performance and "knowledge content" versus "skill content;" and these evaluations then determine the objectives and the content of the units or topics of instruction. Teachers specify in advance these learning objectives and the level of performance that the students are to achieve and demonstrate. "Minimum performance objectives" consistent with the known requirements of the job are set for a passing grade, and course credit is not given until these minimum performance objectives have been achieved.

It can hardly be argued that the excellence of a course in technology is determined by anything other than performance on the job. Technical educators, somewhat belatedly perhaps, are now recognizing what should have been evident all along—that to obtain performance on the job as the output, performance in the classroom and the laboratory must be demanded as the input.

Facility Costs and Capital Expenditures. "Good technical programs cost money" is a statement accepted by most decision-makers in postsecondary education today, even those on legislative appropriations committees. Studies have shown that the annual per student operating cost of industrial and engineering technician programs may be up to 1.54 times as much as straight academic or liberal arts programs (Warren, 1972). Recognizing and accepting such operating costs, technical educators must be more conscious of capital outlay and start-up costs than they have been in the past. Extremely careful estimates of demand for and enrollment in programs must be made, lest there be repetition of the many blunders of the 1960s—spending millions of dollars, for example, on shop space, machines, tools, and instruments, many of which became obsolete in ten years or less, for programs that enroll only ten to twenty students per year. *Need* and *demand,* as noted elsewhere in these pages, are vastly different, and in order to minimize on-campus costs, technical programs should maximize work-experience, internships, in-plant training, field trips, and, to some extent, simulation. There are many good arguments for "realistic" on-campus training, but the same parameters of economies of scale and cost-effectiveness ratios that apply in industry must be applied to technical education as well, and only those elements of the programs that are more effective on campus than on the work site should be retained.

Guidelines for Planners

Planning technician and technologist curriculums for the 1980s will be a challenging business. Many of the suggestions about successful programs and administration that appear later in Chapters Ten and Twelve are as applicable for planners of these programs as for any others. In addition, however, these points warrant particular attention for this science- and engineering-oriented area:

First, survey the need and determine the demand for technician and technologist programs and base plans on demand rather than presumed need.

Second, gauge the abilities, aspirations, and interests of prospective students to devise appropriate programs for them. Are they "regular" students or older persons returning to a "career ladder"?

Third, with the help of an advisory committee, decide on the levels at which technician and technologist programs should be offered and develop the performance objectives to be specified for competency at each level.

Fourth, plan programs with attention to the core-and-ladder concept by developing an employable skill very early and building technical content, supporting theory and science and mathematics knowledge, and general education content into later stages of the program.

Fifth, maximize the use of internships and on-the-job training to provide realism and to keep capital investment to a minimum while extending students' competencies.

And sixth, maintain close contact with industry, business, and government employers of technicians to know their plans and their problems, in order to plan these programs for the future rather than for the past.

7 ◙◙◙◙◙◙◙◙◙◙◙◙◙◙◙

Allied
Health Careers

Despite all his heroism and stamina, man remains a biological organism, a "biosystem," and all such systems operate within inexorable limits.

Alvin Toffler, *Future Shock*

Advances in medical science have occurred at an accelerating pace in the past twenty years. Spurred by research findings in the field of biochemistry and aided by sophisticated instrumentation from the science of electronics, the diagnosis and treatment of disease have made a century of progress in two decades. Concurrently there has been a vast increase in interest in health care occasioned in part by improved communications (notably television) and in part by prepaid health insurance plans and such social legislation as Medicare and Medicaid. Communicable diseases, once the scourge of mankind ("pestilence" was one of the Four Horsemen of the Apocalypse), have largely been brought under effective control; surgery copes ever more successfully with the traumas of accident and the ravages of disease; and such life-sustaining and monitoring systems as heart-lung and kidney dialysis machines, and cardiovascular function monitors provide the surgical team with stand-by equipment while repairs to the patient's "original equipment" are being made. Regrettably, degenerative diseases have not as yet been as susceptible to medical breakthroughs as have communicable diseases and operable illnesses. Heart disease, cancer, arthritis, and mental illness still await the successes that medical science has experienced with tuberculosis, influenza, diabetes, and polio.

Besides the advances in curative medicine, equally important strides are being made in preventive and rehabilitative medicine, all of which have significant health manpower implications. A variety of new approaches are being tried for the delivery of health services. Increased emphasis is being placed on the prevention, rather than only the cure, of disease. Health Maintenance Organizations (HMOs) constitute one such effort, providing "a wide range of medical and hospital services to a defined group of subscribers in return for an annual premium" (Starr, 1976, p. 66). Group health plan hospitals are using computer-coordinated health testing and referral services to regulate the flow of patients and information among their units and to schedule patients, physicians, and allied health workers for maximum efficiency and quality of service. And although the promise of HMOs has been somewhat dimmed by political infighting and the insolvency of some of the units, they do offer a vision of the future, one which could increase the demand for allied health personnel far beyond presently foreseen requirements. The decentralization of large general hospitals and the establishment of community health centers are trends which also indicate increased demand for health paraprofessionals.

One of the disturbing factors about health care, which offsets the "good news" cited above, is the "bad news" of skyrocketing costs. Americans paid more than $130 billion for health care in 1976, making it one of the nation's three largest industries. The past two decades have seen the charge for an office visit, say for a simple sore throat, go from $7 to as much as $30, the cost of a hospital stay from $30 per day to as much as $200 per day, and the charge for such a routine surgical procedure as an appendectomy from $75 to several hundreds of dollars. The current cost of having a baby may exceed $1,500 even for a routine delivery without complications.

The clamor is increasing in many quarters for federal support of health care. Controversy is continuous and heated between those who regard health care as a "right" of citizenship, a free public service, and those who regard it as a professional service of the private sector, to be paid for like any other service. Regardless of who pays for it, of course, it is not free. The major question is who should pay—the user or the public at large? The resolution of this issue in the next few years will have major consequences for planners of career education programs in the health field.

Health Team Approach to Health Care

A more extensive professional hierarchy exists in the health services than in virtually any other occupational area. Medicine, at the top, is an old and honored profession. Practitioners of the healing arts have generally held the esteem of the populace, enjoying what Becker (1962) calls the image criterion of the true profession. For centuries, however, among physicians trained by apprenticeship and even after medical schools came into being in the nineteenth century, professional standards were lax and quality control left much to be desired. Until the early 1900s, many medical schools were owned and operated by groups of doctors on a proprietary basis. But as a result of Abraham Flexner's landmark report of 1910, *Medical Education in the United States and Canada,* medical education in America was brought into universities, given a sound academic and scientific base, and allied with science research. From that time on, the M.D. degree acquired increasing status, and now, in public opinion polls, physicians usually rank at or near the top of the "most admired" professions.

Nursing, too, enjoys an excellent image as a profession. Like medical schools, nursing schools have sought academic affiliation over the past decades. The Bachelor of Science in Nursing is now regarded by the American Nurses' Association as the first professional degree in the field although there is considerable controversy on this matter within the nursing profession itself. "Diploma" nurses—graduates of hospital schools of nursing with typically three-year programs—are still the majority of active nurse practitioners and of course they consider themselves as professional nurses. Associate degree nurses—graduates of two-year college nursing education programs—were initially referred to as "nurse technicians," or "bedside nurses," when these programs were first initiated in the middle 1950s (Montag; 1963); but now that thousands of them are nurse practitioners, they too regard themselves as full-fledged members of the nursing profession. Like the graduates of bachelor's degree programs in four-year colleges and universities and of diploma programs in hospitals, they are qualified to sit for and usually take the same state board examinations for licensure as "registered" nurses. In addition, licensed practical nurses (LPNs) or licensed vocational nurses (LVNs), as they are called in some states, regard themselves as members of the nursing profession, even though they are not eligible for licensure as registered nurses. Thus, while assigning levels of professionalism is difficult in any field, it is most assuredly a sticky wicket in the field of nursing.

Doctors and nurses are still key personnel in the provision of health services, but their knowledge and skills are now supplemented by those of a small army of paraprofessionals and technicians, each with specialized training to perform a task or service essential to the diagnosis and treatment of disease and the recovery of the patient. The extent of this expansion of the "health team" concept for the provision of health services can be seen by noting that in 1900, for every licensed physician, there was less than one allied health worker, while today there are over a dozen, and the ratio is increasing (Gartner, 1971).

Apart from nursing, the field of allied health and the health team approach received its initial impetus in World War II. Army medics and Navy pharmacist's mates rendered service above and beyond their rated competencies in untold isolated and battle emergencies. Time and time again, they proved the potential for medical and health services of persons trained at technician and paraprofessional levels. Further, the team concept for solving many complex problems of science, engineering, and technology—from the Manhattan Project, which produced nuclear fission and the atom bomb, to the joint development of sophisticated radar theory and equipment by British and American electronics scientists—also grew out of World War II. After the war, as medicine became even more scientifically based, as demand for health services outstripped the capabilities of the doctor-nurse team, and as modern management theory made its way into hospitals and clinics; the need for allied health specialties grew by leaps and bounds, until by 1970 over 150 different jobs in the health technologies had been identified and described by Kinsinger (1970). The current relationship between medicine and allied health has been well expressed by the 1975–1976 executive vice president of the American Medical Association, Ernest B. Howard, M.D. (Kuhli, 1974, p. 38): "The two fields—medicine and careers allied to it—are inseparable. They are equal partners working together in a common cause of the highest order."

Manpower Needs in Allied Health

The terms *need* and *demand* are not synonymous when they are employed in the language of manpower forecasting. In the health fields, *need* has been defined as the manpower required to supply the amount and kind of health care judged desirable by social and medical authorities. *Demand,* on the other hand, is based on the numbers of patients actually seeking and using health services, expressed in such absolute terms as hospital admissions or health care expenditures in constant dollars (American Medical Association, 1972). Program planning for allied health education on the basis of current demand might well result in a too-little-and-too-late supply of future allied health manpower; while planning on the basis of future needs, as seen and promulgated by persons making value judgments about desirable health manpower/population ratios, could easily result in a vast oversupply of allied health workers trained at great individual and social cost only to be disillusioned at finding no jobs after graduation. Wise planners make programmatic decisions with these two extremes in mind.

In terms of "need," the U.S. Surgeon General in 1966 estimated that about 100,000 new allied health workers would be required each year during the early and middle 1970s simply to take care of growth in demand and without counting replacements needed because of resignations, retirement, and death (Stewart, 1966). A more recent estimate of the gap between manpower supply and demand in nursing and allied health fields, published by the American Medical Association and based on U.S. Public Health Service projections, appears in Table 12. Here demand, or "estimated manpower requirements," is defined as the number of

Table 12. Estimated Manpower Requirements and Supply in Allied Health, 1975 and 1980.

Requirements and Supply	1975	1980
Allied Medical		
Baccalaureate or Higher Degree:		
Estimated Manpower Requirements	348,000	413,000
Manpower supply	270,000	320,000
Deficit	78,000	93,000
Less than Baccalaureate:		
Estimated Manpower Requirements	488,000	580,000
Manpower Supply	400,000	475,000
Deficit	88,000	105,000
Nursing		
Registered Nurses:		
Estimated Manpower Requirements	1,000,000	—
Manpower supply	816,000	895,000
Deficit	184,000	—
Licensed Practical Nurses:		
Estimated Manpower Requirements	550,000	—
Manpower supply	546,000	675,000
Deficit	4,000	—
Aides, orderlies, attendants, home health aides:		
Estimated Manpower Requirements	1,075,000	1,210,000
Manpower supply	1,000,000	1,150,000
Deficit	75,000	60,000
Total Supply	3,032,000	3,515,000
Deficit without Registered and Licensed Practical Nurses	241,000	258,000
Total Deficit	429,000	—

Souce: American Medical Association (1972, p. 32).

workers who could find employment in these fields without major changes in the health system—rather than as the number "needed" to have an ideal health system.

Table 12 separates demand and supply data for both allied medical and nursing fields into two levels: (1) those requiring a baccalaureate or higher degree for entry, and (2) those open to graduates of less than baccalaureate-level programs. Within the allied medical fields—including medical laboratory staff, physicians' and dental assistants, community health workers, and medical and dental research workers—sizeable deficits at both levels were expected for 1975 and projected to increase appreciably by 1980. In nursing, however, there are signs that the gap between supply and demand is closing. The deficit of aides, orderlies, and other assistants is expected to drop from 75,000 to 60,000 during the five years; and a deficit of only 4,000 licensed practical nurses was estimated for 1975. With preventive health care improving, and with the trend to shorter stays in hospitals, there is some doubt that the demand for nurses will grow at as fast a rate as it has for the past ten years. Consequently, the projections do not include 1980 estimates of demand or deficit for registered and licensed practical nurses, since prediction is too uncertain in these two areas. Moreover, there has been a steady growth in the number of nursing schools, especially in community colleges and area vocational technical schools where both associate-degree (ADN) programs and licensed practical nurse (LPN) programs are now producing thousands of new nurses every year. Thus although on a national basis it is true that there is still a definite shortage of registered nurses, in some localities signs of supply-demand balance are being noted. A significant proportion of entrants to associate-degree nursing programs are mature women with families and roots in the community where they are students. They are not geographically mobile as younger women might be, and, as a consequence, an over-supply of registered nurses is developing in localities where ADN programs are numerous, despite a shortage in regions without these programs. This situation is even more pronounced for licensed practical nurses, since an even larger majority of students in these programs are mature women with little geographic mobility. While Table 12 shows a small deficit of licensed practical nurses in 1975, it is probable that currently there is no real national deficit at all, but instead, areas of shortage and over-supply for these reasons.

It should be pointed out in addition that the Public Health Service projections, which are the source for Table 12, were based on 1970 data. The estimates of 1975 manpower requirements thus may not be highly accurate, and the 1980 requirements easily may be off the mark by 10 to 20 percent. Even with these limitations, however, the demand for allied health workers for the rest of the decade can be interpreted as large and steady, although perhaps not critical.

Turning to the 1980s, the Bureau of Labor Statistics estimates that the number of hospital jobs will grow 2.9 percent a year from 1980 to 1985, while jobs in other health services will increase 2.6 percent a year. Hospitals and other health services are expected to be among the five fastest growing industries out of over a hundred surveyed—growing at more than twice the rate of employment generally, which is projected to rise 1.2 percent during each of these years. Hospitals are likely to add some 460,000 jobs in all categories during those five years, while other health services will add 367,000, for a total of nearly 14 percent of the six million new jobs likely in the economy at large (U.S. Department of Labor, 1974b).

On balance, the forecast for the allied health manpower fields is one of steady growth into the 1980s and beyond, but not one of critical shortages as threatened in the 1960s and early 1970s. College program planners and career guidance workers should adjust their thinking to these new realities rather than continuing to emphasize the critical shortage theme of the past decade. There will be growth, but it should be an ordered growth; new programs will be needed, but decisions to initiate them should be preceded by very careful planning and analysis.

In terms of supply and demand within specific allied health occupations, the following paragraphs summarize employment prospects in those fields particularly well suited to collegiate-level career education, based on estimates from the American Medical

Association, the Bureau of Labor Statistics of the U.S. Department of Labor, the *Occupational Outlook Handbook* for 1976, and the U.S. Public Health Service.

Registered Nurses. The national employment outlook is favorable to excellent. Both the Bureau of Labor Statistics and the U.S. Public Health Service estimate that the demand for registered nurses (whether baccalaureate, associate degree, or diploma) will exceed one million by 1980, compared to the 1975 supply of less than 820,000. When retirements, quits, and deaths are taken into account, the number of new registered nurses needed by 1980 over the 1975 supply is estimated to be of the order of 400,000.

Although the national demand thus appears to be steady for some years ahead, as noted earlier in some localities supply and demand are already in balance. College program planners should watch local and regional trends carefully in cooperation with nursing associations and state licensing boards, which monitor the supply-demand situation, to avoid over-commitment to new programs.

Licensed Practical Nurses. The employment outlook is generally good nationally. Although in 1975 supply and demand were nearly in balance at a figure of nearly 550,000 practitioners, the 1980 need is expected to be in excess of 650,000. Many localities, however, report adequate supply or even small surpluses. "Local demand" is the primary consideration here, since most people entering practical nurse training expect to continue living in the community and will seek employment there. Presently operating programs will probably produce ample numbers of licensed practical nurses for the years ahead, unless the high turnover rate proves to be an even larger factor than expected. Not very many new programs will be needed.

Dental Hygienists. From 16,000 practicing dental hygienists in 1966, this field grew to an estimated 42,000 practitioners in 1976. A steady but unspectacular growth is expected into the 1980s. It is probable that, even taking all aspects of turnover into account, not more than about 5,000 practitioners per year will be needed.

Many dental hygienists are graduates of training programs in university dental schools. Community junior colleges and technical colleges also operate dental hygiene programs (Edgecombe,

1974). In most states eligibility for a dental hygienist's license is limited to graduates of dental hygiene programs accredited by the Council on Dental Education of the American Dental Society.

Dental Assistants. The outlook here is good to excellent. During the latter half of the 1970s the number of employed dental assistants is expected to increase from 125,000 to more than 150,000. In addition to this growth of 25,000 another 25,000 must be trained to replace those who retire, quit, or die. Consequently, a need for about 10,000 new entrants per year is projected.

It is said that a competent dental assistant multiplies a dentist's productivity by a factor of 1.7, but in spite of this reported productivity, pay scales for dental assistants are not very high.

Surgical (Operating Room) Technicians. This relatively new field is expected to grow fairly rapidly. Associate degree graduates will be much sought after, but they must have had adequate on-the-job experience or clinical training. Many operating room technicians are trained in one-year certificate programs. About 27,000 surgical technicians are currently employed, and the need for new entrants is estimated to be about 2,000 per year to balance growth and attrition factors.

Inhalation (Respiratory) Therapy Technicians. The outlook here is good to excellent. Estimated need in 1975 was 12,000, and supply was not up to that level. Programs should be initiated only in regions with a concentration of modern hospitals since these workers are employed only in such settings. Although some schools operate certificate level programs, the trend is toward the associate degree.

Physical Therapy Assistants. The outlook is excellent, especially for two-year associate degree graduates. Pay scales are not attractive, however, and recruitment of students may be a problem. In 1970, about 20,000 physical therapy assistants were employed in hospitals and extended care facilities. About two thousand entrants per year will be needed to meet growth and replacement requirements.

Medical Laboratory Technology. Within this field, *clinical medical laboratory technologists* are ordinarily graduates of four-year colleges who, more often than not, emerge as supervisors, teachers, or laboratory administrators. *Medical laboratory technicians* generally have college training at the two-year level. *Certified laboratory assistants* complete an AMA-approved one-year certificate program in a community college, vocational-technical school, or hospital school (Kahler, 1969). The job outlook is expected to be good for all three levels of medical laboratory staff, according to Bureau of Labor Statistics and Public Health Service manpower forecasts. Over 100,000 medical laboratory technologists, technicians, and assistants were estimated to be employed in hospitals alone in 1975, with another 50,000 or more employed in clinics, doctors' offices, and private laboratories. The effects of automation and instrumentation on the medical laboratory and the impact of increasing numbers of four-year graduates and one-year certified laboratory assistant personnel on technician employment should be carefully monitored.

Radiologic Technicians and Technologists. The outlook is excellent, and the training pattern is mixed. Radiologic technologists are ordinarily graduates of four-year programs, while radiologic technicians come from three-year programs in community and technical colleges or from hospital-operated diploma schools. At least three years are required for a good technician program. Much of the training, even in college-operated programs, must be in the hospital. About 50,000 radiologic technicians and technologists were employed in 1975, and the projected annual need is for about 5,000 new entrants. A local survey should precede serious planning for a new program, although this is a career in which, after full certification, a person can be geographically mobile.

Although the academic demands of all health technology programs are substantial, the rigor of radiologic technology programs is especially to be noted. Only persons with well-above-average ability and high school background in mathematics, physics, and biology are likely to succeed.

These dozen or so specialties merely illustrate likely employment trends. For complete listings of allied health occupations categorized by major field, program planners should consult *Education and Utilization of Allied Health Manpower* (American Medical Association, 1972, pp. 34–37) and *Career Opportunities: Health Technicians* (Kinsinger, 1970, pp. v–vii). Since data on supply and demand are never exact and lag behind the current situation from one to five years, program planners should also seek the most recent available estimates, particularly at the local, state, and regional levels.

In terms of the supply of new practitioners to meet these demands, most program planners are probably aware that beginning about 1972 and apparently as part of the burgeoning interest among students in practical career training rather than in "academic" study, the health fields have become increasingly popular with college students. In 1966, 1968, and 1970, health fields at all levels involved about 12 percent of entering college freshmen. By 1972 that figure had increased to over 18 percent, according to a recent study conducted by the American Council on Education for the U.S. Public Health Service (U.S. Department of Health, Education and Welfare, 1974b). Data for 1973 and 1974 indicate that this interest in health fields continued, particularly among blacks and women, as these two groups participated to a greater extent in postsecondary education. Holmstrom (American Council on Education, 1974, p. 3) summarized the trends in student selection of the health fields as follows: "Many of the recent trends apparent throughout postsecondary education are particularly pronounced in the health fields. For instance, the proportions of blacks and of women have increased over the past several years, perhaps as a result of the new emphasis on equal opportunity and affirmative action. The sex stereotyping of various occupations seems gradually to be breaking down."

One reason for this expansion of enrollments in allied health fields has been the growth and popularity of community colleges in the past ten years. The commitment of these institutions to occupational education, their "second-chance" and open-door admissions policies, their ability to respond more quickly than four-year colleges to manpower needs, and their low-cost access for low-income students, are all factors in the growth of health career enrollments. These same features also explain the similar growth in technical college and area vocational-technical school enrollments in the health fields.

Another causative factor may be increased interest in working with people, both among the population generally and among youth in particular during the past decade. As was pointed out earlier, "working with things" has been tarred with the brush of materialism in the minds of many students, while working with people in the "helping professions" connotes humanitarianism. It is thought to improve the quality of life directly. Besides, it has an aura of professionalism, and its image of "clean jobs" (as exemplified by laboratory smocks and white uniforms) is an attractive consideration for some people.

For these and other reasons, as of 1975, nearly 19 percent of the nation's college freshmen indicated that they were interested in a health career—and nearly 14 percent in health careers other than that of doctor or dentist. Almost as many of them "plan on" allied health careers, in fact, as on careers in business. As Table 13 shows, nearly 5 percent hope to enter nursing, while nearly 9 percent plan on other health professions besides doctor or dentist. (In addition, some 5 percent aim at either the M.D. or the D.D.S.: 6.6 percent of the men and 3.3 percent of the women.)

In contrast to this proportion planning on *careers* in allied health, only 7 percent of the students plan to *major* in a health field as undergraduates. Among them, over seven times as many women plan such majors as do men.

Freshmen in different types of institutions do not vary greatly in their interest in these fields. As Table 13 indicates, the only notable differences occur in terms of career preference: more students at community colleges are interested in nursing than are students at four-year colleges and universities, while slightly more students at universities are interested in other health careers than are those at other four-year colleges and at two-year institutions.

In summary, administrators charged with the responsibility of planning programs for careers in allied health fields must keep up to date on continually shifting developments in the health care system. One group of factors—instrumentation, the "health team" concept, demographic changes, and socio-political pressures—when taken together, supports a thesis of exploding demand for more programs; but another group—skyrocketing costs, medicare and medicaid scandals, depersonalization, the prospect of health care as a political football, the rapid expansion of programs over the past decade, and scattered oversupply of some specialists in some localities—raises questions as to whether extensive expansion is warranted across the board. Educational program planners should be ready with programs as demand becomes evident but should

Table 13. Percent of Incoming Freshmen Planning on Majors or Careers in Allied Health Fields, by Level of Institution, Fall 1975.

Level of Institution	Majors			Careers							
				Nursing			Other Allied Health				
	Men	Women	Total	Men	Women	Total	Men	Women	Total		
Two-Year Colleges	2.0	14.2	7.6	0.5	12.3	5.8	5.2	11.1	7.8		
Four-Year Colleges	1.6	12.4	7.2	0.3	8.7	4.6	5.0	12.7	8.9		
Universities	1.6	12.9	6.9	0.1	7.9	3.7	5.5	15.6	10.1		
All Institutions	1.8	13.2	7.3	0.3	9.9	4.8	5.2	12.8	8.8		

Source: Astin, King, and Richardson (1976, pp. 20, 32, 44).

resist being stampeded into a flurry of new programs on the basis of needs as envisioned and enunciated by socio-medical experts.

Programs for Allied Health Careers

The professional hierarchy that exists in the health services is clearly reflected in training programs for these services.

Physicians are educated in medical schools, most of which are now affiliated with universities, and trained in postgraduate internships and residencies. Baccalaureate schools of nursing are usually affiliated with universities where there is also a medical school or university hospital with teaching, research, clinical, and patient-care facilities. Many of them offer master's programs in clinical specialties and in nursing education, and some offer programs leading to the doctorate in nursing specialties and in administration. But many nurses are educated in other institutions: community junior colleges and technical colleges (associate degree and practical nurses); hospital schools (diploma nurses); area vocational schools (licensed practical nurses); and certain vocational schools and skill centers operated by secondary school districts (licensed practical nurses and nurses' aides).

The many other allied health specialists in medical laboratory technology, radiologic technology, biomedical equipment operation, outpatient office services, and the like, are trained in hospitals, clinics, and doctor's offices, two- and four-year colleges, high schools and vocational schools, and in special programs operated under federal and state funding. They range from less than one-year programs for nursing service workers such as orderlies and nurses' aides, who are not certified by state licensing examination and are more closely related to skilled crafts and trades than to middle-manpower jobs, to high-level research careers in biomedical engineering, which has itself become a recognized professional field for which a number of universities offer graduate programs to health-service oriented engineering students (*Engineering Education,* 1973).

Kinsinger (1970) groups the allied health specialties offered at the undergraduate level, covering the middle-manpower to professional spectrum, into twenty-five "major career areas," as follows, in alphabetical order:

biomedical equipment
   technician
cytotechnologist
dental assistant
dental hygienist
dental laboratory technician
dietetic technician
electroencephalographic
   technician
environmental health
   technician
histologic technician
inhalation (respiratory)
   therapy technician
medical assistant
medical laboratory assistant

medical (or dental) secretary
medical records technician
mental health technician
occupational therapy
   assistant
operating room (surgical)
   technician
optician
optometric technician
orthoptist
physical therapy assistant
practical nurse
prosthetics technician
radiologic technician
registered nurse

There is little long-term stability to this list, since the allied health field remains quite fluid both in terms of occupational categories and training programs. In response to new demands, new concepts of the health team, and new schemes for delivering health services, such new jobs as "emergency medical technician" continue to emerge, and existing jobs merge with others and disappear. For example, the rapid intrusion of machines and electronics into the field has stimulated a demand for such highly specialized personnel as biomedical equipment technicians (BMETs) (Rogers, 1971), cardiopulmonary technicians, renal dialysis technicians, and extracorporeal circulation technicians. The need for physicians' assistants and for independent nurse practitioners is leading to new programs in many states. From the developing relationship between the strictly medical and the social-psychological aspects of health care, a need is emerging for occupational therapy technicians, recreational therapists, and art and music therapists.

Such new and specialized occupations have difficulty in getting established as entities in their own right. Many of them are under constant evaluation until the boundary conditions of their tasks and responsibilities are better defined (Light, 1969). A number are so specialized that for the foreseeable future they will remain the province of well-equipped teaching hospitals and clinics rather than being offered on college campuses. Some still are not yet acceptable to hospitals and individual physicians or other practitioners, even though the medical profession may have authorized their creation and state licensing boards may have established standards for them.

Indeed, the most critical influence on program planners other than supply and demand is the impact of law and professional standards on health practice. As a group, the health fields are controlled by state law, licensure and registration, and by professional association certification, regulation, and codes of ethical practice to a greater extent than any other major group of occupations. The authority to practice hinges in many cases not only on earning a certificate, diploma, or degree, but also on being licensed by state authorities. And even if the force of law does not control program content, national associations, of which the American Medical Association, the American Dental Association, the National League for Nursing, the National Association for Practical Nurse Education Service, the American Association of Medical Assistants, the American Society of Clinical Pathologists, and the American Dental Assistants Association are a representative few, exercise a great deal of influence and control over both practice and training programs. In many states, candidates for licensure cannot sit for the state examination without having completed an educational program approved by state authorities or accredited by the national association governing the field.

As a result of these credentialing and certifying practices, curriculum development for the allied health fields is substantially predetermined in terms of length of program and content and level of instruction. Specifics of curriculum and course content are best obtained from the agencies and associations governing each of the specialized fields.

Accrediting and certifying agencies too often phrase their requirements for program approval in terms of the number of clock hours of instruction and clinical experience to be devoted to particular subjects rather than to the competencies or proficiencies or skills that these hours and subjects should supposedly develop. Despite this problem, innovative program administrators have been able to organize quality programs in ways that fit their local circumstances. Examples at three levels—nondegree certificate or diploma, associate degree, and baccalaureate degree—will be offered here, followed by some general principles applicable to all these levels, including a core-and-career-ladder approach to program development.

Certificate-Level Programs. The Penn Valley Community College of the Metropolitan Community Colleges of Kansas City offers a typical medical assistant program, which was carefully planned with the participation of an active advisory committee. The program is a full year in length and qualifies the successful graduate to take the National Certification Examination given by the American Association of Medical Assistants. The three major areas of competence that the program aims for are office skills, clinical skills, and laboratory skills. Note that even this certificate-level program incorporates some general education in its introductory summer term.

Certificate-Level Medical Assistant Program

	Credit
Summer Term	*Hours*
English Composition	3
Constitution (Social Science)	3
Speech	3
	9
Semester 1	
Medical Terminology I	2
Introduction to Medical Assisting	6
Medical Assistant Procedures I	6
Externship I	5
	19
Semester II	
Medical Assistant Procedures II	6
Medical Assistant Procedures III	6
Medical Assistant Procedures IV	3
Externship II	5
	20

At the same certificate level, the Los Angeles Trade-Technical College offers the following program to train operating room technicians. Entry to the program is not open-door, and previous hospital experience is recommended. At this college, no general education is required. Instead, the program concentrates almost entirely on specific skills needed in the operating room.

Certificate Level Operating Room Technician Program

	Credit Hours
Semester I	
Orientation for Operating Room Technicians	2
Aseptic Techniques	4
Fundamentals of Operating Room Technology I	5
Anatomy and Physiology I	3
Operating Room Procedures I	3
	17
Semester II	
Fundamentals of Operating Room Technology II	3
Anatomy and Physiology II	3
Operating Room Procedures II	5
Operating Room Technician Internship	5
Operating Room Technician Laboratory	1
	17

Associate Degree Programs. Lake Michigan (Community) College in Benton Harbor, Michigan, offers the following associate-degree registered nurse program. A great deal of actual on-the-ward hospital experience is involved in the specialized nursing courses and seminars of such a program. Availability of student stations at hospitals and clinics is often the limiting factor that determines the numbers of students such programs can accept.

Associate Degree Level Registered Nurse Program

First Year

Semester I	Credit Hours	Semester II	Credit Hours
English Composition	3	English Composition	3
Psychology	3	Psychology	3
Human Anatomy	4	Principles of Human	
Introduction to Nursing	5	Physiology	4
		Maternal-Child Health	6
	15		16

Associate Degree Level Registered Nurse Program (Continued)

Second Year

Sociology	3	Political Science	3
Nursing in Physical and		Nursing in Physical and	
Mental Illness	10	Mental Illness	12
Medical Microbiology	4	Nursing Seminar	1
	17		16

Baccalaureate-Level Programs. A good example of a two-plus-two program in environmental health is the baccalaureate program (Bachelor of Science) in environmental health that has been offered for some years at Ferris State College in Michigan. It prepares the student for a career as a professional sanitarian; the junior and senior years at the four-year college build on an associate degree in environmental (sanitary) technology from a two-year college.

Upper Division Baccalaureate-Level Environmental Health Program

Third Year

First Quarter	*Quarter Hours*
	(18)
Introduction to Inorganic Chemistry	2
College Algebra	4
Introduction to Sociology	4
Public Health Administration	4
Publicity Release Writing	4
Second Quarter	(18)
General Inorganic Chemistry	5
Trigonometry	3
Social Problems	4
Communicable Disease Control	3
Elective	3
Third Quarter	(17)
Conservation	5
Technical Report Writing	3
Introduction to Organic Chemistry	5
Air Pollution	4

Upper Division Baccalaureate-Level Environmental Health Program
(Continued)

Fourth Year
First Quarter   *Quarter*
                                                        Hours
                                                        (17)
Environmental Chemistry   5
Physical Geology   4
Introduction to Physics   4
Speech   4

Second Quarter   (15)
Elementary Business Law   4
Environmental Radiation   2
Principles of Economics   4
Electives   5

Third Quarter   (15)
American Political Parties   3
Environmental Engineering   4
Environmental Management   4
Electives   4
Total Upper Division   100

All students, prior to graduation, are expected to have completed a minimum of three months of full-time work experience in a health department or in industrial sanitation responsibilities. Many of the specialized skills are assumed to have been developed in the associate degree program, allowing the upper division program to put more emphasis on theory courses, social studies, and management concepts.

The programs illustrated on the previous pages may imply that career education in college for allied health occupations involves only degree or certificate programs offered on a preemployment basis to full-time students, but this is not the case. Many colleges and vocational-technical schools also provide short-term programs and single courses, seminars, and workshops for updating, upgrading, and certifying people already employed in the health fields. In fact, the provision of short courses of this kind, often in cooperation with local chapters of the professional associations involved, is often the best way for many institutions to get started in allied health career education.

Advantages of a Core Semester—Student Selection

Even without accompanying course descriptions, it may be obvious from the previous outlines that allied health programs involve a considerable content of biological sciences and a strong commitment to the often time-consuming work in clinical internships. Serious, dependable, and capable students are required to attain the specific performance objectives, which are properly based on task analyses of the licensed practitioners' work and on the scientific knowledge needed to perform this work expertly.

Unfortunately many students wanting to enroll in allied health programs know very little of what service in these fields implies and lack the background and academic ability for, or sufficient interest in pursuing collegiate-level study in fields where the biological sciences form the essential underlying academic discipline. Colleges thus have a problem: many students are interested in allied health programs, credentials, and careers; but by and large they are not interested in the disciplines essential to successful practice in these careers. The U.S. Public Health Service reported (U.S. Department of Health, Education and Welfare, 1974b), for example, that although allied health programs gained rapidly in popularity after 1966, the academic health disciplines of biology, biochemistry, biophysics, and zoology experienced decreasing enrollments at the same time. Even though the biological science courses in some of these programs are not extremely demanding, they may pose difficulties for students who have either avoided study in the sciences or who have a record of D's or F's in high school biology or chemistry ("Nursing Programs . . .," 1976).

One way to cope with the problem of inadequate knowledge about the various allied health fields as well as the problem of inadequate preparation in the biological sciences is to adopt a "core semester" plan, which gives all students interested in any of the allied health fields a basic introduction to the health sciences. In some colleges that employ strict screening procedures involving academic aptitude, personality, and previous experience, a core semester may not be essential, since attrition is ordinarily acceptably low. But where there is little or no screening, with students of all ages and degrees of interest and preparation enrolling in allied health career programs, the core semester brings at least some order to an otherwise chaotic situation. As a result, since 1972 a number of colleges and vocational-technical schools have added a core dimension to their allied health programs, and a 1973 study of nine such programs (Burnett, 1973) found that despite numerous problems the merits of the approach outweigh its disadvantages.

The Kellogg Community College at Battle Creek, Michigan, instituted the core approach in both its nursing programs (ADN and LPN) in 1968. Attrition rates in both programs had become worrisome, and there was frequent evidence of uncertainty about career goals even among students with good academic records. After three years of "core" with the nursing programs there was so much positive feeling that a core semester for all allied health programs was planned and initiated. Kellogg now uses the core semester to feed all eight of its allied health programs—dental assisting, dental hygiene, medical assisting, medical laboratory technology, associate degree nursing, practical nursing, physical therapy assisting, and radiologic technology.

Klopfenstein (1973, p. 37) defines the idea of core in allied health career education at Kellogg Community College as follows:

> The rationale for core . . . incorporates several premises. The provision of health care is a team effort. An understanding of the work of the several allied health professions will result in an improvement of attitudes toward other members of the team. Secondly, students will develop an understanding of health-related careers. They will be able to reaffirm initial career choices or make a rational change in career goals. Third, students will be able to enter another related program without loss of credit for work done in the core. Fourth, efficiency will be improved through a reduction in the attrition rate caused by initially inappropriate program selection. Lastly, each program should expect certain outcomes from the core and plan to build upon them in subsequent parts of the specialty.

The core semester at Kellogg Community College consists of the following: English 101 (Freshman Composition); Psychology 201 (Introduction to Psychology); Health Science 90 (Human Anatomy and Physiology); and Health Technology 10 (Integrated Health Services).

Because of limited space and facilities, the core semester at Kellogg Community College is not entirely open-door. Various indicators (high-school record, ACT scores, and so on) are used to predict probable success in the basic freshman courses in English, psychology, and anatomy/physiology. A well-established developmental/remedial program is available at Kellogg to help students bring English, reading, and other basic skills up to levels where success with the core could be expected. Obviously, students in need of considerable remediation might require more than four semesters to complete a career program in allied health.

Kellogg Community College reports the following positive aspects of their core semester for allied health programs.

1. Attrition rates, which typically run from 20 to 40 percent in the first semester of "regular" allied health programs, run only 15 percent in Kellogg's core semester.

2. After completion of the core and election of one of the eight career programs, retention in the programs is very good—from 75 to 100 percent.

3. Data on the success of "core students" who have completed career programs and have taken the appropriate certifying examinations are impressive indeed—approaching 100 percent.

The only negative aspect reported is cost—the core semester being relatively more costly to operate on a per-student basis than the average academic program. The reduced attrition rates in the eight career programs, as a result of the core, however, tend to offset this relatively higher cost.

A somewhat different approach to a health careers core curriculum—as developed at Santa Fe Community College in Florida and further implemented at South Oklahoma City Junior College in Oklahoma—is proposed by Gilliland (1974). Gilliland favors a semiegalitarian approach and warns against an admissions policy based on competitive aptitude measures since these might discriminate and "admit only the most gifted." He proposes the use of *minimum* achievement scores and measures, admitting those who equal or surpass these minimums on a first-come, first-served basis. This would be a defensible and workable proposal as long as the minimums were set at a level that would generally indicate success with programs and courses whose performance objectives accurately reflect the demands of certifying examinations and career practice. The matter of "open access" is one which each college must decide for itself; but open access or not, programs must be competency-based.

The core curriculum approach to allied health education is also a feature of the program at Long Beach (California) City College. One core-and-ladder scheme relates the nurse home health aide course (nine weeks) to the forty-eight-week licensed vocational nursing program. Another provides for a core/spin-off relationship between the licensed vocational nursing and the two-year associate degree nursing program. Still another common core approach has been used to "feed" both the inhalation therapy and the radiologic technology programs.

Career Ladders in Allied Health

The aura of professionalism surrounds the health fields perhaps more completely than it does any other occupational field, and this may account for the great interest in career laddering in the health occupations. For example, nursing services are now rendered on three different levels (nurse's aide, practical nurse, and registered nurse) with pressure mounting for a fourth level of "professional" nurse, or independent nurse practitioner, and there are strong desires and some justification for a career ladder approach to nursing education that permits movement up the ladder to the next step rather than having to go back down and start at a lower rung or even at the bottom again. At the registered nurse level, for example, some baccalaureate programs offer special tracks for graduates of diploma programs to obtain the bachelor's degree without having to repeat subjects they already know. But programs to facilitate upgrading from one level to another remain scattered. Among the pilot programs that have been initiated to facilitate career development from the practical nurse to the registered nurse level is the arrangement between Olive Harvey College (City Colleges of Chicago) and Billings Hospital of the University of Chicago, where a smooth transition awaits qualified licensed practical nurses who, after some years of hospital experience, want to complete requirements for the associate degree in nursing. Articulating associate degree programs with baccalaureate (B.Sc.) nursing programs is also beginning to have some success. As yet, however, these efforts are rather embryonic, and a great deal needs to be done to smooth out progression up the nursing ladder while retaining the competencies and codes of ethics essential to each level. One major problem militating against a more rapid growth of career laddering is the large backlog of applicants at each level. It is difficult, for example, to provide spaces for LPNs to "move up" when hundreds of well-qualified applicants for associate degree RN programs are waiting.

Ferris State College in Michigan reports two examples of "smooth" laddering outside of nursing—one that allows the associate degree environmental health technician to move right on to a bachelor of science in environmental health and another that provides a baccalaureate route to medical records administration for the medical records technician with an associate degree.

The same problem awaits effective articulation measures in the medical laboratory and medical assisting field. It would not seem unduly difficult to work out curriculum and clinical problems in such a way that the climb from medical (office) assistant could proceed step by step to certified laboratory assistant, medical laboratory technician, and on to the baccalaureate degree in clinical medical laboratory technology. The YMCA Community College in Chicago now accepts certified laboratory assistant (CLA) graduates and credits them with one year toward completion of the associate degree medical laboratory technician (MLT) program.

Some colleges also are providing, through a core or other program arrangement, opportunities for *lateral* movement within the allied health field. For example, the move from licensed practical nursing into respiratory therapy, or into medical records, exemplifies this *career lattice* concept in program planning.

The introduction very recently of the concept of *physician's assistant,* a quasiprofessional practitioner who works with and under the direct supervision of a medical doctor, opens up the prospect of an eventual career ladder within medicine itself, beginning with a baccalaureate degree in the life sciences, or possibly with the baccalaureate degree nurse, and proceeding to physician's assistant, then to the full practice of medicine, and on to the graduate specialties that require years of resident training.

These career ladder and lattice possibilities are challenges to practitioners and educators alike. Their implementation will tend to alleviate shortages in health manpower at all levels. Perhaps the next decade will see several such ladders in place with thousands of people making ordered progress toward increased levels of responsibility and service.

Other Issues in Allied Health Education

Some warning flags are flying as the current wave of students rushes into career programs in allied health fields. Planners should give careful consideration to all of the following issues.

The Job Market. Close attention must be paid to the year-by-year actual demand for additional workers in both the total field and the subfields. "Need" is predicated on the hope that money will become available for the salaries required. "Demand" means that the budget is already set, the money is there, and the job is open, ready for applicants. In this era of widespread dissatisfaction with burgeoning budgets and alarming deficits at all levels of government, it would seem imprudent to expand programs and enrollments if the anticipated employment of graduates is largely expected to be in the public sector.

Rigor and Level of Programs. Most allied health careers (especially in nursing, and in the medical laboratory technologies, the electronics-related medical technologies, and the dental fields) require extremely competent and well-prepared workers. The educational programs for these careers must be characterized by high standards of performance. Many such programs have a relatively rigorous science and mathematics content, and all require good reading skills and dedication to academic achievement. Colleges that have attempted to operate these programs on an open-door basis have experienced alarming attrition rates during the instructional program or untenably high failure rates on state licensing board examinations on completion of the program—and usually both. Some community colleges espouse an open-door admissions policy for all of their programs on egalitarian principles. They admit students on a first-come-first-served basis up to the limits set by the resources for the program, regardless of the student's preparation or demonstrated interest. We consider this an ill-advised policy on at least four counts: First, it attempts to be equitable to the student, but fails to consider equity to society—and to the patients whose health (or lives) later may depend on the competency and dependability of the graduates and also to those who support the schools and rightly expect a reasonable social rate of return on the public monies invested. Second, classes with many ill-prepared students often "level down" the achievement of those with proper preparation and motivation. Third, in view of the need for properly certified allied health workers, programs with built-in high attrition rates are not defensible, since they yield relatively few graduates. Fourth and finally, if the program is "adjusted" to the students' abilities all the way through in order to eliminate attrition in the program, then the state or association that certifies examinations will later eliminate the candidate from career practice. (This has been a serious problem with some associate degree nursing programs that feature open-door admissions.)

The egalitarian thesis is best advanced by providing opportunities to succeed, not by providing paths to failure in the name of open-access. The open-door college is a viable concept in a society like ours, but with it comes the responsibility to provide developmental or remedial education, so that educationally disadvantaged persons can try to prepare themselves for entry in and success with college-level academic work. Open-door colleges, in other words, need not—and should not—operate all their programs as open-door curriculums.

Internships and Clinical Experiences. Important as it is in any

middle-manpower or technical field in which technicians are supposed to bridge the gap between theory and practice, work experience or internship on the job is absolutely essential to entry success in the allied health occupations. The safety, health, or even
the life of a patient may depend on how effectively a health paraprofessional performs on the very first day of "regular" employment. If colleges provide only theory and expect hospitals, clinics,
doctors, and dentists to provide months of on-the-job practical
training while paying the new worker full salary, then education
and training for health fields might as well revert back to hospitals,
clinics, and doctor's offices.

The necessity for intensive clinical experience is generally
well recognized, though some colleges have attempted to shorten
the clinical period by utilizing simulation and audiovisual methods.
A serious problem for planners during this era of health program
expansion is the provision of adequate clinical work experiences.
Internships should be long enough to provide a range of experience and should give the student opportunities to perform responsibly under supervision. Many communities just do not have
a sufficient number of hospital and clinic work stations to provide
realistic internships for all potential students. The temptation to
by-pass or short-cut the internship phase of training is ever-present, but health program administrators should resist it. The program, the students, and perhaps some future patients will suffer
as a result of inadequate clinical experience. To prevent misunderstandings that will not adversely affect the program, arrangements for cooperative effort between the college and those agencies and offices providing clinical work stations should be expressed
in formal contractual agreements before students are assigned.
Hospitals, understandably, will set limits on the number of students
that can be accommodated on the wards or in the laboratories. It
is these limits that are often the controlling factor in program
admissions.

Close Association with Advisory Groups. The importance of advisory committees for all of occupational education has been emphasized again and again. In the health field, the advice and counsel of such groups is not just important, it is essential. No allied
health program should be started or operated without an advisory

committee of local physicians, nurses, dentists, and representatives of hospitals and clinics. Their advice may seem unduly restrictive at times, and it may run counter to that of the more vocal advocates of social need and open access, but these are the practitioners in the field and the future employers of the program graduates. Their counsel should always be heard, even if it is not always exactly what program planners and prospective students want to hear.

Curriculum planners often make the mistake of rationalizing a new program on the basis of nebulous estimates of national need, when local surveys indicate little if any employment potential in the local community. Universities and four-year colleges operating professional level programs perhaps can disregard the local need factor and plan on a national or regional basis, but such an approach generally is inadvisable for two-year schools. A good rule of thumb is that the program probably is justified if new entry job potential in the community is at least ten annually. With this small nucleus of local jobs, the program might be planned to produce as many as twenty graduates per year with the expectation that some will seek and find employment elsewhere. State licensing and certification also should be kept in mind. Associate degree graduates who cannot meet these state and professional association competency levels create student disillusionment and lack of public confidence in and support of the college and its programs.

In summary, there is fairly general agreement among the experts, substantiated by various research data, that the demand for new personnel in most allied health fields will continue on into the 1980s and that many students will continue to seek admission to programs in these fields. The important question, however, is not how many students want these programs but how many have both the interest and the ability to succeed in them. Administrators of allied health programs must set up realistic standards for admission, retention, and graduation to assure that allied health practitioners, who deal daily with the health and lives of patients, will bring competence and dedication to their careers. If colleges do not build quality into their programs, training for these careers may (and should) revert to hospitals, clinics, and doctors' offices.

Guidelines for Planners. Beyond the general programmatic and administrative suggestions in Chapters Ten and Twelve, here are several issues and factors that should be specifically evaluated by planners of middle-manpower programs in the health fields:

1. Is there both a national (or regional) and a local need?

2. Besides an indication of current demand, and recalling the lead-time necessary to establish the program and produce graduates, does there appear to be a long-term demand?

3. Is the entry level salary and promotional history for the occupation in a locality competitive with these factors in other fields requiring comparable educational preparation?

4. Are qualified faculty and program directors available at salaries the college can offer?

5. What about equipment, laboratories on campus, supporting science and theory courses, and clinical facilities in the community for internships and work-experience assignments? Can suitable agreements be reached and contracts drawn for the use of these off-campus facilities?

6. Mindful of the extremely high unit cost of nearly all allied health programs, can the college afford to offer the program at the requisite quality level?

7. In view of the uncompromising competency standards required in many allied health occupations, are there sufficient numbers of prospective students with the capability, dependability, and interest that would predict acceptable rates of retention in and completion of the program?

8. Is there interest in and support for the proposed program from the several levels and segments of the profession currently practicing in the community?

8 ▣ ▣ ▣ ▣ ▣ ▣ ▣ ▣ ▣ ▣ ▣ ▣ ▣ ▣ ▣

Public and
Human Service Careers

> *Too many people think of local governments as com-*
> *posed of trash collectors, police, and firemen and fail*
> *to realize the range of tasks to be done and of human*
> *talents needed.*
>
> Municipal Manpower Commission (1962)

The expansion of service related jobs in the United States in the
last ten years has been phenomenal, particularly among those that
are people-oriented. This expansion has created an occupational
category or field at the middle-manpower level broadly defined as
public and human services. This field does not encompass all government related jobs at the technical and paraprofessional level,
since government agencies obviously need workers who span the
whole spectrum of applied knowledge—from agriculture and engineering to the creative and performing arts and the occupations
discussed in previous chapters on business and office jobs, engineering and industrial technology, and the health fields. Instead,
this relatively new area of government service—or perhaps a long-
established government function that is only now moving towards

recognition as an occupational group—centers on those public services that are oriented to meeting the social and personal needs of community residents.

The parameters of public and human services are not precise, but there are two primary criteria which, if taken together, produce an adequate definition of the field. For one thing, these services are firmly based in the applied aspects of the behavioral sciences, particularly psychology and sociology, rather than in such disciplines as the physical or biological sciences. For the other, students are prepared for people-to-people relationships, often on a one-to-one basis, rather than for office work separate from direct contact with citizen problems, or for mass contact, such as information and communications.

DeNure (1973) prefers to divide this field of service into two broad classifications: municipal services and human services, as represented in Figure 4. That figure illustrates the interrelationships between and among major subfields of these two areas. But another classification highlights three categories of service that are emerging within the field. One of these involves the nonmedical

Figure 4. Relationships Among Several Aspects
of Public and Human Services.

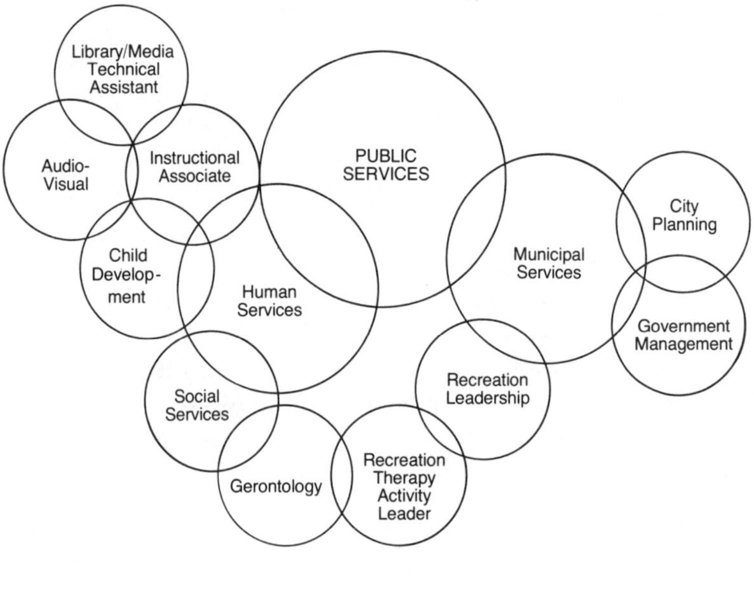

aspects of social welfare, including such areas as social work and recreation. A second group centers in education and includes such jobs as teacher aide and counselor aide. The third relates to the government services of public safety, security, and protection, perhaps best represented by law enforcement.

Fringe areas exist that might be considered to fall within this definition, at least in part. Some, such as fire science, building inspection, and sanitation technology, are oriented to public safety and protection but are based less on the behavioral sciences than on other disciplines. Other occupations, such as paralegal aide or urban planning and environmental technologist, may have some behavioral-science base but they are not largely dependent on public agency employment nor are they engaged primarily in one-to-one relationships with clients. The nucleus of public and human services, however, is in social service, education, and law enforcement and corrections. All three of these areas represent new prospects for the development of postsecondary career education.

Manpower Needs in Public and Human Services

The demand for public and human service paraprofessionals and technicians is merely one aspect of the recent rapid growth of employment in government, which at over 4 percent a year was more than twice the rate of growth of the labor force at large in the decade of the 1960s. During the 1970s, government employment has been increasing at a slower rate—about 2.9 percent a year—but still faster than the rest of the labor force, and it is projected to increase from over 13 million workers at present to approximately 16 million in 1980. From 1980 to 1985 the U.S. Bureau of Labor Statistics estimates it will grow at about 2.5 percent a year to some 18.8 million employees, compared with an annual increase in the total labor force of 1.2 percent.

The slowing rate of growth of total government employment is due almost entirely to a leveling off at the federal level. According to the Bureau of Labor Statistics, federal employment in 1985 is likely to be about the same as it was in 1968. On the other hand, state and local government employment, which is much more closely related to public and human service jobs than is federal employment, is expected to continue expanding rapidly through the rest of the 1970s to some 13 million persons by 1980 (Rotella, 1971). And unless the current strong sentiment against big government markedly slows the growth of government, state and local agencies will add an additional 2.1 million workers to their staffs between 1980 and 1985 (U.S. Department of Labor, 1974b, p. 97).

Within this general pattern of expected increases in government employment, an increasing proportion of workers are involved in human service occupations. An expanded social consciousness has exerted continuing demands on social agencies to provide more services for the disadvantaged, the unemployed, and the handicapped and for preschool children and senior citizens. Civil rights and consumer groups are exerting pressure for more public and human service workers in the areas of affirmative action and consumer protection. The recipients of government services expect that these services, which are supported by their taxes, will be of comparable quality and professionalism, for a comparable price, to similar services provided by the private sector.

Table 14 demonstrates the growth in several service occupations between 1960 and 1970. While the civilian labor force grew by slightly over 18 percent during that decade, the number of recreation workers rose by nearly 32 percent, sheriffs and bailiffs by 44 percent, policemen and detectives by nearly 49 percent, social and welfare workers by nearly 128 percent, and personnel and labor relations workers by nearly 196 percent.

Table 14. Persons Employed in Selected Service Occupations, 1960 and 1970.

	1960	1970	Percent Change
Social and Welfare Workers	95,102	216,623	+127.8%
Personnel and Labor Relations Workers	98,257	290,756	+195.9
Recreation and Group Workers	37,487	49,331	+ 31.6
Policemen and Detectives	252,253	375,494	+ 48.8
Sheriffs and Bailiffs	34,151	34,820	+ 44.2

Source: U.S. Bureau of the Census (1962, 1972).

As one particular example of the demand for human service workers, the development of the specialty of child-care services is a direct response to the growth of child-care and day-care facilities to provide for the children of mothers working outside the home. The percentage of working mothers in the United States has increased from 18 percent in 1948 to more than 40 percent in 1975. This long-range trend has accelerated recently as women have more actively sought parity with men in economic matters. From another perspective, the growth of day-care centers helps to provide jobs for those at the bottom of the economic ladder in many urban areas. Thus, of the 70,000 social service aides, including child-care aides, working in 1974, four out of five were women employed in inner cities (*Occupational Outlook Handbook*, 1977, p. 533). Among social service aides, it is projected that there will be an average of 10,000 openings annually between now and 1985, to reach an anticipated 1985 requirement of 150,000 individuals in this very appropriate category for postsecondary occupational programs (U.S. Department of Labor, 1974b, p. 74).

Overall, in the social work area of the public and human services, approximately 400,000 career openings are expected to materialize over the entire decade of the 1970s. Nearly half of these openings will be suitable for persons with paraprofessional or technical training. Openings in such areas as recreation, child care, and community and group services are expected to increase by over 200 percent during the decade (Korim, 1971b).

In the broad area of law enforcement and corrections, recent changes have created demands on postsecondary institutions similar to those in the social welfare field. With growing crime rates and accelerating urban decay, rich and poor taxpayers alike are insisting on better methods of coping with crime, and on law enforcement and correctional personnel who are better trained to deal with it both before and after the fact. Thus the Bureau of Labor Statistics estimates that 15,000 job opportunities open each year for police personnel in municipal and county agencies, out of a total employment complement of over one-half million (U.S. Department of Health, Education and Welfare, 1975b) and this figure does not include probation and other correctional officers or police at the state level.

The growth in public awareness of the need for more effective public and human service workers has been paralleled since the early 1960s by federal support for training these workers. Assisting in the broad thrust of colleges into all occupational education fields have been the Vocational Education Act of 1963, the Amendments thereto of 1968, and the Education Amendments of 1972 and 1976. These legislative enactments have consistently provided support for many occupationally oriented programs, of which the human services field has been a relatively recent but substantial participant. On top of this broad base of funding, there has been a host of smaller and more specific grants, most of them emanating from various agencies within the Department of Health, Education and Welfare. Even a cursory listing of these would include the New Careers Program, Head Start, and the Model Cities Programs. In the field of geriatrics, the U.S. Administration on Aging, Office of Human Development, has provided support through the American Association of Community and Junior Colleges' Aging Project. In the law enforcement field, many programs never would have developed but for the Law Enforcement Assistance Administration of the 1960s.

In addition to funding, new directions for programs have been recommended, if not mandated, by federal agencies. The concept of differential staffing, for example, which encourages social agencies to team master's degree professionals and associate degree paraprofessionals to work cooperatively, was promoted by the Rehabilitation Services Administration of the Department of Health, Education and Welfare. In the field of mental retardation, federal legislation in 1971 required community plans for funding to allocate services and facilities for retarded persons that were comparable to those for other recipients. The move in the middle 1970s into competency-based instruction in the human services field received impetus from the Office of Child Development of the Department of Health, Education and Welfare. States, counties, and municipalities and many private agencies supported by churches, United Fund drives, and foundations have also been heavily involved in projects demanding paraprofessional workers.

Despite this support for public and human service programs and evidence of expanding employment opportunities, program planners in colleges and universities should not assume that the demand for these workers will continue to exceed supply. The decline in the birth rate, for example, has limited the number of people who can be employed in the elementary schools as teachers' aides, and local oversupply of other workers may occur even with overall shortages at the national level. The justification for any career program is what happens to its graduates, and the probabilities of placement should be reasonable before colleges undertake and expand these programs. A 1970 survey of graduates of social services programs in a number of Florida community colleges revealed that only about one half of these graduates found employment immediately after completing the program and that of all those employed both immediately and subsequently, only a little more than half found jobs in areas directly related to their training. Many of those who did not enter immediate employment enrolled in upper-division programs in the State University of Florida system. One 1972 study of 136 community-college graduates showed that after employment they received salaries ranging from only $3,800 to $9,000—approximately one half of that earned by professionals with advanced degrees in the same fields (McNeer, 1974).

Programs in Public and Human Services

The increased demand for human service workers has been a significant force in developing a division of labor in government agencies that recognizes that paraprofessionals can provide some agency services just as effectively as graduate professionals.

For example, perhaps one of the greatest advances for the paraprofessional level of child care worker is the project program launched in 1971 to create national guidelines for the Child Development Associate (CDA). With direct support from the Office of Child Development, U.S. Department of Health, Education and Welfare, the program has encouraged a nationwide system of training and credentialling for currently employed child care workers as well as for persons preparing for positions. The actual development of the system, the issuance of the credential, the identification of required competencies, and the promotion of the Child Development Associate is in the hands of the Child Development Associate Consortium, made up of representatives from a number of organizations devoted to improved staff competence in child development services.* The CDA program is not based on courses but rather on the acquisition by trainees of the demonstrated competency to provide quality child development services. Nonetheless, the competencies and the training program are readily adaptable to associate degree or certificate programs in postsecondary institutions. The child development curriculum of the City Colleges of Chicago, illustrated on a later page, integrates the CDA competencies as well as state licensing requirements into the required child development courses.

In addition, such national professional associations as the Council on Social Work Education and the National Association of Social Workers have encouraged and legitimized two-year college programs at the associate-degree level in the human services. State agencies in the mental health, child care, family assistance, and corrections fields also have given their support.

The development of these paraprofessional programs has proceeded most rapidly in urban or metropolitan community colleges. Other postsecondary institutions, however, including area vocational-technical schools, private junior colleges, and state systems of technical colleges (as in Ohio and New York), also have added these programs to their offerings, and some colleges not in urban settings but serving smaller or suburban communities, have developed such programs as well.

A partial list of the programs now found in two-year college catalogues includes such specialties as these:

Child Care
Community Development Aid
Counselor Aid
Geriatric Aid
Human Services Associate
Institutional Corrections
   Officer
Labor Relations Aid
Law Enforcement Officer

Legal Services Aid
Mental Health Worker
Probation Officer
Recreation Aid
Social Service Aid
Teacher Aid
Youth Officer

*For further information contact the Child Development Associate Consortium, 7315 Wisconsin Avenue N.W., Washington, D.C. 20014.

The range of programs is surprisingly broad. Responses from 176 colleges to a 1970 survey by Burns (1971) indicated a total of 595 programs in human and public services spread across a dozen broad fields, plus an additional 411 in the allied health or medical field. Korim (1971a) identified 866 programs as of January 1971 and provided not only a rather complete taxonomy of these programs but also sources of further information about them and the careers for which they prepare. Sessoms and Verhoven (1970) identified a wide variety of programs related to recreation leadership alone and have outlined the ways in which two-year colleges are participating in career development in this field. By 1970, some 250 two-year programs were in operation in the area of law enforcement and corrections, and by the mid-1970s, over 400 programs in this field were in operation at either the two-year, four-year, or graduate levels, with greatest concentrations being in California, Florida, New York, Michigan, and Pennsylvania (U.S. Department of Health, Education and Welfare, 1975b, p. 2).

The content of these programs is considered, for convenience, in terms of the three clusters mentioned above: (1) social service, (2) education, and (3) law enforcement and corrections.

Social Services. In this cluster, encompassing such specialties as family assistance, geriatrics, employment counseling, and community development, a professional hierarchy headed by staff members holding the master's degree in social work has been the dominant force for decades. The baccalaureate degree and recently the associate degree have been fitted into the existing hierarchy. This hierarchical structure has encouraged the concept of a curriculum continuum for career laddering, and with some cooperation of the professional associations joint curriculum planning by different educational levels has been a potent factor in the evolution of community college human services programs (Curriculum Building for the Continuum in Social Welfare Education, 1972). The curriculum continuum concept encompasses the idea of a career ladder in which each level or step in the career hierarchy is preparatory to, and can lead to, the next level or step. Curriculums for ladder-type careers are planned so that each level of the program is self-contained, unduplicated at other levels, qualifies the student for immediate employment at a given level, and provides preparation for further study at the next curriculum level. It is essential to provide opportunities for the employed person to get back onto the educational ladder from time to time. Flexible admissions and stop-out provisions recognize the social and economic differences of those attracted to the program and permit adjustment for varying student age levels, family responsibilities, economic circumstances, and work schedules. Furthermore, unlike earlier program development, which was purely vocational and narrowly geared to a single agency, the curriculum continuum concept provides students with the motivation to work toward higher and better-paying career levels.

The development of the curriculum continuum implies that the ideal paraprofessional curriculum should simultaneously provide both transferability and employability. There does not appear to be any single model in use in the hundreds of college programs throughout the United States, however. At one end of the spectrum of human services programs, community and junior colleges have sometimes just "pulled together" existing courses from the liberal arts or transfer areas. A somewhat better approach than this features essentially the liberal arts or the transfer courses, heavy in the general social sciences but augmented with a practicum that allows application of the theory given in the general courses. At the other end of the spectrum are programs of specialized career courses including the practicum and heavily oriented toward "methods" or "how-to" courses, even to the extent of being tailored to the needs of a particular agency (Edman and Collins, 1975). The following curriculum, offered by the City Colleges of Chicago and leading to the associate in applied science, illustrates a two-year program in child development with a preschool education option. It is dual purpose in that it is designed both for students who seek employment as teachers in public and private preschools, day-care centers, or nursery schools or who want to work as teacher aides and activities supervisors as well as for those who intend to transfer to four-year colleges or universities. For the latter students, it is articulated with programs at three such institutions in the Chicago area.

Associate Degree Level Child Development Preschool Education Program

First Year

	Credit Hours		Credit Hours
Semester I		*Semester II*	
Human Growth and Development I	3	Human Growth and Development II	3
Child Development Laboratory or In-Service Seminar	1	Activity Programming	2
		Pre-School Education Laboratory	1
Child Care, Health, and Nutrition	3	Principles of Pre-School Education	3
General Education	9	General Education	6
	16		15

Second Year

	Credit Hours		Credit Hours
Language Arts for the Young Child	3	Music for the Young Child	2
Art for the Young Child	2	Practicum in Nursery School	6
Child Study	3		
General Education	9	General Education	6
	17		14

This program is one of four options in the field of child development. The other three are residential child care, elementary school teacher aide, and special education teacher aide. A common core is basic to all options and includes human growth and development (2 semesters) child care, health and nutrition, activity programming, child study, and a practicum. Specific objectives of the program include (1) setting up and maintaining a safe and healthy learning environment for pre-school children; (2) advancing physical and intellectual competence; (3) building a positive self-concept and individual strength; (4) organizing and sustaining the positive functioning of children and adults in a group within a learning environment; (5) bringing about optimal coordination of home and center child-rearing practices and expectations; and (6) observing, recording and communicating individual and group behavior changes, and planning cooperatively with other staff to adjust the program to these changes.

The following child and family major with a child-care specialization offered at the baccalaureate level by the College of Human Resources of Southern Illinois University is an excellent example of a four-year program for professional service in human service fields. It combines two cores, one in general studies and a second in the child and family major, as do three other related but separate options leading to positions as directors and teachers in pre-school centers, directors and supervisors of residential child care centers, or infant care specialists. Each option involves a dozen or so specialized electives. This child-care option offers basic background leading to positions as nursery school director; teacher in private schools, colleges and universities, or day-care centers; director or teacher in residential living facilities for exceptional children; child care specialist with social, public health, or welfare agencies; home economics extension specialist in child care; and recreation leaders.

Baccalaureate-Level Child and Family Program with a Child-Care Specialization

	Credit Hours
General Studies Requirements, including:	45
Introduction to Psychology	
The Sociological Perspective	
Introduction to American Government and Politics	
Interpersonal Communication	
Requirements for Major in Child and Family	36
Marriage and Family Living	
Child Development	
Advanced Child Development	
Child Development Practicum	
Child Development Practicum	
Family Development	
Electives Recommended for Child Care Specialists	39
Psychology of Personality	
Theory and Practice in the Preschool	
Social Welfare as a Social Institution	
Introduction to Interviewing	
Social Services and Minority Groups	
Consumer Problems	

Baccalaureate-Level Child and Family Program with a Child-Care Specialization

Credit Hours

Consumers and the Market
Management for Low-Income Families
Introduction to Design, Home Furnishings and Interiors
Introduction to Special Education
Social Factors in Personality and Adjustment
Child and Family Workshop
Child and Family Readings
Introduction to Marriage and Family Counseling
Total   120

Education. The same variability identified in social-work oriented programs has been identified in those centering on education, including audiovisual, early childhood education, and teacher aide programs. A review of sixty teacher aide programs across the country by Swift (1970), for example, revealed considerable variation and three generally different types of program. One type was made up of basic general education courses taken from the conventional transfer listings, augmented with clerical skills and business courses to equip the aide to relieve the teacher of attendance chores and other routines. A second type of curriculum was made up largely of courses from the general liberal arts field with emphasis on education, sociology, and psychology. A third category consisted of specially developed teacher aide courses offered in a specific sequence with emphasis on methods and almost always including a practicum.

Law Enforcement and Corrections. Recent and widespread social disorders, crime waves, and drug addiction problems have revealed major problems in training, education, and human relations in law enforcement agencies. Legal restraints on certain police actions were laid down in federal court decisions during the 1960s and early 1970s, and accompanying these changes was a growing belief in the importance of community relations for effective police work. Out of these kinds of pressures have come efforts to professionalize the entire field of law enforcement and corrections.

A companion development to professionalization has been the deemphasis on *institutional* corrections, which removes the offender from society, in favor of such *community* corrections activities as work release, study release, and increased use of probation for first offenders and criminals not considered dangerous to society. These two shifts—toward professionalization and toward community corrections—have brought postsecondary education, particularly two-year college career education, into a close relationship with the entire field of corrections. This relationship has been forged both through programs of preparatory and inservice education for persons seeking employment or already employed in the corrections field and through programs for offenders in prison and in parole status in the community.

In many respects, the field of law enforcement and corrections, including such specialties in the field as youth officer and legal service aide, bears a close relationship to the social and educational service programs described earlier. One author claims, for example, that corrections work is 90 percent behavioral-science oriented (Wallers, 1973). Another cites police authorities who indicate that relations with the public constitute 85 percent of their work (Hulst and Wark, 1975).

The fields of law enforcement and corrections and child development probably constitute the oldest and still most prevalent programs in the public and human services among colleges. California first brought law enforcement and higher education into close relationship. In the early 1900s, Chief August Vollmer at Berkeley, California, advocated professionalizing law enforcement and founded the first school of criminology at the University of California in 1916. Further reinforcement for higher education in law enforcement came from the Wickersham Commission of 1930, which recommended training of law enforcement personnel as part of its nationwide recommendations to handle crime more effectively. Shortly thereafter, Michigan State, San Jose State, Wichita State, and Bernard Baruch College in New York City implemented baccalaureate programs. From this base in four-year institutions higher education programs grew, and, beginning in the 1950s, as the need for paraprofessional level officers became apparent, law enforcement education spread rapidly to two-year colleges.

Many successful law enforcement programs, particularly in community colleges, involve the colleges and local law enforcement agencies in a fully cooperative arrangement. One successful pattern involves the recruitment and hiring of cadets by the law enforcement agency, which then provides instruction in weapons, defense tactics, patrol operations, and investigations, while the community college provides courses to the cadets in communications skills, government, organization and administration, sociology, and criminal law. All of the community-college work may be taken for credit as part of an associate degree program that students may complete part-time after they finish their cadet training.

The obvious advantage of this cooperative relationship is that classroom and practical work experience are combined within the cadet program. Furthermore, the police recruit is already employed, which both simplifies the placement problem and adjusts program size to manpower needs. Useful in this context is the advisory committee, including local, county, and state police administrators who are close to the hiring process and can help integrate the college curriculum with the recruitment and cadet programs.

The following program in law enforcement from Morton College in Berwyn, Illinois, reveals quite well the course content covering basic police skills plus more academically-oriented course work in areas such as law, psychology, and sociology, for students who want a career as law officers either at the city, state, or federal levels, or in retail or industrial security. It is multipurpose in that it serves students who have no previous experience as well as those who are presently employed and are seeking professional advancement, and those seeking immediate employment as well as those planning to transfer to a four-year college.

Associate Degree Level Law Enforcement Program

	Credit Hours
Introduction to Law Enforcement	3
Introduction to Criminology	3
Traffic Law and Control Procedures	3
Police Operations and Procedures I	3
Administration of Justice	3
Police Operations and Procedures II	3

Associate Degree Level Law Enforcement Program (Continued)

	Credit Hours
Juvenile Delinquency	3
Law Enforcement and Community Relations	3
Criminal Law I	3
Criminal Law II	3
Introduction to Criminal Investigation	3
Court Procedure and Evidence	3
Police Organization and Administration	3
Introduction to Psychology*	3
Typing I*	3
Introduction to Sociology*	3
General Education	21
Physical Education (recommended)	4
Total	73

One of the great changes that has brought two-year colleges into direct relationship with the area of corrections has been the decline in the practice of isolating offenders from society. Recent emphasis has been on reintegration, leaving some offenders under supervision in the community and teaching them how to live in and with society. This process, of course, reduces the stigma of being "put away" and also permits family ties to be retained.

As of 1977, there is still much uncertainty and controversy among experts in the criminal justice field about this process, but as reintegration is put into practice in many states and urban areas, community colleges increasingly help prepare such corrections personnel as probation officers, parole officers, and youth officers, while continuing earlier programs for regular police officers and prison guards.

Many of the earlier observations about social-work oriented programs apply to the field of corrections. There is the same need for a close working relationship with the agency. The dual function of attracting and preparing young people fresh out of high school for corrections positions is coupled with in-service programs for employed personnel in institutional and community corrections work. There is a similar need to build dual purpose associate-

These courses may also be applied toward general education requirements.

degree curriculums that provide for job competency and facilitate mobility into higher level education programs.

Two programs in probation services from the Public Service Institute of the City Colleges of Chicago illustrate curricula within corrections. The basic certificate level program may be taken as a free-standing program particularly by employed individuals but may also be used as a fully acceptable module or core of the associate degree program, which provides training in supervision and rehabilitation of offenders and leads to advancement to administrative levels in probation offices.

Basic Certificate Level Probation Services Program

	Credit Hours
Principles and Practices of Probation	3
Probation Counseling and Supervision I	3
Probation Counseling and Supervision II	3
Issues in Probation	3
	12

Associate-Degree Level Probation Services Program

First Year Semester I	Credit Hours	Semester II	Credit Hours
Principles and Practices of Probation	3	Probation Counseling and Supervision I	3
Administration of Criminal Justice	3	Public Administration	3
General Education	6	General Education	3
Elective	3	Electives	6
	15		15
Second Year			
Probation Counseling and Supervision II	3	Issues in Probation	3
General Psychology	3	Social Psychology	3
Introduction to the Study of Society	3	Sociology of Urban Life	3
General Education	3	General Education or Electives	6
Elective	3		
	15		15

A number of senior institutions, for example, have developed baccalaureate programs in law enforcement articulated with the community college programs. In the corrections field, however, the professional hierarchy has never been as well structured or as amenable to a career ladder approach as it is in the social work field, and thus the emphasis on general programs with a high degree of transferability is not as critical in preparing paraprofessionals. Persons desiring to attain *professional* status in the field will, for the most part, have to elect a transfer program in police science or criminal justice with the baccalaureate degree and graduate work in mind from the outset.

Apart from the preparation of corrections personnel, a separate but related development warrants at least brief attention: the development by many community colleges of programs for the further education of offenders themselves. The American Association of Community and Junior Colleges surveyed programs for offenders in 1975 and identified 237 colleges and universities offering offender education. The bulk of these were taught by college and university faculty while approximately one third used correspondence courses, TV instruction, or prison teaching staff [Emmert, 1976]. Some twenty to thirty community colleges are directly involved with state and federal prisons in staff training and inmate education using study-release programs on the community college campus as well as extension courses in the prisons, sometimes with staff and prisoners in the same classroom [McCollum and others, 1975]. The phenomenon of simultaneous inmate education and preservice and inservice training for guard and custodial personnel is evident in a Jackson [Michigan] Community College program started in 1969 which by 1973 had involved 515 persons. The program has used ex-offenders as peer counselors working under the supervision of professional guidance counselors to help inmates plan academic programs [Sheffer, 1973].

In contrast to the social work areas, the field of law enforcement and corrections has had an image problem to overcome. No other function provided by municipal government has more contradictions and ambiguities than does law enforcement and corrections. In no other public service does the citizenry expect the friendly helper, the neighborhood counselor, the tough guy, the information giver, and the law enforcer to be all wrapped together in one individual. Studies of police departments have indicated that they tend toward the paramilitary type of organization, that there is inbreeding within the ranks, and that they are generally conservative in orientation. From this type of outlook and atmosphere many communities expect law enforcement services quite different from the hard line of arrest, detention, arraignment, indictment, imprisonment, and other steps in the formalized criminal justice process (McCollum and others, 1975). Strong differences of opinion about the criminal justice system range from the feeling held by a few citizens that policemen are "fascist pigs," racists, and sadists to that held by most others that policemen generally are protectors of and contributors to the social order. Further, the same dichotomies exist with respect to the courts and the justice system, with cries of "repression" from a few and demands for "the full penalty of the law" from others. Finally, the system of punishment and corrections is a function of society about which there is no great degree of consensus.

It is in these almost schizophrenic situations then that colleges working with law enforcement and corrections agencies have to plan educational programs. The program needs to be responsive to the requirements of the profession, but the profession itself is undergoing critical self-examination and change. The community college program is both a preparatory and an upgrading program for individuals in the system that at the same time attempts to respond to the winds of change that sweep almost daily through the structure of criminal justice in America.

Issues in Public and Human Service Education

Common to all educational programs in the public and human services field are a number of important issues, some related to on-campus problems and others to the larger society, that deserve discussion here.

Students. As with most occupationally oriented programs and with community college programs generally, the perceptions of what the typical college student is like are simply not applicable (see Chapter Two). In general, new types of students are increasingly evident. They follow a pattern typical of most two-year colleges in the 1970s: the average age is close to twenty-eight; Many of them already are employed, married, and have children; minority representation is strong; and in general these students are strongly oriented toward career education. There are some who are interested in working for the baccalaureate degree and who see the two-year college program as a step in that direction. There are young women who plan on only two years of college and seek in the human services field skills that are readily marketable and that may be applicable in marriage. And there are older women in their late thirties or forties who find comfort in a program that relates to skills they already have developed in rearing a family and the practical nature of which overcomes the hesitancy they might have in competing with young students in a strictly academic field. All economic levels may be represented, including the suburban housewife, the working wife whose income supplements her husband's, and the welfare recipient who seeks some degree of independence from public support. These older women with family responsibilities tend to be more sensitive, more concerned about failure, less confident because of age or incomplete education, and more anxious about getting a job. Many of them seek entry to the program with some diffidence and want to make a light commitment of only a course or two at first in order to test out their adequacies.

   The "Open-Door." The issue of the open-door to students in human services programs is ever-present. On the one hand, these programs and the jobs they lead to are seen as opportunities for the economically and educationally disadvantaged, and consequently the open-door concept to the training program has many advocates. On the other hand, it must be remembered that nearly all of the jobs to which public and human services programs lead call for effective and competent service in areas that affect the lives, health, safety, and emotional stability of others. Workers in these services deal on a daily basis with the critical, often traumatic, and frequently confidential problems of other human beings. Persons with serious emotional and personality problems of their own should not be accepted into the program. Consequently, these programs cannot be completely open-door. Emotional stability and maturity are extremely important factors in student selection. And, for two-year paraprofessional programs using the career ladder concept, student selection and counseling should take into account the academic rigor of a curriculum which consists of at least 50 percent transfer courses with substantial academic rigor.

Career Laddering and Latticing. It should be noted that the concept of the curriculum continuum and of career laddering departs radically from that concept of vocational education which holds that occupational preparation should be totally job-oriented and thus terminal, without the possibility of combining transferability with employability. In order to fit into a career-ladder concept, curriculums in the human services field are closely related to programs in senior institutions without being limited by the prescriptive influences of such programs. Often in joint meetings with curriculum planners from four-year colleges the question is asked of two-year human service program planners, "If you provide specific preparation in job skills at the lower division of the undergraduate years, what will we do in the upper division and in the graduate schools?" The emerging answer is that the upper division and the graduate school should deal with essentially the same concepts as the two-year program, blending theory and practice in increasingly complex and theoretical fashion as the student matures and progresses. One authority in the field expresses this idea as follows: "If there are any educational constants to be observed, they are found in the need for both specialized training in certain disciplines and liberal education . . . to start from the first years of college and continue through university education" (Swift, 1971). Methods courses and practicums need to be integrated with general theory and support courses from the very beginning of the student's educational experience. This duality of curriculum—this characteristic that makes programs in the human services both occupational and professional—is what makes them particularly valuable for student motivation. Their concurrent specialization and generalization, although not easy to implement and maintain under all conditions, are obviously easier in such an area as human services where a career hierarchy has already been established, where joint planning across educational levels has been prevalent, and where professional associations have been willing to accept the lower levels of degrees within the career ladder structure, than it is in more rigidly stratified fields such as medicine.

The kind of associate degree most appropriate to the dual-purpose human services program has been a matter of considerable discussion. Traditionally the Associate in Arts degree is transfer oriented, while the Associate in Applied Science or the Associate in Technology degrees are employment oriented. Perhaps more specific degree names, such as Associate in Child Development or Associate in Human Services, would avoid either the label of transferability or the possible stigma of a terminal or vocational degree. In some states, however, specific degree names would run headlong into a management information system and a Higher Education General Information Survey (HEGIS) code that assigns for funding purposes one set of numbers to transfer degrees and a separate and distinct set to occupational programs.

A companion perspective to the career ladder curriculum can be expressed as "career latticing" in terms of horizontal and vertical student mobility. Vertical or upward mobility requires that program components be transferable from two-year to four-year levels and from college to graduate levels. Horizontal mobility is provided at any of these levels by a variety of training and educational experiences that maximize chances for employment in several different positions or agencies in the local community or in other locations. One operational reality that should govern decisions about a narrow or broad program focus with regard to horizontal mobility is the degree to which the program may be focused toward the needs of a specific agency. The narrowness of focus should be directly proportional to the capacity of that agency to absorb not only students for internships but also graduates for permanent placement. If there are no local agencies with large employment capacity for particular jobs, and if there are many small agencies, it would be wiser to develop a broadly focused curriculum in order to permit horizontal mobility.

Just as the degree of generalization or specificity of the curriculum content should be related to the employment market, so the degree of specialization should be consistent with the program title. For example, the curriculum might be very specialized if it were designed to prepare day-care aids but more general for child-care aides and even more broad if its objective were the preparation of human services aides.

The ideal career ladder and lattice curriculum at the two-year college level is often referred to as the *career model.* There are three basic criteria for this model. First, it prepares an individual for immediate employment with a blended body of theory and application. Second, it provides two full years of acceptable college credit work, applicable to upper division work toward a professional degree in at least some four-year colleges. Third, it requires the selection of applicants with acceptable self-awareness and sufficiently well-developed interpersonal and academic skills to cope with transfer-level college work applicable to more than a single job or position.

Internship and Work Experience. One of the major incentives for colleges to develop human services programs was the need for agencies to upgrade and update their staffs, many of whom were hired originally without previous preparation in the human services. Agencies also need to utilize their professional staff more efficiently through a division of labor made possible by employing paraprofessionals. It seems only reasonable, therefore, that the work experience provided by social service agencies should be an integral part of the curriculum.

The question of whether experiences or theory should occur first is probably less important than the question of what experiences are most important or essential. All such programs should start with the specific skills and knowledge required of individuals in performing a job at the entry level or bottom rung of the career ladder. Implied here is the need for a specific task analysis based on what practitioners actually do on the job, on which particular skills they use more than others, which skills are more perishable than others and thus need more review, and on which skills are more difficult to acquire than others. Such a task analysis is essential for a competency-based curriculum that uses these tasks or experiences as the basis for developing the behavioral or performance objectives to be attained through learning sequences in the program (Mager and Beach, 1967). The model may be easier to implement if students are already employed in the field, but in any case the need for a good practicum early in the program is obvious.

Agencies willing to cooperate in providing internships must be in need of the program and the product provided by the college. For effective cooperation, appropriate agencies should have a differential staffing model or at least the willingness to move in that direction. Should the interested agency not have defined positions for associate-degree graduates, the role of the college may have to include helping to effect changes in staffing patterns, job descriptions and qualifications of personnel, and identifying the ways in which the two-year college graduate fits in.

Some of the typical metropolitan agencies that usually cooperate with community colleges offering associate degree human services programs are:

Boys' Clubs	Community action agencies
Day-care centers	Institutions and programs for
Head-Start programs	the mentally, emotionally,
Mental health centers and	or physically handicapped
clinics	Nursing homes
Public housing associations	Public welfare agencies
Public and private school	Recreation agencies
systems	Social service departments in
Senior citizen programs	hospitals
Voluntary family service	Law enforcement agencies
agencies	Prisons and jails

Since the practicum or work experience component of a human services program is so important for the preparation of competent graduates, there are two issues related to education that need to be dealt with: the granting of academic credit for the practicum, and the closely related issue of granting academic credit for independent work experience and other life experience.

In terms of academic credit for the practicum, it should be clear that incidental work experience, inservice training, and on-the-job training are not in themselves the equivalent of a structured and supervised practicum. These are usually somewhat piecemeal approaches to learning with specific and immediate objectives oriented to the needs of the single agency. If, however, work experience, inservice education, and on-the-job training are structured and implemented cooperatively by the human service agency and the college in such a way that principles and practice are integrated and the broad implications of such an integration are developed within the agency setting, then work experience, inservice, and on-the-job training become much more significant and should qualify for academic credit.

In terms of how life experiences relate to human services work as a meaningful or creditable equivalent of a planned educational program, the essential problem is the translation of an infinite variety of life experiences into some standardized system where the "meaningfulness" of the life experience can be equated to the educational program. The disadvantaged person from the ghetto has certainly had more first-hand experiences with social work agencies than the middle-class suburbanite, but even so, this is not enough. Swift observes that "it is the individual's ability to apply and expand upon the learning experiences he has been exposed to, rather than the mere experiencing them, that is important" (1971, p. 47). Thus it should be clear that academic credit *is not and should not* be given for work experience, even with inservice and on-the-job training, or for life experiences per se. It is the ability to apply appropriately the knowledge and skills obtained from these sources and the ability to make proper judgments that should be the basis for giving academic credit. Evaluation mechanisms for equating life experiences and academic credit cannot rely solely upon written examinations but must involve realistic performance of needed competencies and the effective evaluation of such performance.

Finally, all arrangements for the use of off-campus facilities for practicums should be the subject of written agreements between the college and the employer or agency to avoid such questions as whether the agency will provide supervision of the work experience or will expect college faculty to oversee students in the agency's facility and what the expected balance for the student between work and learning during the field experience will be. Particularly in the public and human services and allied health, these agreements should be drawn up with the advice of a competent attorney in order to minimize the chances of litigation.

Since practicums with outside agencies are quite common, the problems that often develop in articulating a college program with an agency program deserve attention. Since the practicum is an integral part of the curriculum, the general and specific objectives should be clearly spelled out and clearly understood by all concerned—the student, the agency, and the college faculty supervisor. The risk encountered if this kind of mutual understanding is not reached is that the agency may very well tend to absorb the students into its general work force and assign them activities needed by the agency but only incidentally related to the skills and knowledge that they need to develop for their college program. The work assignments for students may become so routine that further learning is improbable. Preferably the arrangement should provide the student with a series of graded practice opportunities under supervision, with the expectancy that in some exercises there may be failure but that learning can and will occur even through failure.

There is some difference of opinion as to when the practicum should occur in the educational program. It ought to be continuously integrated, but in some programs it may occur early in the training to provide orientation and to test whether or not the individual really has sufficient interest and ability to succeed. Other programs see it as a wrap-up, a grand finale to demonstrate proficiency. Some programs prefer students to have experience in a number of settings; similar to the associate degree nurse training programs, where students are exposed to a variety of experiences in various specialties in different hospitals. If the student population is made up of young people exploring human services occupations as possible choices, sampling a variety of career settings early in one's experience is preferable. Students who are older and already committed to a particular agency may benefit more from mastering a specific job in a single setting.

Because of difficulties in off-campus internships, the integration of classroom learning with practice is often most effectively accomplished where the college administers its own self-contained program in the human services and operates a child-care center, recreation center, senior-citizens' center, or other facility and uses students to help carry out its activities. For instance, a number of community colleges have set up their own child-care centers where they combine student practice opportunities with service to the young children and working mothers of the community and convenient research facilities for the human services faculty. There are a number of advantages, but also some problems, in this kind of self-contained facility. On the plus side, the college-administered facility can insure that the quality and type of program offered, as well as student involvement in all aspects of the program, are under the direct control of the human services faculty and will thus be consistent with what goes on in the classroom. Spin-off from a self-contained child development center includes utilization of the college facility for classes in psychology, education, nursing, and home economics in order to add more realism to classroom experiences in those fields. On the negative side, the self-contained facility is expensive to set up and to staff. The staffing is particularly difficult to justify to governing boards since the permanent positions of a center director, cook, and perhaps other staff are essential. With the needed utilities, outdoor play area, and normally a first-floor location within a college building, the facility itself may be expensive. To offset these expenses the facility may generate some revenue from fees paid by the families whose children use the center. In addition, public support funds available for children of the working poor in inner-city areas can help to offset operational expenses.

Faculty. Recruiting and selecting faculty for any career program is important, since programs aimed at developing job skills require faculty members with qualifications beyond those required of the academic instructor. The professor whose repertoire is pure theory cannot function effectively in them. But the public and human services demand special personal and professional qualifications of their own, because more than mere teaching is involved in them. The internship and work experience play so important a part in these programs that faculty members with an exclusively academic orientation are not viewed favorably by agencies that provide either practicums or permanent jobs. The classroom and the practicum are in effect laboratories where the interaction of student and instructor is an irreplaceable part of the required experiences. The practice of interpersonal skills demands planning, supervision, and careful and continuous evaluation. Much consultation with the student, as well as close coordination with the agency staff members to whom the student has been assigned, are essential.

The teacher is also a counselor, not only in the classroom but also in small group sessions and individually. In contrast to the typical academic instructor whose acquaintance with the student is a fleeting one, probably limited to a classroom situation three times a week, the human services faculty member will seek more-or-less continuous involvement with the student academically and in the practicum and is with the student through the entire program rather than in just one or two class sessions.

Professionals employed by the agencies are a prime source of faculty since most professional staff fairly early in their employment have acquired teaching skills by being involved in staff development, supervision of other employees, and inservice programs. Similarly, in teacher aide programs the classroom teacher, particularly in the elementary grades, has worked with young people as well as parents and colleagues and is often eager to work in the more formalized and prestigious setting of a college program. Traditional degree requirements for practitioners in the human services field insure that practitioners' graduate degrees will be equal to those of most of the faculty members in academic disciplines.

Program Organization. Public and human service programs admittedly create some confusion regarding educational organization in that they represent career-oriented programs with a client-centered base but also with a strong discipline-oriented base in the behavioral sciences. To resolve some of the difficulties of placing these programs in particular academic departments or disciplinary divisions, some colleges have borrowed an idea from the universities and established special centers or institutes for them. The Public Service Institute of the City Colleges of Chicago, for example, was organized as a "super-department" to administer fifty-six special programs for three thousand city, county, state, and federal government employees. Included were not only such programs as law enforcement and child development, easily categorized as public and human services, but also building inspection, executive development, agency supervision, urban planning, employment service, interviewing, neighborhood relocation advising, community health, and environmental control. These other programs obviously drew heavily on other occupational education fields such as business, health, engineering, and industrial management, yet they have been organized and administered in one unit in the belief that effective administration of programs with public agencies was of higher priority as an organizational base than was discipline cohesiveness.

From an institutional standpoint, public and human service programs are commonly developed for a few large employers in the public sector and require more administrative control, more centralization if they are offered in multiunit educational institutions, and closer articulation with the employing agency than is true in the occupational areas of technology and business which were developed primarily to service the heterogeneous needs of the private sector of the American economy.

As examples of centralized administration and control of public and human services programs in large city community college systems, these programs are coordinated by the Chicago City-Wide College which is a unit of the Chicago City Colleges system. The Los Angeles Community College District has proposed a New Dimensions College, which will, if organized according to current plans, coordinate public and human services programs as well as many other programs in the Los Angeles system; Kansas City is initiating Pioneer College, a new unit in its system of community colleges, to accomplish similar goals; and the Coast Community College District in populous Orange County, California, has a similar project in the planning stages. While these innovative "colleges without walls" are not concerned solely with public and human services programs, the need for expansion and careful coordination of such programs has been a strong factor in their conception and establishment.

Guidelines for Planners. As is true of planners in other career clusters, those in public and human services program planning should consider the suggestions about programs and their administration given in Chapter Ten. In addition, they should pay particular attention to these issues:

First, the demography, social structure, and politics of the local urban community or region has such a marked impact on these public and human service programs that knowledge of these characteristics and skill in working within these settings, are imperative.

Second, in determining the present and estimated future demand for workers in these fields, check which public and private agencies are engaged in this work and whether they are on "soft money" or relatively long-term "hard money" funding.

Third, provide for excellent career counseling and advisement prior to enrollment, to assure the emotional maturity and stability of applicants which are required as special competencies of human services workers.

Fourth, reach contractual agreements with agencies for field-work and internship experiences for students, using competent legal counsel in drafting these contracts to minimize the chances of misunderstanding and litigation.

Fifth, set up an annual review system to gather retention and attrition data, placement data, and follow-up career data in order to determine and improve the cost effectiveness of the programs. Avoid the kind of wide-open door concept that permits anyone to enroll in any program, and often results in devastating attrition rates or incompetent graduates.

And sixth, continue to monitor supply and demand factors with extreme care by keeping up to date on city and county budgets, federal revenue sharing funds, tax revenues, and changing needs for public and human services, since in this field more than in most others, *local* supply and demand factors govern planning decisions. The many mature women who choose these programs are usually not geographically mobile.

9 ◙◙◙◙◙◙◙◙◙◙◙◙◙◙◙

Career Potentials
for the Liberal Arts

Some subjects will inculcate better than other subjects those values we recognize as characteristics of a liberal education. . . . engineering drawing, well taught, will open the windows of the mind, but literature or philosophy, equally well taught, will open many more. The more windows opened for the individual the better, for man does not live by bread alone. But he does live by bread.

Francis H. Horn

One of the tragedies of the 1970s has been the ever-growing discrepancy between the numbers of college graduates and the numbers of jobs in the economy in which these graduates can use their college-level talents and knowledge. The core of this problem is the employment plight of four-year college graduates in the liberal arts and the even more hopeless job prospects of two-year college graduates in liberal arts and general studies. Most of these young people would probably agree that man does not live by bread alone, but unfortunately far too many of them are finding that their liberal arts degrees bring in little bread at all. This chapter takes a positive view of the liberal arts and identifies ways in which both liberal arts colleges and comprehensive two-year colleges can

227

inject an economic dimension or career potential into their liberal arts degree programs while retaining a strong disciplinary or academic studies base.

Loosely defined, the liberal arts include all the physical sciences, biological sciences, social sciences, mathematics, humanities, communications arts, and creative and performing arts. They are the subjects that, in Francis Horn's phrase, seek above all to open the windows of the mind. In both 1975 and 1976, among those freshmen who entered college having already decided on a major, over 30 percent planned to specialize in these subjects (Astin, King, and Richardson, 1976, p. 44; "Characteristics and Attitudes . . .," *Chronicle of Higher Education*, January 10, 1977, pp. 12–13). Moreover, as recently as 1973–1974—the latest year for which earned degree data are available—45 percent of all the nation's undergraduate certificates and degrees were awarded in the liberal arts. As Table 15 indicates, fully 47 percent of students at both the associate-degree and baccalaureate-degree levels specialized in these academic subjects rather than in career-oriented fields. In other words, some 620,000 young people left college in 1974 clutching newly awarded diplomas and credentials with impressive seals— but with little useful currency in the job market.

Developing the Economic Dimension

It is obvious to nearly everyone today that, regardless of the values inherent in college study of the liberal arts (and we hold these values in high esteem), the *economic* value of a liberal arts degree has eroded alarmingly in the past decade. Unlike the period from 1960 to 1972, for which studies indicate ready employment at satisfying jobs for baccalaureate graduates in the liberal arts (CPC Foundation, 1975), the current decade will be disappointing with regard to all three of the factors pertinent to job satisfaction— sheer job availability (*any* job), salary level, and job "suitability."

In Chapter One we discussed the soft job market for liberal arts graduates in some detail, and the facts do not need to be repeated here. They can be summarized, however, by the value of different majors as viewed by employers and as reported by Robert F. Herrick (Southern Regional Education Board, 1974, p. 13), the

Table 15. Certificates and Degrees Awarded in Liberal Arts and Occupational Fields, 1973–1974.

	Arts and Sciences		Occupations		Total	
	Number	Percent	Number	Percent	Number	Percent
Certificates (Less than Two-Year)	794	1.3%	58,970	98.7%	59,764	100.0%
Associate Degrees (Two-Year)	165,520	47.4	181,653	52.3	347,173	100.0
Other Two- or Three-Year Formal Recognition	2,885	12.7	19,885	87.3	22,770	100.0
Bachelor's Degrees (Four- or Five-Year)	453,607	47.7	500,769	52.5	954,376	100.0
Total	622,806	45.0	761,277	55.0	1,384,083	100.0

Source: National Center for Educational Statistics (1976a, 1976b).

executive director of the College Placement Council (CPC), on the basis of a CPC survey: "Engineering is rated as being a strong positive influence on the decision to hire. . . . A major in technology parallels the ratings for engineering. . . . Business receives a strong positive rating from almost all groups. . . . Computer science received positive ratings as did mathematics. The least desirable majors are fine arts, humanities, education, ethnic studies, and social science."

A more recent survey for the CPC Foundation of some 4,138 college graduates who had been freshmen in 1961 reveals that more of them—45 percent—would in retrospect recommend business administration courses as being beneficial than any other courses, with runners-up being courses in English (32 percent), psychology (31 percent), economics (28 percent), and accounting (27 percent) (Bisconti and Solmon, 1976, p. 37). This same study indicates that more than half of these 1960s graduates are in career fields that they had not planned on while in college.

In response to market forces, students by the mid-1970s had begun to turn away from the liberal arts into career-oriented programs in business, allied health, and public and human service occupations. But despite this swing to career-oriented studies (Carnegie Commission on Higher Education, 1973a), there are still thousands of young people in community colleges, liberal arts colleges, and universities whose prospects for satisfying careers after graduation are very discouraging. This large block of academically capable youth constitutes a potential national resource of great promise. But many of its members are likely to become bitter, discouraged, and angry critics of society; others will filter into jobs of little challenge to their talents; and a few may renounce work altogether and make a career of being on public welfare.

There are several options for liberal arts graduates, some of which are listed here. One possibility is to go on with schooling and seek an advanced graduate or professional degree. This option, of course, has its limitations. Its cost is prohibitive for many students; only the top scholars are accepted for Ph.D. and professional school study; many graduate schools are restricting new enrollments because of limited job prospects for their graduates; and in many liberal arts fields an advanced degree does not enhance job possibilities appreciably.

A second option after getting a degree in the liberal arts is to enroll in an occupational degree program—for example, by going to a community or technical college and preparing for a career at the paraprofessional or technical level, with the expectation of upward occupational mobility later.

A third alternative is to take any job at any level available with a big company and "work up." If the adaptive values ascribed to liberal learning are important, promotion may be relatively rapid. This option is automatically rejected by many liberal arts graduates, however.

In an attempt to make higher education more responsive to the career needs of students many colleges are seeking ways to integrate liberal arts and career education, moving away from the sharp divisions of the past. For several decades, forward looking career educators have recognized the values inherent in liberal learning and in both baccalaureate and associate degree career-oriented curriculums have allocated about one fourth of the total credit hours to liberal arts or general studies courses. Only recently, however, have liberal arts traditionalists and humanists reluctantly begun to admit that higher education does indeed have a vocational purpose and to entertain the idea that perhaps one fourth of every liberal arts program should consist of courses or credits in practical career-oriented fields. Sidney Marland, who as U.S. Commissioner of Education in the early 1970s did more than anyone to define, popularize, and operationalize career education, did so out of a humanistic background as a former teacher of English for many years. He has warned his fellow humanities professors (1973b, p. xiii): "Look around. Our beleaguered castle is not really being assaulted by the champions of other disciplines called occupational. They are not attacking our fortress at all, just detouring around it, because so many of them, including students, don't think we guard anything worth taking. If we in the humanities continue to regard more 'practical' people as our enemies, and if we continue to be theirs—it will be our own fault."

With his interest in both the liberal arts and career education,

Marland has exhorted humanists and "practical" people to coop-erate—to replace enmity with good will and, as we suggested in Chapter One, dichotomy with dialogue. Modern humanists need to recognize the importance of work for men and women in our society, and "practical" people need to reexamine the idea that the humanities and the liberal arts are "useless" subjects. Just as there is some question as to whether only the liberal arts can teach one how to live, there is also some question about the premise that they have no use in making a living. Even in these troublesome years of a soft market for liberal arts graduates, there is evidence that such programs do indeed lead to satisfying careers for some college graduates. The problem is not one of no marketability at all but rather one of limited marketability for liberal arts degrees.

A two-pronged attack on this problem is required. First, lib-eral arts students should be able to include a carefully selected set of courses with recognized employment potential in their degree programs. And second, all colleges should provide a career ad-visement and development program, featuring career counseling, faculty advisement, internships, work experience, field trips, and an aggressive placement office. The first several sections of this chapter consider the first of these two strategies at the two-year level and then the four-year level. Then the chapter turns to career advisement and development beyond degree programs.

In terms of the first strategy, a judicious selection of career-oriented courses by liberal arts students—preferably enough to constitute a "minor"—can enhance their employability a great deal. As Herrick of the College Placement Council says in a publication entitled *Integrating Career Development on the Campus* (Southern Re-gional Education Board, 1974, p. 14): "This bears out what many career planning and placement directors have believed for a long time—that far from abandoning liberal arts traditions in a sell-out to vocationalism . . ., all that is required to enhance employability is the inclusion of subject matter from accessible (*presumably career-oriented*) curricula. And given the latitude of liberal arts electives, this should pose no problem." In the early 1970s, the U.S. Office of Education mapped the entire terrain of career options and class-ified it in fifteen clusters or families of occupations, one of which, lo and behold, turned out to be the arts and humanities. Here was recognition that among the 23,000 occupational possibilities available in the United States, a career group of some size is directly related to the arts and humanitistic disciplines. This cluster of arts and humanities careers was fleshed out in considerable detail in the early 1970s issues of the *Occupational Outlook Handbook* of the U.S. Department of Labor's Bureau of Labor Statistics. The 1976–77 *Handbook* identifies thirteen clusters to cover the world of work, of which one is identified as Art, Design, and Communications-Related Occupations.* The focus of this occupational area is centered in creativity and the ability to communicate ideas. Subcategories include (1) the performing arts, with such specific job titles as actor, dancer, singer, and musician; (2) the design occupations, embracing commercial art, architectural design, urban planning, floral design, advertising design, photography, and landscape design; and (3) the communications-related careers covering such workers as interpreters, reporters, journalists, photographers, and technical writers.

Career Outlets for Two-Year College Liberal Arts Programs

Consider career possibilities for two-year college graduates first in the humanities and then in the social sciences, mathematics, and the physical and biological sciences.

Humanities. Occupational possibilities in the humanities have long been recognized by some four-year colleges, as witness those with conservatory-quality programs in the performing arts and specialized programs in the fine and applied arts and the design occupations—essentially the counterparts of professional programs in business, social work, engineering, or education. Now, two-year colleges are finally beginning to identify career opportunities at the middle manpower or semiprofessional level for their arts students and to provide occupationally oriented programs in these fields. If one traces the evolution of occupational programs

*The other twelve are Industrial Production and Related Occupations, Office Occupations, Service Occupations, Education and Related Occupations, Sales Occupations, Construction Occupations, Occupations in Transportation Activities, Scientific and Technical Occupations, Mechanics and Repairers, Health Occupations, Social Scientists, and Social Service Occupations (U.S. Department of Labor, 1976, pp. ix–xii).

in community colleges from the 1950s, it is clear that the first programs were in the business and secretarial field and in the engineering and industrial field. In the 1960s, these programs were supplemented by health career programs led by associate degree curriculums in nursing. About the same time, the human service programs in such fields as child care and law enforcement emerged. But the creative and performing arts—a label growing in popularity among community colleges—were not recognized in the career education upsurge in community colleges until the late 1960s. And it was only very recently that the first serious inquiry into the relationship of the humanities to the role and mission of the two-year college was undertaken (Cohen, 1975).

There are, of course, good and sufficient reasons for this late recognition. Humanities enrollments were comparatively small in most two-year colleges. Many of the subprofessional fields in the creative and performing arts were subsumed under other categories, with commercial art, for example, commonly identified with business offerings. Courses in foreign language, music, art, and speech and drama traditionally had been identified as general education, and it was so difficult to conceive of them in any other role that their career possibilities were either unrecognized or deemphasized; while others such as journalism and theater were deeply entrenched within baccalaureate-oriented transfer programs. Federal agencies excluded liberal arts offerings from occupational categorization as well as from occupational funding. Thus vocational funds under the National Defense Education Act of 1958 and the 1963 Vocational Education Act and its 1968 Amendments were not available to underwrite programs in the humanities, social studies, or arts in any of the approved curriculums then identified as "technical education." Even the very titles used by the Bureau of the Census and the Department of Labor to categorize occupational groups militated against any recognition of the creative and performing arts or the humanities as careers. Where within "Professional and Technical Workers, Managers, Officials, Proprietors, Clerical and Sales Workers, Craftsmen, Operatives, Service Workers, and Farm and Non-Farm Laborers" would the humanities or the creative and performing arts find a palatable identification?

As a consequence, these fields have lagged behind others in developing enough cohesiveness and substance to be identified as a separate area for two-year college career education planning and implementation. A slow change is beginning, however. The following fields are currently recognized as career programs in some community colleges, and a modest number of career openings exist in some regions of the country for persons with the associate degree and demonstrated talent in these fields.

Commercial art provides students with the professional competence needed for employment in such fields as advertising design, interior design, display, graphic design, floral design, and technical illustration. The program leads to employment as a freelance artist or with advertising agencies, department stores, or studios as apprentice or trainee in design, production, and layout.

Communications arts provides the student with a broad background in visual and audio communications—photography, graphics, radio, and television—and leads to employment in advertising, marketing, and audiovisual fields as a trainee, apprentice, or assistant to professional personnel.

Foreign language provides basic and specialized language training and leads to employment in government positions here and abroad, in library work, translating, tour guiding, international trade and foreign industry (when combined with business) and in social agencies dealing with non-English-speaking minority groups. A number of two-year colleges, such as Kirkwood Community College in Cedar Rapids, Iowa, offer associate degree programs in international trade.

Career journalism provides such basic communications skills as reporting, layout, photography, creative writing, and business skills, leading to employment with community newspapers and radio stations, with publishers as a writer or photographer, with professional journalists as an assistant, or to free-lance writing or photography. More than fifty two-year colleges offer "journalism technology" or a similar program under another name, and placement of the graduates is reported to be good in most areas.

Commercial music provides skills in arranging, composing, and performing commercial music and leads to employment as a professional performing musician, private music teacher, arranger for musicians, music publishing house employee, or music store management trainee.

Radio and TV broadcasting provides basic skills in electronic communications, leading to employment as a technician in producing radio and television programs and commercials; as an assistant to engineers and cameramen; or as a trainee in writing, scheduling, or sales.

Theater technology provides students with the technical skills of theater production and leads to employment as set builder, apprentice set painter or stage designer, assistant to costume or make-up designer, model maker, light and sound technician, or assistant to the stage manager.

The job outlook for associate degree graduates in all of these creative and performing arts fields is currently highly competitive. There is always room at the top for persons with real talent and well-developed skills, but job prospects are not good for persons of only modest or average achievement and talent.

When the humanities, including the creative and performing arts, are added to the four occupational clusters discussed in the four previous chapters—business, engineering and industrial technologies, allied health, and the public and human services—then the full spectrum of human knowledge is reasonably well encompassed within five major divisions of an institution.

These five divisions can provide a manageable organizational structure for postsecondary education—a structure that should prove acceptable to colleges and universities since it follows closely the broad divisions of academic disciplines. It permits if not encourages the integration of baccalaureate and occupational programs along common subject-matter lines, thereby promoting unity that increasingly makes sense in institutional operations. With it, one cannot readily separate the theoretical from the applied, and under the general theme that career education embraces all education, the applied becomes paramount and, in contrast to traditional academic organization, the theoretical or cognitive becomes supportive.

Social Studies. Associate degree programs in history, political science, sociology, or economics have very little career potential by themselves, although combinations with business management, urban planning, or human services programs such as social worker aide can increase job prospects. The plethora of associate degree programs designed to increase "awareness," such as Black studies, Chicano studies, environmental studies, and women's studies have had notably poor career potential.

Mathematics and the Sciences. For decades it appeared that there were no career outlets for less-than-baccalaureate programs in mathematics or the natural sciences. To be sure, even today, jobs for associate degree graduates in these fields are limited in number, and they often require the level of ability and insight exhibited by persons in baccalaureate degree programs. Such jobs as are available are frequently considered as "stop-out-and-work" interludes on the career ladder to eventual professional status with a baccalaureate or advanced degree.

Mathematics-based programs that reportedly are successful in placing small numbers of graduates at the associate degree level, despite the quite limited career opportunities, include the following.

Banking and finance requires competency in mathematics through college algebra, mathematics of finance, statistics, and computer science, and prepares for entry (assistant) jobs in banks and credit/loan offices and in general business and industry where statistics and computer analysis are important. The mathematics major should include computer science and, as electives, economics and introduction to accounting.

Insurance, a two-year mathematics program which includes statistics, computer science, and elementary actuarial training, with accounting and insurance courses as electives, prepares for entry jobs with insurance company home offices or serves as a basis for further courses preparing for insurance salesman and eventually agent. Once again, the job market is highly competitive, and only those persons with proven mathematics ability should be encouraged to elect such a program.

Physical and Biological Sciences. In the physical science field, many middle manpower jobs are now being filled by graduates of career-oriented baccalaureate programs. There is, however, a small potential job market for associate-degree graduates in physics, chemistry, and earth sciences as science research assistants, pilot plant assistants, geophysical exploration assistants, and energy research laboratory assistants. If the federal government initiates an all-out energy development program at the level of the space program of the 1960s, job prospects for these graduates will improve remarkably. It hardly need be said, however, that the best option for most such persons is to continue on for a baccalaureate degree.

Physical science technician programs prepare specialists in one field—for example, physics, chemistry, or the earth sciences—and may lead to a job as science laboratory technician, geophysical technician, or, sometimes, engineering aide. Additional specialties will no doubt open up if energy research and development begins in earnest. (But see the discussion of discipline orientation versus job orientation on pages 269–273.) Solar, wind, geothermal, tidal, coal, nuclear, and other energy resource activities may eventually provide many middle manpower jobs for associate degree graduates, but our earlier warning about ·supposed social *need* versus actual job *demand* bears repetition here.

Biological sciences technician programs encompass many specialties requiring a good basis in the biological sciences. Examples of career outlets for associate degree graduates are such fields as forestry technology, fisheries technology, wild life management, marine technology, environmental technology, agriculture and foods technology, dietetics, and biology laboratory research. Since much of biological science research is now highly quantitative, mathematics and data processing skills are important. Once more, only students of relatively high academic ability are likely to succeed, and for the most part these may be persons who will eventually go on to the baccalaureate degree. Thus the importance of career laddering two-year and four-year programs should be kept in mind.

The career potential for associate degree graduates in the liberal arts fields discussed in the foregoing paragraphs is not one of unrelieved gloom, but neither is it one that shows considerable promise. As noted above, only very academically capable students will be successful in these two-year liberal arts programs, and these of course are the very students who are most likely to proceed on to the baccalaureate degree rather than seek permanent employment at the associate degree level. From a career counseling and educational advisement point of view, it is advisable for these students to arrive at a decision about their degree plans by the end of the freshman year so that those who are leaning toward employment rather than transfer to a four-year college can include employment-oriented courses and work-experience or internship assignments in their sophomore year schedules.

Career Prospects for Liberal Arts Baccalaureate Graduates

Four-year colleges must similarly build employability into their liberal arts programs, including occupationally-oriented options, electives, and off-campus experiences. Briefly listed below are some career dimensions that some liberal arts colleges are recommending, or in some cases, requiring, of students in order to increase their career options.

Social Science Majors. Courses and seminars in such fields as business, technology, economics (a desirable course for any student in any major, because of the importance of understanding elementary economic principles), public administration, statistics, urban affairs, labor relations, demography, or computer science will aid employability as will summer job experience in *any* field in order to learn about work.

Science Majors. Seminars and courses in environmental improvement, energy resources development, statistics, and computer science and work experience in laboratories, industry, conservation agencies, or national parks are good background.

Mathematics Majors. Electives or requirements in computer science, actuarial science, statistics, mathematics of finance, accounting, and investments are valuable, as are summer jobs with insurance companies, banks and computer companies.

Humanities and Language Majors. For such fields as history, philosophy, and classical languages, there is little to suggest. But students majoring in modern languages would be well-advised to include courses and seminars in business, finance, international trade, and tourism. Fluency in the language is essential. Summer jobs with import/export companies where the language can be used in the work situation can be helpful.

Fine Arts and Performing Arts Majors. These are exceptionally difficult fields for careers unless one is willing to "go commercial" to assure a living. Many artists, for example, operate pottery shops, art galleries, arts and crafts shops, and hobby shops or teach art in schools, community centers, or YMCAs. Dance and drama majors can often develop satisfying careers in similar activities, even in small towns, as can musicians by running a music shop, teaching, or in the maintenance, tuning, and repair of instruments. The obvious career goal for these majors is, of course, creative performance, but this requires a capability that, unfortunately, only a few possess and a "product" that, equally unfortunately, only a limited number of people are willing to buy at a price that can support the artist or that the artist thinks is adequate.

Cooperation With Two-Year Colleges. If liberal arts colleges cannot offer these courses and experiences for their liberal arts students themselves, they and their students should examine another option carefully: the alternative of using career-oriented courses and skills training experiences at nearby community colleges, technical colleges, and area vocational-technical schools. Not many liberal arts colleges today are geographically isolated. Within a few miles of most of them, one or more two-year colleges offer a broad selection of occupational- and skill-oriented courses—mostly open-door, without prerequisites, and usually at tuition rates not exceeding $10 to $20 per credit hour. The opportunities for fruitful cooperation between these two types of college within easy commuting distance are endless, and articulation efforts between them, directed toward sharing their educational resources for their students, are long overdue. As more and more liberal arts colleges add a career dimension to their degree programs, the best possible way to do so may be to arrange to grant credit toward their baccalaureate degrees for career-oriented or skill development courses taken at nearby two-year colleges, rather than to attempt to initiate these same courses themselves, particularly if suitable specialized facilities and equipment or occupationally qualified faculty are lacking at the four-year college. The opportunities possible with such a course of action are limited only by the interest and imagination of college officials and by their desire that liberal arts students add a career potential to their degrees. The possibilities of positive outcomes are as exciting as the prospects of doing nothing are gloomy.

Indeed, if all colleges—two-year as well as four-year—would begin now to offer all their liberal arts students the option of adding an economic dimension to their programs, perhaps the specter of the unemployed liberal arts graduate would rapidly fade away. Underemployment might still be a problem, but time would remedy that also for those with demonstrated potential.

Cooperative Education for Liberal Arts Students

On other pages, we have emphasized the importance of cooperative education for college students in career-oriented curriculums. But colleges should put much greater emphasis on work opportunities for all their students. For many academically minded youth, just learning about work—any kind of work—is an important factor in their development. But work experience is especially important for students in the humanities and the arts and sciences, particularly since they can take few, if any, practical courses on campus. They should work at summer jobs or part-time jobs during the college year or, better still, take off an entire year for full-time employment in a job related to their major.

Colleges can and should expand their placement and cooperative education services to arrange for work experiences for students in all fields—not just those considered to be "occupational"—and to see that these off-campus experiences are coordinated with on-campus programs (Knowles, 1972). Tyler (in Knowles, 1972, p. 20) cites the particular value of such cooperative work-study programs to liberal arts students in these words: "Many liberal arts students, unsure of their vocational goals, specifically use cooperative education to explore and realistically test different career possibilities. They will first examine, with the help of their cooperative coordinator, their interests, areas of success and difficulty, and other conditions affecting career choice. Based upon this knowledge they will decide upon a job for the next cooperative period. Upon their return to school they and their coordinator will assess the job and its implications for a future career. If it seems to have potential, it will be followed up on the next cooperative term; if not, the information gained will be used to explore further."

Antioch College, Northeastern University, the University of Cincinnati, and the University of Michigan (Dearborn) are just a few examples of four-year colleges and universities that have pioneered in cooperative education. Cooperative education is popular in community and junior colleges also, among them Orange Coast College and the College of San Mateo in California, Alice Lloyd and Lees junior colleges in Kentucky, Sinclair Community College in Dayton, Ohio, Manhattan Community College in New York City, and Mohawk Valley Community College in Utica, New York. In 1971, Knowles (1972) compiled a list of 225 universities, four-year and two-year colleges, and postsecondary technical schools offering cooperative education programs on 235 different campuses. By 1975 the number with cooperative programs had grown to an estimated thousand, (U.S. Dept. of Health, Education and Welfare, 1975, p. 2) as more and more institutions recognized the importance of work experience in the total education of students.

Promotion and exchange of information about cooperative education in colleges is enhanced by the National Commission for Cooperative Education and the Cooperative Education Association, the latter being the national professional organization for persons engaged in any phase of cooperative education. Its national offices are at Drexel University in Philadelphia. Regional associations, of which the Midwest Cooperative Education Association with offices at the University of Detroit is a good example, sponsor workshops, conferences, and special programs for employers, college officials, and students in their respective regions. Educators in the liberal arts who are concerned about improving career opportunities for their students can gain much assistance from such groups.

Providing the Link Between Education and Work

Beyond the curricular adjustments and cooperative education programs mentioned on previous pages, some liberal arts colleges are attempting to add a career dimension to their baccalaureate programs through career counseling and development. For example, Alma College in Michigan is a liberal arts college with a strong commitment to the values that humanists and academicians generally ascribe to the study of the arts and sciences. But concerned about career preparation as well as about liberal arts education, Alma's Advising, Counseling and Career Development Center initiated *The Alma College Career Preparation Program* in the mid-1970s as "a comprehensive four-year plan, totally integrated within the College's liberal arts curriculum" and "designed to maintain and strengthen the traditional liberal arts program while aiding students in developing a variety of skills that will better prepare them to face the job market successfully" (*Alma College Career Preparation Program,* 1976). The Career Preparation Program is offered as an option to every freshman during orientation. Those who elect to participate are programmed into a continuing schedule of activities throughout the four years, including some or all of the following: aptitude and interest testing, career information workshops, career counseling, career seminars with professionals in the field, field trips to job sites, on-campus practicums, summer and part-time employment, job search and interview preparation, specialized career-related courses either at Alma or at other colleges, preparation of a personal career development plan, development of an understanding of the American economy and of the world of work, and development of entry-level skills and knowledge in at least one work role. The program is largely informational and exploratory during the freshman and sophomore years, although summer employment is urged from the outset. Actual career planning, preparation, and implementation take place during the upper division years to "maximize opportunities for satisfactory employment or graduate school placement."

Realizing that the program could founder on the shoals of faculty indifference and resistance, Alma strives for maximum faculty involvement. As an integral part of the total program there is a continuing series of activities for faculty, including workshops; field trips; seminars; opportunities for relationships with business and industry and the professions; and encouragement of faculty to participate as consultants on social, industrial, business, or professional problems of the region.

Oberlin College in Ohio features an "Alumni Career Counseling Program," in which alumni from a broad range of professional, business, and government careers participate in career advisement and counseling for undergraduate students. A joint effort of the Alumni Association and the Oberlin College Office of Career Development and Placement, the program is not a placement activity as such. Instead, it is intended to get Oberlin's undergraduates thinking about careers in time to consider program and course changes or work experiences that will enhance their chances of employment on graduation. Its activities can vary from an alumnus merely talking with a student for an hour or two, to a student visiting the host's office or place of work for a day of observation and participation, and to possible further contacts for the student to study career opportunities in depth in a variety of locations with different companies or agencies. In some cases, arrangements for an internship or for summer employment may result.

Freshmen and sophomores are especially encouraged to participate in the Oberlin program. They can make arrangements through the Office of Career Development and Placement to meet with alumni during semester breaks, summer vacations, weekends, or any other mutually agreeable time. Six urban areas—Boston, Chicago, Cleveland, the District of Columbia, New York City, and the Westchester, New York-Southern Connecticut region—are currently active program centers coordinated by the Oberlin alumni clubs in each area.

Examples of the more than 400 alumni who have participated in the Oberlin program since its origin in 1975 include an orthodontist who as an undergraduate was a philosophy major, a music major who is now an electronics and electrical engineer, a college administrator who formerly was a technician in a cancer research laboratory, and a vice president of a women's sportswear company who majored in French and art history and who is interested in discussing "how to salvage a liberal arts education" (*Oberlin Alumni Career Counseling*, 1975, p. 12).

Pepperdine University in Southern California has implemented a model curriculum including a "career exploration" course for humanities majors; a career-oriented minor in fields like business, international trade, and public service; the option of more specifically career-oriented courses in traditional humanities fields; an internship experience during the final two years of college; and a "job strategies workshop" in the senior year. Conscious of career development, Pepperdine has surveyed what other liberal arts colleges are doing to open up more career options for their graduates and has published the results in a monograph entitled *Career Options in the Humanities* (Goyne, 1975), from which the following three other examples are abstracted.

Coe College in Cedar Rapids, Iowa, has a career counseling program combined with a cooperative work experience program for liberal arts and humanities students. Upon receiving a successful evaluation, academic credit toward graduation is granted for work experience. Lehigh University in Bethlehem, Pennsylvania, features a business minor of thirty-seven semester credits to complement most of its arts, science, and humanities majors. And in Los Angeles, the University of Southern California has developed a joint Spanish and urban studies undergraduate major through the cooperative efforts of its Department of Spanish and Portuguese and its Center for Urban Affairs that prepares graduates for careers in urban affairs in cities where the Spanish language and culture are important.

In 1974, the Southern Regional Education Board sponsored a workshop for colleges in the South to share ideas about improving the career potential and employment prospects for arts and science graduates and summarized the findings in *Integrating Career Development on the Campus* (Southern Regional Education Board, 1974). At that workshop, the Academic and Career Advising Program at the University of North Florida was highlighted as a model for career advisement and development worth emulation by other institutions (pp. 19–21).

Other institutions that report current career enhancement projects designed to ease the dilemma of the liberal arts graduate include Chatham College, DePauw University, The Evergreen State College, Georgetown University, Grinnell College, the State University of New York at Binghamton (in cooperation with Broome Community College), and Warner Pacific College.

Besides such institutions concerned with career development for liberal arts students, several educational organizations are now also involved. In addition to its 1974 workshop mentioned above, the Southern Regional Education Board has devoted an issue of its newsletter, *Regional Spotlight,* to the topic (Southern Regional

Education Board, 1975). The American Association for Higher Education devoted its 1977 National Conference on Higher Education to issues of work and education. And at the American Association for Higher Education, its NEXUS service can provide almost overnight information about innovative programs in career advisement and education as well as other areas.

All in all, liberal arts colleges as well as educational associations are at last beginning to provide better links between the liberal arts and the world of work and ensure that liberal arts students gain before graduation the skills they will need for worthwhile employment.

Conclusion

In selling universal higher education and "the learning society" during the 1960s and 1970s, we continually hammered away at the theme of upward economic mobility as the goal of education instead of emphasizing the intellectual and cultural values of college. We sold a good idea but for the wrong reasons. We cranked up the spring of higher education notch after notch, and now that it is wound up tight, the ratchet does not allow backing off to a more tenable position. The potential energy in the mechanism often is not transmitted to society in beneficial ways but instead whips out at it in counterproductive ways. The millions of students that we asked for have come to college and now they expect an economic return from their attendance, seemingly no matter what they study.

The dedicated humanist, the "true believer" in the liberal arts, the antimaterialist, the traditionalist—all will chafe under the suggestion that colleges have an obligation to prepare their students for economic success. But it must be remembered that of the between 650 and 700 colleges in the United States to which the term *liberal arts college* is applied because they either stress or claim to stress the humanities, the arts, and the sciences, most have been heavily engaged in vocational education for decades—teacher training being the predominant field, with preprofessional education for later graduate study running a close second and with home economics, nursing, business, international trade, music and the performing arts, and even vocational agriculture having found their way into the degree programs of many of them over the years (Mayhew, 1974). Only recently, as teacher education has suffered drastic enrollment losses, have liberal arts colleges of necessity turned to still other programs and devices to establish links between their liberal arts programs and the employment market. The world and society are changing and therefore education must change as well.

Lynn White, Jr., the famed historian of technology, makes a point well worth considering by liberal arts traditionalists (1966, p. 224). "The new world in which we live is so unlike the past, even the past that is close to us, that in proportion that we are saturated with the Western cultural tradition we are incapacitated for looking clearly at our actual situation and thinking constructively about it. The better we are educated, the more we are fitted to live in a world which no longer exists." Humanists may maintain that, instead of including an economic dimension in the liberal arts students' programs in order to prepare students for society *as it is,* society in the form of industry, business, and other employers should adjust to students *as they are.* They cite the experience of the 1900–1965 era, in which liberal arts graduates found ready employment and, on balance, were successful in the economy without an economic dimension built into their education. But they may not realize that in the job seeker's "seller's market" of those decades, a liberal arts graduate was the "best buy" available to the employer. Now such degree holders are not necessarily the best buy because thousands of graduates of career programs are on the job market, already in possession of work-related competencies. Most liberal arts graduates, even in the halcyon days, did not make their living from what they studied in college, anyway. They were hired for their assumed potential, and then once on the job and at the employer's expense, they learned the skills and competencies that later made them valuable to the firm. Today, in a "buyer's market" for talent and in an era of high salaries, high costs, high taxes, and often low profits, employers are demanding not only potential for future growth but also at least some competence for present productivity. Such a demand merely represents good, prudent business sense, and it is a reality that liberal arts graduates will have to face—probably for a long time.

This reality is not cause for gloom. Only those few who believe that the world owes intellectuals a living will think it so. Other advocates of the liberal arts will say with us to today's college youth: Study the liberal arts; there is a joy in knowing them for their own sake; they do open windows of the mind; they do add quality to life. But give your liberal arts program an economic dimension; find out about the world of work and how you can become a part of it; and prepare for your entry into it—for work is perhaps the most satisfying of human endeavors.

The liberal arts are indeed the arts for the free man and woman. But there is no freedom without economic freedom. One is not free who depends on the charity of others or of government for a living. One cannot enhance the quality of life without first enhancing the quality of one's livelihood.

III

Planning,
Finance,
and Governance

10 ▣ ▣ ▣ ▣ ▣ ▣ ▣ ▣ ▣ ▣ ▣ ▣ ▣

Planning and Operating Successful Programs

Efficiency is doing things right; effectiveness is doing the right things.

Anonymous

There is a regrettable tendency in America today to view process as product. Educators, the general public, and even some employers are all victims of the "process syndrome." Students are notorious advocates of process rather than product, as anyone can testify who listens to their plans for "getting these courses out of the way," "getting thirty credits in my major," or "getting my degree." Students and people generally speak of "getting an education" as if it were something that could be bought at a supermarket by waiting in line long enough and then paying the bill. Only infrequently is the emphasis put on learning. Aristotle's ancient admonition that "learning is accompanied by pain" seems to be universally accepted, and since pain is something to avoid, we have finessed the problem by substituting inputs for outputs, course credits for learning, and the degree for knowledge and competence.

New and popular entries in the vocabulary of higher education are such terms as "the educational delivery system," and students as "consumers of education." If such phrases were used only by the lay public or by cost-oriented legislators, the lapse could perhaps be understood or at least forgiven, but the alacrity with which college and university educators have appropriated such nonsense is most disturbing. How, by any stretch of the imagination, can education be *delivered*? How is it possible to *consume* education? And if it could be delivered, garnished with A's and B's, does one consume it on the premises, carry it home for later consumption, or just keep it in the fancy package to impress others?

Education cannot be delivered; it must be sought after, attained by painstaking effort, synthesized by years of personal cognitive action. Neither can learning be consumed; on the contrary, learning eagerly sought consumes the learner and creates a different person.

This infatuation of American education with process rather than product is pervasive enough to be a matter of grave concern not only to education but also to the nation. Complex, finely-tuned, technological societies cannot prosper when their schools and colleges are more concerned with custodial care of students than with achievement and when the credentials of their citizens overstate their capabilities. As a nation we have vitally important work to do, and we will not get the job done with workers whose diplomas and degrees are a facade behind which ignorance and ineptitude dwell.

Career education should reject out of hand the idea that process is product or that education can be delivered and consumed. Degrees and credits are useful parameters of educational progress, and it is not suggested that they be abolished, but they must be based on an honest appraisal of the knowledge and capabilities of those who claim them, rather than merely being evidence of the rites of passage. And while the learning process is important and continues to deserve serious attention, an emphasis on process alone is not enough. Career education must emphasize equally the results of learning—knowledge, skills, abilities, accomplishment. We have traditionally referred to these concepts in terms of "excellence," "quality," and "standards" of attainment. But as these output terms have become unfashionable of late, the educational lexicon has incorporated a whole host of new input terms that are both a reflection and a confirmation of the "process-is-product" malaise. "Noncompetitive" learning, "nonpunitive" grading, "open-door" courses, and "humaneness" in education, often are euphemisms for skidding standards of achievement. The process may be pleasant, but the product is shoddy. "Delivery" may be on time, in a nicely wrapped package, but the contents have no resale value.

Recently there has been increasing recognition of the inadequacy of the "process" approach to education and a renewed interest in excellence, achievement and performance. The almost universal low esteem of the high school diploma as a mere statement of attendance, the alarming decline of scores on nationally administered academic aptitude tests, evidence from community colleges that nearly three fourths of all freshmen enrolled in English and mathematics courses in the late 1960s were in courses of "noncollege" level (Roueche, 1968), and the growing realization among college and university professors that many of their graduate students cannot write acceptable prose—all of these point to the failure of educational policies dictated by permissiveness and based on process theory. Recent demands for accountability, performance objectives, and competency-based learning systems by state legislatures, state boards of education, and taxpayer and employer groups are clear indications that stockholders in the enterprise of education are demanding better dividends than they have been receiving in recent decades. Career education should be in the lead as we recognize again what we really knew all along—that process is not the end but the means in education, that the product is what really counts, and that the product of education must be characterized by quality, excellence, and competence.

Competence and Quality in Career Education

The term *competence* is not easy to define. In some liberal arts fields the term almost defies definition, but in career education the task is somewhat simpler. From a career education standpoint, competence may be defined as *the ability to perform both manipulative and cognitive tasks at levels that meet accepted standards for success in the chosen job field.*

There are, of course, various levels of competence, and some career education programs aim at one level and some at another. In *Individualized Educational Planning* (1975, pp. 30–31), a study group at Metropolitan State University in St. Paul has identified three levels of competence, defined as follows (abstracted with permission of the university):

> *Knowing:* To know means to have *learned and retained* and *be able to recall* the theory and methodology . . . and the context of a particular subject.

> *Applying:* To apply means to be able and willing to *use* the theory and methodology . . . and the context of a subject in new and routine situations.

> *Evaluating:* To evaluate means to be able to *judge the value* of theory and methodology . . . and context of the subject in relation to goals or stated criteria. The evaluation process implies an informed judgment.

The application of this three-level concept to career education is quite direct as the following discussion illustrates.

Knowing. Students who graduate from career education programs at only the "knowing" level of competence are not really ready for fully competent performance on the job, as competence is defined here. Such graduates may have been victims of the process syndrome in education.

They may be ready for entry jobs as interns or apprentices where the "applying" level of competence can be attained through on-the-job training (OJT). This minimal "knowing" level of competence is characteristic of many so-called career education programs that do not provide realistic laboratory work or "hands-on" work experience. Business management majors who "know" marketing and accounting theory from books but who have no experience in actual business operations and technical students who have succeeded in theory classes but who have not had realistic problem-solving laboratory experience with sophisticated instruments and equipment representative of the current state of the art in technology, are both examples of this limited type of program.

Applying. Students who complete career education programs at the "applying" level of competence are ready to go to work with a minimum of job-familiarization training, since they already possess the ability to *perform* at levels that meet accepted standards of success on the job. Many college programs are realistic at this level, providing hundreds of hours of laboratory or shop experience or incorporating internships and other work experience into the curriculum. Examples include such clinic-based allied health programs as associate degree nursing, radiologic technology, and dental assisting and such work-study or laboratory-based technician programs as automotive technology, petroleum technology, and air conditioning technology.

Evaluating. This level of competence is rarely reached by college-age young people who have just graduated from regular-day career education programs. Judgment and evaluation involve an experienced, mature approach to the analysis of problems. Rarely can this talent be attained as a result of simulated experiences in a college laboratory setting. It comes, and then only to some people, from months or even years of coping with responsibility and with the exigencies of day-to-day work situations where productivity, costs, and competition are governing factors. Colleges and technical schools have an important role to play, however, in educating for this most advanced of the three levels of competence through continuing education programs, management training courses, and advanced technological training. Their evening schedules are crowded with persons wanting to achieve this evaluating level of competence, and such innovative instructional modes as case study, simulation, gaming, and of course cooperative work-study all contribute to its attainment.

It is encouraging that competency-based instruction and performance objectives are now receiving long overdue emphasis in career education. They are new ways of assuring that successful completion of an occupational program and the attainment of a certificate or a degree means that students can and will perform at acceptable levels of competence on the job. All career-oriented programs now should involve competency-based learning and performance objectives. The permissive era is over—easy courses and easy grades have no place in career education. Employers and the general public have a right to expect that these programs will be of high quality and that their graduates will possess the performance capabilities for which the programs are planned and operated.

Once initiated, career education programs based on competency and performance must be continuously monitored and evaluated. Subtle forces and pressures will be used to denigrate them. Claims will be made that they are not "humane" and that they discriminate against slow learners. Some faculty may not like to have the results of their teaching measured by the absolute standards of performance expected of their students. Such supporting services as laboratories, educational media, cooperative education work stations, advisory committees, field trips, and testing and counseling services that are required to make competency-based education a success represent an appreciable continuing commitment of time and money.

Despite all these real and fancied objections (and many more are often cited), career education without a competency base is a *non sequitur*. Roueche (1976, p. 11) comments: "The competency-based instructional system is simply a means of linking student performance to institutional accountability." A college that offers career education without setting up performance standards and making sure that students attain them is deluding itself, its students, and its constituency.

Curriculum Content for Competence

Each occupational field and cluster and each level of career program in colleges and technical schools has its own unique curriculum and course requirements. The literature dealing with the content best suited to the hundreds of these programs is voluminous. It is not our purpose here to deal with detailed requirements of specialized curriculums but with some general principles that should guide career education program development: Most career programs are comprised of three kinds of curriculum content—

(1) theoretical and background courses; (2) specialized occupational courses; and (3) general education courses—and each kind should relate to the levels of competence described above.

Theoretical and Background Courses. The theoretical and background course content of middle-manpower education programs makes its greatest contribution to the "knowing" level of competence. The level of rigor of these courses thus depends on the goal of each particular curriculum. For instance, short-term certificate-level programs training students for semiskilled or skilled entry jobs ordinarily feature courses whose academic or theoretical difficulty is minimal, consistent with the relatively modest cognitive demands of those jobs. Associate degree programs intended to train technicians and other semiprofessionals, however, should include theoretical and background courses of collegiate level consistent with the appreciable cognitive and technical content of these occupations. And baccalaureate degree programs producing technologists of one kind or another must feature much more rigorous theoretical courses, especially in the upper division years, along with management and human relations applications to quasi-professional jobs.

Specialized Occupational Courses. These courses aim primarily at developing competencies at the "applying" level. Much of this part of the program is "hands-on" training, working with instruments, tools, equipment, and machinery, and also exercising hand and eye skills. Some students at least can begin to develop competence at the evaluating level in these courses. Much of the instruction in these courses should be in a laboratory or shop setting in which the student encounters problems and performs tasks akin to those found in the actual job situation. Simulation can be used effectively in some fields, actual clinical experience in others, and skill-developing shop work in still others. The use of tools, instruments, and machines comparable in complexity and sophistication to those on the job should be featured.

General Education Courses. A good case can be made for the view that the "evaluating" level of competence is in considerable measure attained through the kind of reflective processes engendered by liberal learning or general education. If, indeed, this is a viable argument, it points up the importance of making the general education content of career education programs interesting, challenging, and demanding. General education is an exceedingly important part of the education of college-trained men and women for another reason as well (Grede, 1973a). Most persons "work" for only about one third of their waking hours. The decisions they make in their "living time" regarding their family, citizenship, culture, religion, and the like are fully as important as the actions they take during their working time. Students in career education courses are not robots to be programmed solely for utilitarian purposes. A prestigious national commission put it in these words: "Technology is not a vessel into which people are to be poured and to which they must be molded. It is something to be adapted to the needs of men and to the furtherance of human ends, including the enrichment of personality and environment" (National Commission on Technology, Automation, and Economic Progress, 1966, p. 1).

Here again, quality and excellence are paramount. Merely "getting the courses out of the way" in order to graduate is a futile exercise. It is this negative approach to "satisfying requirements" in general education courses that has led to the generally low esteem in which liberal learning is held by many career-oriented students.

Faculty

Despite much of the current literature and indeed some evidence to the contrary, the purpose of colleges is teaching and learning. When teachers teach and students learn, the business of a college is being honestly conducted. And if students learn even beyond what teachers teach, either from books and new media or through self-paced instruction modes, so much the better. New learning systems notwithstanding, however, it is the faculty that is at the heart of the process and product of learning. Of all the factors important in attaining programmatic quality and excellent and competent performance of graduates, the most essential one is the faculty. No college can aspire to excellence without an excellent faculty, no learning system is truly effective without faculty effectiveness, and career education graduates are not likely to be competent unless the faculty is competent. It should thus be axiomatic that the faculty's competence must embrace all three levels of competence—knowing, applying and evaluating.

Faculty for Theoretical and Background Courses. Faculty members teaching theory and background courses (such as mathematics, physics, and engineering in technology programs or accounting, economics, and psychology in business management curriculums) should have excellent academic preparation in their subject fields. It is doubtful that anything less than the master's degree *in the field being taught* should be regarded as acceptable. In addition, practical experience in or related to the field should be a prime factor for consideration and encouragement for, indeed insistence upon, maintaining contacts with the field should be standard practice. The farther removed in time a faculty member is from actual practice in the field, the greater is the tendency to emphasize process rather than product.

If the institution is oriented merely to the "knowing" level of competence, there is no real problem of faculty recruitment for theoretical and background courses. As noted in Chapter Eight, however, if it is oriented toward career education with an emphasis on immediately usable skills, then the faculty member whose repertoire is pure theory cannot function effectively. Career education requires more than the traditional academic qualifications from faculty members. More than mere disciplinary teaching is involved. Faculty members teaching theory should be able to relate that theory to practice; they should plan courses and choose instructional materials that emphasize some of the applied aspects of the disciplines being studied; and they should relate their work to that in the specialized occupational courses, even though these may be taught by others. Integration of this kind should not be left to accidental faculty contacts; it should come about as a result of planned curriculum coordination on the part of the faculty and the dean or director of the program, and it is helped by recruiting faculty members interested in the application of their ideas to the world of work.

Faculty for Specialized Occupational Courses. Teachers who provide instruction in the specialized occupational courses of career education programs must, first of all, be competent practitioners in their own fields. Since competencies at the "applying" level must be well developed, the teachers must be capable of demonstrating their own proficiency in the field on an hour-by-hour basis. It is desirable, of course, that faculty members teaching these courses have college training and perhaps even an advanced degree, but the primary requisite is competence and experience in the specialized field.

Faculty for General Education Courses. It would seem that the general education course content of liberal learning in career education programs could be taught by any faculty member who is competent in the particular discipline involved. This is not always true, however. Competence in a discipline, be it mathematics, English, history, psychology, or political science, is of course necessary, but beyond that is the necessity for good rapport with students who are not majoring in that discipline—students who indeed often approach the course with some apprehension and perhaps dislike and who at best regard it as a required "service" course, ancillary if not peripheral to their major interest. With general education objectives in mind, a liberal arts course must stand on its own and be enlightening in and of itself, rather than being just an introduction to a major field where further study is expected. Consequently not all arts and science faculty members are suited to providing general education courses for career education curriculums.

By the opposite token, a proper general education experience hardly can be provided by teaching bits and pieces of the arts and sciences on an "as-needed" basis by vocational teachers in a laboratory or shop setting. For decades the vocational education establishment has promoted this view, and it is just as ill-founded as the claim by some liberal arts advocates that vocational education does not belong in colleges at all.

Ideally, faculty members who teach general education courses to students in occupational programs should have the usual academic preparation in their discipline at the master's degree level or beyond plus significant experience in or familiarity with some aspect of the world of work other than teaching. This is not to say that they should not love their subject-matter field. On the contrary, they should be so completely convinced of its importance for liberal learning that they will exert superhuman effort to motivate these students and convince them, too, of its value. Career education students are thinking people possessed of intellectual curiosity as well as productive skills, and they deserve the best faculty talent available as they sample liberal learning at the college level. Just as they should learn microwave practice from an electronics engineer or nursing practice from a registered professional nurse, so they should learn psychology from a psychologist, history from a historian, and government from a political scientist, each of whom is committed to making general education in career education programs interesting, challenging, and demanding.

The remaining sections of this chapter deal with general principles of career education program development that faculty members and directors of these programs can use in planning their curriculums and courses.

Estimating the Demand for Middle Manpower

Planning and operating successful career education programs in specific fields involves attention, of course, to local, regional, and national manpower needs and demands. Furthermore, as pointed out in earlier chapters, it is essential that program planners understand the difference between *need* and *demand,* as used in manpower forecasting. Manpower "need" speaks to national and regional "goals"—tasks that society ought to undertake or modernization and up-grading that industry ought to be engaging in. "Demand," on the other hand, is concerned with *actual* job openings—with reality rather than possibility, with wage bills already budgeted and personnel directors ready to interview job applicants.

"Bandwagon fever" has afflicted curriculum planners of career programs all too frequently, the most recent outbreak having been the rash of career programs that erupted beginning in 1970 as a result of the proclaimed "national need" for technicians to work on environmental improvement. The need was there, but demand was not. Scores of community and technical colleges initiated carefully planned programs and produced hundreds of graduates, most of whom did not get jobs in environment-related fields at semiprofessional levels.

The "manpower needs" approach to curriculum development (Lecht, 1969) is found to be a valuable planning guide only if the stated needs are carefully evaluated in the light of actual manpower supply and demand. There is no suitable crystal ball, no tea-leaf incantation, no reliable method for reading the palm of the economy to get correct answers to the question of need and demand. Forecasts of future manpower demands are extremely useful when they prove to be correct—but disastrous when they are in error. Actually, the best predictor of future demand is the pattern of past and present employment. If this trend of past and present demand is used as a base for the central thrust of most middle-manpower program development, program planners and administrators can take a modest gamble in a few areas with regard to "new and emerging occupations" (N.C. Harris, 1969), without incurring unacceptable risks for the total program. If, for instance, hospitals are growing, clinics expanding, and medical expenditures mounting, the employment prospects for graduates of allied health programs are promising. Are offices, banks, insurance companies, corporations, and government agencies expanding their operations? Then graduates of secretarial, accounting, finance and credit, and business management programs should find ready employment. Are public utilities, energy companies, mining and the extractive industries, research and development firms, and government agencies hiring engineers and scientists? If so, they will also need technicians and technologists, and the establishment of one or more energy-related technology programs would be a good bet.

In short, curriculum planners need to be wary of writers who take a national or social-needs approach to manpower forecasts rather than an employer-demand approach. They should see if employers are expanding and hiring and, if so, start the program but, if not, wait until need is translated into demand.

Occupational Surveys

National and regional manpower demand can be estimated from data bases compiled by the U.S. Departments of Labor and Commerce and by business- and industry-research units like those maintained by manufacturers' associations or the big chain banking institutions. Local demand, however, ordinarily has to be determined through surveys initiated by the college itself. Such surveys should be conducted or updated at least every five years.

These surveys can be contracted out to management consulting or research firms but usually have the best outcomes if they are locally conducted by the college. Professional consultants may be used to assist in drawing up the research design (N.C. Harris, 1967), but the study itself should be directed by a college staff member, and it should involve the widest possible participation of local citizens and college staff.

In as large and complex an undertaking as a local occupational survey, proper relationships among three particular groups and individuals are essential in order to establish effective channels of communication, avoid unfortunate misunderstandings that otherwise inevitably arise, and facilitate the work.

The Survey Director. Every survey must have a director to coordinate, evaluate, and direct the total effort. The director supervises the work of the research, analysis, and survey report staff, moving everything along at a predetermined rate so that a final report can be ready at the agreed-upon deadline. Critical path technique or Program Evaluation and Review Technique (PERT) is often used to keep all the activities on schedule (Cook, 1966). The director reports progress periodically to the college administration and to the citizens' advisory committee.

Citizens' Committee and Task Groups. This committee is advisory to the survey director. It possesses no legal authority or decision-making power, but it most certainly has the power of influence. A large, broad-based committee is desirable, representing all facets of business, industry, government, and civic development. It has not been uncommon to have a "Committee of 100," since the greater the citizen involvement, the more useful the survey findings are apt to be. From this large group, a much smaller steering committee of from nine to fifteen members is chosen or elected to carry on the week-to-week business of the survey.

The committee as a whole is divided up into task groups to cover such segments of the local economy as allied health, finance and real estate, and manufacturing industries. Consultants may be provided to each task group to assist them with their work. Preliminary reports from the task groups may be made public from time to time to generate interest in the survey, but all such reports should be cleared through the total advisory committee and the survey director's office before distribution.

Research, Analysis, and Survey Report Staff. This group is charged with designing survey instruments, gathering data by questionnaires and interviews, compiling and interpreting the findings, and preparing and publishing the survey report. Copies of the report should be given wide dissemination throughout the region served by the college.

College sponsored and conducted occupational surveys should be related, of course, to other manpower studies in the region. Usually, however, studies done by other agencies have only limited value for college career program planning. As noted in Chapter Three, the breakdown of job titles within occupational categories is not such as to provide useful information for career programs in middle-manpower occupations. Further, federal and state employment service studies usually are directed at manpower supply and demand in skilled, semiskilled, service, and unskilled occupations rather than at job levels requiring college training.

If local surveys reveal a consistent demand for a certain occupational field or cluster of occupations, and an otherwise inadequate supply of workers for it, serious consideration should be given to starting the program. As a general operating guideline, if it appears that local or regional placement of graduates from a career program will exceed fifteen per year for a reasonable planning period such as ten years, then the program could be implemented. Factors still to be considered would, of course, include capital costs, annual operating costs, proximity to institutions already offering the program, availability of qualified faculty, the difficulty level of the program, and its drawing power for potential students.

Determining Drawing Power and Projecting Enrollments

Many a "needed" program, even with demand for its graduates also present, has foundered for lack of student enrollment.

Several different issues are relevant here. One is the image or "prestige index" of the job field. Is it popular? Are income levels satisfactory? Does it have the aura of a near-professional activity? Another issue is the cognitive ability required for success in the educational program and on the job itself. It is well known that students whose capabilities are consistent with semiprofessional and technical careers generally aspire to professional-level programs and jobs, and students who are satisfied with the prestige of middle-manpower jobs all too often lack the academic ability or preparation needed to succeed in the rather demanding courses of these programs. As a consequence, a decision to initiate a new and perhaps very expensive program cannot be made on the basis of manpower demands alone. These factors enter into the dynamics of decision making as well.

A few examples can serve to illustrate the dilemmas that may confront curriculum planners for the next five or ten years regarding these prestige and ability factors in light of need and demand.

Engineering and Science-Related Technologies. The manpower "need" in these fields will be high, but demand will depend on the emphasis the nation puts on such goals as energy independence, space exploration, and national defense. Prestige of these fields is good, but the ability required is usually above that presented by students who want to enroll in these programs.

Health Careers. Need is high and demand is also good but will require careful monitoring. Prestige is good, with needed ability ranging from very high in radiologic technology and nursing to quite low. The difficulty is that most applicants want to take the high ability programs whether or not they are prepared for their academic rigor.

Natural Resources and Environmental Technology. Need is substantial, but demand is still low and may remain so for the decade. Prestige will be high if the demand goes up. Ability required (especially in the natural sciences) is above that possessed by the majority of students in two-year career education programs.

Public and Human Services. Need is high, demand is rather uncertain but perhaps is on the low side, prestige is fairly good but will depend on salaries, while required ability has a wide range. As usual, most students aspire to paraprofessional level programs, and many do not have the ability to cope with that level of academic rigor.

Semi-Skilled and Service Occupations. Need and demand are steady and on the high side, but prestige is very low, since these jobs are considered "dirty work" (Faltermeyer, 1974). Academic ability demanded by them is medium to low, well within the range of most postsecondary career-oriented students.

In summary, then, the crux of the student recruitment problem is that occupations with high need and demand tend to have either low prestige or a requirement of high ability. Or, put another way, students who possess the ability expected in a career education program tend to regard that occupation as having low prestige even when need and demand are high.

Utilizing Advisory Committees

Most colleges engaged in career education find that lay advisory committees are essential to the optimum functioning of their occupational programs. Such advisory committees, it should be emphasized, are just that—advisory. They do not make policy. Only the governing board can do that.

Most colleges find that an overall committee concerned with the total role of the college in its community can serve the interests of the college in many ways, not the least of which is in interpreting its mission and its educational programs to the community and its many publics. Such a committee often consists of from nine to seventeen members chosen from community leaders in many fields— business, industry, education, religion, labor, agriculture, the professions, and government. Appointments may be for four-year periods, with staggered terms to assure continuity of service.

In addition, separate advisory committees for specific career education programs can be of significant value. Such committees should be established to advise the college staff in planning or operating all major occupational programs, with some continuing from year to year with periodic changes in membership and others serving only during the planning period for new courses and curriculums. Some colleges have thirty or more such committees meeting regularly and helping in all of the following ways (Riendeau, 1967): (1) assisting with surveys to determine the need/demand situation in the region; (2) giving expert advice about the competencies required for entry-level jobs in the career field; (3) providing information about the kind and quality of specialized equipment and supplies needed for the laboratory phases of the program; (4) assisting with arrangements for on-the-job training, internships, apprenticeships, and cooperative work experience programs; (5) assisting the college placement office in finding jobs for graduates; and (6) occasionally providing gifts of equipment or even bequests for a new building or laboratory.

Program directors and college officials should choose committee members with care, with the president or provost inviting them to serve for a specific period of time. The advisory committee's role should be clarified at the outset as involving advice and counsel only, with policy and decision making remaining with the governing board and the college administration. Each committee should have a full written agenda for every meeting and keep accurate minutes, elect a lay member as chairman, but provide a college staff member, such as a dean or program chairman, as secretary to assure college-committee liaison; and take suitable follow-up action after every meeting. The college staff member should arrange for frequent visits to the college by committee members, preferably when related classes and laboratories are in session, so that the members get acquainted with students in the program. As each member's term expires, the president should send an official letter of termination, with an expression of appreciation for the service rendered. If it is desired that a member serve for another term, it should nevertheless be officially recognized in the invitation to serve for another stipulated term that the one term has expired.

By judicious use of advisory committees it is possible within a few years to have several hundred active, interested supporters of the college and its career programs from a number of essential constituencies in the community. The good will of these community leaders has incalculable value.

Planning the Level and Breadth of Each Program

When a given career field needs local program development, two associated and very important issues must be resolved: first, at what level should the program be operated—paraprofessional, quasiprofessional, technical, or highly skilled; and second, should the program be *job* oriented to supply workers for a specific occupation, or should it be directed at a broader cluster of occupations by having a strong base in one or more subject matter *disciplines?* Both issues—level of program and job versus discipline orientation—must receive serious consideration by program directors and advisory committees before decisions are made on faculty, facilities, course content, and student recruitment for a new program. Consider some examples that illustrate the two problems.

Program Level. The level at which a program can be offered is often externally controlled by state or national requirements for certification, licensure, or accreditation, with the health careers field being a good example. Advisory committees, as pointed out above, can and should provide local input to decisions about the level of the program, and to some extent at least the availability of students with the required academic aptitude will influence its ultimate level.

In keeping with the national trend for career education to move from the secondary school to postsecondary levels, there is no reason why two-year community and technical colleges should not offer regular degree programs at three levels—paraprofessional, technician, and highly skilled—as well as part-time, short-term, and skill-oriented training and job upgrading courses at the semiskilled level. Universities and four-year colleges, of course, will provide quasiprofessional four-year degree programs for technologists and advanced professional programs for other occupations. Each course and program should be honestly and openly described as to level, and since competency-based education is the only defensible concept in education for careers, its rigor and performance should be held to the level that competence on the job dictates.

It is important for administrators to decide on the appropriate level, with all the factors known and considered, and then to maintain the integrity of the program at that level. If colleges are not honest with their constituents, their students, and themselves about the level of their offerings, can legislated accountability be far away?

In the matter of program level, the field of electronics offers a clear example. Electronics has been popular in colleges for two decades. But how realistic are all the resulting electronics programs? How many of them, for example, train only TV and radio/audio systems repairmen, when there is really a greater demand for industrial electronics and electrical technicians, with more rigorous preparation? And, by the opposite token, how many highly sophisticated microwave engineering technician programs are there in communities where the only need is for TV and radio/audio servicemen?

Program Breadth. The recent history of occupational education program development, spurred by mission-oriented federal appropriations, has been to react to supposed crises or "critical needs" by initiating specific job-oriented occupational programs. Thus ever since the National Defense Education Act of 1958, the federal vocational acts have encouraged, if indeed they have not required, a job-specific approach to vocational-technical education. It is apparent from observations of actual job practice in both the public and private sectors that jobs at the semiskilled and skilled levels (that is, toward the manipulative end of the manipulative-cognitive scale as illustrated in Figures 1 and 2 in Chapters Three and Six) tend to emphasize a rather narrow set of specific skills and require only modest cognitive content. Training programs for these jobs can and probably should be job oriented. But in moving toward the cognitive end of the manpower spectrum, not only does the specificity of manual skills decrease but also the range of cognitive activity increases. Competence now includes not only *knowing* and *applying* but also increasing elements of *evaluating*. Thus in the middle-manpower area, the tasks facing technicians and paraprofessionals are not always routine and repetitive or accomplished by the application of a set of job-specific skills. They call for in-depth theoretical knowledge, the ability to synthesize and apply knowledge from two or more disciplines, and cognitive and evaluative abilities perhaps seasoned by general education or liberal learning. In this respect semiprofessionals and paraprofessionals are more like professionals than they are like skilled trades workers. Consequently, the balance between job-specific training on the one hand and broad discipline orientation on the other must be given intensive consideration by curriculum planners in designing any middle-manpower level programs.

The fields of energy resource development (*Technology Review*, 1972) and environmental improvement provide excellent contexts within which to discuss this job-versus-discipline orientation problem. Both of these fields loom large on the national horizon—they are near the top of the nation's list of urgent priorities. They present technical problems of great magnitude that only improved technology can solve, and to complicate the matter it seems that most of the measures taken to solve the problems in either one of the fields will exacerbate those in the other. Energy and environment do, however, have one thing in common: the solution to their problems will require an entire generation of middle-manpower technologists and technicians and highly-skilled workers prepared for their jobs by career education programs in colleges.

But what kinds and levels of knowledge and skills will these jobs require? What kinds of one-year, two-year, and four-year programs should be initiated or expanded? And how will these programs relate to eventual manpower demands? When systems analysis groups, MBO analysts, and PERT people plan mammoth projects of environmental improvement, will there be a sudden new need for job-oriented curriculums training people in specific fields—for example, will water problems require water treatment technicians; air problems, air pollution technicians; and erosion problems, erosion control technicians, all trained in separate, specialized programs? Or is it more likely that the entire environmental field will require greater emphasis on discipline-oriented workers? If so, the needed semiprofessional and technical personnel may be merely minor variants of the well-known physics technicians, chemical technicians, engineering technicians, biological technicians, and electronics technicians that colleges are already producing.

Considering energy development, since the possible sources of energy to be exploited include coal, geothermal, solar, wind, nuclear fission, and thermonuclear fusion, should we develop two-year and four-year technological degree programs around such specialties as coal gasification, wind energy, solar energy, geothermal energy, and nuclear fission and fusion? Or might sober and careful systems analysis reveal that the best approach would be to improve and perhaps modify slightly the present technologies, built as they are in clusters related to the known disciplines of mechanical and electrical engineering, chemistry, physics and earth sciences, and business management?

Figure 5 attempts to clarify this issue at the two-year college level, using energy resources development as an example and the assumption that the United States will need up to one million semiprofessional, technical, and skilled workers in the energy field by 1990. The top part of the figure depicts the situation if the "job-oriented" alternative is chosen. Job-specific technologies, based on narrowly specialized curriculums, are listed down the left side, with horizontal arrays under the four levels of program. In each space of the matrix, the "Yes," "No," and "Maybe" entries indicate our judgment as to the likely need and demand for middle-manpower workers trained in these narrow specialties and at these levels. Similarly, the bottom half portrays the "discipline-oriented" alternative, with the four levels of middle-manpower workers shown at the left and the disciplinary specialties across the columns. Again, entries in the spaces indicate a judgment as to whether significant numbers of workers at these levels and in the discipline-related fields will be needed in the drive for energy independence.

A judgment as to which of the two alternatives may emerge as a dominant pattern for career education may be premature. Probably, for semi-skilled and skilled levels, job-oriented curriculums will remain popular, and even for technician and semiprofessional levels, categorical funding tends to push curriculum planners toward this job-oriented approach. When one recalls the Manhattan Project of 1942 to 1945 and the Apollo Project of the 1960s and early 1970s, however, it seems that technicians with a discipline orientation buttressed by applied engineering training were better suited to those Herculean national efforts. It is quite apparent by now that energy resources development will "need a crash engineering job comparable to building the atom bomb"

Figure 5. Manpower Development for Energy Independence: Two Alternatives for Technical Educators.

1. *The "Job-Oriented" Program Alternative*
(Assumes each energy problem is discrete and relatively unique. Requires narrowly specialized programs, involving "image" problems, probable high unit costs, and questionable occupational mobility, both laterally and vertically.)

Hypothetical Job Titles	Level of Program			
	Semiskilled (Certificate)	Skilled (Diploma or Apprenticeship)	Technician (Associate Degree)	Semiprofessional (Associate Degree)
Coal Gasification Technician	No	Maybe	Yes	No
Wind Energy Technician	No	Maybe	Yes	No
Solar Energy Technician	No	No	Yes	Yes
Geothermal Energy Technician	No	Yes	Yes	Maybe
Nuclear Fusion Technician	No	No	No	Yes
Petroleum Technician	Maybe	Yes	Yes	Maybe
Coal Mine Mechanic	Yes	Yes	No	No

2. *The "Discipline-Oriented" Program Alternative*
(Assumes energy problems will be solved by a systems approach. Enhances job image, disciplinary association, and occupational mobility.)

Level of Program	Disciplines						
	Engineering	Physics and Earth Sciences	Chemistry	Electricity, Electronics	Business Management	Computer Science	Trades or Crafts
Semiprofessional (Associate Degree)	Yes	Yes	Yes	Yes	Yes	Yes	No
Technician (Associate Degree)	Yes	Maybe	Yes	Yes	Yes	Yes	Maybe
Skilled (Diploma or Apprenticeship)	Maybe	No	No	Yes	Yes	Yes	Yes
Semiskilled (Certificate)	No	No	No	No	Yes	No	Yes

(Lessing, 1973). Narrowly conceived job-training programs featuring "selected content" from the basic disciplines taught on an "as-needed" basis in the shop by shop teachers smack of dilettantism and superficiality, and are not likely to produce the competent technicians needed for an effective national effort. "Technician" programs that offer a little physics here, a little chemistry there, and just enough mathematics to solve shop problems are ill-advised. They claim to be more than they are; they produce industrial workers, not paraprofessionals and technicians; and they increase the probability that graduates will be trapped in the vicious cycle of training, employment, unemployment, and retraining, because the depth necessary in a discipline, that facilitates lateral or upward job mobility, is lacking.

College career education planners thus should not lock in too early on a job-oriented approach to these fields which might produce a score or more of different kinds of narrowly-specialized "technicians" with insufficient depth to cope with the complex and the unexpected. It will be recalled that many of the abortive programs initiated in the mid-1960s in the environmental technology field featured job-oriented curriculums. Was this narrowly specialized curriculum concept one of the factors contributing to the poor employment prospects that faced the many graduates of these programs? If they had graduated in a discipline-based technology such as physics, chemistry, biology, engineering, or computer science, would they not have been just as employable for the few environment-related jobs that were available? And, finding no environment-related job available, would not employment in any science- or engineering-based technology have been an easy lateral move?

Deciding on Teaching and Learning Systems

After resolving the very important issue of job-oriented versus discipline-oriented curriculums, several other vitally important issues must be decided by colleges to assure the success of their career education programs. Chief among them are alternative learning and teaching systems. Not only must faculty be carefully chosen and assigned, but also continuing attention must be given to modes of teaching and learning and to the evaluation and improvement of teaching. Just as there are new career programs in colleges and new subjects to teach, so are there new students (Cross, 1973) with new learning styles. Happily there are also new aids to learning—technology asserting itself in the academic forum (Society for College and University Planning, 1975). To such traditional instructional methods as lecture, discussion, and laboratory, we can now add case-study methods, simulation, small group instruction (Olmstead, 1974), cooperative work experience, improved audiovisual teaching, autotutorial learning, televised teaching, personalized systems of instruction (PSI), and computer-assisted instruction (CAI) (Purdy, 1975). Learning laboratories and clearly stated performance objectives put much of the responsibility for learning on students, who can now play an active rather than a passive role in the learning process. New insights into motivation and new ways of identifying course objectives in behavioral and performance terms have enabled students and instructors to clarify the learning process and improve the learning product. With cognitive mapping techniques (Hill, 1971), it is possible to "match the method to the student" (*Engineering Education*, March 1974), and with suitable learning laboratory hardware and software, self-paced instruction (Rainey, 1971) now becomes a viable option.

We are not as ready as some to "cast the old aside," but neither would we be among the last "by whom the new is tried." If lectures, discussion, and demonstration were not good methods of teaching, would they have lasted 3,000 years? We think not, and we caution against tossing them on the rubbish heap of academic history to be replaced entirely by bright new hardware and dull new software. "Bandwagon fever" has infected hundreds of colleges in this connection. The obviously sane course is to utilize the best of both the traditional and the new in devising learning and teaching systems. Academic deans and division heads should carry on a continuous program of evaluation and improvement of learning and teaching (Pace, 1973), giving just as much emphasis to the improvement of lectures and discussion as to the effective use of the new media.

In order to achieve expected levels of competence, each and

every course and learning sequence in career programs must have clearly stated performance objectives to be attained by *every student* before they complete the program (Mager and Pipe, 1970). Educational technology, open learning laboratories, and self-paced learning methods can be used so that "time can be the variable and learning the constant" (Roueche, Herrscher, and Baker, 1976). Faculty members may need a great deal of urging—perhaps even coercion—before adopting this "mastery learning" approach (Bloom, 1970). A series of faculty workshops may be necessary first, to convince all the instructional staff that programs based on specific performance objectives are essential in career education and second, to acquaint faculty with the steps and methods involved in changing over from the old relativistic standards of performance and evaluation such as grading on the curve, where time was the constant and learning the variable, to absolute standards of performance, regardless of the length of time involved in meeting these standards, as the basis for evaluation.

It should be noted that competency-based programs provide for variation of achievement by stipulating the *minimum* performance standards required for entry employment at a stated job level that must be attained by even the slowest students to pass the course or receive the diploma, certificate, or degree. "Better" students will exceed the minimum requirements throughout the program.

The basics of planning and operating competency-based programs built on performance objectives begins with the concept of *mastery learning* (Bloom, 1970). The competencies required on the job are determined by the process of *job analysis* or *task analysis* (Mager and Beach, 1967). These tasks, and the level of performance required for entry into and success on the job, become the basis for courses, topics, and teaching/learning units (modules) in the program. Each topic or module is learned or practiced under the conditions to be encountered on the job, until performance at the "knowing," "applying," and possibly "evaluating" levels of competence matches that expected on the job within a set of criteria such as time to complete, cost, materials used, and the like, that predict success and advancement (promotion) on the job (D. Brown, 1974).

It should not be inferred from the above that *performance* relates only to manual skills. The performance objectives approach is applicable to all fields of career education—people-related as well as those that emphasize trade and technical skills. When learner performance of interpersonal skills or mechanical abilities is the desired end product, the advantages of discussion methods, simulation, laboratory or shop work, cooperative work experience, case studies, and all such learning and teaching methods that bring activity into the learning process should be apparent.

Implementing Work Experience

There is no satisfactory substitute for work experience. Colleges must make every possible effort to add a cooperative work experience dimension to their career programs. Many advantages accrue to both students and the college. Among them, students gain experience with equipment, materials, time and cost constraints, working conditions, other employees, and foremen and bosses that cannot be duplicated in the college setting; many students need the earnings from paid work experience to continue their schooling; and their work experience often leads to full-time employment. At the same time, the college stays in close contact with the industries and businesses where co-op students are placed, thus getting feedback that helps to keep programs and courses abreast of the times and identifying employers to serve on college advisory committees; and it may receive gifts of materials and equipment and occasional endowment gifts from participating companies.

The Cooperative Education Research Center of the Detroit Institute of Technology recently completed a comprehensive study of employer experience with cooperative education in seventy large and small corporations across the United States. Among the many findings and conclusions was the following (Detroit Institute of Technology, 1974, p. 12): "Co-op graduates have an advantage over recent college grads in terms of productive work performances . . . thereby assisting in management development to meet future needs for supervisory and managerial talent." And a more recent study by the Cooperative Education Research Center at

Northeastern University that compared alumni of cooperative work-study programs with those of regular on-campus programs reveals that although the impact of co-op work experience appears to diminish over the length of the alumni's careers, co-op alumni report having "more complete career information and more adequate information about job opportunities after college," "generally earned higher starting salaries," and "showed greater stability in their overall career choice" than graduates of noncooperative programs (S. J. Brown, 1976, p. 72).

For these several reasons, despite the time, effort, and cost involved in organizing co-op programs, every career-oriented college should use co-op education as a cornerstone of its career education programs. For paraprofessional and technical jobs, internships can usually be arranged with businesses, industries, institutions, and public service agencies. At the trade and craft level, joint management-labor college committees can often work out arrangements whereby a certificate or associate degree can be earned by apprentices within the same time period as their apprenticeship, and for paraprofessional and technician jobs in health and human service fields, internships can usually be arranged with the institution or agency concerned. A great deal of time and effort, and some cost, will be associated with co-op programs, but their benefits are many; all career-oriented colleges should plan to use co-op education.

Using Support Services

The quality of support services for occupational programs appears to be critical for their success. It is one thing for a college to develop a broad and deep spectrum of occupational programs. It is quite another to provide the adequate and sometimes expensive support services that are essential to their effectiveness. One might even say that occupational programs are different in kind rather than in degree from traditional academic programs because they depend so heavily on support services being correlated with classroom education and off-campus training.

Support services include career counseling and guidance, educational advisement, developmental and remedial education, job placement, financial aid, special services for particular groups such as the handicapped, and the collection and dissemination of institutional data for effective decision making about occupational programs, including follow-up studies to evaluate their effectiveness.

Many colleges, anxious to develop new occupational programs, have plunged ahead with curriculum planning, hiring teaching staff, and recruiting students without developing a coordinated structure of these accompanying services. Yet it is extremely difficult to develop and superimpose the full spectrum of these services once the programs are in operation and all available funds have been allocated to them. A fairly common phenomenon, for example, among community colleges and particularly among those in transition from an academic to a career education orientation is that of apparently comprehensive and high quality occupational programs but support services hardly better or more pervasive than those provided for the traditional academic courses and programs. This weakness is particularly unfortunate among urban institutions, because the variety of occupational opportunities in metropolitan areas is especially wide, the range of career offerings is typically broad, and the needs of students for assistance in making wise choices among them are necessarily great.

Among these support services, several deserve special attention:

Counseling and Guidance. Colleges that emphasize career education must offer outstanding career counseling and guidance services. The process begins with *career counseling,* a concerted attempt on the part of counselor and student to clarify career objectives, identify a potential career field, and tentatively decide on a job cluster, in interviews which precede registration for courses. A decision on specific jobs or on the level of employment need not be made at this time, and these options can be kept open if the college properly emphasizes the career ladder approach to curriculum planning.

Despite some well-known limitations of testing, it is nevertheless an important phase of career guidance. Both aptitude tests and interest inventories are valuable checks on the degree of realism of student choice. Prior work experience is one of the best indications of suitability for a career field, and high-school grades are still the best single predictor of academic ability for recent high-school graduates.

Educational Advising. This continuing process begins after a tentative decision has been made on the career field. With test results, the high school or other academic record, and information about work experience, armed forces training, and the like at hand, the counselor and student now agree on the optimum *entry point* into the career education program. Can the student who has chosen medical laboratory technology actually start in microbiology next week with a reasonable chance of success? Is the student who has decided on a career in manufacturing engineering technology ready to begin college physics? Can a student interested in a career as a child care center assistant be enrolled in the basic course in child psychology with a present reading proficiency at the eighth-grade level? These are the problems of educational advisement, and they must be satisfactorily resolved or failure is the sure result.

As a general rule, students' aspirations tend to outstrip their academic ability. Students are often impatient to complete the listed program and are not disposed to take time to remedy past errors and deficiencies with remedial courses prior to "regular" courses. Also, many students at community colleges are convinced that they can "make it" in psychology, microbiology, physics, and similar courses, even though they would avoid these same courses at a four-year college. Images of this kind must be dispelled, unrealistic appraisals of academic ability corrected, and the need to get off to a good start at the proper entry level emphasized. The promise of the open-door college should be one of ultimate success based on careful academic planning, not one of failure based on a policy of allowing students to take any course they want, whether prepared for it or not. Some colleges have used the core-semester approach (see Chapter Seven on allied health careers for examples) to assist students to enter career education programs at the proper level and in the proper specialty. Others use a college-wide developmental or remedial program (see later in chapter). In any event, educational advisement is of overriding importance in the career education decision for most students.

Throughout the counseling and advisement process, mutual agreement between student and counselor is desirable. In career counseling and guidance, the student's final decision about a career field should govern, even if that choice appears to be unwise from the counselor's point of view. In educational advising, however, when decisions about the entry point to the curriculum are being made, *directive* counseling is essential: the counselor is the expert here. If students are consistently allowed to enter courses for which they are unprepared, the counselor's professional judgment is in question.

A career counseling and educational advisement process illustrating the above steps and suited to a comprehensive community college is portrayed in the flow chart of Figure 6 on the next page. In addition to career counseling and educational advising, the full complement of other student personnel services is essential to career education in colleges, including personal counseling, personality and interest inventorying, and referral to financial aid, health, housing, and other services as needed.

Remediation and Developmental Education. As mentioned earlier, nearly all career-oriented colleges, with the possible exception of such specialized schools as technical institutes, enroll large numbers of students whose basic learning skills are inadequate to the educational tasks they have set for themselves (Roueche, 1968). Many such students can be so encouraged and assisted with a good developmental education program that they eventually do succeed in the curriculum of their choice. It is an accepted practice among many two-year colleges that first-time students with ACT scores below 10, or equivalent SAT scores, and with reading and mathematics proficiencies below seventh-grade level are placed in a developmental education program. Most developmental or remedial education programs emphasize reading and language skills improvement and steps to correct deficiencies in mathematics, although some add remedial work in basic social sciences and natural sciences as well.

Three different patterns of organization for developmental education are commonly encountered: first, placing it in the same instructional division with general education but using specially

Figure 6. Place of Career Counseling and Educational
Advising Within Two-Year Career-Oriented College Programs.

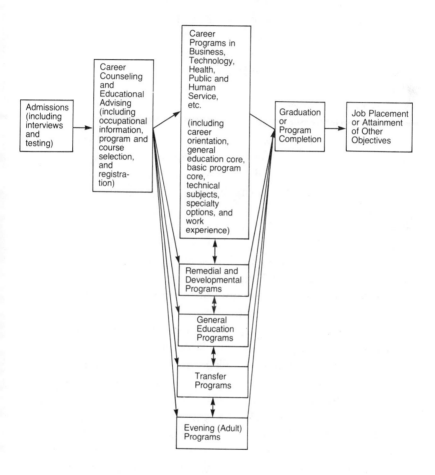

trained teachers and a variety of traditional and new media methods, including learning laboratories; second, assigning it to the library or learning resources center (LLRC), where it may become
almost entirely self-paced or autotutorial, coordinated by a media
specialist or technician; or third, lodging it in the guidance and
counseling center where a semiclinical approach is often used.

No organizational scheme produces magical results—the best records reported thus far not exceeding 25 to 30 percent success in taking students "where they are" and bringing them up to a basic skills level that enables them to perform adequately in the courses of the programs they have selected. Of the three types of organization, we prefer the first, simply because developmental education is an *instructional* function and in our view belongs with the teaching faculty. Furthermore, with this organization it is somewhat easier to schedule remedial students into developmental or elementary level courses in their career areas, thus maintaining a degree of motivation and sense of progress toward their career goal during the sometimes distasteful process of remediation.

Placement. Among all other support services, such as student activities, financial aid, health services, housing, and institutional research and analysis—all of which are a part of exemplary programs—the most critical for successful career programs is placement. Most colleges have placement offices, but they range from being very effective to being almost completely ineffective. It was pointed out in Chapter Four that private and proprietary schools generally maximize the potential of their placement offices, since it is their placement record that attracts students even in the face of high tuition. Most public two-year colleges, however, are not doing a very good job of career placement, and while the record of career-oriented four-year colleges is somewhat better, improvement across the board among public institutions is needed.

First, adequate staffing of the placement office is essential, in terms both of numbers and of experience and dedication. The director and all staff members of the office must be placement- and job-minded. They must know industry and business on a personal basis. They should be out in the field a great deal of the time, calling on businessmen, plant managers, personnel directors, and office managers. Their messages and announcements should continuously remind employers that the college is the place to call when job openings occur. They should make good use of the college's advisory committees in expanding placement prospects. Ideally, as each career education program yields a group of graduates, they should be able to match every one of those graduates to a job that they have identified.

A long-standing argument over the merits of centralized versus decentralized placement remains unresolved. In small colleges, the evidence favors centralized placement, with the responsibility clearly assigned to staff whose performances are evaluated on the basis of their placement results. Coordinators in the various divisions can be used very effectively to improve placement in specialized career areas, but initiative ought to come from the central office. In large colleges with separate schools or divisions for major career fields, sheer size may support a decentralized concept of placement, but it is essential nonetheless to assign clear responsibilities for placement and hold those assigned persons responsible for performance. The weakness of decentralized placement in many colleges is that no one individual recognizes placement as a primary responsibility, and consequently no one really works at it.

In this connection, the all-too-common practice of assigning the placement function to guidance counselors on a part-time basis is ill-advised for several reasons: Counselors may know little about day-to-day business and industry developments and job openings, and although they may have an intellectual interest in employment trends, they may lack visceral involvement in placing students. They may look on their placement job as a sideline—the "real action" being in counseling—and their performance will be evaluated on other-than-placement criteria. Their time devoted to placement is too small to permit the development of off-campus contacts and maintain up-to-date files about job prospects. In truth, counselors' "placement time" in an arrangement of this kind usually is completely absorbed by students needing part-time jobs or "casual" placement while in school, leaving no time for the far more important function of developing an effective career placement service. Finally, the setting is wrong. The college placement office should be visible—a busy, vital place in the midst of the full flow of student traffic, where career information is free for the taking and job information is attractively displayed—not a cubbyhole tucked away in the counseling department. Even today many students still feel a certain reluctance about "going to the counseling office." Placement is too valuable a function to be tacked on to something else and housed in offices where students may be reluctant to go.

Summary and Guidelines for Planners

A low-tide period in occupational education is ending, characterized as it was by infatuation with educational process to the neglect of product, and by disenchantment with technology, applied science, competition, and productivity. It is now becoming clear to more and more people, as it has been clear all along to businessmen, engineers, health educators, and career educators in general that poverty, scarcity, ill health, and deprivation can only be overcome by increased effort and productivity and that the problems created by technology must be solved in a complex society through the application of improved technology. As a result, the demand for quality career education through the 1980s and beyond will probably far exceed our expectations. The challenge to career educators is to plan and operate soundly conceived programs that emphasize excellence in teaching and learning and high standards of performance from students and graduates.

Besides emphasizing the importance of quality and excellence in career education, this chapter has noted the necessity of regarding the learning process as a means and not as a product, of developing competence in each career field at the knowing and applying levels and, if possible, at the evaluating level, and of selecting and assigning faculty to the three major segments of curriculum content in light of these competencies.

Because the specifics of planning and operating occupational curriculums vary a great deal with the career cluster under consideration and with the level of the program, this chapter has dealt only with general guidelines for success. But in summary the following twenty steps apply to the planning and operating of almost all such programs:

1. First of all, survey the *need* and determine the *demand* for manpower in the particular field. Be sure to know the difference between need and demand and base your plans on anticipated demand rather than supposed need. To this end, conduct a local occupational survey and combine its results with information from regional, state, and national sources. Know your city, district, or region thoroughly—its economy, its demography, its social struc-

ture, its history and employment potential. Remember that program planning is not a venture for well-meaning amateurs.

2. Seek answers to these questions. How many other programs for the same occupation are operating or being planned in the region? In light of the long lead-time necessary to get a program established and to produce its first graduates, does there appear to be a long-term demand for new workers in this occupation? What agencies and employers, public and private, will require these workers and in what numbers? Will they employ paraprofessionals and graduates of two-year programs or seek only holders of baccalaureate degrees? With answers to such questions, try to anticipate future manpower supply and demand while staying on top of current supply and demand data. Remember that the only constant in the economic life of a community, as in the nation at large, is change, but remember also that occupational change occurs slowly. Thus plan to provide career education opportunities in all potentially high-demand fields, but by the opposite token do not produce scores or hundreds of graduates for a nonexistent job market.

3. If local need and demand seem to justify the contemplated program, organize a local advisory committee to assist with further planning and select its members with great care in terms of their local experience and employment knowledge. Use ad hoc committees as necessary for special planning projects. And if the approval of particular state agencies or professional associations will be needed later for successful operation of the program, involve these organizations early in the planning process.

4. Make some kind of preliminary determination as to the number of academically qualified students who would enroll in the program. For example, is the entry salary level in the occupation in your locality competitive enough with salaries and wages for other jobs requiring comparable educational preparation that students will be attracted to the program? In terms of the required competencies for successful practice in the occupation and of the interests and ability of potential students, will a sufficient number of qualified students want to enroll? Are there an ample number of clinical work stations in the community for the internship or

field experience phase of the program? And where such experiences are essential, can suitable agreements and contracts be drawn up with the relevant agencies and institutions to permit an adequate enrollment of students?

5. Determine the resources required for the program in terms of money, faculty, space, equipment, and supplies. Compare the likely enrollment with these required resources to see if per-student costs are reasonable. In view of the specialized nature of many of the courses in career programs, per-student unit costs are high in any case and may become untenable if enrollment is low.

6. At this point, assuming there is a decision to proceed, employ the program director or lead teacher. Much of the detailed planning and the recruitment and employment of other well-qualified faculty can proceed under his or her direction.

7. In accordance with realistic job demands, decide on the level or levels at which the program will be offered. Will it be para-professional level, technician level, highly skilled, semiskilled, or will all four levels be established? With the advice of the advisory committee, select the levels to start on—perhaps no more than one at first. Plan articulation of this level with high school and other college programs. Smooth out the steps on the career ladder by judicious planning with educational institutions on other levels. Plan the curriculum with attention to the core-and-ladder concept, with emphasis on developing an employable skill very early in the program.

8. Decide on and set the performance objectives for the program level chosen. Make sure these competencies dovetail with those to be encountered on the job, as determined from a task analysis. Remember that preparation for today's jobs is not a waste of time—in fact, it is probably the best preparation for tomorrow's jobs as well. If accreditation or state approval is involved, plan the details of course content, laboratory work, and clinical experiences with the relevant professional association or state agency.

9. Plan the curriculum in light of these performance objectives and the abilities, aspirations, and interests of prospective students. For example, are they likely to be college-age "regular" students or older persons returning to school to get back on a career ladder? Let your planning reflect the needs of older and part-time

students by remembering that the median age of students in public two-year colleges as of 1976 was over twenty-six years. Adopt a competency-based approach to instruction by awarding credits on the basis of specific performance objectives for each course and program rather than solely on the amount of time enrolled or spent in the classroom.

10. With the assistance of the advisory committee, curriculum consultants, employers, and persons already working at related jobs, decide whether the program should be job-oriented toward narrow specialization or discipline-oriented toward a broader occupational cluster of jobs. Design the curriculum with a proper balance for its particular level among specialized technical content, supporting theory, and general education as these relate to the "knowing," "applying," and "evaluating" competencies demanded in the field.

11. Be sure that faculty recruited to teach these specialized, theory, and general education courses have a good balance of practical and theoretical training themselves and familiarity with the world of work and with the career field involved. Remember that starting a new program with existing faculty is justifiable only if these faculty members are eminently qualified in the career field.

12. Plan and build the necessary on-campus facilities and locate and contract for needed off-campus work stations and internship or work-experience opportunities. Execute written contracts with such agencies as hospitals or clinics that will be involved as intern sites, and with business and industrial employers for co-op work stations. Take cost-effectiveness into account by maximizing the use of these internships, off-campus experiences, and on-the-job training, thus keeping capital investment to a minimum consistent with the performance objectives of the program for entry-level employment.

13. Determine the criteria for student selection and admission into the program at its particular level. Remember that programs at paraprofessional and technician levels are rarely open-door even in open-admissions colleges. If the program is to be offered on an open-door rather than a selective basis, make arrangements for developmental and remedial work and individualized instruction to assure that an open-door admissions policy will have

a chance of success. Make sure that the developmental program offers career students motivation in remedying academic deficiencies by providing employment-oriented training concurrently with remedial education.

14. Decide on the teaching/learning systems to be used. Provide the necessary equipment, supplies, learning laboratories, and autotutorial and other "new media" hardware and software. Select textbooks and other learning resources designed for collegiate-level programs, and make sure the level of these resources matches the level of the program. In instruction, make time the variable and learning the constant through mastery learning of the established performance objectives for all courses and programs. Effective use of auto-tutorial and personalized study systems will be necessary.

15. Make whatever improvements and changes are necessary in student services to provide adequate career counseling, educational advising, and placement services beyond such traditional services as personal counseling, financial aid, and student activities.

16. Finally, begin the student recruitment process. Disseminate information about the program and about occupational opportunities for its graduates, and aim these promotional materials at both youth and adults in the community (Skaggs, 1974). Do not expect that students will flock to new programs automatically. Many a needed program with a steady employment demand for well-trained graduates has failed from a lack of students. Remember that technical education still has an "image" problem, especially among minority students, in contrast to liberal and professional education, and recognize that recruitment may have to be an aggressive and continuing effort.

17. Start the program. Cost it out carefully as it develops and evaluate it yearly. Keep records on attrition rates, completion rates, unit costs, placement in jobs related to the program, and graduates' success over a five-year period after completing the program in order to determine the cost effectiveness of the program and the effectiveness of teaching, counseling, and advising.

18. Maintain close, continuing contact with all existing and potential employers. Visit them frequently, invite them to "open house" on campus, know their problems as well as their plans for

the future, and encourage them to consider hiring graduates of the program. Make adaptations in the program as necessary, in terms of employers' plans for the present and the future.

19. Try to maintain open access to the several levels of the program through developmental or "vestibule" activities and a core-and-ladder approach to promote recurrent and continuing education as well as career laddering and latticing for graduates throughout their careers.

20. Above all, do not compromise on excellence and quality in the program nor on standards of performance expected of the graduates. Award certificates and degrees only when these standards are attained. Avoid the trap of emphasizing educational process rather than product, by orienting the entire program to the results expected from learning: performance and accomplishment.

Additional Suggestions for Four-Year Colleges. Besides these twenty guidelines applicable to any career-oriented institution, the following ideas should be given careful consideration by four-year colleges and universities:

1. Before starting a four-year middle-manpower level program, make sure there is or will be in the immediate future a demand for baccalaureate-degree graduates in the career field.

2. Assure that all the specialized facilities and equipment needed for the program are already available or can be provided immediately—at levels of sophistication consistent with the demands of the career field.

3. Make sure that well-qualified faculty can be found and employed for the program. Starting a career program in order to provide continuing employment for existing faculty is unjustifiable unless the faculty members involved are very well qualified in that career.

4. As suggested in Chapter Four, establish effective articulation with the two-year and other four-year colleges of the region in order to avoid unnecessary duplication of programs and unseemly competition for students.

5. Adopt the "two-plus-two" concept as a general principle and establish only the upper-division level of the program, coordinating it with the relevant associate degree programs being offered in the state's community and technical colleges. And adopt

the "upside-down" concept by structuring the upper division program in such a way that two-year college programs can retain their job-competency emphasis and still meet all the transfer requirements to upper division programs.

6. Finally, do not initiate any associate degree programs unless the demand in the region for manpower in that career field is clearly not being met by two-year colleges. As noted earlier, the picture of four-year colleges and two-year colleges engaged in a recruitment contest for the same students for the same two-year program is one which legislators correctly view with disgust and outrage.

11 ◨◨◨◨◨◨◨◨◨◨◨◨◨

Career Education
in Urban
Community Colleges

*The land grant tradition reaches its urban phase of
growth in the community colleges. The land grant emphasis on technology, agriculture, applied science and
the professions has been translated by the community
colleges into strong support for vocational and technical proficiency of the commuting city-dweller, together with direct service to the practical needs of the
people of the surrounding city and region.*

Buell Gallagher (1974)

Of all the postsecondary institutions that offer career education
and that are described in Chapter Four—from private business,
trade, and technical schools and area vocational-technical schools
to technical institutes, two- and four-year colleges, and universities
—none face the problems in planning and operating successful
programs that confront urban community colleges. The issues with
which these colleges in the forty or fifty largest cities in America

must deal differ not only in degree but often in kind from those of other types of institutions as well as of suburban or rural colleges. As a consequence, these problems warrant special attention in any book dealing with career education in colleges.

Emergence of Urban Community College Systems

Community colleges of the 1970s are increasingly *city* colleges: they are essentially urban in their orientation. In the decade of the 1960s, their flowering was paced by developments in some twenty major American cities, including Phoenix, Denver, Miami, Kansas City, St. Louis, Boston, Detroit, Cleveland, Pittsburgh, Dallas, and Seattle, which joined the older complexes of Los Angeles, Chicago, and New York in developing and expanding multicampus community college systems embracing anywhere from three to nine major units, supplemented by scores of satellite outposts or off-campus centers. Sometimes these systems are coterminous with the city from whose common school system they have emerged as an adjunct of the high school. More commonly, in the newer big-city developments like St. Louis and Cleveland, the system spans the metropolitan area and joins units in the central city with others in the surrounding suburbs. The rise of these urban community college systems has been perhaps the most significant element in the fourfold increase in enrollment in the nation's growing network of community colleges during the 1960s, and in the growth of community college enrollments nationally to 4,069,279 students by 1976 (American Association of Community and Junior Colleges, 1972).

Within community colleges in the big city districts, burgeoning enrollments increasingly have come from adults and the poor. Their average age of students is now 28, and more than half of their students come from families with incomes below the poverty level—and are strongly motivated to qualify for a better job.

Dr. Edmund J. Gleazer, Jr., President of the American Association of Community and Junior Colleges, sees the community college movement as offering increasing opportunities to adults and the economically disadvantaged. He states (1974, p. 11), "Target populations will include a large proportion of personnel not previously found in postsecondary education. These will include persons who have been unable to continue post high school education, adults unemployed or in jobs that are obsolete, the hard core unemployed, women in the community, including young mothers with children at home, and senior citizens. The effects of serving these populations will include a rising age level, higher proportion of students from lower socio-economic levels, and larger numbers of part-time students."

These "new students," seeking training and education either individually or through their present or potential employers, have been the major factor not only in the large and rapid expansion of all postsecondary enrollment but in the conversion of community college programs to a predominantly occupational orientation. In contrast to the 30 percent or more of students who were enrolled in occupational programs in 1965, by 1974 a full 44 percent across the nation identified with courses and programs designed to give them job competence (Hearings on H.R. 14454, 1974).

What characteristics of metropolitan centers are significant for planning and operating successful occupational programs for these students? Several come readily to mind.

One obvious characteristic is that of large numbers of people living and working in close proximity to each other. These large populations are diverse in ethnic and racial background, social class, income, occupation, verbal skills, and job skills. Their sheer volume and density often makes it possible to provide specialized programs for special groups based on such characteristics as verbal skills, age, and occupational experience.

Potential employers are likewise diverse, offering a great number and variety of opportunities for employment and cooperative work experience. They increasingly see upgrading and updating of their employees, particularly those with minimal verbal skills, as a must. Advisory committees and other relationships with industry, business, and public agencies are readily arranged.

In addition, human and public services are badly needed by urban poor people as manufacturing employment declines with the flight to the suburbs. Of highest priority to urban colleges in

the midst of high unemployment in the inner cities is literacy training and job entry training for the poor and inservice education for
adults, particularly for those in public employment.

The planning and operation of successful career programs
cannot deal with these characteristics one at a time in easy isolation,
but must accept them as parts of a consort of complex relationships. Occupational programs for the poor, for example, cannot
be divorced from employment and literacy development any more
than effective career preparation for individuals can be divorced
from the employment needs of business, industry, and public
agencies. Thus a variety of individual and institutional needs must
be serviced simultaneously.

Looking Outward to the City

The first priority in meeting these individual and institutional
needs is for the governing board, administration, and faculty of
the urban community college to adopt an outward look—an external rather than an internal orientation. As the chancellor of an
urban college says, "curricula in the better community colleges
tend to be pragmatically determined, according to the industrial
and commercial demands of the area, embracing the practical and
vocational studies that may be of utility within the region" (Gallagher, 1974, p. 100). The community of outside agencies—public
employers, industries, and business groups—plays a major role in
setting the parameters and the standards of institutional operations. As a study of twenty-three Michigan community colleges revealed, "influence sources external to the college, but in the college
local community, are dominant" (Webster, 1974, p. 89) in the development of new occupational programs.

This looking-outward concept contrasts directly with the conventional faculty view that the determination of curriculums and
courses should be entirely an internal matter and that the faculty
are the only fount of knowledge, the originators and the guardians
of the educational program. In many community colleges, faculty
members now work closely with advisory committees appropriate
to career programs and consider the needs of potential employers
along with their own interests. The problem remains acute, how-

ever, in older and more traditional community colleges, particularly in those that have grown up as junior colleges with a broad liberal arts orientation and a college transfer mission. Here there may be much more resistance to an outward and occupational orientation, particularly in terms of faculty insistence that a large and sometimes undue amount of general education be included in the curriculum. In such institutions, curriculum committees, which internally approve or disapprove new programs, are often loaded with old-line faculty, and internal resistance to change is often institutionalized in a faculty association or union that gets much of its support from older faculty steeped in traditional teaching patterns and subjects and opposed to administrative efforts to adjust to the outside community.

One resolution of this problem is for the administration and governing board simply to take a strong hand in deciding on what curriculums are appropriate and for administrators to take leadership in planning course content, level, and sequence. Community colleges are fortunate in this regard: they have been administrator-influenced institutions without the strong resistance to change that has characterized faculty senates and faculty curriculum committees in four-year colleges, and their administrators have been more ready to support, encourage, and defend this outward thrust in program development in response to community need than have those in other institutions of higher education. This characteristic outward thrust of the community college perhaps distinguishes it most significantly from the traditional college or university with its fairly stable and historically evolved curriculum; its mission, programs, and courses determined essentially by faculty; its "community" defined as a self-contained group of academic scholars; and its students selectively admitted from the four corners of the world to be returned home for eventual leadership roles after prolonged and intensive immersion in the college culture and the community of scholars. In this environment, liberal arts are extolled and practical skills minimized. Learning for learning's sake is emphasized, and learning for career competence, except at professional levels, is soft-pedaled.

Contrast this orientation with the community colleges, where the community served is the district—an area usually coterminous with the city limits or the county—where the entire unselected adult population can find what it wants or needs; and where business, industry, and public agencies see and use the college as a vehicle for producing trained and educated workers and providing inservice education for older workers.

The implications of an external orientation of this kind affect not only how the curriculum, programs, and course content are determined but also what skills and knowledge are deemed essential for students.

Handmaiden to the Establishment?

In terms of developing effective educational programs for students in big city community colleges, the alternatives range between two extremes on a continuum. On the one hand, a community college can offer, as in the past, speculative programs based on past experience in which courses and their content are internally determined, first on the basis of what the faculty can and want to teach, and second on what presumably will attract the most students. Here registration is something of a gamble since there may not be sufficient enrollment to justify the courses on the schedule. This is the so-called cafeteria approach that features an à la carte menu determined by the faculty. At the other end of the continuum is the curriculum based on the needs of private and public agencies and courses developed cooperatively with these agencies, including the tailoring of courses to the needs of particular agencies, hiring and paying agency personnel on a part-time or lectureship basis to teach the courses, and offering the courses to agency employees at their work location during the day, with the employees receiving academic credit as "college students" and their classes given the mantle of approval by the college. This approach contemplates a marriage between the collegiate sector of postsecondary education and employers, in which colleges underwrite, with some financial assistance, inservice education of employed adults on the assumption that such target groups can be better serviced on the job because their educational goals are thereby better focused and that business, industry, and public agencies are entitled to the same educational services as individual taxpayers. This second approach may be called the "handmaiden-to-employers" approach.

Big city community colleges increasingly tend toward this "handmaiden" end of the continuum in their development of inservice programs for employees of business, industry, and public agencies. For example, they offer special banking programs in cooperation with the American Institute of Banking or alternatively with large banks who have their own format for employee education; they provide basic literacy and General Education Development (G.E.D.) test preparation for employees of major industries and businesses; they run programs to upgrade employees of the urban housing authorities, special child development training for staff members of Model Cities day-care centers, and preservice and inservice courses for policemen and firemen. These kinds of programs, particularly in the public sector, appear to be increasing in importance in big cities because of the large numbers of persons involved, the expansion of human service employment, the desperate need for improving the skills of personnel who provide public and human services, and the large concentration of population in urban centers, that makes programs tailored to the needs of specific businesses, industries, and public agencies economically feasible.

When a college becomes a handmaiden to public and private agencies by serving employed adults in closed classes, whether advertised overtly as "blocked" for certain groups or not, the result is restricted class admission by virture of the times the classes are held and the places they are offered. This is a technical violation of open enrollment, but it has distinct advantages and may even in the long run serve a larger number of people, albeit in a more structured arrangement. It ties the college to the needs of community agencies—taxpaying and public—and identifies the college with the public and private power structure of the community. Some humanists see this approach as a departure from the role of higher education as the unrelenting and aloof critic of society and charge such colleges with acquiescence in, if not dowright support of "establishment" goals. This approach does impose on these colleges the role of a full partner to the establishment, immersed in the problems of the city and participating in their solutions. Outward oriented and career oriented institutions generally accept this approach as part of their total philosophy.

Certain operational advantages are inherent in the hand-maiden concept. Employer-related programs normally enroll highly motivated students. Already on the job, their work experience is built in and can be related directly to the educational content of the program. Support in terms of funding or staff assistance is available from the agencies served by the programs. Since the programs provide educational services to the power structure and also to many people, there is in theory at least a more compatible environment for providing other necessary funds through the political process. And class scheduling is ordinarily more predictable than in open classes, although occasionally problems can arise, as when programs dependent on government funds are interrupted for one reason or another—for example, when funds for the Police Recruit Program of the Chicago City Colleges recently were withheld by order of a federal judge.

Some risks exist, however, as colleges move to this kind of program. For one thing, they may have less flexibility in their offerings, which become geared to adults and are therefore not well suited to younger students fresh out of high school who are seeking to prepare for their first jobs. The variety and balance of courses and programs may be affected adversely. The close involvement with the establishment inevitably leads to some politicization. The institution becomes involved in the process of government planning, and its location of off-campus courses or satellite centers may not be institutional choices since they become part of total community planning. Similarily requests for "placement" of people in college jobs, perhaps even verging on political patronage, may be frequent. Furthermore, the presumed stability of programs related to government agencies may not turn out to be a fact because government funding fluctuates with revenues and with the change of political parties in power.

Finally the character of faculty changes significantly as an institution moves toward the handmaiden concept. Experience, and particularly current experience, in the occupation about which a faculty member is teaching becomes far more important than formal academic preparation, even to the point of depending largely on agency staff members without graduate degrees, as in the police and fire departments, to teach specialized courses in their appropriate area. Emphasis tends to be placed more on the realism and effectiveness of instruction based on experience than on formal academic preparation and seniority.

Specialization Versus Comprehensiveness

Up to this point we have noted two emerging characteristics of big city community colleges: their "outward look" toward the city and their role of handmaiden to the establishment. A third characteristic that is emerging as more characteristic of big city community colleges than of others is that of specialization. The big city, of course, offers a great diversity of jobs along with a large population base. In preparing students for these jobs, should programs be duplicated on several campuses or allocated among specialized campuses—and should they be targeted toward the entire city or to sections or neighborhoods of the city? If expensive programs requiring specialized facilities, costly equipment, and low student-instructor ratios could not be duplicated willy-nilly, plans were needed to allocate them to appropriate sites. And if duplicate programs were offered, coordination was needed to insure that individual units within the system were not simultaneously negotiating at cross purposes with the same city agencies, such as the police department or the board of health, or other prospective employers, and not competing among themselves for limited students, faculty, and clinical facilities.

One of the fundamentals of the community college philosophy is the concept of comprehensiveness—the offering of a wide range of programs by a single comprehensive institution to meet the needs of a diverse student body. Historically, however, this concept emerged from single-campus institutions serving relatively small populations. Urban community colleges can be very comprehensive in this sense, since they have a population base large enough to support many more programs than rural or suburban institutions can, but the high density of their population base makes possible the development of specialized facilities and entire campuses for particular programs or clusters of programs. For example, in the public and human service fields, the most frequently encountered specialized programs are probably law enforcement and child care and development. The employing agencies for graduates of these programs are commonly city agencies, and the need for the college to communicate with these agencies about the programs through a single source almost invariably moves these programs toward a specialized location and centralization on one campus. For other reasons also—clear definition of mission, easier public identification, specialized guidance and counseling, cohesiveness of faculty with common interests, better focused general education, and better ethnic and racial integration—the case for specialization makes sense.

Since pressures for specialization are thus inevitable in urban systems, planners of big city colleges can consider the development of specialized units for new metropolitan campuses from the outset. Each unit could have a clearly defined mission to provide for one occupational or divisional area, plus a full range of transfer-oriented programs, career programs, adult and continuing education programs, and community service programs appropriate to that division. If the potential enrollment is adequate to support such specialization and if public transportation makes all units easily accessible, the fringe benefits in terms of clarity of mission, fixing of responsibility, and racial and ethnic integration may complement the obvious economic benefits of specialization (Grede, 1973b).

Even where the units in a big city system are conceived of as independently comprehensive and autonomous—or at least semiautonomous—in developing programs of their own choosing, they ordinarily require some coordination and perhaps even some centralization to prevent competition, avoid unnecessary proliferation, increase economy, and define responsibility. This is true not only in program areas necessitating specialized facilities, sophisticated equipment, and low student-to-faculty ratios, such as the health fields and engineering and industrial technology, but also in student services functions such as testing, career counseling, and job placement. Rather than replicating all of the services at each of the campuses, a centralized city-wide student services approach provides greater visibility and a larger job bank and often is the only cost-effective alternative if the separate units in the system have failed to develop support systems of their own commensurate with the programs they offer.

At the same time, however, it may be necessary to provide educational programs and student services throughout the community in a large number of outposts or satellite center locations if the system is dealing with students who would not normally and voluntarily come into the academic environment. Here it is important to take the programs *out* to the barrios and ghettos. The City Colleges of Chicago, for example, through the Chicago Urban Skills Institute, offer basic education, General Educational Development (G.E.D.) test preparation courses, and instruction in English as a second language at over four hundred off-campus locations, including store fronts, businesses, industries, YMCAs, churches, libraries, and community centers. Such a concept works particularly well for courses using the book-and-lecture learning and teaching format. On the other hand, career education programs that involve laboratory or shop facilities and relatively expensive equipment requiring safety precautions, continuing maintenance, and dependable security are best centered in a relatively few well-established facilities for effective operation.

Some basic problems are often involved in the operation of a network of satellite centers. One stems from requests, if not demands, that such centers take on an ethnic or racial character to provide identity and service in neighborhoods with large concentrations of Blacks, Latinos, or other ethnic or racial groups, and assume community service responsibilities wherein education and training in job skills, basic literacy, G.E.D. preparation, and English as a second language are supplemented by recreation activities, legal services, tenant services, child care, and community counseling. These services often are needed by residents of urban areas, but the college involved in them will have to make some hard decisions as to the allocation of educational dollars to them. Substantial political pressures characteristic of big cities will undoubtedly influence these decisions.

Other problems with satellite centers include meeting building and fire code requirements; providing teaching aids, and access to library and learning resources; and monitoring operations to make certain that teachers are present, registrations are properly completed, and records are being kept and forwarded to the central office.

Cutting across the question of whether or not physical facilities ought to be diffused into the urban landscape or concentrated into a few highly visible campuses is the issue of whether programs should be self-contained within college facilities (even though they be outposts) or whether work experience programs and actual on-the-job training in a realistic field situation is to be promoted. Many colleges have compromised on a combination of providing general skills applicable to a career area in college facilities, while seeing that the more advanced skills and experience on the more sophisticated equipment is gained in realistic job, shop, or clinic situations provided by employers. The argument for a college-based radiology laboratory, for example, is that general skills can be taught to many students in a few hundred hours and thus reduce the time requirements for patient contact experience in a hospital facility. Experience seems to argue for a relatively few well established, well equipped, college-owned facilities for occupational programs, coupled with the maximum utilization of employer locations where work experience may be developed. Neither situation can totally supplant the other.

Literacy and Job Entry Training for Adults. Should a community college in an urban area train the hard-core unemployed and dropouts from high school who are on the streets? Community college faculty might generally say no to such a proposal and argue that basic adult education and literacy training are not collegiate functions but are best left to the lower schools. But the community college that is outward-oriented and not subservient to traditionally narrow faculty perspective of its responsibility will accept this task if the local community has no other adequate training facilities or skill centers to assist the illiterate, the underemployed, and the unemployed in preparing for work. This kind of training is hardly "career education," but it can often stimulate career interest, develop a career goal, lead to job-related education, and result in employment.

Evidence of the need for urban community colleges to accept this kind of role as part of their mission is indicated by a 1971 study by the National Planning Association which found that in the twenty cities studied, only 2.7 percent of the population between nineteen and forty-four years of age were in skill training while many other persons were waiting to be served because programs were not available (Hearings on H.R. 14454, 1974). Furthermore, a recent U.S. Office of Education study revealed that fully 20 percent of all American adults are functionally illiterate, in terms of being incompetent, or functioning with difficulty at ordinary adult tasks. These functionally inept adults tend to be "older, under-educated, unskilled, and perhaps unemployed and living in poverty" ("23 Million Called Illiterate," 1975).

One of the great areas of present or potential growth for the urban community college is among this segment of the adult poor who are inadequate in communication skills, unemployed or marginally employed, and whose native tongue and current family language is frequently not English. Adult basic education is desperately needed for such persons, whose reading levels make the understanding of even simple manuals, work instructions, and safety regulations a difficult hurdle and who have no marketable job skills.

In many urban areas, basic literacy and job entry training for these adults, who may number up to a million, is an accepted responsibility of the secondary schools. In other cities however, economic straits have forced the schools to cut back to their regular "education-for-youth" mandate and to slough off responsibility for adult basic education. Here the community college must assume at least some of this mission. In addition, there is a growing belief that the community college, among all public educational institutions, has the basic responsibility for educating adults who, because of their age and maturity and regardless of their previous schooling, are defined as "postsecondary" students. It is increasingly evident that for many adults who have had unhappy experiences and lack of success in school, the college culture and ethos provide more motivation and a more compatible instructional environment than does the high school.

In recent years, these adults, sometimes defined as disadvantaged and including a disproportionate number of racial and ethnic minority members, have been helped through skill centers supported and regulated by the Department of Labor, first under the Manpower Development and Training Act and later under the Comprehensive Employment Training Act, and operated in some cases by school districts and in many others by community colleges. The simple formula offered by these training programs is prevocational or basic literacy training plus job entry skills development. Federally funded support services for these programs include recruitment from among the unemployed by state employment agencies, orientation, counseling, health services, stipends for living expenses, job placement, and follow-up.

Some basic problems develop for big city community colleges when they take on the mission of providing skill-center type programs. Two basic approaches to the new mission have been used. One is to integrate the skill-center programs into the regular college programs so that the same facilities and the same faculty are used for skill-center students and regular college program students. Strong psychological arguments exist for integrating skill-center programs and regular college programs in the same facilities with the same faculty so that students from both programs intermingle. Skill-center students thus see themselves as part of a college community rather than as persons who are "problems" to society, and the transferability of their work to the regular college program is maximized in the best traditions of the career-ladder concept. Relatively little transfer of credit has actually taken place to date, however, at least in the Chicago area, since the basic desire of most students who complete skill-center programs is for immediate employment.

On the other hand, a number of factors argue for separate satellite centers. For example, the instructional pattern for students in Comprehensive Employment Training Act of 1973 (CETA) programs under Department of Labor guidelines mandates a work week and a work program that simulates actual employment. Students in CETA are tightly programmed in classroom or laboratory and shop instruction for a full seven or eight hours per day, in contrast to the conventional college student who may take only two or three courses meeting for twelve to fifteen hours a week. Skill-center students are conventionally block programmed, particularly where the institution is dealing with sizable numbers. These students receive stipends and are required to sign in and out for receipt of such support funds. Skill-center programs conventionally are offered on a noncredit basis, in contrast to the degree-credit programs of the regular college. And, finally, faculty in skill-center programs do not ordinarily have the same level of academic background as other faculty. Their emphasis is on practical job experience—the *applying* rather than the *knowing* level of competence—and the tendency is to pay them less than conventional faculty in order to keep costs down, since the contracts with funding agencies under which these programs operate are often awarded in competition with alternative institutions, many of which are proprietary. The existence of a faculty union contract can pose problems here, since union negotiators argue for a single salary schedule for both collegiate and skill-center personnel. If this becomes the pattern, there will be few skill centers operated by public colleges since they could not compete with alternative bidders available to the Department of Labor.

It should be apparent from these unresolved problems that maintaining satellite skill centers as integral parts of a community college system presents continuing difficulties because of the different characteristics of the two settings. Actually the difficulty of articulating skill-center programs with regular college programs is merely a facet of the broader nationwide problem of articulation. A recent study of the effect of the funds set aside for vocational education in the CETA legislation found that there has been little impact to date due to poor communication and lack of understanding among educators and concluded that "it is imperative that greater cooperation between vocational education and manpower training programs be established" (National Advisory Council on Vocational Education, 1975, p. 18).

Articulation

The earlier discussion of basic literacy and job skill training of the adult poor in effect deals with internal articulation of college systems in urban areas. This articulation is mandated, of course, by the broad range of verbal and skill training provided within such a system and the need to relate its various programs and campuses to each other in order to provide effective career ladders and lattices through which students may progress to the limit of their interest and ability with a minimum of red tape.

Another aspect of articulation involves the relation of community-college career education to that of the secondary schools on the one hand and the senior colleges and universities on the other. With regard to the secondary schools, and to help counter the high dropout rates of inner-city high schools, community colleges can open their occupational education programs to high school students while they are still enrolled in high school. This cooperative effort serves to tie potential school dropouts to college programs that can be seen as leading to job preparation and employment at middle-manpower levels. Such meaningful and job-oriented high school-college programs encourage many otherwise unmotivated students to stay in school until graduation.

As for articulation between community colleges and four-year institutions, the development in senior institutions of capstone two-plus-two programs geared to two-year community college programs seems to offer great promise. With the development of career education programs and the growing emphasis on career ladders in both community colleges and baccalaureate institutions, career educators at both levels are working for program articulation and attempting to get senior institutions to accept the total associate degree program for transfer rather than limiting transfer to course-by-course evaluation and approval. There is growing support for the idea that all two-year college graduates, whether they follow the baccalaureate-oriented associate in arts program or the career-oriented associate in applied science program, should have access to upper-division education opportunities instead of being forced to meet the lower division requirements of the senior institution for its own freshmen and sophomores.

With its relations with both the high schools and senior institutions, the urban community college has a unique opportunity in the articulation of career education to tie both types of institution to middle-manpower development at the associate degree level. At the same time, it serves career-oriented adults by granting appropriate credit for their prior learning and works closely with business, industry, and public employers and their training programs. Because of these characteristics, it seems to be the agent for linking the elements of the collegiate sector of urban higher education and bridging the gap to the noncollegiate sector—proprietary, military, business, industry, union, and community agency education programs on the one hand and nontraditional students on the other. It has relationships with both the collegiate and noncollegiate arenas, as illustrated in Figure 7 below, and thus may assume the responsibility for promoting a better articulated system of career education. As a *linking pin* or nexus, it can connect people who seek careers with work that needs to be done and programs to prepare them for this work.

Granting Credit for Prior Learning

With over 50 million adults now participating in the so-called noncollegiate sector of postsecondary education, including the military, proprietary schools, and on-the-job training, as noted in Chapter Three, pressure is increasing both within and outside the academic community to assess or evaluate competencies attained through these other sources, equate them with competencies developed in collegiate programs, and translate them into acceptable academic currency by awarding academic credit for them toward degrees. These moves are, of course, highly controversial among tradition-bound educators, and only time will tell whether the practice gains wide acceptance.

Figure 7. The Linking-Pin Concept of the Community College in Career Education Articulation.

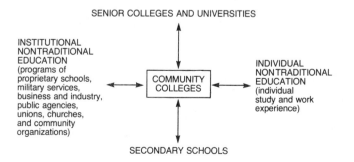

Since urban community colleges increasingly see their educational mission as being related to all adults, it follows that more than most other institutions they are beginning to take on the catalytic role of assessing a great variety of experiences not traditionally classified as collegiate and awarding credit for them as appropriate. These experiences include some from within their own organization, such as skill-center work or special programs for high-school students, which have not been considered "degree-credit" level, as well as a vast range of informal, noncollegiate, and nontraditional learning that adults have accumulated. There is need for competency-based evaluation by performance examinations, interviews, and other procedures to evaluate the several levels of competence in various skill areas so that this learning can be properly credited whenever necessary. The armed forces have already done much experimental work in evaluating various kinds of military training, and colleges have long experience in translating military courses into common academic currency through the work of the Office on Educational Credit (formerly Commission on the Accreditation of Service-Related Experience) of the American Council on Education. More generally applicable is the experimental work now being done for occupational programs by the National Occupational Competency Testing Institute. With initial government funding, it is developing a battery of more than two dozen occupationally oriented tests—both paper and pencil and performance based—to evaluate all kinds of experiences in such occupational fields as the construction trades, electronics, instrumentation, mechanical technology, drafting, and other industrial and engineering areas.

The concept of colleges as competency evaluators is by no means universally accepted, however. Those who hold the view that granting academic credit or "external" degrees for nonacademic learning is merely egalitarianism running rampant over realism, meritocracy, and academic integrity often invoke the following arguments:

First, although colleges may properly offer both academic and job-oriented education, they are basically *teaching and learning* institutions rather than *certifying* agencies for accrediting competencies attained elsewhere.

Second, as a matter of equity, why should persons, no matter how competent they are in a particular job such as wiring or welding be awarded college credits or even an academic degree for that competence, when a bona fide college graduate who has elected to spend two to four or more years in academic study is not certifiable as a journeyman electrician, welder, or other worker despite similar competence? Put more bluntly, why should persons with practical skills (valuable though these are) be presented with *academic* credentials, while the obverse is impossible?

Third, many educators are convinced that the value of the "college experience," the level and kinds of thinking that prolonged college attendance engenders, and the personal growth that extended contact with professors and fellow students fosters are the true basis for awarding the college degree. To award the degree totally or in part by "equating" noncollegiate skills and job experiences to college learning is to them inappropriate, if not a travesty bordering on the ludicrous.

Fourth and finally, certain practices of some colleges engaging in external degree and certifying activities seem to relate as much to maximizing their credit-hour production as to providing legitimate opportunities for students to demonstrate their skill and bypass unnecessary requirements. Interest in external degrees and the equation of off-campus experience to college credits began to burgeon only when full-time, regular-day college enrollments began to taper off, raising the possibility that concern for individual educational advancement may be at least matched by that for institutional financial security.

In one sense, the issues posed by the movement toward external degree competency assessment and credit for experience movement are a part of the ongoing controversy between traditionalists and modernists in education. But transcending that, they have some roots at least in the egalitarianism-meritocracy controversy and involve questions of equity, academic integrity, and fiscal motivation.

Proponents of awarding credit for prior learning argue that the policy has sound historical bases, stretching back to the creation of the University of London in 1836 as a certifying or credentialing institution; that equity now demands that colleges certify the competence of individuals if they have it, regardless of where they learned it (rather than discriminating against nonstudents, even if unions or other groups discriminate against nonmembers); that awarding academic credits and degrees based on demonstrated competence is more appropriate than awarding them primarily for endurance in "chair-sitting" or on the basis of clock hours spent in the classroom; and that the abuses of degree mills and a few desperate institutions should not damn an otherwise desirable practice. New York State has gone so far, in fact, as to create its own Regents External Degree program to award academic degrees on the basis of demonstrated knowledge and skill to people who may never have taken a single course in college.

But to avoid the stigma of overgenerous or illegitimate awards of credit to students for their prior experience, career-oriented colleges should follow the advice of such agencies as the regional accrediting associations, Office on Educational Credit of the American Council on Education, the Council for the Advancement of Experiential Learning (formerly the Cooperative Assessment of Experiential Learning project), and other organizations well versed in the pros and cons of this developing movement.

Attitudes of Minorities Toward Career Education and Job Training

One common problem in the development of occupational programs by big-city community colleges is the frequent rejection by minority groups of middle-manpower and skilled trade programs. As occupational programs have assumed a position of major importance in big city colleges within the last ten years, black college presidents and others have noted that minorities in general and blacks in particular are still grossly underrepresented in the prestigious professions of medicine, law, and engineering, and have argued that young blacks should be encouraged to prepare for these professions rather than for technical or skilled trade careers. This is a point of view that many minority students accept and follow.

Monroe (1972, pp. 94–95) cites another objection on the part of some black students to certain occupational programs: "An ornamental horticulture program failed, not because the planners from both industry and the college had not surveyed the market for horticulturalists but because they did not realize that the students, the majority of whom were black, would reject a field which resembled too closely such menial occupations as cotton planting. White students, however, had no such feelings about ornamental horticulture, a field in which jobs were plentiful and the pay was very good."

Dorothy Knoell (1970), in her study of the interest and abilities of black students in five metropolitan community colleges, confirmed the reluctance of black students to enter employment that they regard as menial and of low prestige, such as hotel or restaurant work, police and fire service, and low-level clerical work in business, particularly when the programs are short-term occupational programs.

Somewhat in contradiction to these findings, however, a study by Willford Wilms (1975), found that minority students, particularly blacks, utilizing funds from financial aid programs enrolled in sizable numbers in proprietary schools, attracted in part at least by their short-term strictly skill-type preparation in contrast to the conventional academic courses that community colleges add to their occupational programs. And in Chicago, at least, black students readily accept vocational-technical programs such as automotive repair and air conditioning, where ready employment awaits the graduates.

It would appear that, while there is a certain amount of voiced opposition by minority *leaders* to minority participation in less prestigious trade-vocational programs, individual students, whatever their racial or ethnic background will participate in training that leads to jobs if the pay is good and if prestige, as in automotive service and air conditioning, is at least satisfactory. Some minority leaders, rather than opposing such programs, openly support minority enrollment in occupational programs, particularly in community colleges. Donald Godbold, (1976, p. 24) president of Merritt College in Oakland, California observes:

> Students who have completed a baccalaureate degree, including blacks and other minorities, frequently return to the

community college to obtain training in occupational areas to provide them with marketable skills. . . . Other blacks and minorities enroll . . . to upgrade themselves in their present occupation or to attain certificates in certain skill areas, to develop basic skills, and to pursue special interests. Blacks and other minorities now attending community colleges are well into their late twenties. . . . (They) have a means of subsistence, and community colleges serve a purpose for them that may enrich their lives and enhance their livelihood, but may not necessarily include transfer to a senior institution for any type of certificate or degree, although this possibility exists.

In essence, Godbold sees minority students getting from community colleges the same range of opportunities and free choice situations as other students and not being "dead-ended" or "tracked" into low-level, noncredit, vocational work that restricts social and economic mobility, as some critics such as Karabel (1972) claim. The restrictions, according to Godbold, are rather with senior institutions where the trend "again appears to be away from egalitarianism and toward meritocracy in consideration of the poor, blacks, and other minorities" (p. 24).

Financial Considerations

Traditionally community colleges derive their funds from state sources, local sources, student tuition, and to some extent from categorical federal funds. Big city community colleges enroll particularly large numbers of students from low income facilities— in Chicago's community colleges, for example, 60 percent are from families with less than $9,000 annual income—and even "low" tuition may be a high hurdle for them. Adequate financial aid is essential to enable many of these students to enroll. Because the cost of occupational programs is generally higher than that of academic programs by a factor of from 1.2 to 2.5, and because tuition increases are not a viable source of revenue to offset their increased cost, financing these programs necessarily falls on public tax sources—local, state, and federal.

Local taxes, however, have generally not provided additional subsidies for vocational programs but instead are used across the board. By contrast, state and federal funds, particularly those from such federal legislation as the Vocational Education Acts of 1963 and 1968 and the Education Amendments of 1972, have generally been depended upon to pick up the "excess costs" of career programs. Unfortunately this additional support has generally been inadequate except in a few states such as Iowa and Wisconsin where considerably more has been available to postsecondary education than the 15 percent "set-aside" specified in the federal acts. The American Association of Community and Junior Colleges and the National Advisory Council on Vocational Education have both recommended that the Congress increase substantially the set-aside for postsecondary education in future major revisions of the federal Vocational Education Acts.

One additional factor is, of course, the amount of state funds that are allocated to match the federal funds. Throughout the country, it is not uncommon for states to provide four to five state dollars for each federal dollar available for postsecondary career education, although some states are barely able to maintain a one-to-one ratio. A serious problem with federal funds is that they have been categorical in nature, and instead of helping local institutions with general funds budgets, they usually call for local matching funds, resulting in greater strain on college general funds budgets.

Another problem of government support of urban community colleges involves job placement of their graduates. Placement in program-related jobs is generally regarded as the single most important item in the evaluation of career education programs, and government funding agencies are particularly prone to judge skill-center programs almost exclusively on their placement records. The use of placement as the primary or sole criterion of program accomplishment or success should be avoided, however, particularly in in-service programs where students are typically already employed before enrollment. What is needed instead are measures of the increment of competence or effectiveness that graduates can utilize for greater job mobility, either lateral or upward, regardless of their immediate placement.

Still another problem for metropolitan colleges involves federal Comprehensive Employment Training Act (CETA) funding for job skill centers and similar programs. These funds frequently can be spread more widely and used more specifically for hands-on training if the vocational or literacy component of the program is funded from other sources, such as Adult Education Act funds, but in a very general sense the funding for these programs discriminates against urban centers. In 1973–1974, the National Advisory Council on Vocational Education held hearings in five major cities that had indicated a great need to improve their vocational education. The hearings revealed that urban areas with the largest concentration of the educationally and economically disadvantaged do not receive funding proportional to their share of the state's population. A National Planning Association study similarly found that in forty-one states, Standard Metropolitan Statistical Areas (SMSAs) received less federal vocational education money than would be expected on the basis of population, and in thirty-seven states they received less state money than their share of the state's population would warrant. Testimony further indicated that most city colleges find their costs are higher for such basic operating expenses as salaries, maintenance, and repair than they are for rural and suburban districts (National Advisory Council on Vocational Education, 1975). Thus many city colleges are caught in a double bind: their funding on a per capita basis is less than that received by other types of districts, while their costs per student generally are higher. There is thus evident need for a program of special funding for urban career education.

Summary

Urbanization brings with it many problems. These are all well known, and reciting the litany of them here would serve no purpose. Many of them however, are either directly or indirectly related to unemployment. To the extent that unemployment can be reduced, urban problems are reduced; and at the same time public revenues are increased so that cities can better cope with the problems which remain.

Education, to be sure, cannot create jobs, but it can provide the skills and the knowledge which enable millions of inner-city residents to qualify for jobs. Urban community colleges, operating in the inner city can bring city residents and city employers together in filling available jobs. To the extent that unemployment can thus be reduced, urban problems are reduced while public revenues are increased. As a result, cities can better cope with their remaining problems.

12 ▣▣▣▣▣▣▣▣▣▣▣▣▣

Economics
of Career Education
in Colleges

*Most people some of the time think that the pursuit of
self-interest and profit is an ignoble pursuit. They are
surely right to take this view, although they preach it
more often than they practice it. Economics has been
(and is) concerned with the less noble side of life—in
part, if not totally—although man is seldom more in-
nocently employed than while making money.*

John Vaizey (1962)

Education has many defenders, though it needs no defense when
pursued for its own sake. It also has its hucksters, whom it would
not need if its perceived value were high enough. The fact that the
lower schooling is free and compulsory in our society and that the
higher learning is expected by most people to "pay off" in the
marketplace says something about the values that the general public ascribes to education. And of all the values associated with

316

higher education, its expected economic value probably looms largest in the minds of most Americans.

A brief historical review of the economic value of education in terms of public support for education will set the stage for further discussion of the current economic returns of college-level career education to Americans individually and to American society.

Education and American Society

Very early in colonial America it was decided that youth should be offered instruction under public auspices. In 1647 the Massachusetts General Court ordered that every town or village of fifty or more households must offer instruction in reading and writing, since "the one chief project of the old deluder Satan (is) to keep men from a knowledge of the Scriptures." Although many school laws and ordinances were enacted in colonial times by various legislative and governmental bodies, the "Old Deluder Satan Act" of 1647 is regarded as the forerunner of public education, and by 1671 all of New England except Rhode Island had some kind of quasicompulsory education for the young (Meyer, 1967). Our forefathers felt that society should provide for the instruction of the young for three reasons, in descending order of importance: (1) to enable youth to read and write, so that Satan's "delusions" could be minimized; (2) to select and instruct the qualified few for later study at a college or university; (3) to provide the rudiments of reading, writing, and "counting" so that the needs of commerce and artificing could be met.

Schooling grew slowly but steadily in popularity, and by the time of the American Revolution, publicly ordained (and partly publicly supported) schools were to be found in nearly all the colonies. Secondary education, for the most part, was still a private affair, and colleges and universities were few and private. Much education was church-related, and very little of the schooling offered at any level could be considered as vocational or occupational except, of course, that offered for persons intending to enter the ministry.

The founding fathers, it seemed, had more pressing problems confronting them than education. Indeed, the idea that education should become an obligation or function of the national government was not at all popular, and the Constitution is silent on the subject of schooling. The Congress, however, in the Ordinance of 1787, "encouraged" education in the newly formed Northwest Territory by stipulating that "since religion, morality, and knowledge are necessary to good government and the happiness of mankind, schools should be ever encouraged." For this purpose each new state to join the Union from the Northwest Territory would be given the sixteenth section in each township for support of schools. With such inducements from the federal government, and in accordance with more definite stipulations in most state constitutions, the concept of publicly supported elementary schooling became an accepted practice throughout the nation in the ensuing century.

Secondary education was much slower in developing. Private academies carried much of this responsibility in colonial times and on into the nineteenth century, when Massachusetts passed the first state law providing for publicly supported education beyond the basics of grammar and arithmetic. The Massachusetts statute of 1827 did not use the term *high school*, but it required every town of five hundred families to provide instruction, paid for by taxation, in such subjects as geometry, bookkeeping, American history, surveying, and advanced, or secondary, instruction in grammar and composition. Larger cities were to provide, in addition, courses in Latin, Greek, logic, and rhetoric (Meyer, 1967).

This Massachusetts law was not implemented with any degree of alacrity, however, and such schools as were established under this and similar laws in other states were generally held in much lower esteem than the private academies of the time. The concept of general taxation to support the common (lower) schools was not yet fully accepted, and the idea of tax-supported public high schools in every city and hamlet was the subject of bitter controversy during the middle half of the nineteenth century. People generally did not see enough value in high school education for all youth to make it a just charge on the taxpayer. It was 1874 before a landmark court case—the "Kalamazoo Decision" of the

Michigan Supreme Court—held that high schools were a legal and justifiable part of a state's public school system to be supported by tax levies on the state's citizens.

Even with this legal sanction, which served as a precedent for other states, another half century would pass before the American high school would be looked upon by most citizens as a useful and necessary institution that all youth should attend tuition free and that society would support because the value to society derived therefrom was deemed greater than its cost. Tuition-free, compulsory public education for all youth became a reality for most Americans by about 1925, and state laws compelling attendance to age sixteen or eighteen were enacted in most states.

Only in very recent times has the idea that education should be provided for all at public expense because it is an ultimate good been extended upward into the realm of higher education. In the euphoric years following victory in World War II, with the great achievements and heroic sacrifices of that conflict fresh in mind, four ideas took embryonic form and began to grow in the minds of many Americans: (1) higher education contains within its content, scope, and method the solution to all or nearly all of the problems of modern societies; (2) the value of higher education to society will be in direct proportion to the number of persons going to college; (3) society owes a college education to anyone who wants to enroll; (4) no matter what it costs, American society can afford it and should provide the funds for universal higher education.

These ideas were reflected in the recommendations of the Commission on Higher Education for American Democracy (the so-called Truman Commission) in 1947, and over the past thirty years they gradually have evolved into a credo of the higher education establishment. By no means is such a credo accepted by Americans generally, and this disagreement is the source of a great deal of controversy.

The Commission's "National Inventory of Talent" (President's Commission on Higher Education, 1947, p. 41) concluded that: "(1) at least 49 percent of our population has the mental ability to complete 14 years of schooling . . . in general and vocational studies that lead to gainful employment or further study at a more advanced level"; and "(2) at least 32 percent . . . has the mental ability to complete advanced liberal or specialized professional education."

In addition to these beginnings of the idea of universal higher education, the Commission's report emphasized throughout the theme that much of the cost of "higher education for American democracy" should be financed from taxes. This report also enunciated the idea that public two-year colleges (up to that time called *junior colleges*) should serve as *community colleges*.

Ten years later President Eisenhower convened a Committee on Education Beyond the High School, and its report (President's Committee on Education Beyond the High School, 1957) further emphasized opportunity for higher education for all youth and reemphasized the idea of low-tuition, publicly supported community colleges, which should be established in "communities or groups of neighboring communities," as being highly effective in providing opportunities for excellent education beyond the high school.

These ideas grew slowly at first, then rapidly, and in the 1960s they culminated in a veritable explosion in the growth of higher education. As the last quarter of the twentieth century began, America had made a commitment to education surpassing that of any other society in history. Universal elementary education is followed by very nearly universal secondary education, and although there is no national consensus, many propose universal higher education as the next step.

By 1972, well over 90 percent of all seventeen-year-olds were in high school, and 75 percent of these were graduating. Of all persons in the twenty-five- to twenty-nine-year cohort, 80 percent had four years of high school or more. In the early 1970s nearly 57 percent of new high school graduates were "going on to college," and in some states this figure was above 70 percent. An indication of the vastness of this enterprise (public and private, elementary through college) can perhaps best be obtained by its price tag—an estimated $130 billion for 1976–1977 ("Schools Expect Fewer Students," 1976). This represents about 8 percent of the Gross National Product (GNP) for 1976 and would require an annual assessment of about $1,480 against *every member of the employed labor force* to pay for it. Nearly $50 billion of the total is expected to go for higher (postsecondary) education.

With nearly one tenth of the GNP going into schooling, it would seem that periodic and serious cost-benefit analyses would be made to determine whether the expenditure is really a good investment or whether alternative investments might yield higher returns. That these analyses are not made supports the contention that education in America is almost a religion—it is an "ultimate good"; to question its value to society is almost the equivalent of blasphemy.

In contrast to the United States, many countries look at public expenditures for education within a context of national priorities and attempt to allocate their limited public funds to those social purposes that seem to promise the best rate of return. Education is therefore looked upon as a *potential good,* an enterprise probably worthy of public investment but one that must continue to justify itself in the crucible of economic analysis. Education in these countries is subject to evaluation and rate-of-return analysis along with all other major public enterprises. If for any reason the rate of return on investment in education proves to be low, relatively less public money will be invested in it.

This market approach to investment in education is unpalatable to many Americans and has not been considered seriously for at least three reasons: (1) the belief held by most Americans that anything we want we can afford; (2) the equally firm conviction that education is an ultimate good, not subject to market analysis; and (3) the fact that Americans generally reject the idea of centralized social and economic planning.

The belief that education is an ultimate good was supported by national trends for many decades. Since the turn of the century it has seemed that the more youth, and later adults, who were schooled, the more society seemed to prosper. Not only did education seem to produce economic prosperity, but also until very recently it appeared that many "social goods" could also be attributed to schooling. Of course, it is quite easy to believe in the moral rewards of a financially rewarding enterprise. For the individual, too, from the turn of the century until 1970, there seemed to be incontrovertible evidence that added increments of education resulted in significant increments of personal income—in other words, education paid off in hard cash.

But 1970 was a turning point, and now we are not so sure that education always pays off either to the individual or to society. And there is the increasing realization that even if education does resemble an "ultimate good," we cannot always afford it. So, after a half-century love affair with education, many Americans are coming to regard it not as the ultimate solution but as just one of many possible avenues to social and economic improvement. They are looking at other options with renewed interest, and they are beginning to look at education from a cost-benefit point of view— they want to know what the rate of return is likely to be before they make additional massive investments.

Although rate-of-return analysis as applied to education is relatively new and somewhat unsophisticated, a considerable amount of work has been done and is currently under way. We turn now to a brief analysis of some of the findings.

Cost-Benefit Considerations in Higher Education

At the outset, let it be noted that we are very much aware of and strongly support those values inherent in the higher learning that are not necessarily associated with individual or societal economic gain. There are indeed significant and enduring values in the study of the arts and sciences for their own sake, for the lift they give to the spirit, for the understanding of the human condition that their study engenders, and just for the joy of knowing. The ongoing argument between the humanists, who would have us believe that education should have no economic dimension, and the economists, whose work sometimes suggests that expected economic returns are the primary purpose of education, has tended to inhibit the realization that for most persons higher education should serve both purposes. Harbison and Myers (1964, p. 12–13) argue this point of view:

> As professional specialists, economists do tend to measure progress exclusively by economic criteria, even if as individual members of society they often have a much broader view of the goals of society. . . . Education for citizenship, education for "life adjustment," or education for enhancement

of freedom, dignity, and worth of man are legitimate goals, but they express only in part the aspirations of modern societies. The purely humanistic approach, like the limited economic approach to human resource development, distorts the true meaning of the aspirations of modern man and modern societies. But, in reality, there need be no conflict between the economists and the humanists. . . . The development of man for himself may still be considered the ultimate end, but economic progress can also be one of the principal means of attaining it.

Rate of Return to the Individual. One way of looking at cost-benefit considerations for the individual in higher education is to sum up the total dollar cost of college attendance to an individual or his family and consider this as a capital investment. The extra or "added income" that the college education produces (over and above what would have been yielded by a high school education alone) is estimated. The average annual individual rate of return on the capital investment, over a working lifetime, can then be calculated.

Before discussing education from a return-on-investment point of view, however, several terms must be clarified.

1. *Economic returns* can be measured in terms of monetary gain. The *individual* rate of return is calculated on the individual's investment as a base; and the rate of return to *society* is calculated on society's investment as a base.

2. *Noneconomic returns,* although they may have some unevaluated relationship to the economic health of the individual and of society, are those returns in the form of personal satisfaction, happiness, improved quality of life, and so on, which are usually difficult to define and to measure in dollars. Noneconomic returns to society are such factors as better citizenship, less crime, improved tolerance, and civic pride.

3. Education as a *consumption item,* refers to learning experiences which are consumed (enjoyed) as of the moment, and have no measurable benefit which accrues to either society or the individual over time.

4. The concept of *human capital* goes beyond Adam Smith's "land, labor, and capital" formulation of economic theory (A. Smith, 1939), and requires what Harbison and Meyers (1964, p. 3) describe as the "economic analysis of investment in man." In addition to land, labor, capital, and investments made in productive equipment and inventories, investment in human resources and building of human capital through education and training are now recognized as essential steps in building the wealth of a nation. It should be noted that the "human capital" theories of economists are rejected by humanists as being degrading, in view of their consideration of humans as another element in economic productivity. Recent events too (notably the energy crisis) are casting some doubt on the promise of human resources development theory, since capital-intensive economies are possible only when energy is abundant.

5. *Annual income* is the dollar value (usually referenced to some "fixed" year) of all income received by an individual in a year.

6. *Lifetime income* is the dollar value (in "constant dollars") of the total earnings, based on means for various groups in the population, for a working lifetime (usually forty years).

7. *Education,* as used in most rate-of-return studies, is taken to mean years of *formal schooling*. Other inputs to learning—experience, on-the-job training, home study, armed forces schools, and the like, are ordinarily not factored in. Much controversy exists about the use of the terms "education" and "schooling." The education "establishment" looks upon them as synonymous terms, but critics of society and education claim that often there is little relationship between schooling and education (Berg, 1971).

8. *Rate-of-return-on-investment* in education is, in effect, a "rate of discount which will equate the stream of *extra earnings* resulting from education (defined as schooling) with the costs incurred in obtaining that education" (Innes, Jacobson, and Pellegrin, 1965).

Note that it is only the *extra earnings* presumed to result from education, that enter into the rate-of-return calculation. It should be noted also that a figure for the total cost of the education must be used, including tuition, books, rent, transportation, extra clothing and supplies—every conceivable expense which going to school entails. Further, an estimated amount for "earnings foregone" is usually included in the cost calculation, since the individual could have been gainfully employed (an assumption of course) had he not been in school.

Serious work on calculating the economic returns of education began only in the early 1960s. Based on separate studies by Schultz, Becker, Miller, and Hansen (who used data from the U.S. Census reports), Innes, Jacobson, and Pellegrin (1965) concluded that the rate of return to the individual on a four-year college education over the period between 1930 and 1960 was in excess of 10 percent. And from the mid-1950s to about 1968, several other researchers have reported that the college graduate derives a monetary return on his investment in a college education (foregone earnings included) of about 12 to 15 percent per year throughout his post-college working life. Wolfle (1973) reports a similar finding, and attributes the earnings advantage of college graduates to three factors: (1) Knowledge and skills enhanced while in college, (2) The self-selection toward higher ability of those who go to college, and (3) The possession of the credential or degree that traditionally has opened the door to the higher status occupations.

Until the late 1960s there was nearly unanimous agreement among educational economists that "going to college" paid off rather handsomely to the individual—that its rate of return was probably higher than could be expected from the investment of a like sum of money (always counting foregone earnings) in almost any other reasonable-risk enterprise. Recent research, however, takes a sharper look and comes up with less positive results. Some of the shortcomings of this early research should be noted, however, in order to obtain a realistic perspective on the results and probabilities identified by the data. First of all, the data base, usually from the U.S. Census, is often unreliable as to the kind and level of education and as to income and foregone earnings. Second, the data cover a period in which higher education was in short supply and therefore of relatively higher value. This was also a period before unionization and divers social pressures pushed up the earnings of blue collar and service workers to a point where differentials between unionized skilled-manual groups and professional-technical-managerial groups are much smaller, or sometimes even reversed. Third, the "screening effect" of college (Taubman and Wales, 1974) was a strong factor then, but with the open-door colleges and universal access of the 1970s this effect is of much smaller import. Are income differentials from a time when only 15 percent of the work force went to college applicable at a time when 55 percent are going to college?

Finally, nearly all of these studies compare the lifetime earnings of persons with four years of college to those of persons with only a high-school diploma. Some compilations from the Census reports and the Labor Department list a "one-to-three-years of college" category, but this aggregation generally represents interrupted, not completed, programs of study. A group that includes a high percentage of drop-outs and academic failures cannot properly be compared with a group of persons who plan, engage in, and *complete* two-year career programs leading to an associate degree. Although many students attend two-year colleges and technical schools without completing a degree or certificate, thousands do finish a planned program each year. In 1974–75 for example, the American Association of Community and Junior Colleges (1977) lists for 1,050 two-year colleges, 314,175 associate degrees, and 89,112 certificates. No field of research in all of higher education is in greater need of study than this—cost-benefit analyses by *field of study* for associate degree career programs in two-year colleges and technical schools.

Based on National Center for Educational Statistics data (1974), the average annual income of men twenty-five years old and over, by amount of education completed, was as follows in 1972:

Elementary school	$ 6,756
High school	10,433
College	
1 to 3 years	11,867
4 years	15,256

As usual, there is no figure for the holder of an associate degree. Also reported are 1972 calculations on lifetime (eighteen years old to death) income of men, by years of school completed, as follows:

Elementary school	$279,997
High School	478,873
College	
1 to 3 years	543,435
4 years	710,569

The absolute dollar values in such tabulations are meaningless today, of course, because of inflation, but the differentials are of interest. As late as 1972 and based on trends that had been continuing for nearly thirty years, a college education seemed to be a good investment, returning excellent "added value" in the form of annual income differentials and anywhere from 10 to 16 percent annually for a working lifetime on the capital invested in a college degree.

Expected lifetime earnings of individuals, broken down by levels of education attained and discounted to give *present value* are another measure used by economists to assess benefits from education. Based on data supplied by the Current Population Survey of the Census Bureau for 1972, giving mean earnings and education levels, Cooper and Brody (1975) have calculated some present values of lifetime earnings. Some of their calculations for "Whites" and "Other Races" for two different age cohorts, based on a 2 percent discount rate, are shown in Table 16. The need for discounting expected lifetime earnings is considered to be essential by economists, since money available now has greater value to most individuals than money that will become available in the future. For example, money available now can be invested or deposited in a savings account and can earn more money. Table 16 points up

Table 16. Present Value of Lifetime Earnings of Males and Females for Two Age Cohorts, by Race and Years of Schooling Completed, Discounted at 2 Percent, 1972.

Race, Sex, and Age Cohorts	Years of School Completed				Mean of All Four Columns
	8 years	12 years	13–15 years	16 years or more	
Whites					
Males					
15–19 years	$197,777	$293,448	$334,083	$433,513	$298,352
20–24 years	210,703	304,792	352,591	466,945	314,652
Females					
15–19 years	145,202	171,202	173,897	218,903	168,118
20–24 years	146,568	170,275	177,251	228,677	170,118
Other Races					
Males					
15–19 years	138,136	191,910	196,383	174,467	174,822
20–24 years	147,264	200,580	208,618	292,033	183,807
Females					
15–19 years	108,305	150,678	141,319	237,620	137,263
20–24 years	108,118	146,252	143,825	247,268	137,524

Source: Cooper and Brody (1975, pp. 5–6).

the usual differentials between incomes of males and females and between whites and minority groups. Looked at from the viewpoint of schooling alone, however, it appears that a high-school diploma is worth a great deal compared to only elementary schooling and that a college degree (note that all advanced degree holders would be included in the column headed "16 years or more"), compared to a high-school education, is worth more than $100,000 "extra" during a lifetime to white males and almost that amount to males of other races.

The lack of any information on associate-degree holders is again regrettable. The column "13-15 years" represents a large group of persons who were academically unsuccessful for one reason or another. Their earnings should not be equated with the earnings of persons *completing* a planned program. The differentials between groups for women are not as great as those for men, partly because many women, regardless of education level, become homemakers or enter fields of employment with relatively low pay scales. The Cooper-Brody research did include the dollar market value of housewives' work, based on age, number of children, and age of youngest child.

As pointed out above, however, these findings must be interpreted with care. Although the data available in 1972 supported the significant added value of a college degree, one cannot conclude that 1982 findings necessarily will be similar. For one thing, due to affirmative action and the increased interest of women in professional and managerial careers, the statistics for females and minority groups will no doubt improve a great deal over the next decade.

Furthermore, if we continue to move toward universal higher education the probability of saturating the market for college graduates will increase and negatively influence 1982 figures. The U.S. economy, though it is one of the most elastic and advanced in the world from a business and technology standpoint, has for decades needed only about 15 to 20 percent of the labor force in the "high-talent"—professional, managerial, and paraprofessional—occupations. And it is the rare college student that does not aspire to a career at professional or managerial levels. Even in community colleges, the stated expectation of over 60 percent of entering students is a professional or managerial career. Figure 8 depicts in

Figure 8. Comparison of College-Going Trends with Growth
in Professional Occupations, United States 1900–1990.

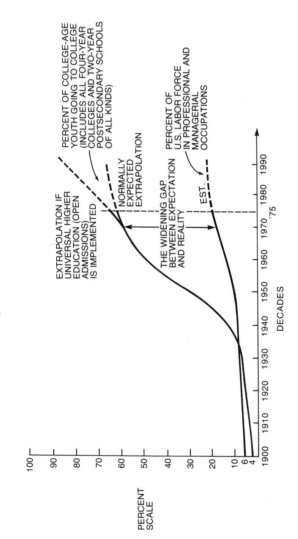

graphic form the rather alarming disparity between growth in demand for high-talent manpower in the United States and growth in college attendance over the past seventy-five years and includes projections to 1990.

As the figure shows, the curve representing the percentage of the U.S. labor force engaged in professional and managerial pursuits has risen very slowly over the years to about 20 percent in 1975. This is in keeping with Flanders' finding that even by 1980 only 20 percent of all jobs will require a baccalaureate or higher college degree (Flanders, 1970). There is little if any evidence to suggest that the nature of economic activities will shift radically to demand significantly greater inputs of high-talent manpower in the next decade. Perhaps the figure could be as high as 24 percent by 1990.

The curve of college-going by college-age youth, over the same time span, more or less paralleled the high-talent manpower curve until 1940, and then it took off under the spur of events already discussed for a steep ride during the golden years of higher education, 1950 to 1970, rising to near the 60 percent level by 1970.

If a "normally expected" extrapolation to 1990 is made, the gap between expectation and reality remains serious, and if a universal higher education pattern is envisioned, the gap becomes catastrophic in its implications. Two trends of the 1970s—the return to schooling of hundreds of thousands of mid-career workers and the sudden increase in women's interest in college-related careers—have tended to exacerbate even further the imbalance between high-talent job availability on the one hand and the expectations of college degree holders on the other.

Freeman and Holloman (1975, p. 24) describe the sudden change in the higher education-job market situation of the early 1970s as follows: "This golden age of higher education came to an abrupt end at the outset of the 1970s, when the twenty-five-year boom in the college job market withered into a major market bust. For the first time in history, new bachelor's graduates began to have difficulty obtaining jobs, and the relative income of college (educated) workers fell significantly."

They proceed to review the underlying reasons for the soft

job market for college graduates since 1970 and come to the same
conclusion as we do—that both unemployment and underemployment of college graduates in general are not merely transitory phenomena resulting from the economic recession of the seventies but
very real and continuing problems resulting from a consistently
greater production of college graduates than the economy can absorb in professional/managerial jobs. When only 20 percent of all
jobs are the desirable professional/managerial, working-with-people
jobs and when nearly 60 percent of youth are electing to go to
college, no great perception is needed to identify the roots of the
dilemma. The phenomenon is not limited to the United States;
nearly all industrialized countries were facing similar problems in
1976 ("Worldwide Job Crisis . . . ," 1976). Many young college
graduates of the mid-1970s are not finding jobs at all, and thousands of others accept employment in jobs that are not of profes-
sional/managerial level.

   Whether this represents "overeducation" or "underemployment" is an exercise in semantics that currently occupies many
pages in the journals and engages the attention of many podium
speakers. In general, economists take the "overeducation" point of
view and remind us of their warnings a decade or more ago that
this might happen (Daniere, 1965; G. Becker, 1960; S. Harris,
1949). Sociologists and educators use the "underemployment" argument and castigate business, industry, and the economy generally for not providing suitable careers for college graduates. The
latter groups, of course, espouse the "ultimate good" theory of education, while economists regard education as just one of many
social goods. Daniere (1965, p. 207) sums it up in economic terms
as follows: "Employers will call for educated employees only so
long as the salary differential is no greater than the value added
to their product. Furthermore, as more educated people enter the
labor force, each one contributes significantly less to productivity."

   According to Freeman and Holloman (1975) the rate of return on investment in a college degree has dropped from perhaps
12 percent in 1968 to as low as 7 percent in 1974. Part of this drop
is due to the fact that many college graduates remain unemployed
and part because many accept low-paying nonprofessional jobs
(underemployment). But a great deal of it is due to the income-
leveling forces exerted by special-interest pressure groups on the

economy. It is doubtful that professionals will ever again enjoy the large income differentials over blue-collar and service workers that they once had. Consequently, college students in arts and sciences fields will have to come to terms with reality—seek a "people-related" or professional/managerial job with the full realization that blue-collar workers may have a comparable income or enter a professional entrepreneurial field where the income (and the risks) are higher, profit is an important motive, and the forty-hour week is forgotten.

In summary, it would appear that the era of handsome economic returns to individuals on investment in arts and sciences college degrees is coming to an end. This is bad news, perhaps, but not necessarily all bad. It will force a rethinking of the goals and purposes of higher education and perhaps it will lead millions of persons in the next few years to more carefully reasoned decisions about career and educational choices.

Higher Education's Returns to Society. The principal reason that societies underwrite the costs of education is that they expect the benefits to outweigh the costs. A major problem is that education's benefits to society are not easily measured. Some are economic, and attempts to measure them have been made; others are non-economic, and these often defy objective measurement.

Denison (1962), in a landmark study, calculated the principal factors affecting economic growth in the United States for the period from 1927 to 1957. He also provided estimates for the period from 1960 to 1980. Table 17 summarizes his findings and projections.

From the vantage point of hindsight, we can make some comments on Denison's estimates. First, he was quite right that the effect of shorter hours on work quality would be minimal in the 1960–1980 period. Indeed, work quality in recent years has appeared to retrograde even as the work week has shortened. Second, in the light of recent findings cited elsewhere in this chapter, it may be that the 40 percent figure projected for dissemination of knowledge (education) for the 1960–1980 period will prove to be too high. Third, the significant advances predicted for both "new knowledge" and "better utilization of women" could both be on target. Finally, the (slight) drop predicted for "capital formation and utilization" may not have been enough. Federal and state tax

Table 17. Estimated Sources of Economic Growth,
United States, 1927–1957 and 1960–1980.

Growth Source	Percent of Growth Rate 1927–1957	1960–1980
Decrease in annual hours worked	−33	−29
Effect of shorter hours on work quality	21	4
Education (dissemination of knowledge)	42	40
Advances in new knowledge	36	46
Better utilization of women	7	16
Capital formation and utilization	9	6
Economies of scale		
National market	17	17
Local markets	4	3
Other factors	−3	−4
Total	100	100

Source: Denison (1962).

policies now absorb so much capital that economic growth may suffer from lack of private capital.

Since "advances in new knowledge" come in large part from educational institutions, according to Denison, the education enterprise in the United States accounted for much of the economic growth of the nation from 1927 to 1957. He felt that an even closer relationship would obtain for the 1960–1980 period. In retrospect, we doubt that this will be the case.

Schultz (1960), utilizing data from the 1927–1957 period, came to similar conclusions: the economic rate of return to society from education was indeed appreciable and that education was not really a societal *cost* but a societal *investment.* Many other researchers in educational economics of the era before the seventies came up with similar conclusions, most of which supported the contention that America was "underinvesting in education."

Calculating economic returns to society is an even greater longitudinal problem than estimating returns to individuals, and no definitive studies similar to Denison's have yet been reported for the period from 1968 to 1976 (for example) to determine whether society's investment in postsecondary education during those years will result in added economic value to society.

Some decidedly negative factors for the 1970s have been of concern, however, to economists, educators, and the general public.

First, society's costs have escalated at an alarming rate as millions of new students have become involved in universal higher education, during a period when tuition charges have decreased as a proportion of total costs and state, federal, and local taxes have increased to cover two thirds or more of the cost. Grants-in-aid to students, federal aid under Title III (Developing Institutions) and other programs, and steadily increasing state and local (community college) appropriations have added billions of dollars to society's annual investment.

Second, economic returns to society cannot yet be calculated or even estimated with any degree of accuracy. The oversupply of college graduates in most liberal arts fields for the past several years is well known. According to Freeman and Holloman (1975, p. 27), "Analysis of the causes of the seventies' turn around suggests that the market developments represent *a major break with the past and are not simply cyclical or temporary phenomena*" (emphasis added).

Finally, in the short term, at least, the hundreds of thousands of unemployed or underemployed college graduates in liberal arts, social studies, and humanities fields are not returning to the GNP in taxes anything like the return on investment that society had come to expect from college-trained workers in the 1930–1965 period. And, as noted earlier, even for the millions who have found suitable employment, the differential or added value attributed to their college degrees has decreased because of the income-leveling effects of collective bargaining in the blue-collar and "no-collar-at-all" occupational groups. And for most members of these latter groups, society has made no higher education investment.

A decade at least will have to pass before definitive research can be done to determine whether or not either the individual *or* society will have received a reasonable economic rate of return on investment in *liberal arts and humanities* college degrees between 1968 and 1980. We predict that the economic returns will be disappointingly small, perhaps less than those that would have been obtained from long-term savings bank deposits or investments in corporate or municipal bonds.

Nonpecuniary Returns. Even though economic returns may be

a disappointment, the individual may yet take great satisfaction from the nonpecuniary returns of his college experience, such as upward social mobility, increased social and political awareness, enhanced cultural appreciation, and the joy of knowing. To the extent that individuals learn to appreciate such returns from the college experience, society too will reap nonpecuniary returns in full measure. Presently, and regrettably, these social benefits are very difficult to establish in fact. Carefully designed longitudinal studies over several decades, with adequate statistical control measures, will have to be conducted to determine whether college experiences of the 1970s will yield a satisfactory social return in the 1980s and beyond.

Short-term observations are interpreted by some as indicating low or even negative rates of return, but this depends on one's definition of *social progress*. Examples of these unsatisfactory social returns include drug addiction, high crime rates, and counterculture activities, including violence and disruption, on and around college and university campuses. There is also the alarming rate of default in the National Student Loan Program recently, with students electing bankruptcy to avoid payment. Student hostility toward "the system," which is, of course, the very society that pays two thirds of the cost of college education in America is another example. All of these tie in with a perceived general breakdown in traditional manners and morality among many college students— new patterns of hetero- and homosexuality; the downgrading of the work ethic; the growth of the "Robin Hood syndrome" ("ripping off" the wealthy or a corporation is really not stealing, but is somehow commendable); and a pervasive lack of concern about the economic future of themselves and the nation.

In summary, there are no answers yet for the current era with respect to individual and societal, economic and noneconomic rates of return in liberal arts and humanities fields. For persons whose interests lie in the traditional liberal arts fields, decisions on college education will have to be made on grounds unrelated to rates of return. The question must be not "What will I get out of it?" but rather "What shall I put into it?" Involvement, participation, enjoyment, consumption, the desire to know—these are the criteria for decision. Having made the decision for college on these grounds, then—grounds that presumably relate to the quality of life—graduates should not later castigate "the system" when their degrees fail to bring them high earnings in the market place.

Returns on Career-Oriented Education

In contrast to unsatisfactory cost-benefit figures for investments in liberal arts and humanities college programs, most career-oriented fields have continued to yield at least minimally satisfactory returns on invested capital. To be sure, this has not been the case for all fields. Teaching, perhaps, is the field with the poorest recent cost-benefit record. Some natural science fields—physics and chemistry, for example—have not been brisk of late, and the behavioral sciences have had a period in the doldrums. On balance, engineering, business, agriculture, health and medicine, industrial management, banking and finance, electronics, and related fields have held up well even in the 1972–1976 recession, and relatively good as these fields have been at baccalaureate and graduate degree levels, they have been fully as good or better at associate-degree, diploma, and certificate levels.

As concerns the economic rate of return to the individual, job opportunities at good salaries have awaited most of the well-qualified graduates in these fields. Beginning salaries for baccalaureate degree holders in career-oriented fields have been running from $10 thousand to as high as $16 thousand annually. Holders of graduate degrees receive commensurately more. Promotions and salary increases have at least kept pace with inflation, and it would appear that the stream of earnings of these career-oriented graduates, over their working lifetimes, will result in a positive rate of return on individual investments in college. Society, too, will receive its economic return in terms of income taxes and production added to the GNP.

As to nonpecuniary returns, the answers are unclear. If, as some humanists claim, engineers and businessmen are engaged in "grubby work" just to make money, perhaps many of these career-oriented graduates will in later years look back on a life that seemed to be lacking in quality. Casual observation does not lend support to this view, however, for it seems that there are just as many happy engineers, businessmen, doctors, and farmers as there are happy historians, philosophers, psychologists, and novelists. As to the relative quality of social participation and the contributions to the good of mankind of such occupational groups, we make no judgment here, since all such judgments are based on the biases of the judges.

Middle-Manpower Fields. As noted above there have been no carefully designed, definitive studies of the rate of return on investment in associate-degree programs. Such studies are sorely needed to give the public some answers as to whether or not the more than four million full-time and part-time students enrolled in the community, junior and technical colleges in 1976 were engaged in pursuits that are worth the time and money invested. The total annual operating cost of this two-year college enterprise (excluding capital outlay) is in the range from six to eight billion dollars (excluding income foregone by students), with society bearing about three-fourths of the cost. Most of the colleges are publicly supported, and tuition is usually low at these institutions, ranging from no tuition at all to a maximum in some states of $800 per year. Typical tuition for a full load of fifteen to seventeen credit hours is $150 to $300 per semester in many states.

If we accept the average annual income and lifetime income figures from the National Center for Educational Statistics calculations reported earlier in the chapter, a few rough generalizations are possible. Discounting native ability, "luck," inherited funds, and other such variables, it would appear that "some college" (one to three years), results in an annual income for men twenty-five years old and older of about $1,400 more than that of the average high-school graduate; and a lifetime income (measured from age eighteen so that the high-school graduate's earnings while the college attender is in college will count) of about $65 thousand more than that of his "high school only" counterpart.

At first glance, these seem to be handsome returns for college attendance. An oversimplification says that the "one to three years of college" is worth $65,000, or $32,500 for each of two college years, but two factors deflate this balloon: First, both foregone earnings and "opportunity costs", the total cost of attending college, must be deducted; and second, it must be remembered that the $65 thousand is not available now but becomes available in small increments over the person's working lifetime. If discounted at even a modest rate of 2 percent to obtain "present value," the added value of the two years of college would be much less.

To balance these rather negative arguments, however, is the fact (referred to earlier) that the group reporting "one to three years of college" is not comparable to a group (if we had research data on them) of associate-degree graduates.

We do know that, even in the recession years of 1972–1975, placement of associate-degree graduates from community college and technical school programs has been excellent across the board—in agriculture, business, engineering and industrial technologies, allied health, and even in the public and human services. Entry salaries vary, of course, being generally low in the public and human services fields; reasonably good in allied health, business, and agriculture; and good to excellent in the engineering/science/industry-related technologies. Starting salaries in such fields as electronics and mechanical and hydraulics technology of $1,000 to $1,400 per month are not uncommon. Semiprofessional technicians with eight to ten years of successful experience often report earnings of $17,000 and more annually. Associate-degree graduates going into business management, sales and advertising, or into business for themselves may in a few years earn $15,000 and more annually.

It is interesting to note that the record of unemployment with respect to education during the recent recession years (1973–1976) has been atypical. As expected, large numbers of persons with less than a high-school education have been unemployed. And, as we have noted elsewhere, inordinately large numbers of liberal arts college graduates were either unemployed or underemployed. High school vocational graduates and two-year college and technical school graduates have fared relatively better. Community and technical colleges generally have reported that 75 to 90 percent of their *associate degree graduates in career fields* found satisfactory immediate employment on graduation, and within a few months after graduation the figure usually exceeded 90 percent. For example, Vincennes University Junior College in Vincennes, Indiana (a community junior college) reported in August 1976 that, of 508 graduates from its career division in June 1976, 77 percent were employed with salaries ranging from $6,500 to $13,400. Sixteen percent reported plans to enroll for upper-division studies at a four-year college. Only 7 percent were unemployed two months after graduation (Report of Career Division, 1976). Similar findings are reported to the authors by Los Angeles Trade-Technical College and Delta College (Michigan) and, in a recent national study, by many other community and technical colleges from coast to coast (Noeth and Hanson, 1976).

In summary, although results from well-designed rate-of-return research are not available, the cost-benefit situation for postsecondary career education in most fields during the period from 1970 to 1976 seems quite favorable. Even in the economic recession, with youth unemployment rates holding in the 10 to 25 percent range, persons completing associate and baccalaureate degree programs in business and agriculture; allied health; engineering, technology, and industrial management; and even in many areas of public and human services have found employment in jobs related to their major field of study. Graduates in the pure sciences, the humanities and social sciences, and teacher education have not fared at all well, and these fields may have an oversupply of qualified job seekers for some time. All-out energy development and a resumption of national efforts in aerospace and defense research, of course, could change the picture almost overnight for science and science technician graduates.

Long-Term Trends

Although qualified graduates from most career-related college programs will continue to find a good demand for their talents, the long-term trend for the added value of college degrees probably will be downward. For several reasons previously outlined, the 12 to 16 percent annual rates of return over a working lifetime reported for the period 1930–1970 are not likely to be realized again very soon.

Besides the reasons adduced above, three additional factors are now operating to reduce the added value of college study. First, the "screening function" and the credentialing function, both former correlates of college attendance, no longer operate as effectively as they did in the past. When only a very few got baccalaureate degrees, and two-year college attendance could be measured in the thousands, there was considerable selectivity in college attendance. The graduates' degrees or credentials represented a collegiate seal of approval on a very select group of academically capable and tenaciously persistent young people. Now that admissions standards are non-existent at most two-year colleges, and much relaxed at many four-year colleges and universities; and with retention and graduation standards also more flexible in many institutions, it is understandable that the millions who graduate today will not continue to command the "differential pay" of the select few who graduated a generation ago.

Second, credentialism is under attack in many quarters. The practice of reserving certain better and higher paying jobs for persons with stipulated college degrees or diplomas, without respect to the actual demands of the job, has been successfully challenged in the courts (*Griggs* v. *Duke Power Co.*, U.S. Supreme Court, March 8, 1971), and this trend will probably continue (Carnegie Commission, *College Graduates and Jobs,* 1973a, p. 167).

Third and finally, as Flanders (1970) and others have reported, only about one job in five requires the level of cognitive or skill performance commensurate with a four-year college degree. If they are to be employed at all, thousands of college graduates probably will continue to take noncollege-level jobs. The work to be performed is only worth so much, no matter who does it, and the artificial upgrading of middle-manpower jobs in an attempt to make them palatable to college graduates is not likely to be a solution to the oversupply of college graduates. If the college graduate is not paid commensurately more, and if the work itself does not become more cognitive or challenging, a mere change in job title would not be very satisfying.

Implications for Career Education

Despite the recent favorable employment experience of career program graduates and the unfavorable experience of liberal arts graduates we hear and read the familiar argument, repeated for decades, that specialized vocational or occupational training is not what employers want; they really want workers with a broad liberal arts background. O'Toole (1975) includes this assertion in one of his recent analyses of the underemployment phenomenon. He projects a dim view of vocational education as a solution to the recurring problems of unemployment and repeats the old cliché that what employers seek are "the adaptive skills of liberal education, not the specific skills of vocational education" (p. 30). Such statements are hardly consistent with the record. *Scientific, Engineering, Technical Manpower Comments* (1976, p. 7) reports, for example, that "among all vocational education graduates available for work in 1973–74, 90 percent found jobs despite a slowdown in the economy."

The persistence of the popular myth that employers really want workers with liberal arts backgrounds is encouraged by company presidents and top-level management personnel, who often expound this theme, largely because it sounds good ("forward-looking, progressive company") and partly because they are thinking primarily of their own executive development program. Sometimes this idea is expressed by personnel directors or managers closer to the actual work force. When pressed for elaboration, their argument usually takes the form of, "Well, we fire a lot more people for lack of good interpersonal relations and lack of adaptability (assumed to be related to liberal arts studies) than we do for not being able to perform the actual job skills".

But when asked if there are to be any new hires this week and, if so, to state the job requirements, the answer is almost invariably in terms of the specific skills required (office skills, machine tool skills, drafting skills, and nursing skills). It is quite apparent that there is one set of requirements to get *hired* (level of performance in *specific job skills*) and a rather different set of requirements to stay on, the lack of which may get you *fired*.

One further observation—the expressed desire for the adaptive skills and the supposed better interpersonal relationships from liberal arts or general education usually is associated with corporate or large-company employers. They can afford to give additional skill training on the job, if the employee has good potential. The small company or the individual entrepreneur, however, (and these account for millions of employees) must "get his money's worth" from the employee from the beginning. No amount of liberal arts adaptability and presumed future promise will substitute for productivity on the job from the very first day of employment. Another writer who is less than enthusiastic about education's relationship to jobs is Ivar Berg (1971), who, as long ago as 1969, when education's halo was still firmly in place, concluded a major study and report with these words: "The results of the present study do not give much weight to the economic argument in its detail, although it would be foolish to deny that education is involved in the nation's capacity to produce goods and services" (p. 29).

Berg correctly pointed out the multitude of factors other than schooling that affect the productivity, paths to promotion, earning power, and occupational level of Americans. Family influences, job experiences, military training, social and political influences, and native intellectual ability, taken individually or severally, may well have a greater effect on career success than the choice of a college or a specific curriculum. The research studies analyzed by Berg, however, gave little if any attention to middle-manpower occupations and to the career education programs of two-year colleges and technical institutes. As usual, they dealt with the traditional three-level system of education—elementary school, high school, and (4-year) college.

Differentiating Among Career Fields. One weakness endemic in nearly all rate-of-return-on-education investment research is that it lumps all college graduates (usually at the baccalaureate level) and all career fields, including the liberal arts, into one mammoth aggregation. Thus everything is blurred, supply-demand factors in the several segments of the economy cannot be identified, and the advisability of investing more in some and less in other kinds and levels of higher education cannot be assessed. Eckhaus (1973) has addressed some of these problems with an occupationally disaggregated approach, and has found significant variations in rate of return from one career field to another. Two serious drawbacks are present in the Eckhaus treatment however: (1) the raw data come from the 1960 Census and the results therefore may not have direct applicability to the 1970s; and (2) the usual "1-to-3 years of college" category is used, with all of the aforementioned disadvantages of such a catch-all grouping.

A good feature of Eckhaus' research is that he adjusted reported annual incomes to a 2000 hours-per-year annual base to correct for the fact that higher reported incomes may be due solely to having worked more hours rather than to occupational status or increased education. Professional and managerial workers, for example, often work 50–60 hours per week and their higher salaries may be due, in part, to this additional dedication to the job.

Eckhaus' detailed calculations are much too extensive to include here, but his results show that, for 1960 data, exceptionally good rates of return resulted from investment in education for the following career categories:

1. *Four years of college compared to high school.*

Engineers and applied scientists	10–20	percent
Pharmacists	9–21	
Managers, buyers	11–30	
Office supervisors	9–30	

2. *One-to-three-years of college compared to high school.*

Accountants	13–17	percent
Aerospace technicians	7–8	
Civil engineer technicians	18–49	
Other technicians	5–11	
Salesmen, agents	9–34	
Carpenters, builders	7–70	
Mechanics, stationary engineers	34–87	

Eckhaus obtained about the same overall (aggregated) figures as have been reported from other researchers on prior pages. For white males he calculated the rates of return as follows, aggregating all of the occupations he sampled: (1) Four years of college compared to high school: 11.5–13 percent; and (2) One-to-three-years' college compared to high school: 7–11.5 percent.

If 1970–76 data were available for similar analysis, it is doubtful that rates of return of this order of magnitude would result. Lacking "hard" calculations, but keeping in mind the relatively high unemployment and underemployment rates among college graduates and the reduced income differentials between white collar and blue collar occupations resulting from unionization and collective bargaining, "best guesses" for the 1970–1976 period would be a rate of return of about 7–9 percent for four years of college and perhaps 5–7 percent for one to three years of college. Based on observations and on scattered but consistently favorable data, the authors believe that if associate degree graduates from career-oriented programs could be studied as a group (disaggregated), the rate of return for the 1970–1976 period would be at least as high as, and perhaps even higher than, that for four-year college graduation.

Summary and Suggestions for Planners

We have seen that education in America is a vast and costly enterprise ($130 billion for 1976–1977). Over one third of the annual education budget (nearly $50 billion) is spent on higher or postsecondary education. Colleges are pretty good at cost accounting, but the accounting of benefits is far less accurate. In fact we are not even agreed on a set of rules for benefits accounting. Economists think of the benefits of education in terms of economic growth and development; humanists think in terms of improved quality of life. The economists' outcomes are perhaps not so noble, but at least they can be defined; the humanists' outcomes defy definition, and involve much disagreement among citizens generally, as to what kinds of behavior actually enhance the quality of life.

There is no question that for the period up to 1970, investment in higher education yielded, in economists' terms, extremely satisfactory "individual and social rates of return on capital invested." From the point of view of human resources—the production of human capital—money spent for education was not a cost but an investment that yielded handsome returns. Since 1970, however, the situation has changed remarkably. Just as wheat futures fall on the commodity market if a glut of grain is expected, so have the expected rates of return on higher education fallen as college graudates have been produced in excess of demand. Disaggregated analyses suggest that going to college is still a good investment in some fields, but that the rate of return in others may be negative. At present and for the near future, business, technology, agriculture, engineering and the applied sciences, health and medicine, and certain public and human service fields are attractive investments at both associate degree and baccalaureate levels. If an all-out national commitment to energy development, aerospace and defense research were made, the pure sciences would also become attractive. Both four-year college degrees and two-year associate degrees in the career fields listed probably will return 7 to 10 percent annually on invested capital.

In contrast to these good investments from an economic point of view are degree programs in the liberal arts, general studies, and "awareness studies." In the first place, there are relatively few jobs for persons with these credentials, and, in the second place, as a result of burgeoning enrollments of students who express a desire for people-related work, there are hundreds of thousands of graduates in these fields, with a like number "in the pipeline" in their undergraduate years. The outlook for many of these persons is not a pleasant one, the alternatives being: (1) to take any job available and thus be underemployed and probably dissatisfied; (2) to remain unemployed and subsist in whatever way is possible; or (3) to obtain further education and training in a field with a good job market. The third alternative is being elected by thousands of college graduates, many of whom are attending community or technical colleges for the career-oriented education they by-passed as undergraduates.

We reaffirm our belief in the value of education for its own sake. Nothing in these pages should be construed as disparaging the value of liberal learning, denigrating the desire just to know, belittling the potential for improving the human condition that is inherent in philosophy and literature, or as minimizing the potential for the enrichment of individual lives that resides in the arts. But we cannot all earn a livelihood as philosophers, poets, and artists. Indeed, only a very, very few possess the rare and unique talents which, when nurtured by the higher learning, eventually produce these practitioners at a level of sophistication and competence such that their "product" becomes marketable. We can all be amateurs in these fields, and that is good, but only a select few can be professionals and get paid for it.

To millions of students of the liberal arts and humanities, higher learning is a consumption item and may have little later value in the market place. It may have a very high rate of return as measured by personal satisfaction, expanded intellectual horizons, new and interesting friends, and by that ineffable concept termed "the quality of life." Such learning should be treasured for its own sake, and the society that provides it (at a great discount off its true cost) should be thanked and praised, not berated and castigated when the low or nonexistent market value of such learning is suddenly realized.

When Americans generally, and college students in particular learn some basic principles of economics: nothing is free; need and demand are not synonymous; the cost of obtaining anything is the value placed on what is sacrificed to obtain it; "cost is the value of opportunities foregone" (Heyne, 1973)—then much of the misunderstanding, disillusionment, and acrimony that characterize the present debate over "education for jobs" versus "education for living" will disappear. In the meantime, the market itself will govern, and its edict to college students is clear—you must learn something that somebody else wants to buy.

The higher education enterprise, too, will have to adjust to market forces. For whatever reasons, we have produced a far greater number of liberal arts graduates in recent years than the market can possibly absorb at any price. The trustees, presidents, deans, division heads, and faculty groups who plan for higher education would do well to consider the following points:

First, administrators of liberal arts colleges and universities should consider the advisability of adding a career dimension to many liberal arts programs (see Chapter Nine). Second, colleges of all kinds and levels, though they have to rely on bureaus and agencies for national and regional manpower needs data, should keep track of the local situation themselves. Reliance on the local or regional branch office of the federal or state employment service for job placements is ill advised. Because these offices have to be crisis-oriented, they often resemble unemployment rather than employment offices. Their overworked staffs have little time to locate highly skilled, technical, paraprofessional, and professional jobs to match with local college students' talents. This is the proper responsibility of the college placement office.

Third, all colleges (not just community colleges and technical institutes) should provide expanded career counseling and educational advisement services. One very serious problem in the past ten years has been the mismatch between students' aspirations and abilities. Exacerbated by open-door admissions and the social pressures for universal higher education, millions of students in the past decade have enrolled in and struggled with courses and programs for which they had neither a consuming interest nor the necessary academic ability. As a result, the quality of the programs has suffered, the graduates' level of competency has fallen, and some colleges have come too close to becoming degree mills. Most of this could be prevented by proper career counseling and realistic, somewhat directive, educational advisement. Fourth, disaggregated cost-benefit research should be encouraged and supported—especially studies that will provide definitive information on the rate of return from investment in associate-degree career education programs. Studies of the emerging baccalaureate-degree occupational fields also are necessary.

Fifth, the facts as we know them about the economics of higher education should be made known to students, preferably while they are underclassmen. Catalogues, brochures, and other public relations and recruitment materials should not continue to impute the affluent life to mere college graduation. Sixth, alternatives and trade-offs should be made clear to students early in their college years. This is not to say that anyone seriously interested in and academically capable of liberal arts and humanistic studies should be discouraged, but these students should have the economic facts at their disposal as they ponder educational decisions.

Seventh, it appears that the job market and the rate of return on investment for paraprofessionals, semiprofessionals, and technicians (middle manpower) will remain good for the foreseeable future. Two-year colleges and technical schools should remain active in the fields and at the levels discussed in Chapters Five–Eight. Minor modifications in courses and curriculums might be considered to enhance transferability into baccalaureate programs in the same or related field, but the occupational integrity of the two-year associate-degree programs should not be compromised. Eighth, we do not know what the rate of return will be on the new four-year quasiprofessional occupational programs. We do not know yet whether the occupational wedge formed by these new groups will push aside the traditional professions or the semiprofessional technicians. On the one hand, the artificial educational upgrading of jobs, which has been a popular response to the pressures of an oversupply of college graduates and has finessed some labor union problems, would seem to predict accelerated acceptance for the graduates of these new programs. The implications of the "Griggs versus Duke Power" case must be evaluated carefully, however. The requirement of a college degree for jobs that do not really require a college degree is apt to lead to further litigation (Carnegie Commission, 1973a).

Ninth, we must look at outputs. Inputs claim too much attention in education, and we often attempt to justify one input by citing other inputs. The output from career education should be well-educated, competent, effective and efficient (remember the difference?) graduates. Such graduates result only from properly conceived and well-taught courses and programs that emphasize quality, competence, and high performance standards. Tenth and finally, the problem confronting decision-makers and planners in technical schools and technological colleges is somewhat less complex than that confronting their counterparts in comprehensive two-year colleges, state colleges, and liberal arts colleges. The students at technical colleges have already decided on a career-oriented college education, and their remaining decisions relate to the choice of a career field and the level of entry into the educational program. Students at comprehensive and liberal arts colleges must first of all be helped to make the *initial* decision—is their education to be largely a consumptive good or is it to have an identifiable career dimension, an economic good?

Thus counselors, advisers, program chairmen, deans, public relations and recruiting personnel, and faculty, too, should take great pains to explain the economics of higher education to all students. America is well on the way to becoming a Learning Society, and that is good; but as students make investments in higher education, they should have a much clearer understanding than they have had in the past about both the rates and the kinds of returns to be expected.

13 🔲🔲🔲🔲🔲🔲🔲🔲🔲🔲🔲🔲🔲

Futurism and Career Education: The Road to 1990

To every thing there is a season
And a time to every purpose under the heaven
A time to be born, and a time to die;
A time to weep, and a time to laugh;
A time to mourn, and a time to dance;
A time to keep silence, and a time to speak.
Ecclesiastes II:16 and III:1–4

This is a time to speak about the purposes and goals of education in the future of America. In fact, it is a time to try to redefine *education* and differentiate it from *schooling*. Somewhere along the road of the last half-century, as education became a central pillar in the political and social structure of America, the facade of schooling came to overshadow the substance of learning in education (Berg, 1971). Schools and colleges adopted a credentialing function, and the measure of a person's education became years attended, units of credit completed, and degrees attained. The concept of compulsory attendance to age sixteen and free schooling through high school graduation, though seemingly a commitment to the improvement of the nation's youth, has actually led to an institutionalized period of marking time for millions. Schooling has thus become what education never should be—a custodial experience—and the more emphasis schools put on custody, the less they can put on learning. It is a time to think through the thicket of the ideological, social, political, and economic factors that force schools to stress custody instead of learning and a time to question labor legislation that makes it nearly impossible for youth who want to work, to work.

There was a time when these issues were of concern only to the elementary and secondary schools, but is it not now time to ask if colleges too are becoming custodial for significant numbers of students? If indeed they are, what should be done about it? Should faculty and administrators participate passively in a collegiate slide from education to schooling to custody? Or should they take the lead in raising these issues with legislators and the public and assuring that postsecondary education continues to be concerned, not with custody and the facade of credentialism—with providing rites of passage and enforcing social policy—but with learning and performance and competence? These are questions for all of higher education, but they are of especial concern to career-oriented colleges.

A Vantage Point for Viewing the Future

The future of career education in colleges must be viewed within the context of the future of the nation, and of course that future can be only dimly perceived and tentatively sketched on the moving canvas of time. But America, as a wonderfully productive nation—advanced industrially, technologically, and scientifically—depends on learning, performance, and competence for its progress. Some say we are a "postindustrial" society (Bell, 1973), but if people believe by this phrase that America no longer needs productive industry, they are certainly mistaken. The term means only that less than half of the American labor force works in industrial production. This is true of other capital-intensive economies as well, but in no sense can it therefore be inferred that such economies are no longer dependent on industry. Insofar as a thriving economy keeps a nation great, productive industry, business, and agriculture will continue to be essential elements in America's greatness.

Once richly endowed with natural resources, the nation now faces a future of scarcity with regard to most of those that are extractive in nature—minerals generally, including petroleum and eventually even coal. On the other hand, the renewable resources of land and seas are adequate to meet foreseen demands and merely await improved management and new or better methods of utilization.

Our greatest resource, however, is our people—a population of some 215 million, still increasing but at a slowing rate, with a prospect of leveling off at something less than 300 million by A.D. 2040. We are a diverse people, gathered from all corners of the earth. As noted earlier, the melting pot has not worked completely—the amalgamated American has not emerged from the "mix"—but any possible disadvantages of the lack of homogeneity have been more than offset by the vitality, innovation, and catalysis provided by our mix of cultures and ethnic groups. Strains and tensions exist, but the common bond of individual freedom and opportunity has so far, at least, been strong enough to provide continuity and progress for a nation "conceived in liberty" and governed by elected representatives of the people.

Three Scenarios: A Look At 1990

Nearly $1 billion a year is being spent on crystal-ball gazing by a self-designated group of "futurists" in the United States. Some of these seers are associated with "think tanks" funded separately or jointly by the federal government and by one or more foundations (Kahn and Weiner, 1967). Realizing that prediction is a precarious business at best, and well aware of the fact that no matter how sophisticated the research design or how competent the computer programmers the basic rule of "garbage in-garbage out" applies no less to production than to description or recapitulation, futurists more and more frequently make their forecasts in the form of "if-then" propositions. That is, they carefully consider and adopt a set of assumptions, and *if* these assumptions hold throughout the time frame of the projection, *then* certain outcomes can be predicted. The set of assumptions or premises on which predictions are made is often called a *scenario*. It is fairly common practice to consider prediction problems in terms of three scenarios—one that assumes the "most favorable" set of conditions and events that could possibly be expected; one that assumes a least favorable set (thus paralleling Murphy's Law that "if anything can go wrong, it will"); and a middle road or "most reasonable expectation" set.

We shall use this approach to initiate a discussion of futurism in career education.

Scenario One: A Future Filled with Promise This scenario assumes that most of the problems that beset mankind, both worldwide and in the United States, will be either solved or on the way to a satisfactory resolution during the time-frame of the 1980s. For example, applied to our 1990 view, it assumes that:

First, there will be no major war, and even brush-fire wars will decrease in frequency and severity. Second, the world economy will improve, and along with it food production and world trade. The U.S. economy will "heat up," with full employment the norm.

Third, with new energy sources just a few "breakthroughs" away, by 1990 effective exploitation of coal, solar, wind, water, and nuclear-fission energy sources will be common everywhere, with thermonuclear (fusion) energy nearly ready for commercial development. Energy for all *stationary* uses will be plentiful; new petroleum fields will meet all demands for propulsion energy; and the United States will have reached energy independence. Fourth, science and technology will produce all the wonders now forecast in the Sunday supplements; the cybernetic age will render manual labor and semiskilled "drudge work" obsolete; medical science will have won the battle against all communicable diseases; control of the degenerative diseases will be much improved; and the concerted application of science and technology to natural resources conservation and environmental improvement will have made great strides toward the restoration of "this plundered planet." Fifth, all nations will have brought population growth under control and will have stanched the flow of people into urban centers. Sixth, America will remain a productive, affluent, nation; a leader in world affairs; a bastion of democracy, with a free-enterprise economy and with maximum individual freedom for its citizens. Seventh, in keeping with the capital-intensive nature of the U.S. economy and with the continuing productivity and affluence of the people, education will remain high on the list of priorities that Americans want and are willing to pay for.

Scenario Two: "No-Growth" Gloom and Doom. Many futurists "see through the glass darkly" and reject most, if not all, of the assumptions of the first scenario. These gloomy futurists like to compare the earth to a spaceship embarked on a journey with a finite supply of energy and materials and an initially small "crew" that has now increased in numbers and in appetite to the point where the ship's life-support systems can no longer cope with the problem. For 1990 this scenario might include the following assumptions: First, world population will zoom to unsupportable levels, and food production will not keep pace (L.R. Brown, 1974)— the result being famine, pestilence, many small wars, and probably World War III as the "have-not" nations obtain nuclear weapons and resort to international blackmail and terrorism. Second, fossil fuels will be well on the way to exhaustion, with only minor successes achieved among alternative forms of energy.

Third, without petroleum for energy and its by-products, productivity will decline, economies will stagnate, and a "disastrous world" will result (Hopkins, 1973). Fourth, with technology seen not as a solution to but a cause of the world's problems, breakthroughs in technology will be viewed as of no value and technological research and career education will wither. Fifth, the United States, as the world's most profligate "spender" of energy, will be seen as the principal culprit. Productivity will be curtailed, technology tamed, life-styles revised backward in time toward a low-energy society and the economy turned back to a labor-intensive model. More people will have jobs, but a subsistence economy will produce less and require fewer technically trained workers.

Sixth, it is unlikely that people will adjust, of their own volition, to the harsh demands of such a "no-growth" society, and concepts like individual freedom and free enterprise consequently may disappear, and powerful central governments (or eventually a one-world government) will enforce the new rules, probably with the aid of behavioral modification programs (Quarton, 1967). Seventh, business, manufacturing, and technology-based activities will be minimized, and career education in these fields will be quite limited, since designing, fabricating, and selling "things" beyond absolute necessities will be antithetical to the tenets of no-growth. With the problem being not how to make a bigger pie but how to divide a smaller one, the social sciences, the humanities, and the arts will be considered more important than education in business, science, engineering, and technology. Technical education will be at a low ebb, although skill training for "cottage industries" requiring low energy input will be popular. Training in subsistence agriculture will flourish, as will programs in animal husbandry—especially those in the breeding and care of draft animals, since the horse will replace the tractor on the farm—and all forms of education and training related to conservation, reforestation, and environmental improvement will be emphasized. As to medical and health education and education in the human services, the scenario is not clear. Where the money would come from to employ millions of these workers is uncertain, to say the least, in a nonproductive economy. Much will depend on how the decision-makers in the new centralized governments come to view the ethical question of whether healing the sick, caring for the indigent, and extending the human lifespan are "feasible" objectives on an already overcrowded planet.

Scenario Three: Balanced Growth and Relative Stability. This scenario presents a vision of steady, ordered progress in a troubled but gradually improving world. Here are some examples of the assumptions associated with it: First, world peace will not be assured: "small" wars will occur; international tensions will ebb and flow; a controlled arms race will continue; and adversarial relationships among nations, groups, and individuals will not abate, but a major war will be avoided (Wynn, Rubin, and Franco, 1973). Second, economic conditions will vary from nation to nation, but the general level of the human condition will improve world-wide (Kahn and Brown, 1975). A gradual leveling effect will take place as poor nations gradually catch up with rich ones. International trade will grow as underdeveloped nations enter world markets. American export-import trade will grow tremendously, and so will investment by Americans abroad and by foreigners in the United States (Ash, 1974).

Third, steady gains will come on the energy front. Coal resource development will make the greatest impact, followed by nuclear (fission) energy, and solar energy in that order. A massive energy development plan will be funded in the United States at the level of $100 billion or more, and "energy independence" by 1990 will be an achievable goal. Along with gains in energy resources, interest will increase in energy conservation, and the "recycle society" may replace the "affluent society" (Seaborg, 1975). The promise of thermonuclear fusion energy will be closer to reality but still a promise for the future. Total energy supplies for stationary use will be in ample supply, but a really satisfactory solution to the mobile energy problem will not yet have been found. Fourth, science, engineering, and technology will have made great advances—perhaps a few "brave new world" fantasies, but mostly steady, worthwhile, effective progress. Medicine will have made further advances but mainly in the field of health care rather than in remarkable cures for organic disability and deterioration.

Fifth, population growth rates in most countries will have slowed ("Women at Work," 1976) but they will still be large enough to be of serious concern. In America and most advanced industrial nations, the birth rate will be near or below the replacement level, with zero population growth (ZPG) expected by about 2040. Sixth, the United States will remain a world leader. Productivity and affluence will increase but probably at a slower rate as the cost of raw materials (largely imported) goes up. The economy will remain basically free enterprise and capital intensive, while the nation continues committed to a political system based on individual freedom and representative government. Seventh, education, as both an economic good and a consumer good, will still be highly valued in America, but the education craze, or cult, of the 1960s will have passed. Education will no longer be regarded as an ultimate good or a neoreligion but will be considered as one among many alternatives for social and individual investment.

Of these three scenarios, given existing realities we regard the first as being overly optimistic and somewhat naive and the second as being a curious mixture of negativism, one-world politics, and distorted views of the simple life envisioned by those who have never had to experience it. The third scenario represents to us the "most probable" view of 1990, and we will base the rest of this futures discussion on its premises. Within these assumptions of balanced growth and relative stability, a look at some future issues for the United States is in order, before identifying some major problems facing career-oriented colleges in the years to 1990.

Seven Future Issues for America and for Career Education

In identifying seven important future issues facing the nation, we realize that there is no general unanimity on such matters. We include these, however, as being the societal issues which may have the greatest inpact on the future development of career education in colleges.

The Energy Crisis. In 1972 the United States imported less than one third of the petroleum it used. By 1976 imports had increased to over 40 percent in spite of the doubling of the price of foreign oil and a continuing effort to develop more domestic production from both new and old oil fields. Not only will the price continue to rise, transferring alarming amounts of capital out of the United States to the OPEC nations—perhaps the most economically disruptive of all world events during this decade—and jacking up the cost of everything from fertilizer to food, but also the probability of another oil embargo at some time within the next decade is quite high.

Energy independence depends on a dual approach—maximum development of new energy sources to take the pressure off fossil fuels and serious attention to energy conservation, so that by 1990 industrial, commercial, and residential demand are reduced by 35 percent below 1974 levels (Train, 1974). The first approach includes creating commercially competitive processes for coal liquefaction and gasification, increasing use of nuclear fission energy, and developing solar energy, geothermal energy, and wind energy. The second approach is one we don't like to think about—drastic reduction in the use of energy with all the associated difficulties attendant thereon, such as a lowered standard of living, reduced comfort, and reduced mobility, a rapid falling off of the gross national product and probable massive unemployment.

The combination of these approaches to move us toward energy independence by 1990 will require the education, training, and employment of hundreds of thousands of new scientists, engineers, technicians, management experts, researchers, and business administrators. The problems are mostly technical, and technologists of all levels and kinds will be necessary to solve them. The *need* for career education in energy research and development is readily evident. When massive funding for research and development is available intense program *demand* will follow.

The Food Crisis. The narrow gap between abundance and scarcity on this earth is a continual source of concern. A drought here, a flood there, or a 3 percent annual increase in a country's population can spell the difference between feast and famine (Canby, 1975). At present, the entire net surplus of food in the world is produced in just a few countries in the north temperate zone—most of it by the United States and Canada. We have the food resources and could greatly expand production, but third-world countries have much of the petroleum from which the energy and fertilizer for this expanded production must come. Moreover, expanding food production to help meet the needs of hungry people throughout the world faces other constraints: farmers caught in the cost-price squeeze, world food prices spiraling upward and causing consternation for American homemakers; the negative environmental effects of putting the plow to millions of new acres; and the fact that relatively well-off foreign nations such as the Soviet Union and oil-rich third world countries can outbid poor nations with famished millions for limited supplies.

In any event, agricultural production and processing will increase markedly over the next decade, and there will be significant increases in the employment of agricultural scientists, technicians, economists, food processors, and possibly even of farmers. The middle-manpower spectrum will account for nearly half of the new workers in agriculture and food processing. These employment trends will lead to a demand for more programs in food production, processing, and technology.

The Environmental Crisis. We have actually made a great deal of progress on environmental problems—particularly air and water pollution—in the last two decades. Very recently some momentum has been lost due to the need to exploit energy sources and the dilemma of unemployment combined with inflation and the mid-1970s recession. This slow-down has not been all bad, however, because it has allowed time for a considered reassessment of interrelated problems. Cleaning up the environment is a highly desirable goal, but like other desirable reforms it is costly and involves many tradeoffs. Not only must we give up trivia and trinkets for it but comforts and necessities as well. For example, the demands of both the energy and the food crises run counter to the desires and demands of environmentalists, as does the need for an economy with full employment. As a national objective we need to decide on a course somewhere between the pristine state visualized by the environmentalists and the deteriorating world that unfettered industrial growth would produce.

Two unanswered questions about the nation's environmental improvement effort involve the kinds of talented manpower needed and the kinds of training programs and degree structures required for that manpower. These questions were considered at some length in Chapter Six, with all the evidence there adduced pointing to a significant *need* for professional, paraprofessional, and technical workers in many different fields of environmental improvement and natural resources conservation, but only a potential need for training programs, waiting on *demand* if massive funding is provided.

International Trade. Coasting on a crest of scientific and technical supremacy over the past forty years and on an earned reputation for aggressive business practices and modern management, Americans have recently grown complacent in the international marketplace. We now find ourselves outhustled all over the world by Japanese, Germans, Italians, Russians, French, and other enterprising folks, and even when we make and sell products and produce, they deliver them in their ships, for we have a very small merchant fleet. In 1976, only 7 percent of America's foreign trade was carried in American flag vessels ("Pressure Builds," 1976).

Two factors govern here: First, our industrial machine will have to be more productive and our workers will have to earn by increased production the wage increases they have already won, and second, we shall have to rebuild our merchant fleet and get back in the business of world shipping.

Along with productivity demands on labor from industry and government, research and development can help with the first goal, and R. and D. will require large numbers of college-trained scientists and technicians. The rebuilding of the merchant marine has already begun, with small but significant financial commitments from Congress and private industry, and shipyards and ship designers will need many new, well-trained personnel—professionals, technicians, and craftsmen. Demand for business managers, accountants, bilingual secretaries, technicians, salesmen, and similar workers will also most likely expand, although there is some doubt about the feasibility of narrowly focused training for them in special international-oriented programs. Existing programs in business, engineering, and technology will probably suffice, with certain minor modifications in the pattern of elective courses or work-experience assignments providing the extra dimension for international trade.

Transportation Versus Communication. For fifty years we have been an increasingly mobile society, but now a few people are beginning to articulate the unthinkable idea that perhaps the gasoline-powered automobile is not here to stay after all. Air pollution, fuel shortages and costs, traffic congestion, and parking problems may combine by 1990 to spawn new solutions to surface transportation problems.

Air travel too will be in for some changes. Bigger planes flying faster somehow create more problems than they solve. Air traffic congestion is already a problem of crisis proportions in some areas, with the only viable solution taking the form of greater airport dispersal. In simple terms this means that when you arrive you are not there yet.

Rail, truck, and water freight transportation and pipeline transport will remain vital elements of an expanding economy, and containerization, and semiautomated merchant vessels will become important factors in maritime transportation. Air cushion vessels and high-speed hydrofoil ships are already in service on bays, harbors, and protected channels, and by 1990 air cushion vehicles and computer-controlled highways could become important elements in surface transportation as well.

But perhaps we will travel less and communicate more. We may not "go to work" on a daily basis or fly all around the country on business trips. By means of computer consoles, conference telephone circuits, videotape machines, and other devices, the day's work might be done at home or at a neighborhood "satellite office." At some near point in time, the exchange of information between computers, recorders, and data storage banks will exceed in volume that between people. Computers as well as people will "go to conferences" ("Future of Computer Conferencing," 1975).

Over the past four decades the useful radio spectrum has been broadened one-thousand fold by new UHF transmitting and receiving circuits and by new antenna designs and transmission techniques. Citizen-band radios are just one manifestation of the new communications era. Solid-state electronic devices have revolutionized computer design and use; new developments in laser technology will affect long-distance communication; orbiting and hovering satellites can place half the world in one vast communications network; and computer networks already being developed may soon link the world's population centers and provide instant access to the known state of the art in any field. It is amazing that man in not much more than one generation has been able to move from sound-wave and line-of-sight communications to Telstar and sophisticated computer networks.

Pierce (1967, p. 910) comments as follows: "As always, man will adapt to this world by apprenticeship, by the same sort of learning-without-understanding that enables him to speak and walk. The man who successfully lives in the world of the future need not understand that world in the sense of scientific understanding, but it is the understanding of science that is bringing that world into being." The hardware and software demands of the new information technologies resulting from this scientific understanding will call for career education programs with a number of new communication specialties.

Modernizing Industry and Making it Competitive. The American economy, as mentioned before, is heavily technological and capital intensive—an investment of more than $40 thousand is necessary to "create" each new basic job in heavy industry. The economy will probably continue to exhibit these same traits in the period to 1990, although there will be much less private capital available than needed for new jobs. Our industrial machine needs modernization and technological upgrading on an intensive basis (Lessing, 1972), and this could well be done over the next ten years as industry adopts the metric system.

American industries encounter particularly tough competition from abroad in producing and selling such mildly labor intensive products as radios, television sets, tape recorders, cameras, toys, and fine fabrics. By the opposite token, being research based and management oriented, they have little effective competition for such capital-intensive products as computers, machine tools, construction equipment, aircraft, and chemicals in their home market and gobble up foreign markets for these products as well.

The high standard of living of American workers is the envy of their counterparts in most nations of the world, but American wage scales and fringe benefit packages have their own built-in booby trap—they force our industry to eschew labor-intensive enterprises and concentrate on complex, high-cost, scientifically sophisticated, and research-connected end products. And these kinds of end products reciprocally demand either a labor force of unusually high levels of education and productivity or a highly automated manufacturing process requiring very few workers. The plight of the untrained and uneducated worker in America is a direct result of the fact that unskilled and many semiskilled jobs have to be done by machine *because a man costs too much.* A highly placed executive with one of the "big three" auto manufacturers puts it this way: "These days a person has to have at least a high school education to compete with a machine." By 1990, as machines get smarter, this necessary educational level well may be the equivalent of the associate degree or beyond.

A safe assumption is that even for more or less standard manufacturing activities, the inputs of science and engineering to industrial processes will increase through the 1980s. And for the newer and more unusual industries such as computers, aerospace, electronics, optics, health and medicine, oceanography, energy development, and defense, manpower development programs will require far greater competence in science, mathematics, and engineering than we have thought possible in the past. Whereas today's industrial needs for new technicians require that perhaps only 10 percent of them be well trained in science and engineering-related technologies, the job demands of 1990 well may require that a third of all technicians be so trained. Increased numbers of programs with a strong science and engineering base to prepare both two-year associate degree technicians and four-year baccalaureate degree technologists will be essential.

Coping With Limits to Growth. The last of the seven sample futurist ideas is that of the "no-growth" society. With its roots in such crises as the population explosion, world food shortages, energy shortages, and environmental degradation, this idea has monopolized the thinking of a number of economists, sociologists, philosophers, political scientists, and futurists in recent years. The sobriquet, "The Club of Rome" has emerged as a generic name for a group which continues its deliberations and writing after its initial meeting in Rome in 1972 (Meadows, and others, 1972). Such thinkers see zero population growth as the first necessary step to avoid catastrophe, followed by a cooling-off of economies to a no-growth level and finally to a life-style that reflects greater concern with the quality of life than with material consumption.

The implications of the no-growth society for the poor and the affluent, and for all nations—advanced, underdeveloped, and emerging—are all discussed in a recent issue of *Daedalus* (Fall, 1973). Clearly the geometrical rates of growth of the past, both in population and in exploitation of the earth's resources, cannot continue indefinitely. If they do, petroleum reserves may be exhausted by 1990 and coal by 2050, and the seven billion inhabitants (double today's population) of an energy-depleted world could by 2010, be constantly on the brink of famine.

On the other hand, the concept of no-growth is not as simple as it seems. Olson (1973, p. 7) observes that "a no-growth society would be torn by conflict over distribution. If there were no growth of income and a constant population, there would be no possibility of anyone having more without someone else having less."

It is interesting to note that the economists, philosophers, and sociologists who favor the no-growth idea are all from relatively affluent nations. There are no champions of no-growth in the poor nations or among poor people anywhere. Crosland (in Johnson, 1974) observes that the intellectuals promoting the no-growth concept "are often kindly and dedicated people. But they are affluent; and fundamentally, though not consciously, they want to kick the ladder down behind them. They are militant mainly about threats to rural peace and wildlife and well-loved beauty spots; but little concerned with the . . . desperate problem of the urban environment in which 80 percent of our citizens live."

The implications for career-oriented colleges of a no-growth economy are difficult to project. As the second scenario earlier in this chapter indicated, there would probably not be a high demand for career education in engineering, industry, and business, although the public and human services might be popular. A vision of low-cost services and extremely high-cost things, with a flourishing black market, comes into focus. Much serious thought will have to be given to the implications of this scenario, if the energy crisis remains unsolved into the 1980s. For instance, one small problem of immediate concern to commuter colleges is what they would do in the case of cuts in transportation caused by oil shortages or embargos accompanied by strict gasoline rationing (Roberts, 1974). The 1974 oil embargo provided a sobering preview of the no-growth society, as many of these colleges closed their campuses for lack of "regular-day" students. In a prolonged recurrence, some two thousand postsecondary institutions with over six million students would be immediately and adversely affected. Enrollment and attendance would fall, perhaps by 50 percent in a few months.

Challenges to Career Education

A great resource of America in adjusting to these developments will be the nation's network of colleges and postsecondary schools and institutes. Described at some length in Chapter Four, the network's strengths and weaknesses for the task ahead require only brief recapitulation here.

First among the strengths of American higher education is its diversity—public and private institutions with many levels and a variety of purposes: four-year colleges and universities, community colleges, technical institutes, vocational-technical schools, and specialized proprietary schools offering hundreds of different programs and thousands of courses on campus, in satellite centers, in urban settings, in the armed forces, in business and industry, and on Main Street.

A second strength is ease of access—colleges so numerous that one or more are within easy commuting distance of most Americans; programs of such diverse scope and level that entrance to career education of some kind for some certificate or degree is possible for nearly everyone; and tuition charges so reasonable and financial aid so readily available that nearly everyone with a serious purpose can attend.

A third is faculty members who, on balance, are well trained by both education and experience to provide good instruction in both the practical and liberal arts.

Other strengths include campuses and learning centers that are well equipped to carry out career education programs, with modern apparatus, instruments, and educational technology; generally adequate financing (although this is a much-discussed and currently critical issue); and a concept of higher education that encompasses both career education and liberal learning—a recognition that, after a thousand years, a rational evolution of education has taken place, melding education for life's work and education for life's quality into one meaningful whole.

Facing the future realistically requires an objective look at weaknesses as well as strengths of the postsecondary system. First among these issues of concern is the continuing emphasis on inputs rather than outputs, as illustrated by the slow but steady emergence of the custodial function within higher education and the gradual erosion of quality, excellence, and standards of performance as a result of sustituting relative standards of achievement for absolute standards. Talking with college administrators and, even more regrettably, with some faculty, it often is difficult to ascertain whether or not the basic purposes of colleges are teaching and learning. One cause of this problem is social, political, and governmental pressures on colleges that require them to act as enforcers of social policy and that blunt the emphasis on learning and divert it to policing and custodial care.

A second is the refusal by many college administrators to accept a "steady state" in terms of enrollments and to emphasize quality of programs rather than the generation of a larger headcount enrollment. Because state funding formulas tie appropriations for public institutions to credit hours generated, a fetish for continued growth has been encouraged, resulting in unseemly and near-disgraceful recruiting policies, duplication of effort, and costly competition between and among colleges and technical schools.

Third is escalating costs that result from several factors—high salaries, reduced class size and fewer teaching hours, a swamp of paperwork to meet federal and state requirements, the rising costs of operating necessities, and overextension of peripheral and often noneducational activities. Severe financial problems plague many colleges for these and other reasons, leading to curtailment of programs and deterioration of facilities and equipment. Their financial squeeze would not be as critical, however, if they reduced their peripheral operations and allocated their resources more directly to teaching and learning.

A fourth cause is the lingering legacy of the outmoded dichotomy discussed in Chapter One between education for leisure for "free" men and women, as represented by the liberal arts, versus practical or vocational education for careers. Although largely overcome within American postsecondary education, this divisive philosophy continues to affect the educational plans of students and to color status differentials between career-oriented programs and more "academic" courses. Trends identified earlier indicating that liberal arts colleges are providing career dimensions in their baccalaureate programs, and that technical and business colleges and programs are recognizing the value of general education in their programs, are an encouraging sign that a new rationality is taking hold in higher education.

Everyone has their own favorite list of other weaknesses, and different types of postsecondary institutions have somewhat different sets of problems that need attention. There are, however, several global issues central to the improvement of career education in all institutions, public or private, and at all levels. Beyond the characteristics of quality career *programs* discussed in Chapter Ten, these issues involve *institutional* characteristics and the interface between colleges and the larger society. They include institutional accountability, quality, finance and governance, and administration.

These are issues to be addressed not only by presidents, deans, division heads, and faculty members but also by board members, legislators, government officials, and other policymakers. Unless they are addressed cooperatively by institutional and civic and political leaders, the problems of higher education will overcome its strengths, and career education will not succeed in meeting the challenges which the economic, social and political trends of the 1980s will bring.

Accountability in Career Education

The crisis of lost public confidence in education was referred to in Chapter One as one of the factors in the "new depression" in higher education. This crisis came about, in large part, from a feeling among citizens generally that higher education was running out of control—free-wheeling without any brakes and with little sense of direction. As the magnitude and cost of the enterprise mounted, there seemed to be less and less accountability to the "stockholders."

To be sure, colleges keep detailed accounts of monies received and expended, and some even provide reasonably good data on per-credit-hour costs of programs and courses and annual costs per full-time-equivalent student. Public community colleges generally provide information on program costs and cost differentials as a part of their cost accounting procedures (Wattenbarger,

1970). And most colleges make available information on budget allocations to teachers' salaries, student personnel services, administration, learning resources, and building construction and maintenance. But these are all *input* data about the educational process— they represent the *cost* part of cost-benefit analysis. The public appreciates knowing these cost data, but the very magnitude of the cost—now at a level of $50 billion dollars annually—demands an accounting of the *benefits* or the *outputs* from the enterprise.

Lessinger (1970, p. 1) makes this distinction between input and output data as he writes, with respect to the public schools: "The American educational commitment has been that every child should have an adequate education. This commitment has been stated in terms of resources such as teachers, books, space, and equipment. . . . Our schools must assume a revised commitment— that every child shall learn . . . in short, to hold the school accountable for results in *terms of student learning,* rather than solely in the use of resources" (emphasis added).

There is no arguing with the premise that colleges must be accountable to students since, on the average, students or their families pay from one fourth to nearly one half of the cost of going to public college. But society, through taxpayers and benefactors, pays almost all of the remaining cost, and accountability is due here, too—not only for how well the student learns but for what he learns. Society establishes and maintains colleges in the belief that they will transmit the culture and improve the human condition. In America, one of the essential elements of the culture is individual freedom, and improving the human condition is seen by most citizens in terms of the maintenance of a free society. It is therefore quite understandable that citizens generally object to attempts to politicize colleges and to indoctrinate students with the ideologies espoused by authoritarian dictatorships, either dynastic or proletarian.

Colleges must be accountable also to employers. This is especially true of all career-oriented colleges, since the implied promise to the employer (who is also heavily taxed for college support) is that graduates will be top-notch employees for his firm. Colleges thus become credentialing agencies, certifying in a very positive way that their graduates are well prepared for stipulated kinds and levels of jobs and that they are worth more to the employer than noncollege-trained employees. Is this promise usually backed up by performance? Employers, as consumers of the product, will hold colleges increasingly accountable on this point.

As the 1970s move to a close, all of higher education will be subjected to increased demands for accountability. Partly because the results of career education are more readily measurable than the results of liberal arts education (graduates either do or do not get jobs in the field for which they prepared, and they either are or are not more successful in them than noncollege-trained workers), career-oriented colleges and technical schools can expect even more insistent calls for accountability than those directed at higher education in general. The current popularity of "consumerism" applied to education; the fact that a college degree per se is no longer a guarantee of a "good job"; and the natural tendency of people to choose more carefully among alternative investments during times of economic stress—all these are indicators for the future of career education. Roueche, Baker, and Brownell (1972), put the challenge to community colleges very bluntly, but they could direct it as well to all of postsecondary education: "Educational accountability is an idea whose time has come. . . . Community college personnel still have the opportunity . . . to define their own responsibilities in a way that focuses upon teaching and learning, those overriding purposes of community colleges. Failure to do so will not delay accountability legislation. It only means that others— state representatives and state boards of education—will define those responsibilities for . . . staff and faculty."

Quality and Excellence in Career Education

We established this theme early in the book and have returned to it repeatedly in the discussion of each of the career education clusters in Part Two. It is important to consider it again in this closing section on futures.

At first thought it would seem that there would be unanimous agreement among college leaders that programmatic quality and excellence in teaching and learning are essential concomitants of the higher education enterprise. But unfortunately the ideas of *quality* and *excellence* have somehow been equated with elitism in the minds of many, and, even more regrettably, have been construed as code words for racism by some. Career-oriented programs can and must provide a climate of *quality within diversity* that blunts the charge of elitism and operating features that include open-door admissions, core-and-ladder programming, developmental education, and learning-teaching systems based on performance objectives—all of which should remove any credence whatever from charges of racism.

As college career education matures in the next decade, a number of extremely important issues will be recognized and dealt with on a continuing basis, to assure that excellence and quality are paramount:

First, there will be a renewal of interest in the art and science of teaching and learning. Teachers must become real professionals—masters of the craft of teaching. Most teachers will need to become expert practitioners not only of lecturing and demonstration but also of small group discussion, laboratory or shop teaching, case study and simulation, television teaching, computer-assisted instruction, learning laboratory and autotutorial instruction, modular learning, and at matching their teaching style to the cognitive style of the learner.

Second, competency-based instruction should become the norm instead of a mere experiment. As outlined in Chapter Ten, minimum performance objectives consistent with the known requirements of the career field should be determined for each unit, module, or course in the program; and mastery of these minimum objectives will be required to pass each segment or course in the program. Garner (1974, p. 64), in describing some of the issues to be faced by colleges in creating performance-based programs points out that "the performance-based campus can serve to diminish the scope of considerations based on faith, and increase the range of those based on evidence and logic." Performance and competency at stipulated levels are already required in a number of paraprofessional fields, notably in the health careers sector, at least insofar as they can be evaluated by state board examinations for licensure. The future will bring certification to many other career fields. It is already beginning with auto mechanics, appliance service technicians, and television technicians in some states, and other trade and technical fields will not be far behind. The competency concept thus ties together education and certification, including program quality, teaching excellence, work experience, and performance standards that can be equally and fairly applied to all in helping insure that employers' and consumers can expect quality service of the graduate.

Third, internships and cooperative work experience will increasingly become a requirement in degree programs. And career development and placement centers will be established and professionally staffed at all colleges with career education programs.

Financing Career Education

It is increasingly apparent that public services, provided by government and paid for by taxation, cannot be extended without limit. The financial crisis of England and, closer to home, the travail of New York City, bear witness to the social disintegration that uncontrolled public spending brings. Educators, including career educators, must face the future realizing that we may be approaching the limits of public funding. Jordan and Hanes (1976, p. 313), assessing the socioeconomic factors that will affect the immediate future of education, suggest that "the time has arrived when efforts to do 'more and more' must be replaced by mutually agreed-upon goals for public education, goals that are *expressed in operational terms and that lend themselves to performance criteria*" (emphasis added).

Career education enjoys a somewhat greater public confidence than is bestowed upon higher education generally, but nevertheless it cannot escape the inevitable belt tightening. The years ahead will be a time of fiscal austerity, a time to trim waste, a time to concentrate on programs that lead to productive careers, and a time to reemphasize the central mission of colleges as being learning and teaching, not providing jobs for administrators, teachers, and support staff at public expense. Prospective sources of funds—from tuition through federal grants—are not boundless.

Tuition. It seems inevitable that tuition will gradually rise as a percentage of total operational income. Since, as noted in Chapter Twelve, the rate of return on investment to the individual in career education remains relatively good and higher than the rate of return to society, the case indeed can be made that a somewhat greater investment by students or their families in career education tuition is justified. But justification or not, the fiscal realities and social priorities facing America on the road to 1990 indicate clearly that persons wanting college-level career education are going to have to pay an increasing share of its cost.

Local Support. Some states, notably many of those with strong community college systems, have a tradition of postsecondary education support from local property taxes. Community colleges, technical colleges, vocational-technical schools, and skill-center districts in many states are governed by locally elected or appointed boards of trustees who are authorized to levy a tax for the partial support of these institutions. In some states, the local district tax supplies 40 percent or more of the total annual operating costs and an even higher proportion of capital outlay costs.

There is, of course, a great deal of controversy over the issue of local tax support. In one camp are those who oppose it on the grounds that reliance on local taxes means that educational opportunity cannot be equal throughout the state and that real property taxes are regressive. In the other camp are those who take pride in their "own" local college and are willing to tax themselves for a substantial measure of its support in order to retain the principle of local control of education or because they feel their college has a better chance at excellence if it escapes the leveling influence of state and federal bureaucracies. This controversy, regardless of its stated reasons is actually the familiar one between egalitarians on the one hand, who generally see their causes enhanced by state or federal control, and individualists on the other, who believe that local citizens should have effective control of their own affairs. In this connection, Medsker and Tillery (1971) identified seven states as pacesetters in the development of high quality systems of public community colleges. Of these seven, it is interesting to note that six of them developed their exemplary systems over a period of years during which there was relatively strong local control and local district tax support.

State Support. State funding of public colleges, including those with a career education emphasis, will be subject to fiscal stringency for at least the next decade, although it is worth noting that in a few states austerity recently has not been applied across the board, in that appropriations to career-oriented institutions have suffered less than those to other colleges and universities. There is some reason to doubt that severe retrenchment will remain a policy after the current recession wanes. Bowen (1976) suggests that *stability* is a better term than retrenchment anyway, an observation that parallels our view set forth in the first chapter that, after the boom of the 1960s, the steady state seemed like a depression. State funding is not actually decreasing—it is merely the rate of increase that has fallen off—and state funding for community colleges, where much of the nation's postsecondary career education takes place, continues to increase. Wattenbarger (1974) reports that, between 1971 and 1974, fifteen states increased their appropriations to community colleges by 50 percent or more. The overall trend reported by the study was for continued increased appropriations, with attention to program orientation and differentiated funding according to costs.

Federal Support. Federal appropriations for career education in colleges may increase somewhat over the years to 1990. It is our view however, that the massive support desired and aggressively lobbied for by some educators will not materialize. For one thing, the national debt is of staggering proportions, and the interest on it is one of the major causes of inflation. For another, competing social demands for welfare, health, energy development, national defense, environmental improvement, and the like will not allow any slack for greatly increased federal support of education. Thus Harcleroad (1973) answers his own question, "Is Federal Financing a Weak Reed?," by concluding that "states should not look to the federal tax power for basic postsecondary education costs, but should push forward on their own."

The categorical nature of federal grants, the untenably complicated process of obtaining and administering them, and the alarming amount of federal control attached to only a few federal dollars are all factors which have a negative effect on the value of federal funding for career education in colleges. Colleges and state postsecondary commissions should aggressively seek new legislation that would place federal appropriations for postsecondary career education under granting authorities and administrative bureaus directly responsible to higher education; and a new concept of federal funding should be sought which does not tie federal funding to specific, narrow, categorical programs requiring local matching dollars and does not require excessive paperwork and supervision.

Summary. In summary, the structure of financing for postsecondary career education during the years to 1990 will probably take shape along these lines:

First, tuition, both in absolute dollars and as a percentage of total cost, is almost certain to increase.

Second, even in states where a local district tax has been a bulwark of support, revenue from this source is likely to decrease as a percentage of total revenue, while many states will continue to make no provision for local tax support of postsecondary education.

Third, state funding will continue to be the major source of operating revenue. Appropriations will continue to increase but at a slower rate. And some type of formula funding that relates appropriations to differentiated program costs will become the norm in most states.

Fourth, federal funding of postsecondary education will remain a relatively small proportion of total revenues. Furthermore, "federal funds" are really taxes levied on citizens which, if levied locally, could be used far more efficiently and satisfactorily to support postsecondary education.

Fifth and last, there will never be enough money to do all the things we will want to do. We will have to be selective about programs, emphasize cost-effective planning, insist on greater productivity, improve learning and teaching, and insure through competency-based programs that the rate of return on investment to both the student and society will be good.

Governance and Administration

The future of postsecondary career education ultimately depends on the decisions made by those who govern and administer postsecondary institutions. By *governance* we mean those actions (many of them with the force of law) taken by groups external to colleges themselves, including voters, boards of trustees, state boards and agencies, legislatures, courts, and such federal authorities as the Congress, executive department bureaus, enforcement and compliance officers, regulatory agencies, and the judicial system. By *administration* we mean the processes internal to institutions by which they are operated on a day-to-day basis within the context of law, the rules of governing bodies, and accepted educational practice.

Trends in Governance

Existing local boards of trustees unfortunately will probably see their power wane as control gravitates to the statehouse. The effectiveness of local boards has already been weakened significantly by the educational consumerism movement (recent court decisions have allowed board members to be sued as individuals for punitive damages stemming from alleged inadequacies and deficiencies of the college) and by rulings in some states allowing students and faculty members to run for election to the board.

Despite the many arguments in favor of local control, the unmistakable trend is toward state and federal control. In the past fifteen years, state after state has enacted master plans for postsecondary education, bringing technical colleges, community colleges, area vocational-technical schools, and four-year colleges and universities under one or more state boards, with the stated goals of "equalizing educational opportunity" and "attaining economies of scale." There is as yet no clear evidence that the first aim has been attained, but there is no doubt whatever that the second objective has not only *not* been attained, it has receded. Bigger systems, it seems, mean bigger bureaucracies as well as bigger budgets. Parkinson's Law, Murphy's Law, and the Peter Principle have all acquired new meaning with respect to the second of these goals. It is to be fervently hoped that Gresham's Law does not become directly associated with the first.

Given the present sociopolitical climate, one can only assume that the trend toward increased state governance and control will continue. State-mandated management information systems (MIS) and planning, programming, and budgeting systems (PPBS) will probably increase; program-differentiated budgeting will be required; record-keeping and reporting will grow exponentially; rule books will outgrow their bindings; and power will move closer to the capitol and the courtroom. The "1202" state postsecondary commissions, now sputtering along on a lean mixture of underfunding, could become a powerful controlling force at the state level if full funding of Title X of the Education Amendments of 1972 ever becomes a reality, even though the governors of some states oppose them, and as yet in most states they have had little real impact (Fenske, 1975).

Several steps should be taken to maximize the alleged advantages and minimize the disadvantages of state control for college-level career education.

First, while striving for equal opportunity, states should allow for *flexibility*, local initiative, and institutional differences so that equal opportunity does not end up as equal mediocrity. Second, they should emphasize service and leadership, not rules and regulations, by streamlining bureaus, reducing the number of bureaucrats, and cutting down paper work.

Third, they should staff such bureaus and agencies as are actually needed with persons who have a background of college administration and a knowledge of college-level career education. Fourth, they should provide methods for selecting persons of unquestioned ability for the top administrative posts at state colleges and technical schools and then given them the responsibility and the authority to administer these institutions. They should insist on results and evaluate presidents on the results they produce. State-fabricated hurdles in the form of nit-picking rules and regulations, should not be set in the path of progress.

Fifth, they should provide for differentiation of function among institutions through cooperative planning, with basic courses and popular programs on all campuses and highly specialized programs only at selected institutions. If necessary, they should provide residence halls at some regional campuses offering these specialized programs. And sixth, since most of the cost of postsecondary education is in faculty and staff salaries, state leaders should exert every effort to create a climate of faculty productivity, with emphasis on the theme that a faculty member's job is to teach and see that students learn.

At the national level, the federal "presence" will increase geometrically if federal appropriations increase. As stated above, however, we do not see significantly increased federal funding for college-level career education, given the crisis of the federal budget. Even though federal funds for occupational education are not likely to increase markedly, there is always pressure for increased federal control. A major difficulty with federal funding for education is the debilitating bureaucratic controls associated with its acceptance. Acts of Congress, drawn with the best of intentions and with reasonable simplicity, become Machiavellian monsters by the time the federal and state bureaucracies finish preparing the "guidelines" for implementing them. Every federal dollar has a "leverage" on, or controls, at least six state dollars and infects them with essentially the same malady of restrictions, rules, and regulations that surround the federal dollars. The paper work, reports, retroactive audits, and control systems associated with obtaining federal dollars are so onerous and costly that many college presidents feel that seeking federal money for occupational education is an exercise in futility. Based on a professional lifetime as a community-college administrator and consultant-researcher, Lombardi (1972, p. 23) concludes that "vocational education grants invariably include requirements for supervisory and administrative personnel whose cost may be greater than all the money in the grant."

Moreover, funds intended for college-level career education are still controlled and administered by a vocational education establishment whose modus operandi stems from the 1917 Smith-Hughes Act and whose orientation for fifty years has been toward the secondary school, not the college. Unless colleges can mount a successful effort for passage of their own career education bill by the Congress, categorical grants will continue to be the mode of providing federal funds for most middle-manpower programs, and the present machinery for the allocation and distribution of federal vocational education funds through state vocational education departments will remain in vogue.

One possible change should be mentioned, however. If an all-out energy resources development bill emerges from the Congress, financed at the level of $80 to $100 billion, no doubt several billions will be earmarked for energy resources manpower development. If the usual type of secondary-school-oriented bureaus and agencies are not to exercise a governance function with respect to colleges that establish programs in the energy field, colleges and their national associations should work for direct access by colleges to these funds to prevent their control by and distribution through the present vocational education establishment.

A final caveat is in order with respect to federal governance and controls. There is strong pressure to base federal and state support for career education in colleges primarily on forecasts of manpower "need" in semiprofessional and technical occupations. By their very nature, however, societies based on free enterprise economic systems do not engage in highly specific long-range planning, since it is the ebb and flow of the marketplace that governs the pulse of the economy. Since the economy itself is not planned, manpower supply and demand cannot be subjected to detailed planning and management. Not only are accurate manpower needs projections for a five- or ten-year period impossible to arrive at, but also in a free society there is no way to "pour into the pipeline" this year the required number of student trainees to meet the supposed job requirements in a future year. In America we have used the "market adjustment approach," which is based on the principle that a manpower shortage will create its own demand and lead to higher levels of income or more attractive conditions of employment or both and that these facts will become well enough known that persons will of their own volition seek the necessary education and training for those careers. The Carnegie Commission on Higher Education (1973a, p. 11) in its intensive studies of the relationship between higher education and jobs, came out strongly on the side of the "free-choice principle," as opposed to "target-setting" manpower planning. They wisely state: "We are totally opposed, with a few special exceptions, to a 'manpower planning' approach to higher education; we believe that reliance on student choice is superior. . . . Manpower planning leads toward rigidities and toward controls, and we find it, by and large, both an ineffective and a repugnant mechanism and probably also an unenforceable one as well. . . . The 'free choice principle' is generally superior to the 'manpower principle.' "

With respect to external controls inposed on institutions from all levels of government, familiarity with the old adage of science that "nature abhors a vacuum," should remind us that power is much like nature in this regard. If institutional leadership is weak and inept, if the reins of local power are slack, the state will step in, and if states allow a leadership and power vacuum to exist, it will quickly be filled by federal action. Shared local and state governance and control are the best guarantee of excellence in career education. The strength of postsecondary career education stems from this partnership.

Patterns of Administration. There is a great deal of ferment and experimentation going on with regard to the local administration of colleges and technical schools. The future will see continuing and perhaps radical experimentation with administrative organization patterns and administrative styles, and college administration in the years to 1990 will be a rapidly changing and increasingly demanding profession.

Two factors are paramount in forcing changes in college administrative structures: first, the need to economize on administrative costs, as the "steady state" replaces the "crisis of growth"; and second, the need to establish an administrative organization that can cope with faculty and staff collective bargaining. In terms of the second challenge, the facetious query, "Who's in charge here?" has become a deadly serious question, and any vision of the future has to include the expectation that faculty unions will increase, both in numbers and demands, as part of the general increase in adversarial relations characteristic of modern life. From a time when the unprotected worker organized against the "greedy, inhumane employer," we have arrived now in an era when everybody seems organized against everybody else. The extent to which this mania has now been carried is exemplified by colleges where not only the faculty is organized for bargaining with the "administration" but also all the second- and third-echelon administrators are organized for disputations with the president. In this situation presidents tend to reflect on "the loneliness of power" until they suddenly realize that they have precious little power left. They also do not have much help.

Much has been written about the impact of collective bargaining on students (Bond, 1974), on institutional policymaking

(Bucklew, 1974; Kemerer and Baldridge, 1975), and on communnity colleges in general (ERIC Clearinghouse, 1974); and no purpose would be served here by extended discourse on the subject. Its impact on academic administration, however, deserves attention. Sadly, as collective bargaining and union activities in general are adopted by the faculty and by other job families on campus, the idea of a college as a common effort among scholars becomes untenable. Decision-making discussion among colleagues is replaced by an industrial model collective negotiations process that produces a legal contract between the faculty as employees and the president and the board (or the state) as the employer. These trends may eventually be reversed, but at present there is only hope and no evidence that this will be so. Patterns of administration will have to adjust to the new reality. This model of employer-employee relationships allows, indeed almost dictates, streamlining administrative functions, tightening the administrative organization, assigning definite responsibilities, demanding results by defining objectives, and clarifying roles so that administrator-faculty ambiguities disappear. Staff members are either bosses or workers—they can't be both at different times of the day or week.

In response to the need to reduce costs and consolidate administrative power, colleges are trying a number of new administrative patterns. True, the traditional structure of president, deans, program directors, and department heads probably remains the dominant mode, but other schemes appear with increasing frequency, and organizational theorists are proposing that each college engage in simulation modeling to determine the administrative pattern best suited to its own conditions (F. Wise, 1971).

Administratively, the place of career education programs within the institutional decision-making structure has been, and still is, a matter of much discussion and in some colleges even of some dissension. By 1950, as two-year colleges began to move aggressively into occupational education, there arose real and imagined problems of administering this new dimension of the college. Faculty members in liberal arts and transfer programs were not even sure vocational-technical education belonged in the college, while occupational faculty, as a general rule, wanted to keep "their"

programs and "their" students to themselves for a variety of reasons, one of which was the special funding they received from federal vocational education acts. With these two groups of strange
bedfellows, it was almost inevitable that an administrative bundling
board would be used, and most junior colleges effectively sepa-
rated themselves into two institutions operating on the same campus: one for the academic arts and sciences programs and another
for occupational programs. This left some faculty, as in business
education, in a quandary—should they go with the occupational
division or stay with arts and sciences? Some institutions decided
one way, some the other, the decision being complicated by the fact
that such business courses as accounting, business law, data programming, mathematics of finance, and economics are often bona
fide lower-division college parallel or transfer courses.

Recently, in recognition of the increasing comprehensiveness
of community colleges and as a result of gradual acceptance of the
philosophy that nearly all education is career education, a number
of institutions have initiated a "career division" administrative and
organizational model proposed by Grede (1971) and others. This
concept rests on the idea that nearly all college courses and programs can be fitted quite well into five or six major divisions, each
of which has career goals and a career ladder with steps that lead
either to entry-level employment in a career field or into four-year
and even advanced graduate programs.

In this model, the president selects and appoints the administrators necessary to direct student services, business operations,
and planning and development activities and to keep these support
functions within carefully controlled budgetary limits. With regard
to the instructional program of the college, a vice-president is made
responsible for the entire operation in order to point up the career
orientation of the college and put an end to the left-over dualities
and invidious distinctions between "vocational" and "academic"
education or "terminal" and "transfer" programs (Borow, 1972).
The career-oriented college admits no such dichotomies and combines liberal arts and career courses in each of the divisions, which
bear such labels as these: (1) Agriculture, Science, and Technology,
including mathematics and the physical sciences; (2) Business and
Economics; (3) Health and Life Sciences; (4) Public and Human

Services, including behavioral and political science, and (5) Liberal Arts and Humanities, including music, theater, dance, and art, and also including general education.

These five divisions, each of which emphasizes one area or career cluster discussed earlier in Chapters Five through Nine, cover the full spectrum of human knowledge, from the physical sciences to the fine arts, as well as the broad spectrum of all middle-manpower occupational programs. Such a division-based organizational pattern not only represents what has actually evolved as two-year colleges have espoused career education but also provides an acceptable organizational structure for postsecondary institutions at large, since it follows closely the broad divisions of academic disciplines while it supports the philosophical concept of a unified curriculum that relates occupational to nonoccupational courses in a close structure. One cannot readily separate the theoretical from the applied under this arrangement, and the general theme that career education embraces all education becomes explicit. It differs from traditional departmental or divisional structures by equating applied knowledge with theoretical learning and making them mutually supportive.

Reduced to a typical organizational chart, this career division arrangement is shown in Figure 9. Courses and programs of all levels—short term, certificate and diploma, associate degree, and college parallel and preprofessional—are offered within a given division if they relate to that career field. Core-and-ladder arrangements and career advisement and placement services (coordinated through the college's career development and placement center) are provided within each division.

Neither students nor faculty wear "vocational" or "academic" labels. A faculty member may teach technical mathematics one hour and calculus the next, and a student in an associate degree business program may enroll in "transfer" courses in economics or political science. The emphasis is on the career goal and the student's academic abilities, not on separate "tracks" or degree levels. Options are kept open, so that students who complete one-year skill-oriented programs can return later and take supporting theory and general education courses and complete an associate degree. In like manner, students completing associate degrees at

Figure 9. Suggested Administrative Organization for a Two-Year College, Illustrating the "Career Division" Concept.

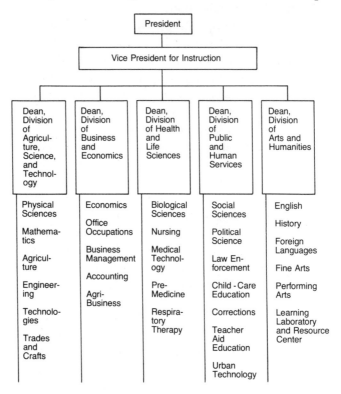

skilled or technician levels can return for the preprofessional theory and liberal arts courses that enable them to transfer to upper-division status at four-year colleges. Advisers work with their colleagues in other divisions to plan curriculums that include necessary developmental and remedial work as well as general education required for associate degree and baccalaureate degree programs. Students in short-term job-upgrading courses and one-year certificate programs are usually not required to take general education work unless remediation is necessary for success in their occupational courses.

Many four-year colleges have had this general type of organization for some years, and it holds a great deal of promise for community junior colleges and technical schools. It not only provides a much better mechanism for a career-ladder approach to education but also eases implementation of a competency-based approach to learning, gives more visibility to careers, and discourages the image of occupational departments as places offering little more than typing or shop. Administratively, the plan offers good span-of-control—three or four persons reporting to the president, five or six to the vice-president for instruction, and probably not more than seven or eight program directors reporting to each division head or dean. The size of the institution and the number of students and faculty involved determine the number of full-time administrators needed for the several career programs in each division. Authority can be delegated, responsibilities can be clearly assigned, and administrators at all levels can be held accountable for their performance. A management-by-objectives (MBO) system can be initiated fairly easily if the president prefers it.

Operating this administrative pattern in a college with a faculty union presents no unusual problems and involves only one requirement: The break between administration and the faculty, or "bargaining unit," should place program directors in the administration, since these key officers are often involved in policy matters. Small programs may need to be combined until their responsibilities warrant a full-time director or administrator.

Summary and Conclusions

Contemplation is an activity neglected by most of us. And even when we do lapse into an interlude of thinking, all too often it is the issues and crises of the moment, rather than the possibilities and potentials of the future, that capture our thoughts. Career education has its share of transient problems, and they often demand attention with an insistence that brooks no delay. Good administrators, effective decision makers, concerned legislators, and involved citizens properly devote much of their thinking time to current problems in college operations, because efficiency is a necessary attribute of colleges. But beyond the present lies the future, and beyond efficiency is the issue of effectiveness.

The enterprise of higher education now enrolls over ten million students and its annual cost of some $50 billion amounts in some years to nearly $580 for every person in the labor force.

Educators and those who help them make decisions need to insure that so large an enterprise remains cost-effective; that it will be used for teaching and learning rather than for custodial purposes; and that product will be emphasized rather than process. They should set aside time to create scenarios for the future, such as those advanced here; and time to weigh alternative courses of action with respect to administration, governance, finance, and institutional outcomes.

Without a doubt we will be faced with rapid, perhaps even dramatic, changes in the years stretching ahead to 1990. The youth who joins the labor force tomorrow will face as many changes in his career as did last week's new retiree. But this is not to say that we cannot design career education programs that will help tomorrow's workers adapt to change.

Some alarmists foresee such drastic change that they claim career education is a waste of time and that the liberal arts and humanities are the only viable approach to education for the future, thus saying, in effect, that to prepare for the future we should return to higher education patterns of the past. Other observers foresee so little change or such slow changes that they advocate narrowly focused job-specific occupational programs limited to jobs that exist today rather than broad-gauged discipline-oriented or job-cluster programs. This is the restricted vocational education approach to career education.

Neither of these extremes is adequate for the probable developments of the 1980s. There is change in the labor force, but there is also stability. The economy's need for particular specialized skills will continue to be affected by new technologies as it has in the past, but career education based on a broad cluster of knowledge and skill competencies will never become outdated. Planners of career programs—adventurers in futurism—realize that the strength of a free and open society is in the productivity and competence of its people. Career education in colleges seeks to strengthen this productivity and competence. Thus, although not true in the past, perhaps in the future all of education will be recognized as career education.

References

Adler, M. J., and Mayer, M. *The Revolution in Education.* Chicago: University of Chicago Press, 1958.

Alma College Career Preparation Program, The. Alma, Mich.: Advising, Counseling, and Career Development Center, Alma College, 1976 (multilithed).

Almarode, R. L. *Guidelines for Hospitality Education in Junior Colleges.* Washington, D.C.: American Association of Junior Colleges, 1968.

American Association of Community and Junior Colleges. *1977 Community, Junior, and Technical College Directory.* Washington, D.C.: AACJC, 1977.

American Council on Education. *Guidelines For Improving Articulation Between Junior and Senior Colleges.* Washington, D.C.: ACE, 1967.

American Council on Education. *Policy Briefs.* Bulletin of the Policy Analysis Service, Vol. 1, No. 2. Washington, D.C.: ACE, 1974.

American Medical Association. *A Report on Education and Utilization of Allied Health Manpower.* Chicago: AMA, 1972.

American Society for Engineering Education. *Characteristics of Excellence in Engineering Technology Education.* Washington, D.C.: ASEE, 1962.

American Society for Engineering Education. *Final Report: Engineering Technology Education Study.* Washington, D.C.: ASEE, 1972.

American Technical Education Association. *Technical Education Newsletter,* May–June 1976.

"An Engineer Shortage." *Business Week,* November 4, 1972, p. 33.

Ash, R. L. (Ed.) "A Report of the White House's Office of Management and Budget." *The Futurist,* 1974, *8* (4) 192–194.

Astin, A. W., King, M. R., and Richardson, G. T. *The American Freshman: National Norms for Fall 1975.* Los Angeles: Cooperative Institutional Research Program, Laboratory for Research in Higher Education, Graduate School of Education, University of California, Los Angeles, 1976.

Becker, G. S. "Underinvestment in College Education?" *American Economic Review,* 1960, *50* (2).

Becker, H. "The Nature of a Profession," *Education for the Professions,* Yearbook of the National Society for the Study of Education, Part II. Chicago: University of Chicago Press, 1962.

Bell, D. *The Coming of Post-Industrial Society: A Venture in Social Forecasting.* New York: Basic Books, 1973.

Berg, I. *Education and Jobs: The Great Training Robbery.* Boston: Beacon Press, 1971.

Bisconti, A. S., and Solmon, L. C. *College Education On the Job . . . The Graduates' Viewpoint.* Bethlehem, Penn.: CPC Foundation, 1976.

Bloom, B. S. "Learning for Mastery." *Instruction and Curriculum.* Regional Education Laboratory for the Carolinas and Virginia Topical Paper, Reprint No. 1. Durham, N.C.: RELCV, 1970.

Bolick, G. M., and Cooper, L. "Bachelor of Technology Degree: Link in the Career Ladder." *Community and Junior College Journal,* June/July, 1974, pp. 26–27.

Bond, L. "Impact of Collective Bargaining on Students." In D. W. Vermilye (Ed.), *Lifelong Learners—A New Clientele for Higher Education: Current Issues in Higher Education 1974.* San Francisco: Jossey-Bass, 1974.

Borow, H. "Student Decision Making: When and How." *College/ Career Choice: Right Student, Right Time, Right Place.* Monograph Nine. Iowa City: American College Testing Program, 1972.

Bowen, F. "State Fiscal Stringency and Public Higher Education." *The Research Reporter,* 1976, *10*(1). (A publication of the Center for Research and Development in Higher Education, University of California, Berkeley.)

Branscomb, L. M. "Taming Technology." *Science,* March 12, 1971, p. 171.

Brown, D. *Performance Objectives Development Project.* Lansing: Michigan Department of Education, Vocational-Technical Education Service, 1974.

Brown, L. R. "Global Food Insecurity." *The Futurist,* 1974, *8* (2), 56–64.

Brown, R. L. *Cooperative Education.* Washington, D.C.: American Association of Community and Junior Colleges, 1971.

Brown, S. J. *Cooperative Education and Career Development: A Comparative Study of Alumni.* Boston: Cooperative Education Research Center, Northeastern University, 1976.

Brubacher, J. S. *Bases for Policy in Higher Education.* New York: McGraw-Hill, 1965.

Bucklew, N. S. "Collective Bargaining and Policymaking." In D. W. Vermilye (Ed.), *Lifelong Learners—A New Clientele for Higher Education: Current Issues in Higher Education 1974.* San Francisco: Jossey-Bass, 1974.

"Burgeoning Benefits of a Lower Birth Rate." *Business Week,* December 15, 1973, p. 41.

Burnett, C. "Core Concept in Allied Health: A Summary of the ASAHP Report." *Journal of Allied Health,* June 1973.

Burns, M. A. *New Careers in Human Service: A Challenge to the Two-Year College.* Report No. 8. University Park: Center for the Study of Higher Education, Pennsylvania State University, 1971.

California State Colleges. *Industrial Arts/Industrial Technology.* Sacramento: Office of the Chancellor, Division of Academic Planning, California State Colleges, 1970.

Canby, T. Y. "Can The World Feed Its People?" *National Geographic,* July 1975, *148* (1), 2–39.

"Careers and the Community Colleges." *American Education,* March 1972, pp. 11–20.

Carnegie Commission on Higher Education, The. *College Graduates and Jobs.* New York: McGraw-Hill, 1973a.

Carnegie Commission on Higher Education, The. *Toward a Learning Society.* New York: McGraw-Hill, 1973b.

Carp, A., Peterson, R., and Roelfs, P. "Adult Learning Interests and Experiences." In K.P. Cross and J.R. Valley (Eds.), *Planning Non-Traditional Programs: An Analysis of the Issues for Postsecondary Education.* San Francisco: Jossey-Bass, 1974.

"Characteristics and Attitudes of 1976–77 Freshmen." *Chronicle of Higher Education,* January 10, 1977, pp. 12–13.

Cheit, E. F. *The New Depression in Higher Education: A Study of Financial Conditions in 41 Colleges and Universities.* New York: McGraw-Hill, 1971.

Clark, H. F., and Sloan, H. S. *Classrooms on Main Street.* New York: Teachers College Press, Columbia University, 1966.

Clarke, J. R. "Emerging Students: Career Education and Career Goals." *Emerging Students and the New Career Thrust in Higher Education.* Iowa City: American College Testing Program, 1971.

Cohen, A., and Brawer, F. *The Humanities In Two-Year Colleges.* Los Angeles: ERIC Clearinghouse for Junior Colleges, University of California, 1975.

College Board News. New York: College Entrance Examination Board, September 1975.

College Placement Council Foundation, The. *The Hard-to-Place Majority.* Report No. 5. Bethlehem, Pa.: CPC Foundation, 1975.

Community and Junior College News, April 1975, *1* (9), pp. 4–5.

Conference Board, The. *Technician Education—Who Chooses It?* New York: The Conference Board, 1972.

Cook, D.L. *Program Evaluation and Review Technique—Applications in Education.* OE-12024. Monograph 17. Washington, D.C.: U.S. Department of Health, Education and Welfare, 1966.

Cooper, B. S., and Brody, W. "1972 Lifetime Earnings by Age, Sex, Race, and Education Level." *Research and Statistics Note.* DHEW Publication No. (SSA) 75-11701. Washington, D.C.: U.S. Department of Health, Education and Welfare, Social Security Administration, 1975.

Corcoran, T. B. "Community Colleges: The Coming Slums of Education?" *Change,* September 1972.

"Courses That Lead to Jobs Are Taking Over on Campus." *U.S. News and World Report,* December 15, 1975, p. 50.

Cross, K. P. "New Students of the 1970s." *The Research Reporter,*

1971, 6 (4). (A publication of the Center for Research and Development in Higher Education, University of California, Berkeley.)

Cross, K. P. "New Students in a New World." In D. W. Vermilye (Ed.), *The Future In The Making: Current Issues in Higher Education 1973.* San Francisco: Jossey-Bass, 1973.

Curriculum Building for the Continuum in Social Welfare Education. Tallahassee: State University System of Florida, 1972.

Daniere, A. "Planning Education for Economic Productivity." In S. Harris (Ed.), *Challenge and Change in American Education.* Berkeley; Calif.: McCutchan, 1965.

Davis, D. "The 'Relevance' of Accountability." *The School Administrator,* April 1970.

Davis, K. "Zero Population Growth: The Goal and the Means." *Daedalus,* Fall 1973, p. 24.

DeBernardis, A. "What Career Education Means to the Community College." *Community and Junior College Journal,* May 1973, p. 9.

Defore, J. J. "Technology Education Comments," *Engineering Education,* February 1974a.

Defore, J. J. "Technology Education Comments." *Engineering Education,* May 1974b, p. 562.

Denison, E. F. *The Sources of Economic Growth in the United States and the Alternatives Before Us.* Supplemental Paper No. 13. New York: Committee for Economic Development, 1962.

DeNure, M. E. "Public Service Education Programs." In N.C. Harris (Ed.), *New Directions for Community Colleges: Updating Occupational Education,* no. 4. San Francisco: Jossey-Bass, 1973.

Detroit Institute of Technology. *Employer Experience With Cooperative Education: Analysis of Costs and Benefits.* Detroit: DIT, 1974.

Drucker, P. "Pension Fund Socialism." *The Public Interest,* Winter 1976 (42), 34–36.

Dunham, E. A. *Colleges of the Forgotten Americans.* New York: McGraw-Hill, 1969.

Eckhaus, R. S. *Estimating the Returns to Education: A Disaggregated Approach.* New York: McGraw-Hill, 1973.

Edgecombe, W. I. "A Community College Dental Clinic." *Community and Junior College Journal,* March 1974, p. 32.

Edman, E., and Collins, J. "Human Behavior in Human Services."

Community and Junior College Journal, December–January, 1975.

Ellis, M. "Women in Technical Education." Speech delivered at the National Clinic on Technical Education, Oklahoma City, March 26, 1971 (mimeograph).

Emmert, E. B. *Offender Assistance Programs Operated by Postsecondary Institutions of Education, 1975–76.* Washington, D.C.: American Association of Community and Junior Colleges, 1976.

Engineering Education, December 1973, (entire issue).

Engineering Education, March 1974, (entire issue).

Engineering Manpower Commission. In *Business Week,* November 4, 1972.

ERIC Clearinghouse for Junior Colleges. *Implications for Community College Governance Under Collective Bargaining.* Los Angeles: ERIC Clearinghouse for Junior Colleges, University of California, 1974.

ERIC Junior College Research Review. "Cooperative Work-Experience Education Programs in Junior Colleges," 1970, *5* (2).

Erwin, J. M. *The Proprietary School: Assessing Its Impact on the Collegiate Sector.* Ann Arbor: Center for the Study of Higher Education, University of Michigan, 1975.

"Ethics of Recruiting Stirs Spirited Debate." *College Board News,* January 1975, p. 1.

Faltermeyer, E. "Who Will Do The Dirty Work Tomorrow?" *Fortune,* January 1974, p. 132.

Feldman, M. "Feldman Rebuts Attack on Career and Voc-Ed." *Newsletter* of the National Advisory Council on Vocational Education, May–June 1976, p. 1.

Fenske, R. *Current Status, Planning and Prospects of the 1202 State Postsecondary Education Commissions.* Tempe: Center for the Study of Higher Education, Arizona State University, 1975.

Flanders, R. "Employment Patterns for the Seventies." *Compact,* August 1970.

Flexner, A. *Medical Education in the United States and Canada.* Bulletin No. 4. New York: Carnegie Foundation for the Advancement of Teaching, 1910.

Freeman, R., and Hollomon, J. H. "The Declining Value of College Going." *Change,* September 1975, p. 24.

"Future of Computer Conferencing." *Futurist,* August 1975, *9* (4), 182–195.

Gallagher, B. *Campus in Crisis.* New York: Harper & Row, 1974.

Garner, A. "Performance-Based Campus." In D. W. Vermilye (Ed.), *Lifelong Learners—A New Clientele for Higher Education: Current Issues In Higher Education 1974.* San Francisco: Jossey-Bass, 1974.

Gartner, A. *Paraprofessionals and Their Performance.* New York: Praeger, 1971.

Gilliland, R., Jr. "Maximizing Student Success." *Community and Junior College Journal,* March 1974, pp. 13–15.

Ginzberg, E. *The Manpower Connection: Education and Work.* Cambridge, Mass.: Harvard University Press, 1975.

Gladieux, L. E., and Wolanin, T. R. *Congress and the Colleges.* Lexington, Mass.: Heath, 1976.

Gleazer, E. J. "After the Boom—What Now for Community Colleges?" *Community and Junior College Journal,* December–January, 1974.

Glenny, L. A. "The '60s in Reverse." *The Research Reporter,* 1973, *8* (3), 1. (A publication of the Center for Research and Development in Higher Education, University of California, Berkeley.)

Godbold, D. H. "Most Valuable Medium for Blacks." *Community and Junior College Journal,* September 1976, p. 24–29.

Goyne, G. *Career Options in the Humanities: A Bibliography and Program Guide.* Los Angeles: Pepperdine University, 1975.

Graney, M. *The Technical Institute.* New York: Center for Applied Research in Education, 1965.

Grede, J. "Career Education for Community Colleges." *Illinois Career Education Journal,* Autumn 1972, pp. 31–35.

Grede, J. "The Role of the Community Colleges in Career Education." *Essays on Career Education.* Portland, Ore.: Northwest Regional Educational Laboratory, 1973a.

Grede, J. "The Untried Model of the Urban Community College." In N.C. Harris (Ed.), *New Directions for Community Colleges: Updating Occupational Education,* no. 4. San Francisco: Jossey-Bass, 1973b.

Greene, E. "Taking the 'Higher' Out of Higher Education." *College and University Journal,* 1974, *13* (1), 19.

Hamilton, A. "Career Education Working Model." *American Education,* December 1975, pp. 22–25.

Harbison, F., and Myers, C. *Education, Manpower, and Economic Growth.* New York: McGraw-Hill, 1964.

Harcleroad, F. "Is Federal Financing a Weak Reed?" Speech presented at the annual meeting of the American Association of Community College Trustees, New Orleans, November 2, 1973 (mimeograph).

Harcleroad, F. F., Molen, C. T., Jr., and Rayman, J. R. *The Regional State Colleges and Universities Enter the 1970s: ACT Special Report Ten.* Iowa City: The American College Testing Program, 1973.

Harris, N. C. *Technical Education in the Junior College: New Programs for New Jobs.* Washington, D.C.: American Association of Junior Colleges, 1964.

Harris, N. C. "On Being a Consultant." *Junior College Journal,* April 1967.

Harris, N. C. "Identifying New and Emerging Occupations." *Occupations and Education: Leaders in the Field Speak Out.* OEG3-7-000158-2037. Washington, D.C.: U.S. Department of Health, Education and Welfare, Office of Education, Bureau of Research, 1969.

Harris, N.C. "Technicians in the Energy Pipeline." *Technical Education News.* May–June 1975, p. 2.

Harris, S. *The Market for College Graduates.* Cambridge, Mass.: Harvard University Press, 1949.

Hayakawa, S.I. "Are the Colleges Educating too Well?" *Honolulu Star Bulletin,* February 4, 1970, editorial page.

Haynes, W. O. *Guidelines for Supermarket Management Programs in the Community College.* Washington, D.C.: American Association of Junior Colleges, 1968.

Hearings on H.R. 14454. House of Representatives, 93rd Congress, Second Session, August 13, 1974, p. 817.

Heinich, R. "Technology and the Student." In F. Harcleroad (Ed.), *Issues of the Seventies: The Future of Higher Education.* San Francisco: Jossey-Bass, 1970.

Henninger, G. R. *The Technical Institute in America.* New York: McGraw-Hill, 1959.

Heyne, P. T. *The Economic Way of Thinking.* Chicago: Science Research Associates, 1973.

Hill, J. *The Educational Sciences.* Bloomfield Hills, Mich.: Oakland Community College, 1971.

Hopkins, F. S. "The Postulated Future, The Invented Future, and an Ameliorated World." *The Futurist,* December 1973, *8* (5), 254–258.

Horn, F. H. "Liberal Education Reexamined." *Harvard Educational Review,* Fall 1956, *26,* 303–314.

Houston, J. "U.S. Predicts 10-Year Jobs Increase of 20 Percent." *Chicago Tribune,* November 16, 1975, Section 12, p. 1.

"How Your Life Will Change." *U.S. News and World Report,* March 3, 1975, p. 35.

Hulst, T. R., and Wark, R. G. "The Community in the Classroom." *Community and Junior College Journal,* February 1975, p. 17.

Indiana Plan for Postsecondary Education. Indianapolis: Commission for Higher Education of the State of Indiana, 1973.

Individualized Educational Planning. St. Paul: Minnesota Metropolitan State College, June 1975.

Innes, J. T., Jacobson, P. B., and Pellegrin, R. J. *The Economic Returns to Education: A Survey of the Findings.* Eugene: University of Oregon Press, 1965.

Jacob, P. E. *Changing Values in College.* New York: Harper & Row, 1957.

Johnson, W. R. "Should the Poor Buy No-Growth?" *Daedalus,* Fall 1973, p. 165.

Jordan, K. F., and Hanes, C. "Funding Public Education: Have We Reached the Limits?" *North Central Association Quarterly,* Winter 1976, *50* (3), 312–320.

Juster, T. (Ed.). *Education, Income, and Human Behavior.* New York: McGraw-Hill, 1975.

Kahler, C. (Ed.). *Guide for Program Planning: Medical Laboratory Technician.* Washington, D.C.: American Association of Junior Colleges, 1969.

Kahn, H., and Brown, W. "A Turning Point: And a Better Prospect for the Future." *The Futurist,* December 1975, *9* (6), 284–292.

Kahn, H., and Weiner, A. "The Next Thirty-Three Years: A Framework for Speculation." *Daedalus,* Summer 1967, pp. 705–732.

Kalani, H. *Curriculum Guide for Hospitality Education.* Honolulu: Kapiolani Community College, 1975.

Karabel, J. "Open Admissions: Toward Meritocracy or Democracy?" *Change,* May 1972, p. 38.

Kemerer, F. R., and Baldridge, J. V. *Unions on Campus: A National Study of the Consequences of Faculty Bargaining.* San Francisco: Jossey-Bass, 1975.

Kinsinger, R. E. (Ed.). *Career Opportunities: Health Technicians.* Chicago: Ferguson, 1970.

Klopfenstein, T. D. "The Core Is Not the Part You Throw Away: Allied Health Education." In N.C. Harris (Ed.), *New Directions for Community Colleges: Updating Occupational Education,* no. 4. San Francisco: Jossey-Bass, 1973.

Knoell, D. M. *People Who Need College: A Report on Students We Have Yet to Serve.* Washington, D.C.: American Association of Junior Colleges, 1970.

Knoell, D. *Through the Open Door: A Study of Enrollment and Performance in California Community Colleges.* Sacramento: California Postsecondary Education Commission, 1976.

Knowles, A. S., and Associates. *Handbook of Cooperative Education.* San Francisco: Jossey-Bass, 1971.

Korim, A. S. "Focusing on the Future." In J. W. Swift (Ed.), *Human Services Career Programs and the Community College.* Washington, D.C.: American Association of Junior Colleges, 1971a.

Korim, A. S. *Government Careers and the Community College.* Washington, D.C.: American Association of Junior Colleges, 1971b.

Kuhli, R. C. "Economics of Allied Health Education." *Human Resource Development—Technical Education's Challenge.* Proceedings of the twelfth annual national clinic on technical education, the American Technical Education Association, Wahpeton, North Dakota State School of Science, 1974.

Lecht, L. A. *Manpower Needs for National Goals in the 1970s.* New York: Praeger, 1969.

Lessing, L. "The Senseless War on Science." *Fortune,* March 1971, pp. 88–91.

Lessing, L. "Why The U.S. Lags in Technology." *Fortune,* April 1972, p. 69.

Lessing, L. "Capturing Clean Gas and Oil From Coal." *Fortune,* November 1973, p. 129.

Lessinger, L. *Accountability in Education.* Washington, D.C.: National Committee for Support of the Public Schools, 1970.

"Liberal Arts Students and the Job Market." *Chronicle of Higher Education,* May 5, 1975, pp. 27–31.

Light, I. "Development and Growth of New Allied Health Fields." *Journal of the American Medical Association,* October 1969.

Lombardi, J. *The Financial Crisis in the Community College.* Topical Paper No. 29. Los Angeles: ERIC Clearinghouse for Community Colleges, University of California, 1972.

Lombardi, J. *The Department/Division Structure in the Community College.* Topical Paper No. 38. Los Angeles: ERIC Clearinghouse for Junior Colleges, University of California, 1973.

McCollum, S., and others. "The Conversation: Community-Based Corrections in Community-Based Colleges." *Community and Junior College Journal,* February 1975, pp. 7–10.

McNeer, L. W. "Human Services." *Community and Junior College Journal,* March 1974, pp. 25–27.

McNett, I.E. "Legal Constraints to External Degrees." *American Education,* April 1976.

Mager, R. F. *Preparing Instructional Objectives.* Belmont, Calif.: Fearon, 1975.

Mager, R. F., and Beach, K. *Developing Vocational Instruction.* Belmont, Calif.: Fearon, 1967.

Mager, R. F., and Pipe, P. *Analyzing Performance Problems.* Belmont, Calif.: Fearon, 1970.

Mangelson, W. L., and others. *Projecting College and University Enrollments: Analyzing the Past and Focusing the Future.* Ann Arbor: Center for the Study of Higher Education, University of Michigan, 1974.

Marland, S. P., Jr. "Education and Public Confidence." *American Education,* May 1973a, pp. 5–10.

Marland, S. P., Jr. "Meeting Our Enemies, Career Education and the Humanities." *English Journal,* September 1973b, p. 900–906.

Marland, S. P., Jr. *Career Education.* New York: McGraw-Hill, 1974.

Marshall, A. *Principles of Economics.* (8th ed.) New York: Macmillan, 1949.

Martorana, S. V. "State-Level Planning for Community Colleges: Are the 1202 Commissions a Centripetal or Centrifugal Force

References

in Postsecondary Education?" *Essays on Education,* No. 4. Iowa City: American College Testing Program, 1973.

Mayhew, L. B. *Higher Education for Occupations.* Research Monograph No. 20. Atlanta: Southern Regional Education Board, 1974.

Meadows, D. L., and others. *The Limits to Growth.* New York: Potomac Associates, 1972.

Medsker, L., and Tillery, D. *Breaking the Access Barriers.* New York: McGraw-Hill, 1971.

Meyer, A. *An Educational History of the Western World.* New York: McGraw-Hill, 1965.

Meyer, A. *An Educational History of the American People* (2nd ed.) New York: McGraw-Hill, 1967.

Micheels, W. J. "Career Education at the Postsecondary Level: A Mission for the Four-Year Colleges." In S.P. Marland (Ed.), *Essays on Career Education.* Portland, Ore.: Northwest Regional Educational Laboratory, 1973.

Michigan State Department of Education. *Annual Report of Private Trade Schools, Business Schools, and Institutes, 1972–73.* Lansing, September 1973.

Millard, R. M. "Vocation: Central Aim of Education." *Essays on Education,* No. 2. Iowa City: American College Testing Program, 1973.

Minter, C., and Cacciola, R. "The Welder Is a Woman." *Community and Junior College Journal,* November 1976, pp. 6–7.

"Money Magazine Looks at the Two-Year College Option." *Higher Education Daily,* September 5, 1975, p. 6.

Monroe, C. R. *Profile of the Community College: A Handbook.* San Francisco: Jossey-Bass, 1972.

Montag, M. L. "Technical Education in Nursing." *The American Journal of Nursing,* May 1963, p. 100.

Moore, J. H., and Will, R. K. "Baccalaureate Programs in Engineering Technology." *Engineering Education,* October 1973, pp. 34–38.

Moore, J. H., and Will, R. K. "Baccalaureate Programs in Engineering Technology." *Engineering Education,* November 1974.

Moses, S. *The Learning Force: A More Comprehensive Framework for Educational Policy.* Syracuse, N.Y.: Publications in Continuing Education, Syracuse University, 1971.

National Advisory Council on Vocational Education. Testimony before the Education Subcommittee of the Committee on Labor and Public Welfare, U.S. Senate, Washington, D.C., April 11, 1975.

National Center for Educational Statistics. *Projections of Educational Statistics to 1983–84.* Washington, D.C.: U.S. Department of Health, Education and Welfare, 1974.

National Center for Educational Statistics. *Digest of Educational Statistics, 1974.* Washington, D.C.: U.S. Department of Health, Education and Welfare, 1975a.

National Center for Educational Statistics. *Federal Policy Issues and Data Needs In Postsecondary Education.* Washington, D.C.: U.S. Department of Health, Education and Welfare, 1975b.

National Center for Educational Statistics. *Associate Degrees and Other Formal Awards Below the Baccalaureate, 1972–73 and 1973–74.* (NCES 76-10) Washington, D.C.: U.S. Government Printing Office, 1976a.

National Center for Educational Statistics. *Earned Degrees Conferred 1972–73 and 1973–74. Summary Data.* (NCES 76-105.) Washington, D.C.: U.S. Government Printing Office, 1976b.

National Commission on Technology, Automation, and Economic Progress. *Technology and the American Economy.* Vol. 1. Washington, D.C.: National Commission on Technology, Automation and Economic Progress, 1966.

National Commission on the Financing of Posecondary Education. *Financing Postsecondary Education in the United States.* Washington, D.C.: U.S. Government Printing Office, 1973.

National Industrial Conference Board. *The Technical Manpower Shortage: How Acute?* New York: National Industrial Conference Board, 1970.

"News You Can Use: College and Jobs." *U.S. News and World Report,* November 22, 1976, p. 78.

1974–75 Placement Report: Career Planning and Placement Services. Menomonie: University of Wisconsin–Stout, 1975.

Noeth, R. J., and Hanson, G. "Occupational Programs Do the Job." *Community and Junior College Journal,* November 1976, pp. 28–30.

"Nursing Programs in Massachusetts' State College and University System." *Higher Education Daily,* August 26, 1976, p. 6.

Oberlin Alumni Career Counseling. Oberlin, Ohio: Office of Career Development and Placement, Oberlin College, 1975.

Occupational Manpower and Training Needs. Bulletin 1824. Washington, D.C.: U.S. Department of Labor, Bureau of Labor Statistics, 1974.

Occupational Outlook Handbook, 1976–77. Washington, D.C.: U.S. Department of Labor, 1977.

Olmstead, J. A. *Small-Group Instruction: Theory and Practice.* Alexandria, Va.: Human Resources Research Organization, 1974.

Olson, M. "Introduction." *Daedalus,* Fall 1973, p. 7.

O'Toole, J. "The Reserve Army of the Underemployed." *Change,* June 1975, p. 30.

Pace, C. R. (Ed.). *New Directions for Higher Education: Evaluating Learning and Teaching,* no. 4. San Francisco: Jossey-Bass, 1973.

Parker, G. "Enrollments in American Two-Year Colleges, 1973–74." *Intellect,* April 1974, p. 469.

Parker, G. *Collegiate Enrollments in American Two-Year Institutions, 1974–75.* Iowa City: American College Testing Program, 1975.

Parker, G. *Collegiate Enrollments in American Two-Year Institutions, 1975–76.* Iowa City: American College Testing Program, 1976.

Pierce, J. R. "Communication." *Daedalus,* Summer 1967, p. 910.

"Population Implosion." *Newsweek,* December 6, 1976, p. 58.

Poulton, N. L. *Enrollment Analysis Project.* Ann Arbor: Office of Academic Planning and Analysis, University of Michigan, 1975.

President's Commission on Higher Education. *Higher Education for American Democracy.* New York: Harper & Row, 1947.

President's Committee on Education Beyond the High School. *Second Report to the President.* Washington, D.C.: U.S. Government Printing Office, 1957.

"Pressure Builds for Fair Share Legislation." *Sea Power*, August 1976, p. 19.

Purdy, L. "Community College Instructors and the New Media: Why Some Do and Others Don't." *Educational Technology*, March 1975.

Quarton, G. C. "Deliberate Efforts To Control Human Behavior and Modify Personality." *Daedalus*, Summer 1967, pp. 837–853.

Rainey, G. "How To Avoid Mistakes in Individual-Paced Instruction." West Lafayette, Ind.: Purdue University, Department of Electrical Technology, 1971 (mimeograph).

Report of Career Division. Vincennes, Ind.: Vincennes University Junior College, 1976 (mimeograph).

Research Coordinating Unit for Vocational Education. *The Perceptions of Selected Male Public High School Seniors Concerning Specialized and Comprehensive Postsecondary Schools in Minnesota.* Minneapolis: University of Minnesota, 1972.

Richardson, E. "The Decline of Initiative." *Change*, April 1973, p. 16.

Riendeau, A. J. *The Role of the Advisory Committee in Occupational Education in the Junior College.* Washington, D.C.: American Association of Junior Colleges, 1967.

Rinehart, R. L. "Articulating Career Education at Associate-Degree and Baccalaureate-Degree Levels." In N.C. Harris (Ed.), *New Directions for Community Colleges: Updating Occupational Education*, no. 4. San Francisco: Jossey-Bass, 1973.

Roberts, R. "Energy Crisis: Colleges Aren't Taking it Lightly." *College and University Business*, February 1974, pp. 44–46.

Rochester Institute of Technology. Letter to the authors from the Provost. Rochester, N.Y., November 1976.

Rogers, J. A. "The Bio-Medical Equipment Technician." *Industrial Arts and Vocational Education*, Technical Education Supplement. January 1971.

Rotella, S. "College Education for Government Service." Speech delivered at the International Congress of Administrative Science, Rome, Italy, September 1971. (Available from Chicago City-Wide College, Chicago City Colleges, 185 North Wabash Avenue, Chicago.)

Roueche, J. *Salvage, Redirection, or Custody? Remedial Education in the Community Junior College.* Washington, D.C.: American Association of Junior Colleges, 1968.

Roueche, J., Baker, G., and Brownell, R. *Accountability and the Community College.* Washington, D.C.: American Association of Community and Junior Colleges, 1972.

Roueche, J., Herrscher, B., and Baker, G. *Time as the Variable, Achievement as the Constant: Competency-Based Instruction in the Community College.* Washington, D.C.: American Association of Community and Junior Colleges, 1976.

"Schools Expect Fewer Students." *Ann Arbor* (Mich.) *News,* September 15, 1976, p. 13.

Schultz, T. W. "Capital Formation by Education." *Journal of Political Economy,* December 1960, *68.*

Scientific, Engineering, Technical Manpower Comments. November 1975, *12* (9), 1.

Scientific, Engineering, Technical Manpower Comments. July–August 1976, *13* (6), 7.

Seaborg, G. "Opportunities in Today's Energy Milieu." *The Futurist,* February 1975, *9* (1), 22–37.

Sessoms, H. D., and Verhoven, P. J. *Recreation Program Leadership and the Community College.* Washington, D.C.: American Association of Junior Colleges, 1970.

Sheffer, H. V. "Directed Corrections or Corrected Directions?" *Community and Junior College Journal,* August–September 1973, pp. 22–24.

Silberman, C. "The Public Business: The Remaking of American Education," *Fortune,* April 1961, p. 125–131.

Skaggs, K. G. "Health Technology Programs: A Brief Review." *Community and Junior College Journal,* March 1974, pp. 7–8.

Smith, A. *An Inquiry into the Nature and Causes of the Wealth of Nations.* New York: Random House, 1939.

Smith, S. M. "Career Education For Women: An Opportunity To Change the Theme." *Essays on Career Education.* Portland, Ore.: Northwest Regional Educational Laboratory, 1973.

Society for College and University Planning. "Media Marshalled by Community College." *Planning for Higher Education,* August 1975, Profile 8, *4,* (4).

Southern Regional Education Board. *Integrating Career Development on Campus.* Report of a Workshop. Atlanta: SREB, 1974.

Southern Regional Education Board. *Regional Spotlight,* November 1975, *10* (2).

Sprick, W. J. "Try It, You'll Like It—Business Simulation, That Is." In N. C. Harris (Ed.), *New Directions for Community Colleges: Updating Occupational Education,* no. 4. San Francisco: Jossey-Bass, 1973.

Starr, P. "The Undelivered Health System." *The Public Interest,* Winter 1976 (42), 66.

Stewart, W. A. "Manpower for Better Health Services." *Public Health Reports.* Washington, D.C.: U.S. Public Health Service, 1966.

"Student Tests Hit New Lows." *Detroit Free Press,* September 12, 1976, p. 9A.

Study of 1974–75 Grads and Their Beginning Salaries. Ferris State College. Big Rapids, Mich.: Placement and Career Education Center, 1975.

Swift, J. W. "The Teacher Aide Program and the Baccalaureate Degree: Junior College Point of View." In *Proceedings: Statewide Articulation Conference in Professional Education.* Springfield: Illinois Junior College Board, 1970.

Swift, J. W. *Human Services Career Programs and the Community College.* Washington, D.C.: American Association of Community and Junior Colleges, 1971.

Taubman, P., and Wales, T. *Higher Education and Earnings.* New York: McGraw-Hill, 1974.

Technology Review, December 1972 (entire issue).

Technology Review, December 1973 (entire issue).

Technology Review, May 1974 (entire issue).

Thornton, J. W. *The Community Junior College.* (2nd ed.) New York: Wiley, 1972.

Tonsor, S. "Commentary: Who Should Decide Who Goes to College?" In P. R. Rever (Ed.), *Open Admissions and Equal Access.* Monograph 4. Iowa City: American College Testing Program, 1971.

Trachtenberg, S. J., and Levy, L. C. "In Search of Warm Bodies." *Change,* Summer 1973, pp. 54–57.

Train, R. "The Long-Term Value of the Energy Crisis." *Futurist,* February 1974, *8* (1), 14–18.

"Training for Jobs." *Business Week,* February 9, 1976, p. 104.

"Training More People for Jobs in the 'Real World'." *U.S. News and World Report,* June 1973, p. 50.

"Trend of American Business." *U.S. News and World Report,* May 3, 1976, p. 56.

Trivett, D. A. "Postsecondary Education: The New Meaning." *ERIC Higher Education Research Currents,* October 1973, p. 5.

Trivett, D. A. *Proprietary Schools and Postsecondary Education.* ERIC Higher Education Research Report No. 2. Washington, D.C.: American Association for Higher Education, 1974.

Trivett, D. A. "Open Admissions and the CUNY Experience." *ERIC Higher Education Research Currents,* March 1976.

Turner, R., and Shelding, A. "Students and the Curriculum Continuum." In *Curriculum Building for the Continuum in Social Welfare Education.* Tallahassee: State University System of Florida, 1972.

"23 Million Called Illiterate." *Chicago Daily News,* October 29, 1975, p. 1.

U.S Bureau of the Census. *Census of Population 1960 Subject Reports: Occupation by Industry.* Washington, D.C.: U.S. Government Printing Office, 1962.

U.S. Bureau of the Census. *Census of Population 1970 Subject Reports: Occupation by Industry.* Washington, D.C.: U.S. Government Printing Office, 1972.

U.S. Bureau of the Census. *Special Report on Youth.* Washington, D.C.: U.S. Government Printing Office, 1973.

U.S. Congress. *Education Amendments of 1972,* May 1972.

U.S. Department of Health, Education and Welfare, Office of Education. *Criteria for Technician Education: A Suggested Guide.* OE-80056. Washington, D.C.: U.S. Government Printing Office, 1968.

U.S. Department of Health, Education and Welfare, Office of Education. *Selected Statistical Notes on American Education.* Washington, D.C.: U.S. Government Printing Office, 1974a.

U.S. Department of Health, Education and Welfare, Public Health

Service. *Trends and Career Changes of College Students in the Health Fields.* Publication No. (HRA) 76-54. Washington, D.C.: U.S. Government Printing Office, 1974b.

U.S. Department of Health, Education and Welfare, Office of Education. "Cooperative Education." *Education Briefing Paper.* Washington, D.C.: U.S. Government Printing Office, 1975a.

U.S. Department of Health, Education and Welfare, Office of Education, Division of Vocational and Technical Education. *Law Enforcement Technology.* Washington, D.C.: U.S. Government Printing Office, 1975b.

U.S. Department of Labor. *Employment Outlook for Technicians Who Work With Engineers and Physical Scientists.* BLS Bulletin No. 1300-96. Washington, D.C.: U.S. Government Printing Office, 1962.

U.S. Department of Labor, Bureau of Labor Statistics. *Occupational Manpower and Training Needs.* BLS Bulletin No. 1824. Washington, D.C.: U.S. Government Printing Office, 1974a.

U.S. Department of Labor, Bureau of Labor Statistics. *The Structure of the U.S. Economy in 1980 and 1985.* BLS Bulletin No. 1831. Washington, D.C.: U.S. Government Printing Office, 1974b.

U.S. Department of Labor, Bureau of Labor Statistics. *Employment of High School Graduates and Dropouts. Special Labor Force Report 168.* Washington, D.C.: U.S. Government Printing Office, 1974c.

U.S. Department of Labor, Bureau of Labor Statistics. *Handbook of Labor Statistics 1975.* Washington, D.C.: U.S. Government Printing Office, 1975.

U.S. Department of Labor, Bureau of Labor Statistics. *The Occupational Outlook Handbook, 1976–77.* Washington, D.C.: U.S. Government Printing Office, 1976.

Vaizey, J. *The Economics of Education* (introduction to). London: Faber and Faber, 1962.

Venn, G. *Man, Education, and Work: Postsecondary Vocational and Technical Education.* Washington, D.C.: American Council on Education, 1963.

Wallers, R.I. "Education by Infusion." *Community and Junior College Journal,* August–September 1973, p. 50.

Warren, J. T. "Differential Costs of Curricula in Illinois Public Junior Colleges." Unpublished doctoral dissertation. Urbana: University of Illinois, 1972.

Watkins, B. T. "Student Demands for 'Practical' Education Are Forcing Major Changes in Curricula." *Chronicle of Higher Education,* November 26, 1973.

Wattenbarger, J. L. *The Community Junior College: Target Population, Program Costs and Cost Differentials.* National Educational Finance Project, Special Study No. 6. Gainesville: Institute of Higher Education, University of Florida, 1970.

Wattenbarger, J., and Starnes, P. *Financial Support For Community. Colleges, 1974.* Gainesville: Institute of Higher Education, University of Florida, 1974.

Webster, R. S. "Community College Occupational Programs: An Investigation of the Planning Process." Unpublished doctoral dissertation. Ann Arbor: University of Michigan, 1974.

White, L. T., Jr. "On Intellectual Gloom." *The American Scholar,* Spring 1966, *35* (2), 223–226; quoted by Robert Heinich in F. F. Harcleroad (Ed.) *Issues of the Seventies: The Future of Higher Education.* San Francisco: Jossey-Bass, 1970.

Whitehead, A. N. "Technical Education and Its Relation to Science and Literature." Presidential Address to the Mathematical Association of England, 1917, reproduced as Chapter 4 in *The Aims of Education and Other Essays.* New York: New American Library, 1949.

Wiggs, G. D. (Ed.). *Career Opportunities—Marketing, Business, and Office Specialists.* Chicago: Ferguson, 1970.

Willers, J. C. "The Quality of Life in the Seventies and Implications for Vocational Teacher Education." In R.N. Evans and D.R. Terry (Eds.), *Changing the Role of Vocational Teacher Education.* Bloomington, Ind.: McKnight and McKnight, 1971.

Wilms, W. "Controversial Research and Its Critics." *Change,* November 1975, pp. 44, 45, 61.

Wise, F. "Simulation Models in College Planning and Administration." In J. Bolin (Ed.), *Management Information for College Administrators.* Athens, Ga.: Institute of Higher Education, 1971.

Wise, M. *They Come For The Best of Reasons.* Washington, D.C.: American Council on Education, 1958.

Withey, Stephen B. (Ed.). *A Degree and What Else? Correlates and Consequences of a College Education.* New York: McGraw-Hill, 1971.

Wolfle, D. "To What Extent Do Monetary Returns to Education Vary with Family Background, Mental Ability and School Quality?" In L. C. Solmon and P. J. Taubman (Eds.), *Does College Matter?* New York: Academic Press, 1973.

"Women at Work." *Newsweek,* December 6, 1976, pp. 68–81.

"Worldwide Job Crisis Faces University Graduates." *Chronicle of Higher Education,* September 27, 1976, p. 1.

Wynn, M., Rubin, T., and Franco, G. R. "New Ways to Measure and Forecast International Affairs." *Futurist,* December 1973, 7 (5), 244–249.

Index

Accountability: in career education, 368–370; related to educational inputs and outputs, 349

ADLER, M. J., 21

Administration in career education, 380–385; career-division model of, 382–385

Adult Education Act, 314

Advisory committees, 128–129, 194–195, 263, 266–267

Aerospace technicians, 149

Age shift of U.S. Population, 46–47

Agri-business programs, 119–121

Air conditioning, heating, and refrigeration technicians, 144, 147

Alice Lloyd College (Kentucky), 242

Allied health careers: freshmen planning to enter training for, 179; list of major career areas in, 180–181; manpower needs and supply in, 170–180; types of schools offering training programs for, 180

Allied health programs, 180–187; advisory groups for, 194–195; and associate degree level, 184–185; and baccalaureate level, 185–186; and certificate level, 183–184; core semester play for, 187–190; expansion of enrollments in, 177; intern-ships and clinical experiences in, 193–194; problems of quality and level of rigor in, 192–193

Alma College (Michigan), 242–243

ALMARODE, R. L., 116

American Association of Collegiate Schools of Business (AACSB), 121, 126

American Association of Community and Junior Colleges (AACJC), 33, 68, 71, 71n, 214, 292, 313, 326

American Association for Higher Education (AAHE), 246

American Association of Medical Assistants, 182–183

American Association of State Colleges and Universities, 89

American College Testing (ACT) Program, 36, 129, 154

American Council on Education (ACE), 20, 95, 105, 177; Office of Educational Credit of, 308, 310

American Dental Assistants' Association, 182

American Dental Association (ADA): Council on Dental Education of, 175, 182

American Institute of Banking (AIB), 112–113, 297

409

American Medical Association (AMA), 170, 171, 176, 182
American Nurses' Association (ANA), 168
American Society of Clinical Pathologists (ASCP), 182
American Society for Engineering Education (ASEE), 79, 80, 134, 141, 143, 151, 155, 157, 160
American Vocational Association (AVA), 67
Antiintellectualism in America, 18
Antioch College (Ohio), 242
Appliance repair technicians, 144
Area vocational-technical schools (AVTSs), 81–84; characteristics of, 83; enrollments in, 82–83; strengths and weaknesses of, 83–84
ASH, R. L., 357
Associate degree programs in four-year colleges, 94–96
ASTIN, A. W., 35, 105, 179, 228
Auto service technicians, 144

Baccalaureate degree occupational programs, 57, 91–97, 124–126, 141–142, 155–160, 185–186
BAKER, G., 130, 275, 370
Bakersfield College (California), 71
BALDRIDGE, J. V., 381
Banking, careers in, 112–113, 237
BEACH, K., 275
BECKER, G. S., 332
BECKER, H., 39, 168
BELL, D., 352
BERG, I., 324, 343, 351
Bernard Baruch College (New York), 210
BISCONTI, A. S., 230
BLOOM, B., 76, 163, 275
BOLICK, G. M., 156
BOND, L., 380
BOROW, H., 382
BOWEN, F., 374
BRANSCOMB, L. M., 17, 132
BRODY, W., 327, 329
Broome Community College (New York), 245

BROWN, D., 76, 163
BROWN, L. R., 355
BROWN, R. L., 126
BROWN, S. J., 277
BROWN, W., 357
BROWNELL, R., 370
BRUBACHER, J. S., 16, 21
BUCKLEW, N., 381
BURNETT, C., 188
BURNS, M. A., 205
Business: enployment in, 102–105; as a foundation of the economy, 101–102
Business careers: and automation, 105; education and training for, 106; and middle manpower, 104
Business and office careers, workers in, 102–104
Business management: associate degree program in, 124; baccalaureate program in, 125; careers in, 121–123
Business management laboratory, 127–128
Business programs: advisory committees for, 128–129; freshmen interest in, 105–106; kinds offered by various institutions, 106–107; quality and level of, 129–130

CACCIOLA, R., 59
California Polytechnic State University, 89
Capstone programs. See Two-Plus-Two programs
Career education: accountability in, 368–370; attitudes of minorities toward, 310–312; and college level, 10–13; and communication, 361–363; competence, excellence, and quality in, 251–256, 370–372; definitions of, 8–11; and the energy crisis, 358–359; and the environmental crisis, 360; federal funding and control of, 378–380; financing of, 372–375; and the food crisis, 359–360; future of, 351–386; governance and administration of,

375–385; and industrial modernization, 363–364; and international
trade, 360–361; local patterns of
organization and administration
of, 380–385; and the "no-growth"
society, 364–365; return on investment in, 337–350; and transportation and communications, 361–363
Career ladder and lattice concepts, 10,
108, 118, 161–163, 190–192, 217–
219
Career-oriented studies, increase in
enrollments in, 33–35
Career programs: curriculum content
of, 256–258; level and breadth of,
192–193; 268–273; planning for,
130, 164–165, 195–196, 225–226,
251–290, 345–350; projecting enrollments in, 264–266; teaching
and learning systems for, 273–276
Carnegie Commission on Higher Education, 30–31, 45, 56, 66, 69, 90,
230, 341, 349, 379
CARP, A., 35
Case study methods in business, 127;
business simulation as a variant of,
127–128
Chartered Life Underwriters, 114
Chatham College (Pennsylvania), 245
CHEIT, E. F., 4
Chemical technicians, 149
Child development: associate degree
programs in, 203–204, 207; bac-
calaureate program in, 208
Child Development Associate Con-
sortium, 203
City Colleges of Chicago, 71, 74, 191,
204, 206, 213, 224–225, 298, 301
Civil engineering technicians, 149
Civil Rights Act of 1964, 156
CLARK, H. F., 85
CLARKE, J. R., 9
Clerk-typist programs, 108–109
Coast Community College (California),
225
Coe College (Iowa), 245
COHEN, A., 234
Collective bargaining, as a factor in the

administration of career-oriented
colleges, 380–381
College attendance: and demand for
professional manpower, 329–331;
effect of birth rate on predictions of,
29–30
College Entrance Examination Board,
129
College Placement Council (CPC),
230, 232
College of San Mateo (California), 242
College students, changing goals and
attitudes of, 27–41
COLLINS, J., 206
Commercial art, 235
Commercial music, 235
Communications arts, 235
Community colleges: admission to,
36–37; and articulation with other
institutions, 305–307; career programs in, 74–75; characteristics of,
70–77, 295–296; development of,
71; enrollment by programs in,
34; financing career programs in,
312–314; in-service programs for
business, industry, and public
agencies in, 296–298; "linking pin"
concept of, 307; list of, 71n; literacy
and job–entry training for adults
in, 302–305; noncampus colleges
in, 74; problems of, 75–77; programs for unemployed in, 302–303;
skill centers in, 303–305; students
in, 73; trends for the future of, 76–
77; urban organization of career
programs in, 298; urban satellite
centers in, 301–302; urban systems
in, 292–294
Competence: curriculum content for
development of, 256–258; definitions and levels of 254–255
Competency-based evaluation of non-
traditional learning, 307–310
Competency-based instruction, 163,
255–256, 274–276, 371–372
Comprehensive Employment Training Act (CETA) of 1973, 304–305,
313–314

Conference Board, The, 143–148, 154
Construction technicians, 145
COOK, D. L., 262
COOPER, B. S., 327–329
Cooperative education. *See* Work experience and internship
Cooperative Education Association, 242
Cooperative Institutional Research Program (UCLA), 105
CORCORAN, T. B., 76
Core and ladder approach: in allied health, 187–190; in technical education, 161–163
Corrections. *See* Law enforcement and corrections
Council for the Advancement of Experiential Learning, 310
Council on Hotel, Restaurant, and Institutional Education, 116
Council on Social Work Education, 204
Counseling and guidance, 277–280; flow chart for, 281
CROSS, K. P., 73, 274

DANIERE, A., 332
DE BERNARDIS, A., 75
DEFORE, J. J., 152, 154
Delta College (Michigan), 151–340
DENISON, E. F., 333–334
Dental assistants, 175
DE NURE, M. E., 198
Dental hygienists, 174
Detail draftsmen, 144
De Pauw University (Indiana), 245
Detroit Institute of Technology, 276
Developmental and remedial education, 280–282
DEWEY, J., 21
Dichotomy and dialogue in higher education, 13–23
Diversity, problems of, 35–38
Drafting (design) technicians, 150
Drexel University (Pennsylvania), 242
DRUCKER, P., 49, 104
Dualism in education, 15–19
DUNHAM, E. A., 89

ECKHAUS, R. S., 343–344
Economic growth, sources of in the U.S., 334
Economic returns on investment in higher education, 6–8, 322–333
EDGECOMB, W. I., 174–175
EDMAN, E., 206
Education: current annual cost of in U.S., 320–321; history of in U.S., 316–322; as an "ultimate good," 321; versus schooling and custody, 352
Education Amendments Act of 1972, 67, 69, 70, 82, 84, 202, 313, 377
Education Amendments Act of 1976, 202
Education for middle manpower, 60–62
Education requirements of jobs, 56; and artificial educational upgrading, 57. *See also* Griggs *v.* Duke Power Company
Educational Testing Service, 35
Egalitarianism versus meritocracy in higher education, 37–38, 76
Electronics and electrical technicians, 150
ELLIS, M., 58–59
EMMERT, E. B., 214
Energy resources, 270–272, 358–359
Engineering and industrial technology: ASEE definitions of, 141. *See also* Technologists, engineering and industrial
Engineering Manpower Commission, 136, 148, 155
Engineering technology education, 79–80; degree programs in, 91, 152–153, 156–160
Engineers Council for Professional Development (ECPD), 79, 81, 87, 151, 154
Enrollment distribution by program, two-year colleges, 34; among adults, 35
Environment and ecology as problems for technology, 360
Environmental health program, 185–186

ERWIN, J. M., 85–86
Evergreen State College (Washington), 245

Faculty in career programs, 223–224, 258–261
FALTERMEYER, E., 17, 266
FELDMAN, M., 20
FENSKE, R., 377
Ferris State College (Michigan), 89, 92, 124, 155, 185, 191
Finance, insurance and real estate: careers in, 111–115
Financing career education: and federal appropriations, 374; and local taxation, 373; and state appropriations, 373–374; and tuition charges, 372
FLANDERS, R., 56, 331, 341
FLEXNER, A., 168
Food crisis, implications for middle manpower education, 359–360
Foreign language, career potentials for persons fluent in, 235
Four-year colleges and universities, 89–96; and articulation with two-year colleges, 94–96; career programs in, 91–93; and characteristics of "state colleges," 89; "two-plus-two" programs in, 93–94
FRANCO, G. R., 356
FREEMAN, R., 50, 331, 332, 335
Full employment, definition of, 104n

GALLAGHER, B., 294
GARNER, A., 393
GARTNER, A., 169
General education in career programs: faculty for, 260–261; relationship of to competence, 257–258
General Education Development Tests, (G.E.D.), 287, 301
Georgetown University (Washington, D.C.), 245
GILLILAND, R., JR., 190
GLADIEUX, L. E., 69
GLEAZER, E. J., 76, 292
GLENNY, L. A., 5
GODBOLD, D., 311–312

Golden West College (California), 123
Governance and administration of career education, 375–385; impact of collective bargaining on, 380
GRANEY, M., 77, 134
GREDE, J., 76, 258, 322
GREENE, E., 5
Griggs v. Duke Power Company, 156, 341, 349
Grinnell College (Iowa), 245

HAMILTON, A., 10
HANES, C., 372
HANSON, J., 340
HARBISON, F., 24, 322, 324
HARCLEROAD, F., 89, 374
HARRIS, N. C., 58, 68, 262, 263
HARRIS, S., 332
Harvard Graduate School of Business Administration, 127
HAYAKAWA, S. A., 18
HAYNES, W. O., 129
Head Start Program, 202
Health care: costs of, 167–168; team approach to, 168–170
Health Maintenance Organizations (HMOs), 167
Health occupations: manpower requirements, "need" and "demand," 170–174
Health team: and approach to health care, 168–170; personnel in, 168–170
HENNINGER, G. R., 134
HERRSCHER, B., 130, 275
HEYNE, P. T., 347
High school graduates going to college, percent of, 28
High talent manpower, 49–51
Higher education: and changing job markets, 330–333; characteristics of four-year colleges and universities in, 89–96; in competition with other social goals, 4; cost benefit considerations in, 322–350; decline of enrollment in, 5; decline of public confidence in, 4–8; dichotomy between liberal and practical arts

in, 15–23; and early development
in U.S., 13–15, 64–65, 316–322;
economic returns on, 321–335; and
market forces, 347–348; "new
depression" in, 4–8; nonpecuniary
returns on, 335–337; percent of
new high school graduates in, 28;
societal changes and, 14–15; transi-
tion to career education, 3–25;
universal, 319–322
Higher Education General Information
Survey (HEGIS), 218
Highly-skilled workers, 55
HILL, J., 274
HOLLOMON, J. H., 50, 331, 332, 335
HOPKINS, F. S., 355
HORN, F. H., 228
Hospitality industry, careers in, 115–119
Hotel and restaurant management pro-
grams, 117
HOUSTON, J., 123
HOWARD, E. B., 170
HULST, T. R., 210

In loco parentis, 39–40
Industrial management technicians,
144
Industrial modernization, need for,
363–364
Inhalation (respiratory) therapy tech-
nicians, 175
INNES, J. T., 324–325
Instrument repair technicians, 144
Insurance, careers in, 114, 237
International trade, 360–361

Jackson Community College (Michi-
gan), 214
JACOB, P. E., 6
JACOBSON, P. B., 324–325
JOHNSON, W. R., 365
JORDAN, K. F., 372
Journalism, careers in, 235
Junior colleges, 71. See also Community
colleges
JUSTER, T., 6

KAHLER, C., 176
KAHN, H., 353–357
Kansas City, Metropolitan Junior Col-
lege District of, 74, 183, 225
Kapiolani Community College (Hawaii),
119
KARABEL, J., 75, 312
Katherine Gibbs Schools, 85
Kellogg Community College (Michi-
gan), 188
KEMERER, F. R., 381
KING, M. R., 35, 105, 179, 228
KINSINGER, R. E., 170, 176, 180
Kirkwood Community College (Iowa),
235
KLOPFENSTEIN, T. D., 188
KNOELL, D. M., 311
KNOWLES, A., 241
KORIM, A. S., 201, 205
KUHLI, R. C., 170

Labor force in U.S., 43–63; defined,
47–49; distribution by occupational
groups in, 48, 52; major occupa-
tional groups in, 48; women in
the, 47–48
Lake Michigan College (Michigan), 184
Law Enforcement Assistance Administration, 202
Law enforcement and corrections,
209–215; associate degree programs in, 211–214; and further
education of offenders, 214–215
Law Enforcement Program, 211–212
Learning Society, 31–33
LECHT, L. A., 133
Lees Junior College (Kentucky), 242
Lehigh University (Pennsylvania), 245
LESSING, L., 40, 273, 363
LESSINGER, L., 369
LEVY, L. C., 91
Liberal arts, 227–248; associate degree
career programs in, 233–239;
career options for baccalaureate
graduates in, 230, 239–241; de-
fined, 228; foundations of the,
16–20; limited market for gradu-

ates in, 227–232; and practical arts contrasted, 17–19; work experience for students in, 241–246

Liberal arts colleges, as providing link between college and work, 242–246

LIGHT, I., 181

Lifelong learning, 29, 32–33. *See also* Learning Society

Lifetime earnings of males and females, table of, 328

LOMBARDI, J., 22, 378

Long Beach City College (California), 190

Los Angeles Community College District, 71–74, 183, 225, 340

McCOLLUM, S., 214–215

Machine draftsman program, 146

Machine tool technicians, 144

McNEER, L. W., 203

McNETT, I. E., 88

MAGER, R. F., 76, 163, 219, 275

Management programs, 121–126

MANGELSON, W. L., 30

Manhattan Community College (New York), 242

Manpower demands and needs, contrasted, 170

Manpower development: defined, 44–45, 65; and the labor force, 43–49

Manpower Development and Training Act of 1963, 304

Market forces, as factor in student career choice, 41

MARLAND, S. P., 8, 22, 231–232

MARSHALL, A., 44

Mastery learning. *See* Competency-based instruction

MAYER, M., 21

MAYHEW, L. B., 128, 247

MEADOWS, D. L., 364

Mechanical engineering technicians, 150

Medical assistant program, 183

Medical laboratory technology, 175–176

Medical science, advances in, 166–167

MEDSKER, L., 71, 373

Merritt College (California), 311

Metropolitan State University (Minnesota), 254

MEYER, A., 38, 317–318

MICHEELS, W. J., 11

Michigan State Department of Education, 85

Michigan State University, 210

Middle manpower, 51–63; defined, 51–53; education for, 60–63; educational requirements for jobs in, 56–57, 139; estimating demand for, 261–262; relative proportions of cognitive and manipulative activities in, 53–54; skilled workers in, 55–56; supply and demand for jobs in, 57–58; technicians in, 53–55; women and, 58–60

Midwest Cooperative Education Association, 242

MILLARD, R., 21, 65, 67

Mining technicians, 144

Minorities: Enrolling in colleges, 27–28, 32. *See also* Community colleges, Middle manpower, Students

MINTER, C., 59

Model Cities Program, 202, 297

Mohawk Valley Community College (New York), 242

MOLEN, C. T., 89

MONROE, C. R., 71, 310

MONTAG, M. L., 169

MOORE, J. H., 91, 155

Morrill Land-Grant Colleges Act of 1862, 18, 64

Morton College (Illinois), 211

MOSES, S., 30, 45

Mott, C. S., Community College (Michigan), 146

MYERS, C., 24, 322, 324

National Advisory Council on Vocational Education, 305, 313, 314

National Association of Manufacturers, 143

National Association for Practical Nurse Education Service, 182
National Association of Social Workers, 204
National Association of Trade and Technical Schools, 87
National Bureau of Standards, 132
National Center for Educational Statistics, 84, 229, 326, 338
National Commission for Cooperative Education, 242
National Commission on the Financing of Postsecondary Education, 70, 84–85
National Commission on Technology, Automation, and Economic Progress, 62, 258
National Defense Education Act of 1958, 68, 134, 234, 269
National Industrial Conference Board (now The Conference Board), 135
National League for Nursing, 182
National Occupational Competency Testing Institute, 308
National Planning Association, 303, 314
National Science Foundation, 143
National Student Loan Program, 336
Need versus demand in manpower forecasting, 261–262
New Careers Program, 202
"New Depression" in higher education, 4, 8
Newman Report, 69
NEXUS, 246
NOETH, R. J., 340
No-Growth Society, 355, 364–366
Noncollegiate sector of post-secondary education, 29–31
Nontraditional learning, awarding credit for, 307–310
Northeastern University (Massachusetts), 242, 277
Nurses, licensed practical, 174
Nurses, registered, 174, 184–185
Nursing, 168–169, 172, 174, 184–185
Nursing programs, 169; and associate degree (ADN), 184; baccalaureate (BSN), 180; practical (LPN), 180

Oberlin College (Ohio), 243–244
Occupational education, 68; compared to vocational education and technical education, 68–70
Occupational structure in U.S., changing patterns in, 49–60
Occupational surveys, 262–264
Office careers: major types of programs in, 108–111; persons employed in, 107–108
Ohio College of Applied Science (University of Cincinnati), 77
OLMSTEAD, J. A., 128, 274
OLSON, M., 365
"Open-door" colleges, 36
Orange Coast College (California), 242
Orange County Consortium Career Education Project, 10
O'TOOLE, J., 342

PACE, C. R., 274
Paraprofessionals, 53; in the health field; 181; in public and human services fields, 204. See also Middle manpower, Technicians
PARKER, G., 33–35, 72, 80, 82
PELLEGRIN, R. J., 324–325
Pepperdine University (California), 244–245
Peralta Community College (California), 74
Performance objectives in competency-based education, 163
Performance standards for job entry, 275–276
PETERSON, R. E., 35
Physical therapy assistants, 175
Physician's assistant, 192
PIERCE, J. R., 362
PIPE, P., 275
Placement, 76–77, 92–93, 230, 232; the office of, 282–283; of associate degree graduates, 282–283, 339–340
Planning career education programs, 268–273; considerations of breadth versus narrow specialization in, 269–273

Police Recruit Program, 298
Population trends in the U.S., 45–47
Postsecondary education: defined, 70; development of, in America, 64–65; in Education Amendments Act of 1972, 69; and higher education, 69–70; noncollegiate institutional enrollment in, 30–31; private schools involved in, 85
POULTON, N. L., 29
President's Commission on Education Beyond the High School, 320
President's Commission on Higher Education, 319–320
Private business, trade, and technical schools, 84–88, 97, 145; characteristics of, 84–86; strengths and weaknesses of, 86–88
Probation Services Program, 213
"Process," contrasted with "product," in education, 251–253
Projecting enrollments in career education programs, 264–266
Proprietary schools. See Private, business, trade, and technical schools
Public and Human Services, 197–226; admissions to programs in, 216–217; centralized administration and control of, 224–225; defined, 197–199; faculty in, 223–224; four-year college sample program in, 208; internship and work experience in, 219–223; manpower supply and demand in, 199–203; persons employed in selected fields of, 200; relationships among sub-fields of, 198; special issues related to program operation in, 215–225; students in, 215–216; two-year college programs in, 205
PURDY, L., 274

Quality and diversity in post-secondary education, 36–38
QUARTON, G. C., 356

Radio and TV broadcasting, 236
Radiologic technicians and technologists, 176

RAINEY, G., 274
Rate of return on investment in higher education, 323–337; in career oriented programs, 337–340; to the individual, 323–333; to society, 333–337
RAYMAN, J. R., 89
Real estate, careers in, 113–114
Remediation and developmental education, 280–282
RICHARDSON, G. T., 35, 105, 179, 228
RINEHART, R., 91, 122, 141
Rochester Institute of Technology (New York), 89, 155
ROELFS, P., 35
ROGERS, J. A., 181
ROUECHE, J., 37, 130, 253, 256, 275, 370
RUBIN, T., 356

Sales careers, 115
San Francisco City College (California), 71
San Jose State University (California), 210
Santa Fe Community College (Florida), 189
Scenarios for the future, 352–358
Scholastic Aptitude Test, 73–129
SCHULTZ, T. W., 334
SEABORG, G., 357
Secretarial programs, 109–111
Semiprofessional occupations, 53. See also Middle manpower
Senior citizens, 32
SESSOMS, H. D., 205
SHEFFER, H. V., 214
SILBERMAN, C., 61
Simulation, instruction by, 127–128
Sinclair Community College (Ohio), 242
SKAGGS, K. G., 288
SLOAN, H. S., 85
Small business, programs for, 122–123
SMITH, A., 43–44, 324
SMITH, S. M., 59
Smith-Hughes Act, 66–70

Social returns on investment in higher education, 6–8, 333–337
Social services, programs in, 205–206
Society for College and University Planning, 274
SOLMON, L. C., 230
Southern Illinois University, 208
Southern Regional Education Board, 228, 232, 245
South Oklahoma City Junior College, 190
SPRICK, W. J., 127–128
SPUTNIK, I., 131
STARR, P., 167
State colleges. See Higher education
State University of New York at Binghamton, 245
Stenographer programs, 109–111
Students, 2–42; academic aptitude scores of, 37; age-mix of, 28–30; attitudes of in the 1960s, 39–41; changing characteristics of, 26–42, 73; as a class in society, 38–39; diversity of goals and aspirations of, 35–38; minority, 27, 32, 73, 310, 312; recruitment of, 27; senior citizens as, 32; shift of, to career-oriented studies, 33–35; women, 27, 32, 73
Subprofessional. See Middle manpower
Support services for career education, 277–283
Surgical (operating room) technicians, 175, 184
SWIFT, J. W., 209

Target-setting approach to manpower planning, 379
TAUBMAN, P., 326
Teacher aide programs, 209
Teaching and learning systems, 273–276
Technical colleges, 81–82
Technical education: articulation of two- and four-year programs in, 160–163; changing attitudes toward, 131–133; competency-based instruction in, 163; core and ladder approach in, 161–163; costs of, 163–164; defined, 68; historical development of, 133–135; postsecondary programs in, 134–135; problems of quality in, 151–154
Technical institutes, 77–81, 134, 151; common characteristics of, 78–79; strengths and weaknesses of, 80–81
Technical occupations: employment in, 136; manpower forecasts for, 142–145, 148–151; and place in industry, 136–142
Technicians, industrial: characteristics of, 140; demand for various kinds of, 143–145; postsecondary programs to prepare, 145–148
Technicians, science and engineering: characteristics of, 137–141; demand for various kinds of, 145–151; postsecondary programs to prepare, 151–155
Technological change and career education, 62–63
Technologists, engineering and industrial: baccalaureate programs to prepare, 155–160; characteristics of, 141–142; demand for, 155; place of, in industry, 155
Technology, negative attitudes toward, 131–133
Theater technology, 236
THORNTON, J. W., 71
TILLERY, D., 71, 373
TONSOR, S., 40
TRACHTENBERG, S. J., 91
TRAIN, R., 358
TRIVETT, D. A., 85–86, 129
Two-Plus-Two programs, 93
Two-year colleges. See Community colleges, Junior colleges

Urban community colleges: credit for prior learning given by, 307–310; development of, 292; as handmaiden to the establishment, 296–298; problems of comprehensiveness in, 298–301; relationships of, to skill centers and CETA programs, 304–305; satellite learning centers of, 301–302; special financial problems of, 312–314

U.S. Administration on Aging, Office of Human Development, 202

U.S. Bureau of the Census, 29–30, 51, 103, 107, 135–136, 200, 234, 326, 327, 343

U.S. Chamber of Commerce, 143

U.S. Department of Commerce, 102, 262

U.S. Department of Health, Education, and Welfare, 27, 30, 69, 201–202, 205; and Office of Child Development, 202–203; and Office of Education, 142, 153, 154, 202, 232, 303; and Public Health Service, 171, 173, 174, 176, 177, 187; and Rehabilitation Services Administration, 142, 153–154, 202, 232, 242

U.S. Department of Labor, 48, 49, 102, 136, 137, 149, 173, 200–201, 234, 262, 304–305, 326

U.S. Department of Labor, Bureau of Labor Statistics, 7, 28, 47, 48, 51, 52, 63, 142–143, 173–174, 176, 199, 201, 233

University of California at Los Angeles, 105

University of Chicago, 191

University of Cincinnati, 242

University of Detroit, 242

University of Michigan at Dearborn, 242

University of North Florida, 245

University of Southern California, 245

University of Wisconsin-Stout, 11, 89, 92, 155

VENN, G., 20

VERHOVEN, P. J., 205

Vincennes University Junior College (Indiana), 151, 339

Vocational education: as the central aim of all education, 21; defined, 66–67

Vocational Amendments of 1968, 67, 67n, 82, 202, 234, 313

Vocational Education Act of 1963; 67n, 82, 202, 234, 313

VOLLMER, A., 210

WALES, T., 326

WALLERS, R. I., 210

WARK, R. G., 210

Warner Pacific College (Oregon), 245

WARREN, J. T., 163

WATKINS, B. T., 94

WATTENBARGER, J. L., 368, 374

Wayne County Community College (Michigan), 210

WEBSTER, R. S., 294

WEINER, A., 353

Western Michigan University, 129

WHITE, L. T., JR., 247

WHITEHEAD, A. N., 23

Wichita State University (Kansas), 210

Wickersham Commission, 210

WIGGS, G. D., 112

WILL, R. K., 91, 155

WILMS, W., 311

WISE, F., 381

WISE, M., 33

WITHEY, S. B., 6

WOLANIN, T. R., 69

WOLFLE, D., 325

Women: career opportunities for, 32, 58–60; in colleges, 27; in the labor force, 47; as technicians, 149

Work experience and internships, 115, 126, 193–194, 219, 223, 241–246, 276–277

WYNN, M., 356

Y.M.C.A. Community College (Chicago), 191

Zero population growth (ZPG), 357, 364–365